The We

The
Weston Sisters

An American Abolitionist Family

LEE V. CHAMBERS

The University of North Carolina Press   Chapel Hill

This book was published with the assistance of the
Thornton H. Brooks Fund
of the University of North Carolina Press.

© 2014 The University of North Carolina Press
All rights reserved
Manufactured in the United States of America
Set in Miller types by codeMantra
The paper in this book meets the guidelines for permanence and durability
of the Committee on Production Guidelines for Book Longevity of the Council
on Library Resources. The University of North Carolina Press has been a
member of the Green Press Initiative since 2003.

Complete cataloging information for this title is available from the
Library of Congress
978-1-4696-1817-3 (pbk.: alk. paper)
978-1-4696-1818-0 (ebook)

THIS BOOK WAS DIGITALLY PRINTED.

For my siblings,
William Bell Chambers,
Leslie Chambers Trujillo, and Kenneth Carter Chambers,
and my son,
Devon Leith Schiller

Contents

The Weston Sisters

INTRODUCTION

A Household Band

On a winter's eve in 1840, Caroline Weston of Weymouth, Massachusetts, ruminated on the traumatic schism that had divided American abolitionists and ended the collective social activism of Boston's antislavery women. While there had been differences of opinion over ideology and tactics, the sisters Weston believed that the conflict that tore asunder the Boston Female Anti-Slavery Society (BFAS) had to do with gender: gender ideals and roles, the civil rights and moral obligations of women, and the appropriate relations of the "sisters" to the "brethren."[1] Over a three-year period, from 1837 to 1840, these differences built to the point that a group led by president Mary Parker and the sisters Lucy and Martha Ball called for a vote to dissolve the BFAS. They would form the new, anti-Garrisonian Massachusetts Female Emancipation Society, which allied with the "new" Massachusetts Abolition Society. Another group, led by Maria Weston Chapman and her sisters Weston, reconstituted the BFAS and carried on its cooperation with the "promiscuous"[2] and Garrisonian Massachusetts Anti-Slavery Society (MAS), in which several served as officers and committee members.[3]

While the new Massachusetts Abolition Society opposed "the introduction into our cause of what is technically called the 'Woman's Rights question'" and the appointment of women to the association's business committee, Caroline Weston's charismatic elder sister, Maria Weston Chapman, argued vigorously that "for the slave's sake we [antislavery women] are bound to urge on all his advocates the use of all their powers according to their own consciences."[4] Believing that many of her fictive sisters had fallen short of the glory of God, Caroline Weston turned to her siblings

1

to carry on without flagging. "[S]uppose the love of many waxes cold," she wrote, "what of that? suppose that—organization gets out of fashion because people are too stupid and too impatient to discern the signs of the times—what matter? do we not know that if three persons remain who choose to do so—they alone can rock the land with excitement. I bless God our own Family I think without more help might fight this battle out."[5]

Caroline was not alone in holding this view. In 1855, Oliver Johnson, a founding member of the New England Anti-Slavery Society and its agent for many years,[6] was asked by Maria to join Sydney H. Gay[7] as editor of the *National Anti-Slavery Standard* and "to plough and sow N[ew] York city, for $150 a year." Johnson asked only one question: "You know the main body of the cause don't see much use in the Standard:—what probability is there—what guaranty that it will be kept up?" Maria responded: "As to that, Mr. Johnson, you know all I can say. You know the women of my family for 20 years in the cause. There are six of us not yet past middle life. It depends upon the lives of this family." Replied Johnson, "It is enough!"[8]

In speaking of "this family," both Maria and Caroline meant themselves and their younger sisters—Anne, Debora, Lucia, and Emma Weston, abolitionists all. "A family of marked genius," according to Lucia's close friend Sarah Southwick, the Weston daughters were "very unlike, but all talented."[9] The eldest, Maria Ann, dominated the family circle by virtue of age and personality. Lydia Maria Child called her "one of the most remarkable women of the age. Her heart is as large and magnanimous as her intellect is clear, vigorous, and brilliant."[10] British political economist Harriet Martineau,[11] in awe of Maria's intelligence, learning, and political savvy, described her as having "reasoning powers which can never be baffled[;] learning and literary *fullness* I cannot fathom or compass; and knowledge of the world which the worldling cannot suppress." Attracted as well to Maria's personal qualities, Martineau ascribed to her "the sweetest womanly tenderness that woman ever manifested."[12] Others took a dimmer view of Maria's wicked wit and of the exquisite confidence, bordering on arrogance, that earned her such nicknames as "her Lordship" or the "elect Lady."[13]

Two years younger than Maria, Caroline was said to be "a delightful woman, not so handsome or majestic looking as [Maria], but with perhaps more sweetness of manner and a good deal of the same energetic frame of mind." Among family, friends, and colleagues Caroline was known as one who "attempted impossibilities," continuously giving her life and labor for others. Abolitionist Edmund Quincy, with whom she exchanged daily correspondence, called her a "sincere warm-hearted friend" who "would stand by us to the death and do any possible service to us or ours." William Lloyd Garrison, founder and editor of the antislavery newspaper the *Liberator*, described her as "one of the rare women of the world for moral heroism and intellectual acumen" and a "most effective" laborer in the cause.[14] Despite the nickname "Duchess of Sutherland," attached after her sojourn abroad in the late 1840s and early 1850s, Caroline demonstrated a less imperious manner and more pragmatic mind than Maria. She spoke bluntly but with less acerbity than her older sister. She had a ready and subtle sense of humor—fewer puns than Maria and less saucy than Anne. Temperamentally, Caroline had more in common with her younger sister Debora, although she proved less tolerant of incompetence and less patient with foolishness. Goal oriented, Caroline was no one's pushover. She commanded her troops, familial and associational, with a manner both firm and generous.

Anne Warren Weston saw herself as molded in a "less heroic strain" than her elder sisters, a descendent of John Bunyan's "Much Afraid." Philadelphia Quaker and abolitionist Sarah Pugh acknowledged, "Ann[e] is weak" in contrast to Caroline, who was "strong and able *to do* for herself and others." Yet if prone to hypochondria, Anne was also popular. Quincy described her as the best conversationalist, male or female, whom he had ever met: "charming, fresh, and original." According to abolitionist lecturer Sallie Holley,[15] Anne was "a most ladylike and agreeable person . . . full of intelligence and a great talker. Mr. Garrison says she talks the best, for a person who talks so much, of any woman he ever knew. She is small in stature, with a light, delicate complexion, light hair, and hazel eyes." Samuel J. May Jr. described Anne as having "a great being in that little body. Her spirits, her animation, her earnestness, her deep and clear insight, her flow of language in conversation, her manner of speech—and all together, are very taking with most people, and make her a great favorite." While William Lloyd Garrison Jr. found Maria "indisputably the most ablest intellectual" among the Westons, he believed "Anne must come next." Friends called her "the Great Weston," a pun upon the name of the *Great Western* steamship, and a nod to both her popularity and her capacity to steam full ahead and dominate every conversation.[16]

Debora, nicknamed Dora or Bella by the family, was "famous" for "having a great deal . . . to do at once." Viewed as the family's "indispensable housekeeper and care-taker," Debora served as favorite teacher, devoted nurse, beloved aunt, and neighborhood benefactor. She attended to all "the thousand little duties of a country neighborhood. . . . Visits, parties, hikes, road mending, sewing meetings, Freedman's Aid Societies, all are in her hands and keep her very busy." Although she was known as "a very bright, animated, cheerful girl," it was Debora's capability that struck even relative strangers, for she was "very efficient & smart." Debora declined any formal position officiating over female antislavery societies, although she played a crucial role in getting New Bedford's onto solid ground. Despite her antipathy for the spotlight, Debora worked as hard as her sisters to manage their business, whether passing petitions, making and selling fair goods, or working behind the scenes to uphold the weary, strengthen the dispirited, and calm the provoked.[17]

By all accounts the sweetest Weston was Lucia, openly affectionate with family and "cordial and confiding" to others. She had "an easy quietness of disposition," a patient, self-effacing, staunch, and good-spirited manner that made her both an excellent nurse and a charming invalid. Indeed, she made of her consumption, which lasted almost twenty years, a social affair.[18] Lucia had a marvelous sense of humor, full of fun and lacking the barbed witticisms of her three eldest sisters. Despite the physical weakness she began to manifest in the 1840s, Lucia determined to live as fully as possible. Her adventurous spirit took her to France, Italy, and Switzerland with her sisters. She climbed mountains by foot, on horseback, and in a chair, searching for improved health and distraction. After 1853 she convalesced in Italy, attracting a circle of notable European and American expatriates and visitors.[19]

Strangers as well as friends saw in Emma Forbes Weston "the beauty of the family." A "bright vision," she was described in terms of light: "very striking with her blonde complexion and abundance of flaxen hair." Distingué and flirtatious, she was as "*spirituelle*, witty, well read and amiable as she is pretty."[20] Emma lived abroad a great deal after 1849, content to circulate in the London society provided by her uncle, banker Joshua Bates, or the cosmopolitan society of Paris embraced by her older sisters and her niece Elizabeth Bates Chapman, who married and took up housekeeping there. In 1854, when Lucia settled in Rome for her lungs, Emma joined her as companion. Massachusetts abolitionists saw Emma as having acquired "an air of ceremonial reserve" in Europe, less haute than that of Caroline yet refined and genteel.[21]

Lucia and Emma, the youngest Weston sisters, were born three years apart. Sixteen and nineteen years younger than Maria, they engaged in politics first as girls. Lucia was just old enough to follow discussions of abolition in the Weston and Chapman households during the early years of organizing the Weymouth and Braintree Female Emancipation Society and the BFAS. Only ten in 1835, when anti-abolitionists mobbed her elder sisters in Boston, Emma evidenced less of an activist bent than they. Nevertheless she shared their politics, attended conventions, and sewed for and sold at the annual Boston antislavery bazaar. Her correspondence served to inform those of her sisters away from home about important political developments.[22] Lucia and Emma spent as much time with their nieces, Maria's daughters, as with their older sisters (and Emma had more in common with the Chapman girls).[23]

Together, the four elder Weston sisters led three female antislavery societies and a national women's antislavery organization. Maria and Anne served on the governing boards of the Boston, Massachusetts, New England, and American Anti-Slavery Societies, while Caroline and Debora served actively in three local associations in Boston, Weymouth, and New Bedford. The sisters all supported the instruments and agents of these associations, largely through the mechanism of the Boston fair that they helped organize from 1834 to 1838 and administered from 1839 to 1858. Maria also wrote the annual reports of the BFAS, turning them into a collective history of the early movement and a testament to the tactics, ideology, and meaning of Garrisonian abolition. "One and all we sympathize not with the oppressors, but with the oppressed," she wrote of her family, "and would infinitely prefer to be stoned or scourged to death, (*lynched* as it is called here) to supporting slavery even by the lesser crime of silence."[24]

In constructing this sibling band as "abolitionists one and all," the Westons gendered it female. Captain Warren and Ann Bates Weston seem to have been little influenced by the winds of religious and reform enthusiasm that swept their community and captivated their daughters, who, along with Warren's sister Mary, helped organize the Weymouth community for abolition.[25] The Westons lived for many years in the northeastern part of Weymouth called "the Landing." Cousin Edmund Soper Hunt deemed it "much in advance of the other parts of town, for here we had all the 'isms' of the day, abolitionists, total abstainers, non-resistants, come-outers—in fact we entertained all the cranks there were at the time."[26]

Brothers Hervey and Richard Warren did not share in their sisters' gender-specific antislavery labor, nor was abolition so central a component of their gender and familial identities. The brothers made their own, albeit episodic and far more modest, contributions to the cause.[27] Hervey Eliphas Weston signed an 1836 Weymouth men's petition seeking to end slavery in the nation's capital. Additionally, his name appeared among those of his townsmen who convened at the Methodist Chapel on 13 November 1837 to form a local antislavery society.[28] While remaining more observer than activist, Hervey avidly reported on anti-abolitionist activity at Yale during his college years. He attended various conventions of the MAS, ran errands for the Boston bazaar, and casually garnered subscriptions for antislavery newspapers.[29] In 1850, Hervey joined the Boston Vigilance Committee, formed to secure the freedom of runaways in the aftermath of the Fugitive Slave Act, which authorized southern agents and northern law enforcement to seize and return fugitive slaves to their owners.[30] As the committee's rescue work grew increasingly violent, Hervey's willingness to adopt physical force as a legitimate means of defying the law violated his sisters' profound belief in nonresistance.[31]

Maria described Richard Warren Weston (called "Warren" by the family) as "a common worldly gentleman" who had the capacity to be shocked by hypocrisy and immorality but only in passing and "not technically an abolitionist."[32] He signed, at age seventeen, the same 1836 petition as his brother,[33] and extended himself to aid his sisters with their commitments. For example, in the 1850s he arranged through his shipping business to transport across the Atlantic goods that his sisters purchased in Europe for the Boston antislavery bazaar. He helped out occasionally, as when, during the political crisis surrounding the fugitive slave George Latimer, abolitionists scurried to place an observer of their own at the U.S. Capitol. Caroline reported that Maria "pitched in like a flood—& the universe is turning over to get [David L.] Child right on to Washington. *Warren* is going up to Northampton at 3 o'clock to see the Child."[34] Maria, in her role as a member of the executive committee of the American Anti-Slavery Society (AAS), sent Warren to Northampton with a letter asking Child to accept the position and ensured his swift response by having Warren conduct him to the train.[35] Warren's actions, however, seemed to express sibling accommodation as much as any political engagement.

In contrast to their brothers, the Weston sisters understood their abolitionism as key to the identity of the "House of Weston."[36] The next-to-youngest sister, Lucia, had, by age fourteen, so internalized the family narrative that she utilized its terms to proudly announce her election to the presidency of the Massachusetts Juvenile Anti-Slavery Society in January 1837. "We were counting up the number of officers in the whole family and we thought we made a goodly array," she wrote. "Maria, Caroline, Anne[,] Secretaries [of the Boston Female] and also Lucretia [Cowing, a cousin, of the Weymouth Female], Aunt Mary [Weston] Vice President [of the Weymouth Female], Henry [Grafton Chapman, Maria's husband] Treasurer [of the MAS], and though last not least [myself] President."[37]

Many of their peers saw the Weston sisters as they saw themselves— not only abolitionists all but abolition itself. Educator Ebenezer Bailey hailed Debora on a Boston street with "How do you do Abolition?" Edmund Quincy denominated the Westons the "Weymouth sisterhood," an appellation that bore a cultural meaning beyond literal consanguinity.[38] The term "sisterhood" evoked a community of women, usually religious but also, in this era of association, a female voluntary society active in benevolence, moral reform, or the spread of Christianity.[39] Quincy intended the designation to acknowledge not only a consociation whose adhesion reflected sororal feelings of connection, exclusivity, equality, companionship, mutual devotion, and love but also one whose identity and purpose took root in an enterprise of moral and political import. In the eyes of many, the Weston sisters constituted an antislavery society all their own.

Such a "family culture" bore a performance imperative.[40] As Maria put it, in a time when "Boston has been quite as strongly convulsed as any southern city, at the distinct assertion of the abolitionists that slavery is a sin," when "[e]verybody is compelled to take sides by the earnest inquiry on all hands 'what is your opinion? Not for the abolition of slavery I hope' or 'not for the perpetuation of slavery I hope' as the case may be," these sisters held it as a matter of faith that none of them "suffered so great an obscuration of the moral sense as to be in doubt as to what answer duty requires Americans to make."[41] "Being too good Westons," they could not "think of turning back" or giving up. They believed the cause would "succeed & be victorious" because "it finds enough (*few* but *enough*) to live & die by it." Among those few, as Anne said of Sarah Rugg, president of the Groton Female Anti-Slavery Society, abolition was their "Alpha & Omega," and the Westons were "prepared to do any thing, to go any lengths" to accomplish emancipation.[42] The performance imperative embedded in the term "abolitionists all" demanded that the Weymouth sisterhood commit their souls, thought, time, financial resources, and labor to the cause, adopting all possible means and turning every opportunity toward sustaining their affiliation and achieving its purpose. At times it surely seemed to the Westons, as to their friends and enemies alike, as though the Weymouth sisterhood *were* the Boston Female.

Abolitionists in need of aid or advice turned to these siblings, viewing them not only as a collective but also as interchangeable. Again and again the cry arose, "Can you help me? Or can any of your sisters?"[43] George Foster of Haverhill, for example, requested of Maria, "If anything should prevent you (I hope there may be nothing) from attending [the quarterly conference of the female abolitionists of Essex County] send one of your sisters." Edmund Quincy begged her "or one of your sisters" to proofread his newspaper article. Lydia Jones of Holliston excused the "liberty" she took of addressing Anne, "as I knew not whom else in Mrs Chapman's absence." MAS agent John A. Collins, then in New Bedford, sought advice from Anne, saying, "Debora, who has resided so long in the regions of sperm and blubber, would in this trying hour, be of great service. But she made her exit this A.M. at 7 o'clock, and I am left without a counselor. You can atone for this obvious neglect of duty only by throwing yourself into the breach and see that the most extensive notice is given of [MAS agent George] Bradburn's Meeting on Wednesday evening." Harriet Hayden begged from New York for "a letter from you or your sister," as antislavery people "are rare both here & among our correspondents."[44]

Those outside the Weston family assumed that any one sister might speak or act for the others.[45] From within the sisterhood, however, the Westons viewed themselves as partners in a common enterprise. They might, and did, disagree on details; as Caroline put it, "I don't dictate." Quincy viewed their temperaments and intellects as diverse, contradicting a colleague who assumed that they necessarily all thought alike. "You know them very little if you think they are influenced by [Maria] or anybody in making up their minds," he explained. "Mrs. C[hapman] has no more influence over them, nor they over her than you or I have. . . . They differ in the most animated way on all kinds of subjects but without the least *aigresse* and with perfect good temper." Even as these sisters debated strategies, personalities, and ideas, they jousted over tasks and opportunities. Yet they worked as a team to complete the tasks they deemed essential to the success of the abolitionist movement.[46]

The Westons exemplify a sororal model of female social activism in antebellum New England. The more general model features sisters—though seldom so many—who remained single, lived and worked together in or from the same household, and committed their lives and resources (time, money, and labor) to social reform or benevolence.[47] The marriage of Maria Ann Weston did not reduce her effectiveness as part of this sibling cohort because her five unwed sisters shared her child-rearing and domestic responsibilities (in addition to fulfilling those of their natal household), enabling this housewife and mother to engage continuously in antislavery work even when pregnant, child-rearing, and nursing a dying husband.[48] Singlehood in numbers contributed to the Westons' impact on the cause.

As distinct from the workings of other sibling bands, those of the Weymouth sisterhood offer students of antebellum America a large body of surviving correspondence with which to reconstruct their activism.[49] But can we really base a model upon the study of one family? I argue that even if the Weston venture was exceptional, it did represent a broader sororal practice among antislavery women. The BFAS included several sisterhoods. The Parkers—Mary (who presided over the society through the 1830s), Abigail, Lucy, and Eliza—provide one example. They operated a boardinghouse patronized by abolitionists such as William Lloyd Garrison and his family.

Also active among the officers of the society were such siblings as Lucy, Martha, and Hannah Ball, who lived together (with their mother, Mary Drew Ball) after the 1837 death of their father, Joseph. The Sargent sisters, Catherine and Henrietta, shared a house provided them by their well-to-do father, merchant Epes Sargent. The similarly situated Southwicks—Abby, Anna, Elizabeth, and Sarah—lived with one another in the home of their abolitionist parents, Thankful Hussey and Joseph Southwick.[50] Janette and Rebecca Louge were childhood friends of the Westons; the widow Eliza Lee Cabot Follen and her sister Susan Cabot were their friends as adults; BFAS activists Mary Gray Chapman and Ann Greene Chapman became Weston in-laws when Maria Ann Weston married their brother Henry Grafton Chapman in 1830. Other sisters fit the profile, such as African Americans Ann Jennett Jackson and Sarah Jackson.[51]

Similar sister groupings (unwed, living and working in the same household) played a significant role in other female antislavery societies. Mary and Susan Grew, among the founding members of the BFAS in 1833, left Boston for Philadelphia in the mid-1830s and continued their antislavery labors as members of the Philadelphia Female Anti-Slavery Society. Other Philadelphians included African Americans Grace and Sarah Douglass, and Sarah and Margaretta Forten. The Thoreau sisters, Susan and Helen, not only shared a home with their abolitionist mother, Cynthia Dunbar Thoreau, while providing occupational assistance and domestic labor to their brother, Henry David, but also helped found the Concord, Massachusetts, female antislavery society. In Worcester, Massachusetts, Matilda and Lucy Chase devoted themselves to the Female Anti-Slavery Society Sewing Circle while African Americans Caroline, Susan, and Sarah Remond joined their mother, Nancy, in the Salem Female Anti-Slavery Society. Several abolitionist siblings in Rhode Island followed suit: Susan and Anna Sisson of Pawtucket; their cousins Hannah, Lydia, and Sarah Sisson of Kent County; Harriett, Mary Ann, and Joanna Peck, along with Susan and Mary Anthony, also of Kent County; Caroline and Susan Little of Newport; the Thurber sisters, Rachel and Abby, as well as Sarah and Ann Pratt, of Providence.[52] The Tappans of New York City and Bensons of Brooklyn, Connecticut, offer additional examples.[53]

Perhaps the most famous, or infamous, antislavery sisters were the Grimkés of South Carolina and Philadelphia, who provide a complex example of the importance of sororal support for activism. At first, the two sustained one another as they lectured to groups of strangers in New York, Connecticut, and Massachusetts. When the younger Angelina married Theodore Weld just before the second Anti-Slavery Convention of American Women in 1838, *both* she and her older sibling, Sarah, retired from their agency for the AAS. The marriage and childbearing of one removed both from the movement.[54] Similarly, three of the five daughters of merchant Phillip Ammidon—Angelina, Melania, and Sylvia—married conservative clergymen and left organized abolition in the late 1830s.

Shared labor in the cause constructed and reinforced the ties of affection that bound together the Weymouth sisterhood and others of its kind. Caroline Weston's invocation of her sisters as soldiers both necessary and sufficient to carry the battle forward to emancipation emphasized the nature of the relationship between these sisters by blood *and* election.[55] The unsentimental Maria wrote, "Jeremy Taylor thought Friendship an eminently *useful* thing:—that its main characteristic was its utility. There are a contrary-minded set of people who guard it from such an imputation as from the charge of meanness. I am not one of these latter."[56] She might have said the same about siblicity—that its paramount quality was utility—without either denying or denigrating the love and affection that infused and reinforced her sibling relations.[57]

In asserting the importance of siblicity in understanding how the Westons viewed and organized their lives, both political and domestic, this study builds upon the research of historians of eighteenth- and early nineteenth-century American sociability who have argued that the affection that bound kin together grew from shared labor. Daniel Scott Smith and Catherine E. Kelly, for example, have drawn upon Adam Smith's definition of affection as "habitual sympathy." Adam Smith theorized that affective relations among kin required interaction within a common household,[58] though affective ties might also emerge as a characteristic of neighborliness, which Daniel Scott Smith defined as living within five houses in either direction.[59] By the mid-1830s, the Weston aunts— Phebe, Priscilla, and Mary—lived across the street from their nieces, a proximity that helped sustain Mary's antislavery activism during Priscilla's long mental and physical decline. Mary's labor in the Weymouth and Braintree Female Anti-Slavery Society in turn supported the Weston sisters' local antislavery commitments during periods when one or another was away from home.

Kelly has accepted periodic cohabitation as sufficient for generating affection, given a practice of shared labor among siblings.[60] And other historians have suggested that affective ties among kin might span considerable distances. Women, in particular, contributed to these durable bonds by fostering marital matches for their brothers and otherwise augmenting kinship ties through shared tasks, hospitality, correspondence, and conversation.[61] Such kin-work provided not only psychological and social nurturing, housekeeping, education, and nursing but also intellectual stimulation. This study adds politicization to the uses of sibling affection and the facilitation of social activism to the portfolio of sibling tasks.[62]

The Weston sisters functioned as a political entity, an economic corporation, and a domestic concern. Their complex works involved organizing, administering, and financing various antislavery bodies, as well as earning their own income and much of the natal household's. The sisters jointly managed both Maria's marital household in Boston and the family home in Weymouth, while educating the Weston and Chapman young and caring for all family members. These interactions wove a complex web of mutual responsibility and obligation that bound the sisters together through both utility and the feelings of satisfaction and appreciation generated by the exchange of labor and favors. As members of a household, the Weston siblings developed their housewifery and their social and occupational relationships, and in these working connections they rooted their political practice.

This study emphasizes the Westons' shared labor in manufacturing the Weymouth sisterhood. The sisters conducted virtually all tasks in common. Even when temporarily separated (by occupational necessity, for example), they remained closely connected to the Weymouth and Boston households through commissions, correspondence, and visitation. The longevity of their sisterhood illustrates Daniel Scott Smith's insight that shared activity prevents the attenuation of social relations and sentimentalization of affection.[63]

But Weston lives and labors expand the historiography of kinship in that these were public and political. The sisters' mutual regard encouraged in one another the development of political consciousness. In turn, their conduct of abolition constructed and kept current the ties of reciprocity that sustained sibling affection. In families such as the Westons, sisters educated and honed one another's political analysis, reinforced each other's civic participation, directed their sibship toward public ends, and organized the means by which they worked politically. That the Weymouth sisterhood bonded as a political enterprise was among the most consequential uses of their siblicity.

Despite the potential richness of such investigations for the fields of political, family, social, women's, and gender history, there has been remarkably little interest among historians in siblings.[64] The existing work shows that sibling relations shape inheritance of land and other real property, as well as less clear-cut transfers of labor and income such as housekeeping and capital investment.[65] Siblings have helped with each other's education, migration, access to housing, and job opportunities through patronage and exchange networks, nepotism, and information sharing.[66] Leonore Davidoff has reminded us that siblings "have acted as surrogate parents (and children), informal teachers, adult co-residents, friends and even, on occasion, lovers," providing child and parental care, nursing, and other forms of personal assistance.[67] This is the work of kin-keeping, largely viewed as women's work, and usually that of unwed sisters, cousins, or aunts.[68]

Nineteenth-century leisure, social life, and courtship all took place within a context of social relations constructed largely by the horizontal family. C. Dallett Hemphill has argued that in the aftermath of the American Revolution, older siblings took on new responsibilities advising younger ones. Sibling relations provided a space "unfettered" by the restraints of patriarchal gender relations in the early republic, where "old social controls were ebbing before new social safeguards were erected."[69] These norms in sibling culture encouraged intimacy between siblings as older brothers took on primary responsibility for advising their younger sisters and brothers. But American sibling culture also encouraged sisters (and particularly elder sisters) to guide their brothers in the ways they should act in the world.[70] Through the 1830s, Hemphill argues, the influence of sisters softened the republican political and economic "rule of the brother." New, more democratic sibling ideals among northern, middle-class families compensated women culturally for their political and economic inequality by encouraging brothers to perform deference rituals that provided their sisters with a token social precedence.[71] This sentimental "rule of the sister" did not signify women's social or political equality,[72] as the Westons certainly recognized, although some antislavery women took satisfaction in such ritualized homage. Indeed, symbolic deference toward (some) female abolitionists by the more conservative antislavery brethren inflamed the conflict among female activists over woman's role in the movement by masking male power and authority with polite manners, pretty words, and petty rewards. The Westons, and others of their persuasion, demanded more substantive participation.

The Weston sisters remained relatively immune to, even suspicious of, male flattery. The elder four had established a female cohort within the

Weymouth household before their younger brothers arrived some three to five years after Debora's birth and eleven to thirteen after Maria's. This sibling culture more easily incorporated the youngest sisters than it did the intervening brothers. Well before northern sibling culture urged sisters to undertake for brothers the roles of guide, teacher, and disciplinarian, Hervey and Richard Warren had failed as protectors of their younger sisters and behaved in ways that called for the oversight of elder ones. By 1840, the elder Weston sisters had been working to improve their brothers' behavior and character for some fifteen years. Their intimate acquaintance with unpredictable and derelict male behavior, rooted in their father's alcoholism and brothers' unruliness, ensured skepticism of patriarchal authority and impatience with what they saw as irresponsible or negligent behavior on the part of antislavery brethren across the ideological spectrum—whether the hypochondria of editor William Lloyd Garrison, the condescension of Rev. Jonas Perkins of Union Church, Weymouth, or the dismissiveness of AAS executive secretary Elizur Wright Jr.

Historians have focused on the role of the middle-class horizontal family in coping with rapid social change in early nineteenth-century New England. Mary Ryan has proposed that middle-class women met new social and economic challenges by viewing the home as a prime location for cultivating religious feeling and inculcating Christian morality in younger brothers, sons, and husbands. These mothers joined voluntary associations of fictive siblings to further their goals at a time when the surveillance and support networks of church and community became attenuated through geographical mobility even as parents lacked the resources and authority to fill the vacuum.[73]

In the first decades of the nineteenth century, siblings forged the social networks necessary for establishing social status, political success, and business advancement. Middle-class men used kinship ties to coordinate their economic interests and mobilize capital while women, through their domestic and social activities, worked to maintain family solidarity and to preserve the family as an economic institution by organizing appropriate marriages. Sibling exchange marriages, marriages to a dead wife's sister, and first-cousin marriages served these pragmatic ends.[74] Artisans and small shopkeepers brought brothers and brothers-in-law into business partnerships, replacing an earlier pattern of fathers and sons. In tracing the decline of the corporate family on the New York frontier during the canal era, Ryan has shown that sons who could no longer find a place on their father's land migrated to manufacturing towns, commercial entrepôts, and cities, where they worked and lived with siblings, attended school on the wages of unmarried sisters, and married their siblings' in-laws.[75]

Scholarly work on the role of women in developing and nurturing sibling ties has focused largely on building political and economic alliances through marriage formation; few family or women's historians have examined how sibship fostered female political consciousness or politicking. An exception is Catherine Allgor, who has found that in the early Republic, women "of elite, politically connected families" understood political patronage and utilized family connections to provide staffing for the new federal government despite the antipatronage rhetoric of republicanism. While she has not used siblicity as an analytical category, some of Allgor's best examples have demonstrated its import. Bayard Smith, for example, provided employment assistance to her nephew, the son of her sister Jane Bayard Kirkpatrick. Allgor has viewed finding employment for male family members to be an extension of women's duty "as loving, responsible mothers," but in this case it was also an extension of sister relations.[76]

Historians have noted the role of kinship in general in recruitment for reform organizations, benevolent societies, and religious institutions. According to Debra Gold Hansen, some 70 percent of women who joined abolitionist societies did so as part of a family unit. Julie Roy Jeffrey has argued that "some grew up in abolitionism" and "as wives, sisters, daughters, and cousins they naturally sympathized with and supported antislavery."[77] However, such sympathy may have been less "natural" than constructed and maintained.[78] Abolitionist sentiments divided families as well as brought them together. Among the Sargent sisters of Boston, for example, Henrietta and Catherine lived together and were ardent Garrisonian abolitionists, friends of the Westons, and members of the BFAS. But their married sister, Anna Sargent Parker, who lived only a few blocks away, refused to have tea with them more than twice a year because, as Henrietta wrote, "my Abolition has disgusted her with me. I am sorry but I cannot help it. God knows I love her."[79]

While noting that family ties may have recruited women into social activism, scholars Jeffrey and Boylan have asserted that kinship did not keep them there.[80] The Weston model suggests that sibship did accomplish retention of married women—provided that at least one sister was both active and unwed. In families such as the Westons, single sisters kept married ones informed and engaged when pregnancy, sickness, childcare, or household labor temporarily reduced their political or benevolent activity. Moreover, unwed sisters aided in domestic work not simply as family dependents earning their keep but so as to release their siblings for public duty as part of their contribution to a corporate entity (the household) that shared domestic, economic, and political concerns.[81]

For example, Susan Cabot lived with her sister, Elizabeth Lee Cabot Follen. During Eliza's marriage and widowhood, Susan passed antislavery petitions and participated in BFAS meetings, but she also helped to care for her nephew and the Follen household while Eliza wrote and published antislavery tracts, children's literature, and a biography of her husband, abolitionist and Unitarian minister Rev. Charles Follen. Eliza accomplished this work not only to meet the household's financial needs but also to fulfill political commitments shared by her sister. She served as "counsellor" to the MAS in the early 1840s alongside her beloved friend Maria Weston Chapman.[82]

Although Cabot did not play so visible a role as Follen in the BFAS, she and other such unwed sisters empowered themselves through the collaborative approach to life's labors and political passions provided by shared household arrangements.[83] As Hansen found, about half of the women in the BFAS never married. Those who remained single were "the most active in the society." They included the organization's presidents, vice presidents, secretaries, and treasurer. Indeed the BFAS had only two presidents, both single women: Mary Grew and Mary S. Parker. Looking closely at the marital status of a broader range of reform women, Boylan has concluded, "In their desire to challenge hierarchies beyond those of race and thralldom, including the hierarchy of marital status, [the BFAS] were very unusual."[84] Unusual certainly, and yet also highly visible and influential. Female abolitionists in other associations had strong role models in the Westons and not infrequently sought their advice and the support of the BFAS.

Thus the second historiography upon which this study draws is that of singlehood. This field of study has developed slowly over the past two decades, struggling against the dominant flow of historical research that assumes marriage to be the natural and normative female state.[85] Historians of nineteenth-century America, and Britain as well, have tended to describe unmarried women as unattached or dependent, exchanging their services for protection and economic support while living in the households of fathers, brothers, or brothers-in-law. Such women, it has been argued, learned a gendered dependency within the household that prepared them for marriage or, if marriage did not occur, took the form of subordination and obedience to male kin. An alternative interpretation has suggested that some, perhaps many, single women had greater autonomy (and greater responsibility) than this image offers. Particularly among the growing numbers of female-headed households appearing in American cities as a result of deaths and population displacement in the Revolutionary War or rising opportunities and geographic mobility in the new commercial economy, unwed women not only supported themselves but also housed, cared for, and supported dependents of their own—younger siblings both male and female, nieces and nephews, and/or widowed sisters and mothers, for example.[86]

Economic dependency did not characterize the Weston sisters' experience. In whole and in part, the elder sisters supported themselves, their younger siblings, and, for a long time, their parents as well. They did so while living in and caring for two primary households: the marital household of the eldest sister in Boston and the natal home in Weymouth. As individuals and in groups they came and went between the two, with Maria's no less critical to the family's economic, social, and domestic goals while somewhat more central to its political ones. While each Weston sibling pursued a living, an education, or better health elsewhere for some period of time, they all returned to Weymouth—not only to succor their parents and support one another but also to aid their cause.

This study looks to the household as an incubator of female political activism. It attempts to complicate the tendency of historians to view family and household structure as primarily a result rather than a cause of political events. This presumption, as Carole Shammas has observed, has had "the effect of relegating these to the private and non-governmental social realm."[87] Instead, I emphasize the significance of both sibling relations and marital status in forging the Weymouth sisterhood from the Weston sisters. Indeed, for these women, the social categories single and sibling proved mutually constitutive. In speaking of being "married to the cause," the Westons acknowledged the cultural assumption that marriage was the primary source of meaning in women's lives (and labors) even as they largely rejected the institution for themselves.[88] Siblicity and singlehood in numbers functioned to structure the Weston household(s), the family's social relations, the gendering of relationships and responsibilities, and the sisters' political enterprise.

This inquiry also draws upon scholarly interest in the geography of space with a view to understanding how the emergence of clubs, libraries, voluntary organization headquarters, and other centers of activity encouraged sociability and political development. The Weston household in Weymouth and, to a greater extent, the Chapman town house in Boston collected abolitionists and organized considerable antislavery activism. In the words of Edmund Quincy, Boston abolition "wobbled" around

Maria's town house, the symbolic and practical "center" of the Garrisonian world, standing as it did between the offices of the MAS and the houses of key Garrisonians south and southeast of the Boston Common.[89] On West Street, it stood within easy walking distance of the *Liberator* office, as well, allowing the Westons to dispatch and retrieve political correspondence and acquire the latest political news.

The Chapman household, which the Weston sisters (in various configurations) routinely shared, was organized to abet, sustain, support, and promote the antislavery labor of the Weymouth sisterhood. In its special relation to other Garrisonian centers in the city of Boston and state of Massachusetts, it contributed to the development of political consciousness and the growth of a reform community.[90] This work looks to the Weston household for the "tactics of habitat" by which its inhabitants experienced and learned to wield social power. The household was no more an "empty container, filled by ready-made subjects" in nineteenth-century New England than it was elsewhere in place and time.[91]

Defined culturally as private rather than public space, the household remains underappreciated for its role in shaping women's political work. The Westons' relations of gender, siblicity, and labor were created, adopted, and refined within the natal household in Weymouth. There, and in the Chapman marital household in Boston, a dynamic of female cooperation shaped feminist subjectivity. The work habits, independent-mindedness, sibling cohesion, and intellectual assurance of the Weymouth sisterhood also took shape in a household characterized by paternal alcoholism and fraternal debility. These two factors contributed to the Weston critique of "the rule of the brother" that informed their views of women's roles in the movement.[92]

Briefly, the book is organized as follows. Chapter 1 situates the Westons within the abolition movement that gave meaning and structure to their lives and to which they contributed as innovative fund-raisers, organizational leaders, propagandists, and petition bearers. Chapter 2 addresses the structure and relationships in the Weston family and Weymouth household. Among key aspects of its organization were inconsistent paternal governance and the necessity for the elder sisters to assume responsibility for the family's well-being. The chapter examines the meaning of the sisters' determined singlehood.

Chapter 3 recounts the economic struggle of these sisters to support the household. The earnings of the eldest daughters served to educate their younger siblings and provide for the upkeep of the natal home. Chapter 4 analyzes the conduct and organization of domestic labor in both the natal and Maria's marital households. The unwed sisters shared the labor involved in nursing and clothing three generations of Westons and rearing the children of two. Chapter 5 explores the extension of kinship duties and ties—including political responsibilities—beyond the natal household as familial, occupational, and political work took the Weston sisters away from Weymouth and Boston (within customary walking distance of one another) to Roxbury, New Bedford, Paris, and Rome.

Chapter 6 discusses the negotiations required of the sisters in order to meet their multiple responsibilities. These demonstrated the privileging of antislavery duties among the sisters' concerns and the nature of their relationships as to both affection and utility. Chapter 7 focuses specifically on the importance of the sibling relation to the Westons' political labor and the centrality of the household in its conduct. Chapter 8 assesses what some viewed as the "impudence" of the sisters Weston and the significance of this construction of political womanliness for understanding the import of horizontal kinship structures and the language of fictive kinship in antebellum reform.

The argument has several parts. In tune with the instrumental insights of Adam Smith, Jeremy Taylor, Daniel Scott Smith, and Catherine E. Kelly, this study emphasizes the roots of sororal affection in reciprocal obligations, mutual responsibilities, and shared labor—a goodly portion of which in this case went beyond kin-work and sociability to political activism. Mutual affection and shared labor generated a common political identity among the Weston sisters from which a political sisterhood was forged. Mutual reliance reinforced, extended, and maintained the bonds of sisterhood beyond the household(s) that nurtured and organized these sibling relations. The Weston example suggests that sibship and singlehood may serve political innovation, encourage resistance to female dependency, inspire a critique of the "rule of the brother," and generate creative forms of politicking not only against so entrenched a social and economic institution as slavery but also against patriarchy.

1

MARRIED TO THE CAUSE

The Weston Sisters and Antislavery

In January 1837 several male abolitionists addressed a meeting of the Boston Female Anti-Slavery Society (BFAS). Among them were Henry B. Stanton, the Reverend Amos Dresser, and the Reverend Samuel J. May.[1] Lucia Weston, at fifteen the next-to-youngest Weston sister, reported that the meeting was "very full and we had a very good time and they got many new members. In the evening Maria [Weston Chapman, Lucia's eldest sibling and an officer of the BFAS] had a pow wow [at her home] and all the brethren were there including the sisters. [B]rother May said at one of the meetings that the women of the Society were the most efficient brethren and the men their weak and less efficient sisters. [T]his was clapped."[2]

Among the most "efficient" of the "female brethren"—a term that was picked up with glee by anti-abolitionists—the Westons joined the movement in 1834–35. They helped organize female antislavery in Roxbury and New Bedford, Massachusetts; managed the BFAS and, with their aunt Mary Weston, the Weymouth and Braintree Female Emancipation Society; assumed responsibility for antislavery fund-raising by organizing the "cent box" campaign and sustaining the BFAS annual fair (from 1835 to 1858), which supported antislavery agents, organs, and associations in Massachusetts; wrote such significant propaganda as *Right and Wrong in Boston* (1836), which detailed mob violence and social intimidation of abolitionists in the city, and *Right and Wrong in Massachusetts* (1839), which decried the efforts of some antislavery activists to isolate William Lloyd Garrison and female abolitionists who espoused immediatism, disunion, and independent female activism; and served as editors and authors for such abolitionist and reform newspapers as the *Liberator*, the

National Anti-Slavery Standard, and the *Non-Resistant*. In an effort to appeal to genteel, cultivated readers who shied away from these newspapers, the Westons also created and produced the *Liberty Bell*, a magazine of poetry, short essays, biographical sketches, and short fiction. (As Maria put it, the American public "must be treated like children, to whom a medicine is made as pleasant as it[s] nature admits. A childish mind desires a small measure of truth in gilt edges, when it would reject it in whitty-brown.")[3]

The Westons helped organize and conduct a massive, multiyear campaign throughout the state of Massachusetts petitioning the federal government to end slavery. As part of this effort they solicited individuals in their assigned counties to take responsibility for organizing local campaigns, provided these men and women with petition forms, and bundled the signatures for presentation to Congress. They themselves went door-to-door in Boston, Roxbury, Weymouth, Fall River, and New Bedford in an effort to educate women about slavery and enroll female assistance in challenging the laws sustaining it. The sisters helped coordinate and accompanied the first abolitionist speaking tour by female agents (the Grimké sisters of South Carolina and Philadelphia), and wrote volumes of letters, newspaper articles, organizational documents, tracts, hymns, and poetry in the process of shaping public opinion and recording the movement's history. One or more Westons served, at any given time, as officer(s) of the BFAS from 1835 through the lifetime of the association, and of the MAS and AAS from 1840 to 1865. The Weston and Chapman homes in Weymouth and Boston served as centers of abolition organization and sociability.

Thus, among the many women and men who engaged in abolition, the Weston sisters occupied a position of unusual visibility, even notoriety. For decades they provided leadership while working to exhaustion in the trenches of reform. As individuals and as a group they were renowned, both loved and despised within and without the antislavery movement. Yet exactly how and why the Westons came to abolition remains unclear.

Maria, Caroline, and Anne were teachers or students in Boston when its black and white communities first embraced antislavery activism, and various evidence suggests that they came to abolition in part through an interest in education and child welfare, particularly that of black students and orphans.[4] They may well have heard or read about the controversial lectures given by Maria [Miller] W. Stewart in 1832 as she made the case for improved education to better African American lives. The earliest actual evidence of Weston engagement in the cause of racial equality is provided by a September 1832 fund-raiser, possibly to support Prudence Crandall's school in Canterbury, Connecticut, as she considered admitting a mixed-race student body.[5]

Another draw was certainly temperance reform.[6] Probably as a result of their father's drinking, the Weston daughters closely followed temperance efforts in Weymouth and Boston. Maria encouraged her sisters to canvass for votes in 1834 when Boston first proposed laws limiting the retail sale of liquor, and then again in the 1835 Norfolk and Suffolk county commissioner elections, in which temperance candidates who advocated restricted licensing won 52 percent of the vote.[7] In 1838, Boston proposed the first law in the nation limiting retail sales of distilled spirits to less than fifteen gallons.[8] Hoping "the Temperance folks may prevail," Anne urged her sisters "to go out and canvass for votes."[9] Thereafter, even as nonresistants, the Westons consistently campaigned among their male kin, fellow abolitionists, and friends on behalf of temperate Whigs and against "democratic rum drinkers" in local elections.[10]

Weymouth embraced temperance. Well-known lecturers such as Dr. Charles Jewett and Edwin Thompson campaigned there. Members of the Washington Total Abstinence Society of Weymouth and Braintree conducted a pledge drive shortly after it was founded in March 1842,[11] and they gathered the signatures of 639 locals (about 16 percent of the population) who affirmed their desire to give up liquor. Weston cousin Edmund Hunt reported, "Everyone signed the pledge"; his father, Major Elias Hunt, "signed with the rest." However, when the local visiting committee came around to police those who continued to drink, Hunt rejected their belief that he had broken his oath. "They said, 'Major Hunt, we understand you have broken the pledge.' With much surprise, [Hunt] replied, 'No I have not.' They said, 'We are told you drink gin.' 'Of course I do. I always have, and have to,' was the reply. And so the Major was turned out of the 'Cold Water Army.'"[12] There is no evidence as to whether or not Captain Warren Weston signed the pledge, but his understanding likely mirrored that of his stepfather.

Also as a result of Warren Weston's drinking, character formed a central theme in the lives and works of his daughters. As Maria wrote of her father, "What a fine mind was wrecked by his want of self-government! I sometimes think that his family are possibly superior to what they would have been, through the powerful admonition that his defects have given them."[13] In 1837, she reported (perhaps overoptimistically) to her abstemious uncle, banker Joshua Bates, that her fifty-six-year-old father was "now a temperate man."[14]

For the Westons, as for many of their contemporaries, enslavement meant not only a physical but also a mental process affecting anyone who could not exercise his or her own will for lack of self-mastery, whether due to drink, greed, lust, cruelty, or laziness.[15] Just as alcohol enslaved the drinker, the enslaving of human beings aroused passions of brutality and lust in masters while encouraging indolence and immorality in slaves.[16]

Weston abolitionism was also encouraged by means of marital ties. Maria Ann Weston married Henry Grafton Chapman in 1830. Henry's cousin Ann T. Greene, a niece of Maria's mother-in-law, Sarah Greene Chapman, was an invalid who lived with Henry's parents at their home in Boston's Chauncy Place in the early 1830s,[17] and Ann's cousins, Susan and Mary Grew, were very early abolitionists. No evidence remains of discussions about slavery or abolition between the Grew sisters and their relatives, but by January 1834, Anne Warren Weston had announced her decision to attend a recruitment meeting of the Middlesex County Abolitionist Society.[18] That March, against a rising tide of antiblack and anti-abolitionist violence across the Northeast, the women of the newly constituted BFAS elected Mary Grew its first secretary, passed a constitution, and issued a call for additional members.[19] The following spring, when Grew moved to Philadelphia, Anne Warren Weston replaced her as corresponding secretary of the BFAS.[20]

During this period, Maria Weston Chapman sought to rally Bostonians of means to purchase a membership in the Boston Athenaeum for Lydia Maria Child, whose borrowing privileges had been revoked by the library's directors after she published *An Appeal in Favor of That Class of Americans Called Africans*. Chapman collected the necessary $100 fee to enable Child to finish her feminist work, *The History and Condition of Women in Various Ages and Nations*.[21]

According to Sarah Southwick, who was present at the time,[22] Maria Weston Chapman formally declared her desire to join the BFAS in June 1835.[23] In November, when the society undertook its second fund-raising fair,[24] Maria greeted participants as Anne worked the tables alongside Maria's sisters-in-law Ann Greene Chapman and Mary Gray Chapman. The BFAS raised some $300 for the New England Anti-Slavery Society (NEAS).[25]

By midsummer 1835 the campaign against slavery had inspired the destruction of antislavery literature by postal agents and rioting by anti-abolitionist and antiblack mobs. Visiting British "agitator" George Thompson received death threats, and after his 1 August 1835 commemoration of the end to British slavery in the Caribbean, antislavery women covered his retreat to a waiting carriage. Over the next two months, tensions built between abolitionists and Boston's mercantile elite, who sought to protect their southern trade. The announcement that Thompson would speak to the BFAS the second week in October produced such a public uproar that the women postponed the event for a month before substituting Garrison for the "foreign incendiary."

Thompson played an important role in the founding of many local antislavery societies, including Weymouth's. Maria and Anne drove out to Weymouth from Boston to attend Thompson's September lectures and follow up with an organizational meeting. Some thirty "well-disposed" women signed a call to join the nascent Weymouth and Braintree Female Emancipation Society.[26] During the first year of their association these women circulated to every family in town an antislavery appeal aimed at raising abolitionist consciousness. Aunt Mary Weston wrote the annual report, crafting it as an appeal to Weymouth women: "Let every member of this society act in all respects as she would be induced to do, if her father, her mother, her child, her sister, or her brother was in slavery." These beginnings were slow to catch on, however, and the society held no quarterly meeting in January 1836.[27] A second association, the South Weymouth Female Anti-Slavery Society, emerged on 19 November 1835; it was generally more gradualist in practice and ameliorist in ideology, though the two groups occasionally met and worked together. Their difference reflected broader fractures in the movement that would become septic some four to five years later.

Meanwhile in Boston, the merchants of Washington Street sought from Mayor Theodore Lyman an injunction to prevent the women's society from meeting to hear George Thompson. A group of businessmen operating on Boston's Central Wharf, alongside the chandlery owned and operated by Maria's father-in-law and husband, organized an effort "to snake out . . . the infamous foreign scoundrel," and an anonymous broadsheet offered $100 to the first man to lay "violent hands" on him. Some 500 copies were distributed across the North End wharfs and along State Street, the city's commercial center. By midafternoon on the October day of the BFAS meeting, the streets around the antislavery offices were crowded with angry men and unruly boys.[28] They filled the stairwell and blocked the entryway to the Washington Street building where the women's meeting was to take place. While Garrison addressed the twenty-five to thirty women gathered for the occasion, another hundred or so found themselves unable to gain entrance. Among these were Caroline Weston and Garrison's wife Helen Benson Garrison.[29]

As the crowd grew in noise, numbers, and threat, BFAS president Mary Parker urged Garrison to leave for his own safety. He withdrew to the *Liberator* office. Pushing his way through the crowd, Mayor Lyman urged the women to disperse for their own safety. Parker questioned the need, and Chapman challenged the mayor to use his influence to subdue and disperse the mob. After all, she charged, his "personal friends" had instigated the crisis. Lyman reiterated that the women endangered themselves if they chose to remain. Parker asked Lyman whether he would guarantee their safety if they withdrew; only, he replied, if they left immediately.[30]

In pairs, the women walked bravely through the amassed crowd and down Washington Street to the home of Francis Jackson.[31] Dispersing from there, some retired to Maria's home in nearby West Street, where another crowd had gathered, fueled by the rumor that Thompson hid there. Gradually that crowd disbanded as well, although the house continued to draw anti-abolitionist protesters. A group of newspaper editors and merchants attempted to blackmail Maria's husband into giving up Thompson's hiding place and withdrawing his own public support for abolition.[32]

Meanwhile, Garrison fled the Washington Street building, escaping through a window and dropping to the street below. The crowd recognized and seized him. Two teamsters driving by rescued him and fled to City Hall, where Mayor Lyman swore out a warrant authorizing Garrison's overnight incarceration, ostensibly for his protection. Garrison closed his Boston household, stored his furnishings with Caroline and Anne Warren Weston, who were setting up a private school on Boylston Street, and joined his pregnant wife in Brooklyn, Connecticut, to await the birth of their first child. George Thompson hid from pursuit at the Boston home of Joseph and Thankful Hussey Southwick.[33] Concerned for Thompson's life, Henry G. Chapman escorted him to the wharf and put him safely on a boat back to England.

That winter, the BFAS held another fund-raiser—in the Chauncy Place home of Maria's in-laws, as the society feared that, after the mob, the Washington Street hall would prove "especially repulsive to purchasers" and no commercial landlord would rent them space. Maria insisted that the traumatized members must stand up for their cause, even if this meant performing "a service of danger."

In December 1835, William Ellery Channing, revered minister of the Federal Street Unitarian Church, broke his silence on the subject of slavery with a 160-page pamphlet in which he made the philosophical case against it. Channing criticized anti-abolitionist mobs but also abolitionists who sought support from an "excitable and unenlightened" African

American community. The Westons thought him "a milksop," and Maria called him "a tender spirited saintly sort of man, to whom the evil not before his eyes, (and they were not sharp eyes) was mere abstraction." Channing had "entreated" Maria "not to hold a ladies meeting, as if it were a crime, dangerous & against humanity to protest slavery."[34]

Although Garrison continued to absent himself from Boston through the spring of 1836, the AAS doubled in size to more than 500 auxiliaries in fifteen states. Among the primary activities of these societies were well-organized and carefully orchestrated campaigns petitioning for an end to slavery. As Caroline informed Anne from Boston, "We have devised a magnificent plan about petitions—there is a committee of 14 raised—each member of that committee is to take the responsibility of seeing a petition for abolition circulated in every town in some one county." Maria took Norfolk (Boston), Ann Greene Chapman chose Worcester ("with its 55 towns!!"), and Anne selected Bristol (Fall River, Taunton, and New Bedford). For the next twenty-five years, the Weston sisters continued to petition Congress on behalf of the slave. With one Saturday's effort, Debora celebrated her addition of 27 names to the almost 300 collected by members of the BFAS (who divided Boston's wards as they had the state's cities). She set herself the goal of obtaining 100 signatures.[35]

By January 1837, Mary Weston could report that she had sent 248 signatures from Weymouth and 130 from Braintree to Maria, who gathered them together in Boston for shipment to Washington, D.C.[36] Debora deemed petitioning so important that she urged Anne's presence in town to aid her, directed Lucia to stay in Boston to assist Maria, and commanded Caroline, who was teaching in Roxbury, to "use her Saturdays for a few weeks for nothing else."[37] So successful were the petition campaigns in raising the political consciousness of the North that the House of Representatives adopted a "gag rule" tabling any discussion in chambers. Although Massachusetts representative John Quincy Adams ably attacked the gag on the House floor, it was renewed every session into the 1840s.[38]

In the face of spreading anti-abolitionist and antiblack violence in the North, Garrison began writing of nonresistance and disunion, issues that Boston's conservative elite perceived as radical and tangential to the main abolitionist agenda; the Garrisonians also became increasingly alienated from the clergy. At midsummer 1836, he attacked Rev. Lyman Beecher in the *Liberator*, impugning the motives of Congregational ministers in Massachusetts and Connecticut who closed their pulpits to sermons or lectures on slavery and notices of antislavery meetings. Boston and Weymouth churches, like most in Massachusetts, shut their doors to such abolitionist preachers as the Reverend Charles Follen, husband of Maria's close friend Elizabeth Cabot Follen. As female abolitionists heightened the pressure with a campaign to deliver notices of their meetings to every church in Boston on Sundays, several men, including Henry G. Chapman, organized a "Free Church" to serve as a religious haven for antislavery thought and practice.[39]

At the behest of slave owners and their agents, local authorities began searching private residences in Boston for runaway slaves. The BFAS expressed concern about the plight of a woman arrested in one such search and offered legal assistance to two others who, despite having carried their emancipation papers on their persons, were taken from the brig *Chicasaw* in Boston harbor and detained as fugitives. The Westons visited the women in jail. Along with other members of the BFAS, they attended hearings before the Massachusetts Supreme Court and celebrated the decision of Justice Lemuel Shaw, who ruled the "fugitives" falsely imprisoned and ordered their release.[40]

Maria further challenged the legal and political culture of Boston in the case of child slave Med Sommersett, brought to the city by her mistress on a visit from New Orleans. Posing as a Sunday school teacher, Maria went with two other BFAS members to 21 Pinckney Street, the residence of Thomas Aves, hoping to convince her owner, Samuel Slater, to free the child and place her in Boston's new black orphanage. He refused. While a group of African American men planned Med's rescue, lawyer Ellis G. Loring obtained a writ of habeas corpus and persuaded Aves to surrender her.[41]

Upon investigating Med's legal situation, members of the BFAS discovered that she was to be sold to cover the cost of her mistress's trip north. They secured a second writ of habeas corpus, setting in motion a case that came before the Massachusetts Supreme Court in late August. The BFAS asked Daniel Webster to plead the case. He agreed but was not immediately available, so the society engaged Rufus Choate.[42] Ellis Gray Loring and Samuel Sewall filed suit against Thomas Aves and Samuel Slater for unlawful imprisonment. Sarah Greene Chapman, Maria's mother-in-law, paid the fifty-dollar filing fee to put the case on the court's docket. With Weston fund-raising, the BFAS paid the lawyers.[43] In an unprecedented decision, Justice Shaw declared a slave's right to remain in a free state into which she or he had been temporarily brought.[44]

One thousand participants attended the January 1837 meeting of the MAS, held in the loft of a horse barn attached to the Marlboro Hotel.

Although offered another venue, the society chose to highlight the strain between abolitionists and those churches that were reluctant to take a stand on slavery. The meeting marked the beginning of a highly divisive struggle between conservative clerical authority and the Weston brand of female abolition.

The conflict had begun in fall 1836 when the Philadelphia Female Anti-Slavery Society (PFAS) announced it would send delegates to the annual convention of the American Anti-Slavery Society (AAS) and urged other female associations to follow suit. Sarah Pugh penned a request for female credentialing to Elizur Wright Jr., executive secretary of the AAS. He assured the PFAS that women "would doubtless be received with the courtesy and high respect which it is the glory of the *Christian* religion to pay to the *better half* of human nature."[45] Such condescension, posing as polite deference, spurred a wider discussion of the notion of appointing formal delegates from female societies. A BFAS proposal to this end lost on a close vote among the female associations. Mary Clark, corresponding secretary for the Concord [New Hampshire] Society, spoke for others that declined direct representation: "Our more experienced *brethren* who are accustomed to speak in such assemblies can more justly represent us than we could represent ourselves."[46]

Unwilling to drop the matter, Maria pushed to form an executive committee drawn from members of female societies "to devise plans for the advancement of this cause." As corresponding secretary for the BFAS, she wrote to all female associations, declaring, "Great good might result from the collision of such minds as those of A. E. Grimké, Lucretia Mott, Mary Parker, Mary Clark of Concord, the Balls, the Westons, the Childs & others."[47] A positive response to her suggestion led to the May 1837 Anti-Slavery Convention of American Women in New York City.[48] Some 200 attended the three sessions. Anne Warren Weston's detailed notes circulated through the family and to Garrison, who drew upon them for a report in the *Liberator*.[49]

Among the many resolutions brought before this first woman's convention was one proposed by Angelina Grimké. Signaling a growing independence among antislavery women as to their proper sphere, she charged that "corrupt custom and a perverted application of Scripture" had "circumscribed" woman's duty. Grimké's resolution encouraged antislavery women "to plead the cause of the oppressed in our land" by every means— voice, pen, and purse. Following intense debate, the resolution won approval. However, twelve delegates, mostly from New York City, requested that the minutes record their dissent.[50]

A month later, on 7 June 1837, the BFAS sent a letter addressed to "all Female Anti-Slavery Societies throughout New England." Written by Maria in her official capacity as corresponding secretary, the letter was also signed by President Mary S. Parker. "In all spiritual things," Maria insisted, men's and women's "functions are identical;—both are created to be parents and educators;—both for all the duties growing out of that spiritual equality . . . neither for helplessness or dependence—neither for arbitrary dictation;—each to obey the commands of God as responsible to him alone." However, Maria allowed, "with respect to secondary pursuits—whether mercantile, mechanical, domestic or professional—the machinery of mortal existence,—'the tools to whosoever can use them.'"[51] It was a position to which she and her sisters would closely adhere thereafter.

That same month began the highly successful, and controversial, public speaking tour of AAS agents Angelina and Sarah Grimké. Maria and Anne accompanied them and, on behalf of the BFAS, undertook to ensure local sponsors and appropriate speaking and hospitality arrangements.[52] Some 500 women showed up to greet the Grimkés at the Lynn, Massachusetts, Female Anti-Slavery Association meeting of 21 June 1837.

A week later, on 27 June 1837, the General Association of Congregational Ministers meeting in North Brookfield, Massachusetts, issued a "Pastoral Letter" addressed to all orthodox congregations. Written by Rev. Nehemiah Adams in three parts, the epistle insisted that discussion of abolition "should not be FORCED upon any church as matters for debate *at the hazard of alienation and division.*" Adams particularly decried what he saw as a loss of deference to the pastoral office among antislavery women. The entire second part of his letter addressed such disrespectful behaviors as parishioner attendance at antislavery lectures held *"within the parochial limits of settled pastors without their consent."* Seeking to curb abolitionist pressure on clergy members to preach on the subject of slavery and to open their pulpits to antislavery notices and speakers, Adams enjoined the female brethren to "obey them that have the rule over you and submit yourselves."[53]

Of particular concern to the orthodox clergy was the proper deference of women to clerical office and subordination to their pastors. The "Pastoral Letter" invited attention "to the dangers which at present seem to threaten the FEMALE CHARACTER with wide-spread and permanent injury." Adams admitted the duty of sisters-in-Christ to guide and influence their brothers, thus acknowledging the gender roles of contemporary sibling culture,[54] but insisted that "those duties and that influence are unobtrusive and private." The letter emphasized the boundaries and limitations of female usefulness. "[W]hen [woman] assumes the place and tone of man as a public reformer, . . . her character becomes unnatural."[55] This barb took direct aim at the Grimkés, as well as at women in antislavery associations.

Debate over the "Pastoral Letter" reflected all shades of opinion, as demonstrated by the numerous sermons offered throughout New England over the following months. Rev. Parsons Cooke reminded his congregation, "It is made the duty of woman so far as religious assemblies are concerned, to learn and not to teach—to learn in silence." Speaking "would be an unseemly usurping of authority, for one who should bear the marks of subjection." Rev. Winslow Hubbard agreed: a female transformed her naturally "delicate voice" by taking it "house to house, or in social assemblies, rising in harsh unnatural tones of denunciation against civil laws and rulers, against measures involving political and State affairs of which she is nearly as ignorant as the child she left at home in the cradle." Surely, he insisted, such women had "usurp[ed] authority over the man" and earned Samuel J. May's denomination "the female brethren."[56]

Heaping fuel on the fire, Maria wrote and published a poem, "The Times That Try Men's Souls," belittling orthodox clergymen and making fun of their outrage:

Confusion has seized us, and all things go wrong,
The women have leaped from "their spheres,"
And, instead of fixed stars, shoot as comets along,
And are setting the world by the ears! . . .
They've taken a notion to speak for themselves,
And are wielding the tongue and the pen;
They've mounted the rostrum; the termagant elves,
And—oh horrid!—are talking to men![57]

The clerical directive had an immediate effect. Juliana A. Tappan of the New York society wrote Anne Warren Weston to ask whether addressing gentlemen might not go over the line of appropriate female behavior. While she appreciated the difficulty of steering a course between "servile submission to the opinions of the other sex" and the "equal danger of losing that modesty and instinctive delicacy of feeling, which our Creator has given as a safeguard . . . on account of our weakness," Tappan chose to err on the side of female modesty.[58] On the other hand, Mrs. George Tailor of the Groton, Massachusetts, Female Anti-Slavery Society was so shocked by her minister's refusal to take his place in the pulpit with the Grimkés in attendance that she left his church.[59]

As BFAS secretary, Anne constructed her own missive and addressed it to the female antislavery societies, pleading for mutual support among "all who hold the Abolition faith 'undimmed & pure.'" She affirmed the Grimkés' call to public speaking but acknowledged to her readers, "If you cannot conscientiously support these views we would not ask you to do so." However, she urged, "we would earnestly & faithfully entreat you to do more, far more, in those ways that *do* approve themselves to your consciences than you ever yet have done." Anne argued that the problem rested not with the antislavery sisters but with the clerical brothers: "[W]ho are those who are now opposing woman's influence as exercised in favour of the Emancipation? As a general thing are they not the men whose opposition to the cause of the injured and outraged slave has ever been bitter and unrelenting?"[60] Anne showed her draft to Maria and to Mary Parker. While the former thought the letter ought to be sent, the latter disagreed because the timing was sufficiently close to that of the society's annual report that what should be said could be said in it. A meeting of the BFAS board discussed the issue, and Parker's view carried the day.[61]

Reports in the *Liberator* further inflamed the conflict. Garrison, preoccupied with the slow death of his father-in-law, had left the paper in the hands of Oliver Johnson. Johnson published an inflammatory denunciation of the General Assembly of the Presbyterian Church by Rev. Eliphaz White, a Massachusetts native attached to a southern church but preaching temporarily in Boston: "My presbytery will never, o never, give up their right to hold slaves."[62] Both Amos Phelps, general agent for the MAS, and Garrison himself responded in the *Liberator* that not all ministers were necessarily "excellent Christians"; indeed, "Christianity indignantly rejects the sanctimonious pretensions of the great mass of the clergy in our land. . . . They are nothing better than hirelings. . . . hindrances to the march of human freedom, and to the enfranchisement of the souls of men."[63]

In August 1837 a group of Congregational clergy followed the "Pastoral Letter" with an "Appeal of Clerical Abolitionists on Anti-slavery Measures" that deepened the split among abolitionists by explicitly attacking Garrison. Among these was the Westons' own Rev. Jonas Perkins of Weymouth's Union Church.[64] Perkins and his fellow signatories charged that Garrison had been "hasty, unsparing, almost ferocious" in his denunciation of Eliphaz White; had insinuated that George Blagden, a former minister at the Salem Street Congregational Church, was a slaveholder; had, through the *Liberator*, supported the campaign of female congregants to have notices of their antislavery meetings read to Boston congregations; and had publicly abused ministers and other Christians who did not join antislavery societies. The authors of the "Appeal" threatened that unless Garrison and his followers changed their language and tactics, some antislavery clergy would abandon the movement.[65]

Maria leapt to Garrison's defense. Seeking the support of the AAS, she wrote Elizur Wright Jr. of her "deep conviction of the necessity—the *absolute necessity* of holding by Garrison with a giant grasp at this moment." She challenged Wright's intellectual honesty and courage, demanding to know whether he was fooled by "the black hearted ministry," and added, "My prayer has ever been that the ecclesiastical despotism of this land be abolished at the same stroke that freed the slave and I see now, that without the abolition of the former the latter cannot be."[66]

The entire matter of Garrison, the *Liberator*, and relations with the antislavery clergy was put on the agenda of the MAS quarterly meeting held in Worcester that October. The executive committee of the AAS assured Garrison, in Anne's words, that the problem was "a quarrel between brethren." However, by September, she feared that only Rev. Amos Phelps, general agent of the MAS, could be counted on to carry forward the fight for Garrison from within the religious establishment. Leaving as little to chance as possible, she asked Debora to ensure that the antislavery brethren in New Bedford would come to Worcester to support the *Liberator* and Garrison. "I trust that God will overrule matters at Worcester," she wrote, "for the prospect seems to me dark."[67] In his position as MAS treasurer, Henry G. Chapman attended the meeting, as did Maria, Caroline, and Hervey Weston on his return home from Yale. Caroline reported to Debora on many of the speeches and wrote with relief that the crowd received Garrison with "*deafening thundrus* of applaus [*sic*]," saying that only then did she believe all would be well.[68]

Rather than building bridges to the disaffected, however, Garrison continued to attack the clergy in such a way that even Amos Phelps was dismayed. Garrison defended his harsh language and, as Caroline reported, "left the door open to them only as they might confess and repent." Thus began Phelps's alienation from Garrison and the Westons, who should have recognized the significance of the breach when the MAS agent agreed to preach at Jonas Perkins's Weymouth pulpit on the subject of "Christian Affection" before giving an evening antislavery lecture following the MAS meeting in October.[69]

The Union Religious Society of Weymouth rebuked Perkins for his role in the "Appeal," insisting, "We consider it the duty of ministers of the gospel to give all notices of meetings, handed to them to be publicly read from the pulpit, on all subjects, which have for their object the promotion of virtue or suppression of vice, when couched in proper and respectful language."[70] At a meeting of the Weymouth and Braintree Female Emancipation Society, Mary Weston carried the day, proposing and passing resolutions supportive of Garrison and the *Liberator* despite the presiding of Rhoda (Mrs. Jonas) Perkins.[71]

In November 1837, the murder of Elijah Lovejoy, editor and publisher of an antislavery newspaper in Alton, Illinois, created a public outcry against anti-abolitionist violence. Rev. William Ellery Channing called for a meeting in Boston's Faneuil Hall to address the matter on 8 December 1837. When civic authorities denied this use of the building, his outrage forced them to back down. On the night, some 5,000 people filled the hall to overflowing. Among those attending was a group of antislavery women. Sarah Southwick later reported that Maria had "sent word to our family" that she and her sisters wished to attend the meeting and invited Southwick to join them. "Women," she noted, "were not then in the habit of attending political meetings, and had never been to any in Faneuil Hall." Maria wanted sufficient women present to "keep one another in countenance" and make a statement. Thirteen women "ranged ourselves in the front seat of the right gallery."[72] At the meeting, in attacking abolitionists for inciting southern fears of slave rebellion, Massachusetts attorney general James T. Austin implied that Lovejoy had only himself to blame for his death. Wendell Phillips, a Weston cousin by marriage, rose to object. In his first public antislavery speech, Phillips defended Lovejoy and attacked Austin's view of Lovejoy's murderers as patriots.[73]

The AAS grew significantly in 1838, fielding thirty-eight agents who inspired 350 new societies. The number of local affiliates expanded to over 1,000. The association printed some 600,000 antislavery pamphlets, including Maria's *Pinda: A True Tale* (the story of a fugitive slave who made her way to the Chapman home, was taken under the Weston wing, and was covertly reunited with her husband in New Bedford),[74] an antislavery hymnal she collated with Elizabeth Cabot Follen, and her primer, *How Can I Become an Abolitionist?*. During this period antislavery societies forwarded some 400,000 petitions to Congress with nearly 1,000,000 signatures,[75] the bulk gathered in drives organized and conducted by women, because antislavery men increasingly saw the petition as an impotent political instrument after the congressional gag left these unopened and unread.[76] Antislavery women forwarded no fewer than 50,000 names from Massachusetts alone.[77]

In May 1838, many who attended the annual AAS meeting in New York City went on to Philadelphia to celebrate the dedication of the newly built

Pennsylvania Hall, a civic monument to free speech. Maria and Anne also attended the wedding of Theodore Weld and Angelina Grimké on 14 May in an extraordinary ceremony overseen by two ministers, one black and one white. Quaker abolitionist Lucretia Mott refused to attend because Angelina married outside her faith. Garrison read aloud the wedding certificate signed by the guests.

Delegates to the second antislavery women's convention faced verbal abuse and physical harassment on the streets of Philadelphia, especially when walking in mixed-race groups. Maria made her first public speech from the stage of Pennsylvania Hall amid the violence of a proslavery mob that eventually forced the delegates from the building before burning it to the ground. Despite such intimidation, the antislavery women continued their meetings the following day. However, as mobs roamed the streets of the city, Maria and Anne fled for their own safety and that of their hosts, James and Lucretia Mott.[78]

At the end of May, the NEAS convention met, without incident, in Boston's recently built Marlboro Chapel. Some 500 participants attended. A resolution passed admitting the sixty to seventy women present with rights to speak and vote. Despite the objections of those who suggested it would be unseemly for a woman to work so closely with men, the convention appointed female lecturer Abigail Kelley[79] to a committee charged with developing a call to churches to sustain the cause. Conservatives who had opposed Kelley's appointment then moved to reconsider the equal admission of women to the convention on the grounds that the indecent mixing of women with men would cast the committee's work in an "unscriptural" light. When this motion failed, many delegates walked out, protesting the injection of a "foreign" issue, woman's rights, into an antislavery meeting.

In September 1838, Garrison called for a discussion of peaceful methods to resolve social conflict and resist government's physical coercion of citizens. The meeting would consider the legitimacy of a standing army and of conscientious objection to military service, the immorality of capital punishment, and whether nonresistants should participate, by voting, in a government that used force to uphold its laws. Most delegates who convened in Marlboro Chapel on 20 September 1838 were local, although antislavery activists also came from Rhode Island, New Hampshire, and even Pennsylvania. Many were Quakers. The Westons competed with one another to attend the convention and sign the Declaration of Sentiments establishing the Non-Resistance Society. Anne and Maria served on the governing board until fall 1843, and the society frequently met in Maria's Boston home.[80]

Anne, who had signed the Declaration of Sentiments, took on Garrison, insisting "that the non resistance society should possess an organ of communication with the public other than the *Liberator*, and this as well on account of the one cause as the other." She feared—correctly, as it turned out—that nonresistance articles in the *Liberator* would "prove a source of vexation and discord to the Abolitionists." She particularly feared the effect of "recreant" ministers' "allegations that we are contending for the abolition of government rather than that of anti slavery."[81] Garrison eventually acquiesced, and Edmund Quincy took responsibility for editing the *Non Resistant*, with the not inconsiderable help of the Westons, who wrote copy. Over the years, the Westons maintained their nonresistance even in the face of such grave temptations as using force to rescue fugitive slaves and marshalling the potential power of woman's suffrage.[82] Maria and Caroline attended the Congress of Peace in Versailles in 1851 and continued the discussion of nonresistance with such British abolitionists as Elizabeth Pease and Richard D. Webb during the second congress in London in 1855.

Weston concerns about the efforts of clerical abolitionists to subvert the MAS continued to grow as some agents insisted that electoral activism was "a Christian duty." At the annual AAS meeting in January 1839, delegates voted to end their financial support of the *Liberator* and expressed a desire for an alternative. The Westons also feared duplicity in the national office. Elizur Wright Jr. had urged Garrison to withdraw from the movement after the nonresistance convention of the previous year, and Henry B. Stanton argued that it might be a good idea to purge the Massachusetts leadership from the AAS. The two men insisted that the AAS constitution required abolitionists to exercise the franchise, so, in questioning whether nonresistants should vote, Garrison had abandoned the organization's principles.

The MAS meeting that began on 23 January 1839 lasted three days. Rev. Amos Phelps, who had resigned his agency for the society, denounced Garrison as unfit to lead a moral enterprise. Stanton, who was not a MAS member, argued that a new antislavery newspaper had become a necessity given the ideological sympathies of the *Liberator*. He demanded of Garrison directly whether he thought it a sin to vote and insisted that the AAS constitution mandated its exercise. Garrison replied, "Sin for *me*." Furious, Maria insisted that no abolitionist had ever presented "a creed-measure to his brethren."[83] When a resolution affirming the franchise as an antislavery measure was rejected, the anti-Garrisonians challenged the right of women to vote on it. In the end, the incumbent board was reelected.

Although the majority of association members continued to support the *Liberator*, others turned to the rival *Massachusetts Abolitionist* as their official organ.

Although women had long voted in both MAS and NEAS conventions, before 1839 the AAS had not considered the matter of enfranchising female members of and delegates to the national association and its meetings. Antislavery women had held their own conventions concurrently with the AAS annual meetings in New York in 1837 and Philadelphia in 1838. But in 1839, these same women expected to participate fully in the national association convention.

The MAS sent female delegates to represent it. Elizur Wright Jr. expressed "opposition to hens crowing" and worried that the woman question would dominate the meeting. James G. Birney and Arthur Tappan, among others, recognized that to succeed in limiting Garrison's influence they would have to bar his female supporters from active participation.[84] Hence, the 1839 annual meeting began with a debate on qualifications for membership. Abigail Kelley, a Quaker from Worcester, Massachusetts, and Eliza Barney, a Quaker from Nantucket, spoke to the issue.[85] When the convention voted on whether the roll should be made up of men or of persons, the female brethren succeeded in achieving admission as equals. The ultimate outcome of this dissension in the AAS would be the breakaway of the anti-Garrisonian, anti–woman's rights group led by Arthur and Lewis Tappan and Elizur Wright Jr., and the 1840 formation of the American and Foreign Anti-Slavery Society.

In Massachusetts, opponents again tried and failed to limit women's antislavery activism at the May 1839 meeting of the MAS. A "sifting" on "the woman's rights question" resulted in the formation of a second statewide association, the Massachusetts Abolition Society on 27 May, which required that members be male and committed to electioneering, limited participation in business meetings solely to officers and agents of the organization, and rationed local auxiliaries to one convention delegate for every twenty-five members, to reduce the impact of "disorganizers" and "woman's rights men" (male Garrisonians) and "Amazons" (female Garrisonians).[86]

Arguably, the primary "success" of the "new organization" in Massachusetts was its impact on the division of the BFAS. The Parker and Ball sisters, along with their supporters, announced the end of the association in January 1840, even as the Westons and their allies objected to the vote count and Maria called for another meeting to prove the group's ongoing viability. Similar splits followed across the Northeast. For example, by a vote of twenty-seven to eighteen, two-thirds of the Dedham Female Anti-Slavery Society transferred their "auxiliaryship" to the new Massachusetts Female Emancipation Society, which was allied with the Massachusetts Abolition Society.

Edmund Quincy urged the Westons to heed Dedham's example, as "the other women's societies in the country . . . are no doubt all to go through the same process." He warned that the "new organization" had successfully defined women's antislavery activism as a danger to the church. The Dedham vote "was accomplished," he wrote, "by drawing up all manner of women . . . many who had taken no interest in the cause. . . . The rallying word was 'the church is in danger!' & these new Joans of Arc hastened to the rescue of the idol in which they put their trust."[87] While the Westons saw this reaction against female abolitionists as a denial of women's contributions to the cause and a prohibition of their right to act upon their own consciences, many antislavery women retreated into confusion. In some societies with histories of women and men working together, women's right to participate and vote in antislavery meetings was circumscribed. In others, such as the Newport Female Society, women closed their same-sex auxiliary and joined the male association on equal terms. In Boston, Caroline characterized the BFAS quarterly meeting as a "desperate struggle" and acknowledged that the organization could "do nothing at all at present either for good or evil," though she hoped that it would soon "be quietly at work in the old way."[88]

At the national level, efforts to dissolve the AAS continued even as the quarrel over "new organization" reduced the treasury. Lewis Tappan hoped to replace the AAS with a self-perpetuating national board of commissioners similar to those governing some evangelical missionary efforts. The Westons feared that his goal was to dissolve the national antislavery society completely. When the AAS executive committee transferred ownership of the association's newspaper, the *Emancipator*, to Joshua Leavitt (a clerical abolitionist and third political party advocate), they and other Garrisonians identified the move as a step in that direction. As Lydia Maria Child warned that Henry B. Stanton and Amos Phelps had engaged in a whispering campaign against the association, the still-Garrisonian MAS put out a call for support. It warned that the AAS might try to limit the number of delegates to the annual meeting or form an independent board of commissioners in order to bring an end to the national organization.

On 11 May 1840 Massachusetts delegates and observers made their way to New York City to attend the AAS annual meeting. Hervey Weston represented the Garrisonian Weymouth and Braintree men's society; Anne and Caroline Weston went from the BFAS.[89] As the meeting opened at the Free Church on 12 May 1840, Arthur Tappan sent word that he was retiring from the AAS presidency and would not attend. Vice President Francis Jackson of Boston took the gavel and presented a balanced list of candidates for board positions. For the business committee he announced both anti-Garrisonians Lewis Tappan and Amos Phelps and Garrisonians Abby Kelley and Charles C. Burleigh.

According to Anne, the vote on this slate went on steadily until it came to Kelley, at which point "there was first, an immense *yes*—then a superb *no*." Jackson asked those supporting Kelley to stand. So crowded were the pews that the tellers had trouble counting votes, but eventually they announced 571 for approval. When Jackson asked the opponents to stand, one minister urged the ladies to refrain from voting in this case, and Phelps shouted that women should not be voting on either side. The tally was 451 negative votes. Tappan announced he would not serve on a mixed-gender committee, and other conservatives insisted that such a composition defied scripture and ran contrary to the society's charter and custom. "It held on till near dark," Anne wrote, "and when we broke up it was settled that we had achieved a glorious victory."[90]

Anne supposed that the anti-Garrisonians would "make an attempt to reconsider" the following day. Instead, Lewis Tappan met with thirty like-minded individuals later that same evening to discuss a draft of a new antislavery organization. The following morning, 13 May 1840, he asked all who objected to placing a woman on the business committee to meet in the church basement later that afternoon for the purpose of forming the American and Foreign Anti-Slavery Society. Clerical dissidents and those who sought to pursue emancipation through the electoral process walked out of the convention. Although Edmund Quincy joked, "After tea we went to a caucus at [black caterer] Thomas Van Rensellaer's to see what we should do with the Society now we have got it," the Garrisonians held only the executive committee. Seated on that committee were Maria Weston Chapman, Lydia Maria Child, and Lucretia Mott.

In mid-June 1840, a number of Americans traveled to London to participate in an international antislavery convention sponsored by the newly formed British and Foreign Anti-Slavery Society. Before the AAS divided in May, its executive committee had voted to subsidize the attendance of James G. Birney and Henry B. Stanton. Mott thus met Elizabeth Cady Stanton, an encounter that would bear fruit at Seneca Falls in 1848.[91] Although nominated as a delegate, Maria had just given birth to her fourth child, was nursing an ill husband, and chose not to attend. Once in

London, the Garrisonian delegates refused to participate because, despite its invitation to the "peoples of all clime," the convention excluded female delegates.[92]

When abolitionist James G. Birney ran for U.S. president on the Liberty Party ticket in the fall of 1840 and lost to Whig candidate William Henry Harrison, Garrison charged that "third party" was simply another name for the "new organization." The Westons continued to support Garrison and the AAS, MAS, and BFAS. When the *Union Herald* misquoted the *Liberator* to suggest that the BFAS had dissolved, the newly elected officers provided an "emphatic *denial*" and pointed to a "*living Boston Female Anti-Slavery Society*" of 120 members.[93] When the PFAS called for unity, Sarah Southwick, Maria Weston Chapman, and Lydia Maria Child replied that its exhortation was irrelevant under current circumstances.[94] Chapman sent copies of her account of the division, *Right and Wrong in Massachusetts*, asking that these circulate among Pennsylvania abolitionists.

In the midst of much divisiveness and confusion, Maria kept her eye on movement finances. In May 1840 she sent a letter asking members of the BFAS to gather after the morning session of the NEAS convention to raise a subscription from among those present to fund a national anti-slavery newspaper. She hoped to convince 150 people to contribute two to five dollars each; personally she would contribute fifteen dollars. As she looked toward the annual bazaar in December, she insisted, "These sort of [donor] fountains get *chocked up* if they are not kept in continual flow."[95]

On behalf of the board of managers of the MAS, she offered a "*weekly contribution*" plan to encourage the "flow." She sought twelve men and women in each community who would each sign up ten others. Average donations of six cents each would produce $374.20 a year for the cause. Even the poorest individuals, she noted, might proffer a "cent a week." To inspire and remind participants of the value of their contributions, Maria offered each one a moneybox "*manufactured for this purpose, with appropriate devices & inscriptions*." The money put aside was to be sent to Henry G. Chapman, MAS treasurer, for the association's use. Maria pointed out that such a plan had been tried and proved effective on a small scale, accruing some twenty or thirty dollars as the highest weekly collections.[96] Debora reported that the annual meeting of the New Bedford society voted to take fifty boxes.[97] The "Cent Box" campaign proved an effective plan for reinforcing familial and community commitment and encouraging financial support for the cause among Massachusetts abolitionists.

Briefly, the case of the *Amistad* rebels brought some unanimity to the divided abolitionists as Tappan, Birney, Garrison, and what Elizabeth R.

Varon has called "the Whig antislavery lobby in Congress" came together to support the captives for differing reasons.[98] In February 1841 the U.S. Supreme Court upheld the January 1840 ruling of Connecticut District Court judge Andrew T. Judson that the *Amistad* rebels should be freed "under the rule of self-defense in international waters" and returned to Africa. But the fugitive slave issue blew up again on 4 October 1842 with the Boston arrest and jailing of George Latimer on charges made by James Gray, a Norfolk, Virginia, planter.

At the time, Justice Joseph Story, who had freed the *Amistad* captives, was beginning a term on the federal circuit court that held jurisdiction in the case. Story had ruled earlier in the year, in *Prigg v. Pennsylvania*, that the states could not interfere with the federal regulation of commerce by hindering a master's repossession of his slave property.[99] Story incarcerated Latimer for ten days to give Gray time to produce evidence of the man's status. In a rowdy Faneuil Hall rally on 30 October, Edmund Quincy denounced Story as "the-slave-catcher-in-chief for the New England states." Abolitionist lawyer Samuel Sewall filed a brief of habeas corpus seeking Latimer's release, and Judge Lemuel Shaw heard arguments in the jail-house. While sympathetic, Shaw ruled that because the case was properly pending in federal court, the state court could not interfere.[100]

Abolitionists, even some known to Anne Warren Weston as advocates of nonresistance, joined in the public calls to free Latimer, through violence if necessary. Although deeply conflicted (she noted that she would feel "dreadfully let the case go as it may"), Anne chastised Garrison for "forgetting that now is the especial trial for his nonresistance faith." Insisting, "I *do* think that Non Resistants should . . . not countenance bloodshed," she also admitted, "I say this actually under a sense of duty for I have felt at times to have Latimer rescued if Boston streets were a mile deep with blood."[101]

Meanwhile, Boston patricians Henry I. Bowditch, William F. Channing, and Frederick S. Cabot formed the Latimer Committee to pursue Latimer's freedom while circulating a petition to the Massachusetts General Court asking it to forbid all persons holding state office from aiding and abetting the arrest or detention of a person claimed within the commonwealth as a fugitive.[102] The Weston sisters undertook production of a newssheet, the *Latimer Journal and North Star*, which came out three times a week beginning 11 November.[103] The heart of the *Journal*, and perhaps the Latimer Committee as well, was the Chapman household, where, only weeks after Henry G. Chapman's death on 3 October, the Westons wrote copy, organized the contributions of authors such as

Edmund Quincy and Elizabeth Cabot Follen, and raised funds to pay for publication.[104] Maria's grief over her husband's death, particularly as it followed so closely upon the loss of her daughter Gertrude the previous winter, was shared by her sisters, whose nursing, housework, and childcare had released her to focus on Henry's care. Anne closed her New Bedford school to move into Maria's house for the duration. She remained to see Maria and the children through their mourning and to conduct the *Latimer Journal*. Lucia reported to Debora, "The Latimer journal is going on well and I will send you a copy by mail as soon as out[—]it will be out Sat[urday] I expect. Channing and Bowditch are in every few minutes."[105]

The sisters also organized petition campaigns for a new "personal liberty law" that would forbid state officers to recover runaways, use state facilities to hold hearings, or incarcerate fugitives. Maria grew increasingly angry with Unitarian minister Theodore Parker, who, although nominally an abolitionist, remained silent and aloof when she took these petitions to his Park Street Chapel and asked him to announce their availability for signatures at the entrance to the church. She concluded scathingly that "he had just moral courage enough for his own use, but none to spare for the Cause."[106] She was similarly upset with Lydia Maria Child, whom she had strong-armed into becoming the editor of the *National Anti-Slavery Standard* in hopes that Child might provide a more appealing, literary voice to the paper in a time of internecine warfare, but who refused to engage in the level of partisanship Chapman desired.[107]

Meanwhile, the Latimer case was postponed and Judge Story withdrew. Boston's sheriff, worried that efforts to rescue the fugitive might lead to violence, ruled that slave masters could not use the jail to retain their "property" while asserting their claims through northern courts. He ordered Latimer released. Gray conceded defeat and manumitted Latimer for $400. Both men signed quitclaims. The Massachusetts state legislature passed the personal liberty law demanded by some 65,000 petitioners. Garrison issued a public address urging slaves to emancipate themselves by running away, then left the *Liberator* to the editorship of Edmund Quincy and Maria Weston Chapman as he took off for New York.[108]

Late in 1842, Henry I. Bowditch suggested that a reporter was needed in Washington, D.C., to cover the Latimer case as it came before Congress. He offered twenty-five dollars toward a salary. Maria pursued David L. Child, who agreed to go.[109] Within six months, by June 1843, Child had replaced his wife as editor of the *Standard* in an effort to provide a more aggressive tone and political emphasis to the newspaper.[110] The following May, Sydney H. Gay of New York City undertook the editorship for what would become a thirteen-year commitment. Because of their joint experience editing the *Liberator* in Garrison's absence, the *Standard* masthead bore Edmund Quincy's and Maria's names as well.[111]

The next few years proved highly stressful for the Westons, personally and politically. In 1844, Lucia began to show serious symptoms of the tuberculosis that had killed Ann Greene Chapman and Henry G. Chapman. The BFAS continued with its primary function, the annual antislavery bazaar. Nathanial Rogers, a longtime Garrisonian, attempted to seize ownership of the *Herald of Freedom* newspaper, which he had edited for the New Hampshire Anti-Slavery Society. Anne worried about the situation. "I really do not like all Rogers writes," she told Mary Weston. "If he disapproves of calling the common people names, (and he does) he ought not to call the ministers names any more. Such expressions as 'fat bellied priests' I do not like and I wish he would alter a little."[112] The annual meeting of the MAS addressed disunion directly. Two Weston allies, Wendell Phillips and Francis Jackson, "came-out" from civil responsibility. Phillips closed his law office, insisting that he would not take an oath to uphold the laws of the state of Massachusetts or the government of the United States, and Jackson resigned his position as justice of the peace for the same reason.

After the 1840–42 division between Garrisonians and anti-Garrisonians, the Westons served as leaders of the reconstructed MAS. Caroline acted as a vice president, while Anne and Maria took office as counselors. So too, Caroline served as vice president and a counselor of the Boston Female, Maria as foreign corresponding secretary, and Anne as a counselor. Maria moved her family to smaller quarters and expanded to the entire summer the month she usually spent in Weymouth with her younger children. First her father-in-law, Henry Chapman, then her mother-in-law, Sarah Greene Chapman, died, in 1846 and 1847, respectively. This substantially changed Maria's financial circumstances, as she inherited half the elder Chapmans' wealth. She continued to edit the *Liberator* when Garrison absented himself from Boston to assume a mission to England in 1846, and she served on the editorial board of the *Anti-Slavery Standard* under Sydney H. Gay.

By 1843, the relationship between Frederick Douglass and the Westons had begun to deteriorate. That year, he, along with Charles L. Remond, George Bradburn, and John A. Collins, undertook an antislavery speaking tour as part of a campaign in which thirty agents held 100 local conventions across the Northeast. The AAS board relied upon the Westons to find ways to support the tour financially. However, as the lecture circuit tested the patience of its agents, group cohesion floundered under the weight of competing egos and fraying tempers. Frustration exploded at Syracuse, New York, when Collins, who was increasingly turning his attention to property reform, discussed his "associationist" ideas from the antislavery platform. Remond and Douglass objected. Collins retaliated by making a speech about "the bigotry and narrow mindedness of abolitionists."[113]

While anti-Garrisonians and Liberty Party men had a public relations field day over the dissension, Ellis Gray Loring tasked Maria with writing the agents in the name of the AAS board and advising them against public bickering.[114] Douglass took umbrage at the tone of her missive, as did Bradburn, who refused to accept the idea that a woman spoke for the board. Maria herself seemed deaf to her patronizing language. While Bradburn chastised Chapman as "insolent," Douglass proved more circumspect if no less furious. He accepted that Maria spoke for the board and offered a no-nonsense version of events that nevertheless revealed deep anger at his fellow agents and a firm belief that they were at fault in upending the mission.[115]

When Douglass again received well-intentioned but unsolicited advice from Chapman during his 1845 antislavery mission to England, and learned that she feared the British and Foreign Anti-Slavery Society would appeal to his vanity or poverty and induce him to contradict Garrisonian ideology, he viewed her as arrogant, even racist. Deeply insulted, he accused Maria of attempting to constrain his behavior by organizing a circle of "watchers" (as, indeed, she had). "If you wish to drive me from the Anti-slavery society put me under overseership and the work is done," he wrote.[116] Their relationship fractured irreparably when Douglass began to solicit financial aid from the women of Great Britain for his *North Star* newspaper, an act Maria saw as undermining British support for the Boston antislavery fair. Despite an admonition that "an open breach there would do us injury," Anne proved unable to curb Maria's open disapprobation of Douglass. In her communications with British Garrisonians, Maria brought about the very fissure Anne feared, as some among the Irish and Scottish contributors to the Boston fair sent their usual contributions to Douglass.[117]

For all intents and purposes the BFAS ceased to exist in 1848. The annual bazaar, including the associated publication of the *Liberty Bell*, became the Westons' primary, ongoing contribution to the cause. Known as the Massachusetts Anti-Slavery Society Fair from 1834 to 1844, and the National Bazaar of the American Anti-Slavery Society from 1845 to 1858, the fair was replaced by Maria with a direct monetary subscription in 1859. What had begun as a $300 sale of "useful articles" held in a private home and attracting a small circle of supporters became a lucrative money-maker and principle attraction of the Boston holiday season. By 1848 it was raising upwards of $3,000 a year, and its culture, procedures, and organization were primarily determined by the Westons, who, over the years, adopted a number of innovations, some controversial, that built an extensive and increasingly fashionable customer base.[118]

Maria's move to France in 1848 brought to an end the shared Boston and Weymouth households in which the Weston sororal reform culture emerged. Caroline went with Maria and the children. The invalided Lucia and Emma joined them, splitting their time between France and Italy. Anne and Debora remained behind in Massachusetts, with Anne undertaking the bulk of the work necessary to organize and conduct the annual bazaar and remaining in close contact with Maria, Caroline, and Debora by post. While the sisters Weston continued to support the antislavery fair and to share family responsibilities, the density of their intertwined living and working relationships thinned. Debora would spend the largest part of her time in New Bedford teaching. She worked with the local female antislavery society, continued to pass petitions, and raised contributions for the fair. She traveled to Weymouth and Boston to work the event and felt lonely for the first time in her life.

The Chapman household in Paris, as it had in Boston, served as a center of hospitality and antislavery discourse during the sisters' seven-year stay in France. European Garrisonians made pilgrimages to visit with them. Irish abolitionist Richard D. Webb traveled to Paris for three weeks in 1849. Mary A. Estlin of Bristol's active female society visited in 1850. George Thompson spent a month with the sisters in 1851. So too Maria made frequent visits across the channel on antislavery missions. She visited Harriet Martineau often during these years, to nurse, provide company, and edit Harriet's autobiography. When in the north of England, she also visited Elizabeth Pease, a Quaker much beloved by her sisters. The Westons made annual trips to Bristol to see John B. and Mary A. Estlin, and to speak at antislavery meetings in an enclave that had provided considerable financial support to the Boston fair and the *Liberator*. In 1851, the sisters attended the International Peace Conference, spending two months in London. Elizabeth Pease joined them for several weeks, during which the Estlins, Webbs, and even the invalided Harriet Martineau arrived to tour the Crystal Palace Exhibition with the Westons.[119]

Maria returned to Massachusetts from Europe in 1855, after her daughter Elizabeth's marriage to Auguste Laugel in Paris and her father's death. She lived in the Weymouth natal home, where she continued her antislavery activism in the MAS and AAS. She turned down the salaried editorship of the *Anti-Slavery Standard* in 1858. Despite her nonresistance ideals, she contributed needlework to the Boston Women's Aid Society fairs that supported the Massachusetts troops on the Civil War battlefront. Occasionally, she rented a domicile in New York City near that of her son, Henry Jr., who worked in the financial business with his uncle Warren and married Eleanor Jay, daughter of abolitionist John Jay. In 1867, Maria's youngest child, Ann Greene Chapman, married journalist Edward James Steven Dicey in England. Like her sister Elizabeth, Anne would live abroad for the rest of her life, dying in a road accident with her son in 1877. Anne and Caroline Weston returned to Weymouth from Europe but often traveled abroad to visit relatives and friends in London, Paris, and Rome. Lucia remained largely in Rome, struggling with her health. Emma, who found European society more to her taste than American, moved between the abodes of her maternal uncle Joshua Bates and his family in Great Britain, Lucia in Rome, and her niece Elizabeth Chapman Laugel in Paris with occasional return visits to Weymouth. Lucia died in 1861, the first of the sisters to pass.

In January 1865, Abigail Kelley objected to the reelection of Maria Weston Chapman and Anne Warren Weston to the MAS board of managers because the two sisters believed that the work of the society had come to an end. In May, Kelley and Caroline Remond replaced them, and in 1867, the sisters ceased their support of the Massachusetts Anti-Slavery Society Fair. The Reverend John T. Sargent and his wife, Mary, carried on the fund-raiser for a time but with far less panache and success than had the Westons. The final meeting of the AAS was held on 9 April 1869, following ratification of the Fifteenth Amendment to the U.S. Constitution. Neither William Lloyd Garrison nor any Weston sister attended.

2

MARRIED TO EACH OTHER

Marriage, Singlehood, and Sororal Practice

Edmund Quincy knew something about sisters. He had five, three of whom—Eliza, Abigail, and Maria—remained single. Like the Westons, they lived together, summering in their natal home in Quincy, Massachusetts, or wintering in Boston or Cambridge near their brothers, Edmund and Josiah.[1] An intimate of the Weston family, Edmund exchanged daily letters with one or another of these sisters. He saw himself as closer to them than "any of my blood relations" and, speaking from this intimacy, assessed the cause of their single status: "[N]one of those sisters will ever marry if they can help it. Nothing but a most desperate falling in love could carry them off. They are married to each other and cannot imagine at present, that any possible man could supply the society of their sisters."[2]

Given the high rate of female singlehood in antebellum Massachusetts, sibling troops such as the Quincys and Westons were not unusual.[3] Quincy's observation that the Westons chose their single status because they valued sibling relations above all others raises questions as to the nature and meaning of that choice. What about the Weston family culture encouraged these sisters to resist cultural norms as well as social and economic inducements to wed? What ties bound these sisters together with such affection, exclusivity, and longevity? How were these ties formed?

While affection rooted in shared activity and mutual reliance forged from family a political sisterhood of this sibling band, singleness in numbers produced the abundant labor that made their activism both possible and powerfully effective. Many factors contributed to Weston singlehood, some individual and personal, others more broadly social or cultural. No one contingency, circumstance, or decision necessarily resulted in their common status. Nevertheless, together and over time, the following factors contributed: domestic life with irresponsible and alcoholic males; a high standard for judging the character of potential mates and a low tolerance for connubial deference; a realistic assessment of how social activism affected their standing in the marriage market, particularly in the 1830s and early 1840s, and a choice as to the import of abolition to themselves and their country; the ubiquitous singlehood of female friends and acquaintances; and the belief that while desirable, marriage was not necessary for (and was sometimes deleterious to) an emotionally fulfilling, socially acceptable, or economically sustainable life. Making marriage a woman's chief goal in life and motherhood a woman's primary role, they believed, was irreligious.[4]

The household in which the Weston siblings grew up bore little resemblance to the republican model in which benevolent paternal governance, when combined with moral motherhood, induced children to internalize proper conduct and discipline in an effort to gain their father's approval and mother's affection.[5] Although nominally head of household, Captain Warren Weston did not rule at home. His lack of employment undermined his ability to control either the labor of his sons or the marriages of his daughters. Called Nancy, Ann Bates Weston appears in her daughters' letters as a superb housewife and steady soul, known for her pickles and her "loveable ways of doing all the things essential to be done for people's comfort that no one else liked to do."[6] She must also have had enormous strength of mind and character, however, to keep track of the household accounts and raise a prize bull with seemingly the same equanimity as she managed an erratic drunkard of a husband, reared eight lively, headstrong, and intelligent children, and helped care for three similarly endowed grandchildren.[7]

When Captain Warren Weston and Ann Bates married on 17 November 1805, he was twenty-four and she twenty years of age. Both were slightly younger than the average marital age in Massachusetts at the time of twenty-five for men and twenty-two for women.[8] Both lacked fathers to contract their marriage and ensure their transition to a new household. In 1792, at age eleven, Warren had lost his father, Eliphaz Weston.[9] His widowed mother, Deborah Nash Weston, shared a home with her mariner son and three daughters, Priscilla, Phebe, and Mary, who, at the time of their brother's marriage, ranged in age from twenty-eight to thirteen.[10] None married. They lived together throughout their lives in their father's "old fashioned cottage" on Front Street, Weymouth, providing a model of single blessedness, mutual support, and social activism.[11] Ann's father, Colonel Joshua Bates, died in February 1804, a factor that may have encouraged her mother, Tirzah Pratt Bates, to see her elder daughter (and eldest child) settled.[12]

These years in Weymouth proved difficult for the newly married. As one local historian wrote, "Ship-building was the most interesting business in the village. There were quaint men from the South Shore towns who worked on these vessels. They seemed to have the flavor of the sea about them. As I remember, they were men of consequence, who attended church, drank New England rum, and, in truth, verified Byron's lines: 'There's naught, no doubt, so much the spirit calms / As rum and true religion.'"[13] These men, and such a life, drew Warren Weston.

Even as Weston men, from Duxbury to Boston, engaged in the building and manning of ships, Massachusetts mariners struggled to make a living during the quasi war with France that preceded the Embargo and Non-Intercourse Acts of 1807 and 1809. During these years, French and British naval ships seized and burned many New England vessels, including the *Gershom*, built by Ezra Weston, Warren's uncle and a well-regarded entrepreneur and shipbuilder. During the War of 1812, a British naval squadron patrolled the Cape Cod and Massachusetts Bays, confiscating cargoes and seizing sailors in a search for privateers. Indeed, the British man-of-war *Bulwark* nearly destroyed the fishing fleet of Scituate, Massachusetts, a coastal town just south of Weymouth.[14]

Like many Massachusetts sailors, Captain Warren Weston lost his ship and his livelihood to the British blockade. His family believed that the war brought personal as well as financial ruin to Captain Weston, for, "when there was nothing to do" during the embargo, he "got the habit of intemperance."[15] With the sea closed to New England mariners, Weston turned to farming, although without much love or aptitude for it. In 1813, eight years after his marriage and with three daughters to support, he bought from J. John Eaton Jr., for $688, slightly more than ten acres of mowing and pasture land in North Weymouth, on which stood a house and barn. Warren held this property in common with his widowed mother, Deborah Nash Weston, who lent him part of the purchase price, enabling him to establish his own marital household.[16] Generally speaking, new households formed with marriage in early nineteenth-century New England.[17] But ten acres provided a small living, and the family's economic situation remained precarious.

A premarital pregnancy may have influenced the timing of the Weston marriage. Warren's and Ann's first child, Maria Ann, arrived on 20 July

1806, thirty-five weeks after they wed 11 November 1805.[18] Premarital pregnancy was hardly unusual at the time. In 1801, some 23.7 percent of American brides married while pregnant with their first child.[19] If that was the case here, such a pregnancy was neither the first nor the last in the Bates family. Ann Bates herself had been born four months after Colonel Joshua Bates married Tirzah Pratt on 17 February 1785. Ann's younger sister Cynthia's first child, Joshua Bates Cowing, arrived a little over four months after Cynthia married Balch Cowing in 1809.[20] Historians explain the high premarital pregnancy rate in early national New England as having to do with geographical mobility, increased sexual misbehavior, and decreased parental authority.[21] In the case of Warren Weston and Ann Bates, the distraction or even tacit approval of widowed and economically vulnerable mothers may have encouraged (and failed to inhibit) the premarital sexual activity of their son and daughter.[22]

Ann and Warren Weston's eight children arrived on average every two years. The longest gap was the three-year, ten-month period between Caroline's birth 13 September 1808 and Anne Warren's 13 July 1812, and the shortest spacing the one-year, three-month period between Anne's birth and Debora's on 22 October 1814. Both may be explained by the instability of the political and economic circumstances in which young Captain Weston sought to establish himself as a seafaring man and ship's master, struggling to get work during the embargo and war, and commiserating with fellow seamen on their common failure to do so. Certainly he spent considerable time drinking with his equally underemployed peers. Perhaps Ann suffered a miscarriage during this period or, after two children in two years, acted to limit conception for personal or economic reasons. In any case, both the numbers of Weston children and their spacing fit the general New England pattern for married women of the day.[23]

By age thirty-nine, Captain Weston had a large household of six children. Yet not until 1825, at age forty-five, did he complete his family with the birth of his youngest child, Emma Forbes. His eldest, nineteen-year-old Maria Ann, continued to live at home for three more years. Over time, the Weymouth household flexed in size as both children and grandchildren came and went. Ann Bates Weston outlived her husband, her daughter Lucia, and her younger son, Richard Warren, dying at home in 1878 at age ninety-three.[24] The five Weston children who remained single used the Weymouth house as their primary abode throughout their adulthood. Most ended their days there. Even the widowed Maria returned to the natal home to live with her mother for some years before her own death seven years later, in 1885.[25]

Among the Weston siblings only the eldest daughter and younger son married, both at higher than average ages—Maria to Henry Grafton Chapman in 1830 at age twenty-four, and Robert Warren to Sarah Maria Grant in 1847 at age twenty-eight. While Maria extended her education and worked for a time as a teacher before marrying, Warren's late marriage resulted from a misspent youth. Like his father, young Warren developed a drinking problem. For some time his sisters sought to counteract his bad habits, a project they pursued vigorously, unrelentingly, and collectively. Indeed Caroline introduced Warren to his future wife when he boarded with her in Roxbury as part of a family effort to oversee and constrain his carousing in Boston. His courtship of Sarah M. Grant may have inspired and certainly reinforced Warren's reform.[26] After proving himself a new man and buckling down to the business of merchant shipping (with the financial support and advice of his uncle Joshua Bates), Warren married Sarah and sired four children, who spent almost as much time in Weymouth with their aunts and grandmother as in Staten Island while their father sought to recover his health there and conduct his business in New York City.[27]

Positioned in the middle of the sibling band, and requiring considerable attention and care, both Weston brothers tried their sisters' patience. Loved by and at times a disappointment to sisters who worried endlessly about their health and character, Warren and Hervey exhibited mood disorders and behavioral problems perhaps caused by and certainly treated with opiates and alcohol. Substantial imbibing routinely accompanied the fast company and late hours Warren kept as he immersed himself in Boston's fast urban youth culture, drinking to excess and enjoying the theater far too often for his sisters' taste.

One mid-1830s binge occurred while Warren worked as a clerk in the Boston mercantile house of John Tyler at 9 Central Wharf and lived, as many clerks did, in the nearby rooming house of Mary Easton at 18 Pearl Street.[28] As Anne reported from Maria's Boston townhome, "About 10 Warren came in quite poorly, said he had the diarrhea; whether he has or not, I dont know. He said he did not go out of town last night, but staid at the Broomfield [hotel], therefore I think it like enough he had a night of it." Anne prepared Warren some arrowroot tea to clean out his system and cure his hangover, saying, "I shall do what I can for him, but if all he suffers does not warn him my talk will be of no use."[29] She offered a progress report featuring news that his closest pal was leaving town (and with him a negative influence): "R. W. goes on *pretty* well. He went to the theatre last evening, but—Rome was not built in a day &c. His fidus Achates, John has gone to St Louis, at which I rejoice."[30]

Warren's sisters evidenced considerable relief during his more settled periods—those he spent "at home almost every evening"—and reacted with alarm when "*Porto Rico*" (rum) resurfaced.[31] They attempted to curtail his drinking by checking up on him at his rooming house and bringing him home to Weymouth when he proved incapable of resisting the urban haunts of young working men like himself. In 1836, for example, his sisters arranged for Warren to spend the winter under Maria's and Henry's roof and supervision. To make the added trouble and responsibility more palatable, Ann Bates Weston offered to keep Maria's three-year-old son and second child, Henry Grafton Chapman Jr., under her care at Weymouth.[32] When Warren relapsed, resuming his drinking and carousing about town, he was sent farther away from the city and its temptations to board with Caroline in Roxbury. Once again he blamed nausea and poor health on bowel problems rather than drunkenness and poor sleep. Wrote Anne with disgust, "I no more think he had the diarrhea than I think he had the lumbago."[33]

Warren's older brother, Hervey, so turned the Weymouth household upside down with his mood swings that Emma called him the "raging bear."[34] An indifferent student, Hervey attended Yale, graduating in 1839.[35] During his college years, word of a student riot worried his sisters, who feared, on the basis of Hervey's generally rebellious demeanor, that he must have participated. Indeed, the faculty questioned him about the affair but chose to believe Hervey's denial of any involvement. Nevertheless, they critiqued his erratic classroom attendance and suggested that poor academic performance had raised their suspicion. Hervey assured his sisters that he had had nothing to do with the riot but "acknowledged that he had neglected his studies," his excuse being that he had "not had a well day this term." His sisters questioned both his self-awareness and his veracity. As Anne put it, "I had a letter from Hervey in which he says all things are going on well. I hope they are. He wrote in good spirits but I never know what to think of his accounts."[36] On another occasion she noted wryly, "Hervey is, or says he is still poorly. He looks pretty well."[37]

After graduating from Yale, Hervey descended into lethargy. Despite his assertions that he had "got some plans in my head to employ me for a year or two," he returned to Weymouth to "remain there awhile." His sisters recognized that he "of course, has no part," by which they meant no plans and no job.[38] They attributed his inability to settle down into "the land of steady habits" to "a disinclination to assume any responsibilities" rather than to illness.[39]

In the end, Hervey trained for a medical career at Harvard in the early 1840s and took an additional three years at the School of Medicine in

Paris. He attempted to establish a practice in Boston even as he suffered malaise, what Anne called his "common poorliness." Early in the 1850s, incapacitated by "an obscure spinal malady," Hervey gave up his formal medical practice, although he continued to treat family and an occasional Weymouth neighbor. As one kinsman wrote, Hervey "was an eccentric man, and unlike the other doctors: if his patient was poor, he made no charge. His profession seemed to him more a pleasure than a means of gaining a livelihood."[40]

At the age of forty, Hervey gave himself over to invalidism. In the summer of 1866, for example, he "threaten[ed his sisters] with losing the use of his limb" to rheumatism as a mode of seeking their attention, resisting their imposition on his time, and explaining his "disinclination" to practice medicine. Said Anne in weary resignation, "The worst of rheumatism is that you never feel as if one were fairly rid of it."[41] Hervey's primary occupation became the study of numismatics, and he developed a reputation as something of an expert on the subject. For a time he moved back and forth to Rome, monitoring Lucia's consumption. Otherwise, he lived and studied in the natal home, a bachelor dependent upon his mother's care and sisters' keeping.[42]

Life with such brothers, and the father in whose steps they followed, may have contributed to the Weston sisters' desire to remain single, as they resisted the idea of subordinating themselves personally and legally to a potentially mercurial, irascible, unreliable, or intemperate spouse.[43] Even after he was said to have stopped drinking, Captain Warren Weston's behavior tended toward the unpredictable. When he felt a sudden desire to shave off the dog's fur, the family feared it would suffer in the cold and removed it to their aunts' abode across the street.[44] His poor judgment in buying horses became a running family joke, all the more irritating when Pa Weston asserted his paternal prerogative to refuse his footsore daughters the use of the animals. On occasion, his high spirits and misjudgment had disastrous effects.[45] In one instance, Emma reported sarcastically that her father suddenly, and "most *un*characteristically," set the horse going full speed down a steep hill in a pouring rain, thereby crashing the wagon, knocking the horse to the ground, and so frightening the dog that it refused to return. Thrown from the wagon, Emma and her mother trudged some distance to the nearest house, where they attempted to calm their nerves, tend to their aches and pains, dry their feet, and ward off the chill.[46]

Nevertheless, however erratically a husband might act, he retained authority over his household, wife, and children according to American custom and law. On the defensive in the second quarter of the nineteenth century, husbands and fathers became more aggressive in their assertions of pater familias status when the state asserted an interest in such matters as the adoption of children, contracting of apprenticeships, divorce, and married women's control over their earnings and property.[47] Protective toward their mother, the Weston daughters aided her in limiting the damage their father might do during his drinking bouts and dry rages. They adopted a practice of keeping at least one daughter at home to help with household matters and manage their father. For example, Debora asked anxiously about a visit Emma made to Boston, "How did pa get along during her absence?" On another occasion Anne reassured her, "Lucia is out to Weymouth keeping house for Pa."[48]

When in Boston, the Weston daughters insisted their mother visit them so that she might have a change of scene and recoup her energy. "Ma is expected in town daily and I trust that then she will be better," wrote Anne from Maria's marital household, where the Weston girls stayed when in the city. She hoped their mother would remain for two or three weeks; however, reluctant to be away so long, Ma Weston returned to Weymouth in less than one. Nevertheless, her daughters persisted. When all else failed, they cajoled their mother into bringing their father into the city so they might relieve her of some of the burden of watching over and caring for him. "I am in hopes to prevail upon Ma and Pa to come in and take up their abode with us this winter," wrote Caroline. "Mom is very desirous of coming but your father holds out still—I see however that he will knock under—It will save much expense and some trouble—and be more comfortable for them."[49]

Across the back lot from the natal home, Warren's sisters noted the comings and goings of their nieces from their brother's household. Aunt Mary Weston alerted Debora to what was clearly an unusual circumstance: "Your father and mother are now living in single blessedness, as Emma left them last Saturday morning with Nancy Cowing [a cousin] in a wagon."[50] In so writing, Mary humorously addressed the possibilities inherent in the situation of a married couple whose many children continued to live at home when finding themselves unexpectedly in sole possession of the house. Her choice of language offered an ironic commentary on the tradeoff suggested in Shakespeare's original:

Thrice blessed they that master so their blood,
To undergo such maiden pilgrimage;
But earthlier happy is the rose distill'd

Than that which withering on the virgin thorn
Grows, lives, and dies in single blessedness.[51]

Mary embraced single blessedness. She questioned her sister-in-law's capacity to cope with her husband without the assistance and, perhaps, the mediation of a daughter at home. She saw Ann as not necessarily "earthlier happy" and certainly not as blessed as she was, living with her sisters rather than her difficult brother and deeply engaged with abolition. As for her nieces, the deleterious impact of coping with such a father educated them about the potential trials of married life.

The eldest, Maria, made a great splash in the Boston marriage market. She was beautiful and accomplished, though lacking in material wealth, and her education and foreign polish were desirable attributes in a wife. Henry Grafton Chapman offered handsome looks and solid economic prospects as an urbane scion of Boston's commercial elite.[52] His grandson John Jay Chapman reported that Henry had been preparing for the clergy when he met the young teacher: "My grandmother told me that she first saw him as a handsome young man behind the chancel rail where he was serving the communion table."[53] That Henry turned away from a pastoral profession was, if anything, appealing to the Westons, who, while churchgoing and characterized by a spiritual cast of mind, had little religiosity and maintained independence in their denominational and institutional affiliations.[54] The Westons required political and intellectual compatibility as well as a serious engagement of the heart. Caroline's description of her brother-in-law as a fervent abolitionist who gave himself, his children, and his household up to the management of his wife and her sisters, and who made no effort to come between them emotionally, suggests her view of the model husband.[55]

Anne's analysis of the marriage of her abolitionist friend Mary Merrick Brooks of Concord provides insight into the Weston sisters' beau ideal. Anne liked Brooks exceedingly: "I *never* saw a woman more truly independent & conscientious. She is very lively and very good tempered, & perfectly fearless—what the transcendentalists might hail as 'the truest of women.'" Anne described Nathan Brooks as "a pleasant looking and highly gentlemanly man. He is, I think considerably older than herself and as far as such a woman as Mrs B can stand in that relation to a man, she is his *petkin*. You only need to hear him say what 'Mary thinks' to know the very loving terms on which they stand to each other." Brooks had received Anne's visit gratefully because he had a court appointment at Lowell and would "not have to leave [Mary] alone." Yet despite his apparent care and affection for his wife, and his tolerance of her social activism, such a man as Mr. Brooks would never do for a Weston. Anne assessed his intellect and character as "a little too slow & plodding." She noted the same of his politics, calling Brooks "as good an Abolitionist as his social standing will permit." By this she meant that he was not a reader or an independent thinker and would risk far less than her brother-in-law Henry G. Chapman in the service of the cause.[56]

The elder Weston sisters understood how the politics of antislavery affected their marital eligibility. They encouraged the youngest, Emma, to pay attention to the social opportunities made available to her by her uncle Bates's position in British society, reminding her that "if she ever means to enter the married state she must do it while she is abroad for she never will in America." Debora acknowledged, "Emma does not need this admonition, as she knows it as well as I do."[57]

Edmund Quincy teased the sisters about Emma's "entrance into the world" of fashion and society when, after her husband's death, Maria took her children and Emma to London in 1844. "I hope the fair Emma will escape the machinations of the . . . gay hornets and wicked lords, who no doubt abound in that gay capital, and who have contracted habits of running away with young ladies in post chaises and fours." Forecasting that "the unpretentious village of Boston" would appear "but dull and tame after the jackties [ostentatious braggarts] of that great metropolis," he held that "it would be positive cruelty to bring [the] girls [Emma Weston and Elizabeth B. Chapman] back to America," and wished that "they could both get well married abroad for their chance would be much less here." Samuel May Jr. also advocated such a course. In October 1848 he wrote to Caroline, then in Paris with Maria and the children, "I hope the Cafes and Restaurants of the Palais Royal will be in their best estate of brilliancy & coziness for you to visit, in company with some *male* friend, at least once."[58]

Emma Forbes Weston took a good look around when she found herself in the sparkling arena of upper-class British society. Owing to her uncle Joshua Bates's position at Barings Bank, his wife Lucretia Sturgis Bates and daughter Elizabeth were formally presented at court to Queen Victoria.[59] In consequence and because of her family ties, Emma had a "brilliant" London social season.[60] A bright vision at twenty-seven, Emma was old to come out into society.[61] Nevertheless, she met "everybody that was worth seeing almost, of literary celebrities as well as fashionable." She attended society balls, "flirting for half an hour with Disraeli on Lady Darby's staircase, on the night of Lord D's first official reception while the Duke of Buccleugh had gone to fetch her cloak! Then she went to balls at Northumberland House, Bridgewater House, the Duchess of Bedford's and any quantity of others."[62] In Paris, too, the family received invitations to the Hotel De Ville ball and other elite gaieties.[63] Emma was reputed to have had a romance, even become engaged to Lucia's Italian physician while acting as nurse and companion during her sister's long convalescence in Italy.[64] Yet, despite "plenty of offers," Emma chose not to marry.

The elder Weston sisters recognized that their insistence upon a husband who would share their political beliefs and support their labor in the antislavery cause affected their eligibility. In the 1830s their abolition was viewed as a negative factor for any but other abolitionists, and in the 1840s the division in the movement further limited the field of potential suitors. Leery of celebrity-seekers and hangers-on, and suspicious of insincere pursuit by wife-hunters, Debora cooled the ardor of young Mr. Hawes, an assistant principal in John F. Emerson's New Bedford school where she taught. As with George Emerson (John's son, who attached himself to Debora), she supplied Hawes with antislavery literature and labored over his conversion to the cause. Over time, however, Debora became more and more uncomfortable in his presence. Hawes "takes to me rather too warmly, indeed," she confided. "I hear that nobody ever knew any thing about his abolition till now."[65] Debora would accept none but a full commitment to abolition from suitor or spouse. She had reason to fear opportunistic courtship, having witnessed at first hand the emotional devastation and damaged reputation of Mary G. Chapman in one such case.

Late in April 1840, Mary took her family by surprise in announcing her engagement to William M. Chace. A mature woman of forty-two, Mary was sixteen years older than her fiancé. Chace was a Providence, Rhode Island, wool merchant, the recording secretary of the Providence Anti-Slavery Society and onetime partner of George W. Benson, father-in-law to William Lloyd Garrison. A close friend of Helen Benson Garrison, Eliza J. Chace (William's sister) participated in organizing the Providence Female Anti-Slavery Society. A longtime abolitionist and agent for the *Liberator*, William attended the 1838 women's national antislavery convention in Philadelphia. There the couple met and found themselves "much pleased with each other." Maria joked that an anti-abolitionist mob, such as the one marring the convention, might seem "a strange place to make up a match," but "the abolitionists are like Croaker's household, in the good natured man—'my insensible crew would fry beef-steaks at a volcano.'"[66]

When she first heard of the engagement, Maria believed Chace "a most excellent man," whose character reflected "true integrity and worth." She approved of his "solid ability" and his devotion "to every good word and work—particularly abolition." She noted the couple's "warm attachment on both sides" and called upon her sisters to "rejoice with them that rejoice." Maria, perhaps relieved, as she lacked fondness for the histrionic and narcissistic Mary, remembered the charge given her by Mary's sister, the beloved Ann Chapman. "One of her last thoughts was to commend Mary to me in a particular manner. 'She will be now,' said Ann, 'without companionship—alone.' We never thought to see Ann die, or Mary marry. Yet we see both."[67] Nevertheless Maria felt some foreboding about the relationship, and within the year William had broken the engagement. Stunned, the Westons could only guess at his reasons. "We have yet *no light* upon the *why* the engagement was off—and probably shall never have," exclaimed Caroline.[68] The family came to believe they had been deceived in Chace's character.

The devoted Edmund Quincy viewed Chace as living "in a morbid state," his private and public behavior "a manifestation of the distemperation." The breaking up of the engagement coincided with Chace's resignation from the governing board of the American Anti-Slavery Society (AAS), in which he accused the members of "sectarianism and love of power," charges that Quincy characterized as "adding insult to injury." Following the Reverend William E. Channing, Chace apparently had come to believe that abolition should be carried out by individuals acting privately, because organizations offered the potential for tyranny in coercing members to espouse an antithetical point of view or practice. The Westons had opposed Channing, publicly attacking his view of voluntary associations.[69]

Quincy feared that in the engagement, the breaking of it, and the resignation from the AAS board, Chace was motivated by "something of vanity, wounded pride, desire of greater prominence than he has had."[70] Maria agreed, also believing that Chace had turned against Mary when clerical opposition to abolition made the Westons notorious and thus unsuitable in-laws. She requested of the family that "we may never mention [the Chaces], in any but a private way, for I suppose they are doing all this vast amount of nothing [by which she meant considerable gossiping] for the sake of being talked of." Anne advised Mary to have no conversation and engage in no written communication with Chace or "any of his friends." She confided that "individuals who had been told by members of the C[hace] family the circumstances connected with the separation had told me, and that it was a duty she owed to herself."[71] The entire affair left a foul taste in Weston mouths, and the public humiliation augmented Mary's emotional fragility.[72]

Neither as state nor as status did singlehood hold anxiety for the Weston women. None was willing to marry for "an establishment," a widespread, thoroughly respectable, and often economically necessary practice for women. In 1843, for example, Henrietta Sargent, a single woman who lived with her beloved sister Catherine, a close friend and sister abolitionist of Anne's, bemoaned the untimely death of acquaintance John Brooks because it left his only sibling, Lucy, in dire economic need and without home or protector.[73] To Henrietta's horror, Lucy Brooks resolved her situation through a swift and less than eligible marriage "as it respects the fortune or character of her husband." Deprecating a brother's failure to think ahead and provide adequately for his sister, as had her own father for her, Sargent worried about the young woman's "dreadful fate": "I wonder more married people do not run away from each other, or kill themselves, when they find their partner uncongenial, or unkind, or crooked—or extravagant, or untidy, or lazy, or too talkative, or dumb—or unchristian—or unfaithful." She believed that "men when in this shocking dilemma, can seek some employment abroad, or travel for [their] health, or remove [their] better half to some remote retreat," but wondered "what can a poor woman do[? M]any a one, I believe dies broken hearted!"[74] While the Westons could appreciate Lucy's desperation, no such concern moved them to take marriage vows.[75]

After all, they had grown up with a model of sisterly devotion, mutual reliance, and singlehood among their paternal aunts: Priscilla, Phebe, and Mary Weston.[76] When they died (in 1852, 1861, and 1860, respectively), these aunts left wills ensuring that their "unmarried nieces" would receive all their real property and the bulk of their personal property. As Mary Weston stipulated, "Should any of my nieces . . . hereafter marry, it is my will that they lose all right, claim and title in the above bequest, which shall, in that case, revert immediately to my nieces remaining unmarried."[77] She and her sisters ensured that in the next generation disinheritance would follow marriage and singlehood receive what economic support they could provide.[78] A common practice in New England, such arrangements served as a financial and social safety net of the sort that Lucy Brooks could have used to advantage. The combination of an engaging life (which included antislavery activism on Mary's part) with love and mutual reliance, sociability, and family connection powerfully reinforced all other factors influencing Weston views of single life.

The sisters did not dislike (though they often disrespected) men. Indeed, they appreciated male companionship and generally found courtship an interesting and often agreeable rite. They speculated among themselves about potential suitors and embraced opportunities to socialize with eligible men. Caroline, for example, looked at her Boston boarding school venture as providing a more likely situation in which to meet marital prospects than would a rural school. She enjoyed this "gayer world" of private parties, sleigh rides, public lectures, readings, and concerts, to which she had many and overlapping invitations. She regaled Debora with tales of the twenty calls she received in one day, of taking tea and spending a Saturday evening "with a private party at Mr Smith's & in order to do so declined a sleighride to Smith's tavern that the gayer world attended & to which I was invited by 2 gentlemen." The weekend's festivities were followed on Monday by her efforts to console an unwanted suitor named Farley and an afternoon drinking yet more tea at the home of Luther Lincoln. She "went with him at eight oclock—to Mr Smith's to meet the reading Society—but what then befell—I reserve until I see you," she teased. So great was the approbation directed her way that Caroline began "to entertain the idea that I was really something very extraordinary—the smoke of it is even now in my nostrils a sweet smelling savor."[79] So too, Anne teased Lucia about her many beaux. "Do you really think that any of your present swains have serious designs?" she asked. "I never was so amused as at Emma's witticism about firing at random."[80]

Eligible men called frequently upon the Westons. To their amusement, a Mr. Jones arrived, for whom "getting a wife was very evidently on his mind," and surveyed the entire sibling circle. Anne confided laughingly, however, "We all bore such a very full testimony on the woman question, and it was evidently such a very strange doctrine to him that I do not apprehend that he will respect any of us with a preference." But if Mr. Jones did not suit, other men offered greater potential. Debora, for example, acknowledged antislavery agent John A. Collins to be "a perfect jewel—I must say I should like to own him myself." Anne agreed: "We are all carried away with him, even thinking we could walk through life by his side."[81]

One or possibly two of the sisters may have found themselves emotionally attached to ineligible men and may have mourned what might have been. Evidence in diaries and letters suggests that Anne, for example, was enamored of the married George Thompson.[82] In 1850, she wrote somewhat ambiguously, "Fifteen years have elapsed since we met, & I felt myself so extremely changed in mind & person that I feared to observe a great change in him. In one respect *I* was unaltered. I experienced as great a desire to burn incense before him now, as when an enthusiastic young girl." Feeling self-conscious about having "not outlived such follies," she acknowledged how thankful she was for the experience. "[S]o few people carry me completely away that you must allow me to be thankful for the luxury of unboundedly admiring," she wrote Mary A. Estlin. Two years later she remarked, "The strong friendship that I have for Mr Thompson is some thing entirely personal to myself not specially connected with his gifts as an orator, or his labours as an Abolitionist. I was drawn to him at first by these circumstances undoubtedly but were he to never speak publicly again, and were every slave in the world emancipated tomorrow, it would make no difference in my friendship for him." It was an enchantment that had worried her sisters, but Anne embraced the emotions aroused, acknowledging that she felt this way "of but very few people, for the tie that binds me to the great majority of my fellow labourers this side the water is the identity of feeling and opinion *on one topic* [abolition]. I esteem them very highly in love for their works sake, as says the apostle. But this is a very different matter from a personal friendship."[83]

When, in 1864, Thompson returned to Massachusetts, Anne told Ann T. G. Phillips that he was invited to visit at Weymouth. She admitted, "[I]t is a dreadful trial to me to see him. He recalls to me so much 'The memory of what has been and never more shall be.' He is so associated with all I have lost that the idea of meeting him under the circumstances so painfully altered, is something that I can hardly bear."[84] While her "loss" may have had to do with the particular camaraderie of the "Boston clique"[85] of Garrisonians in the early and dangerous years of antislavery agitation or the deaths of beloved family members who had passed away since Thompson's previous visit (including her father, sister Lucia, and sister-in-law Ann Chapman), she may have meant an old romantic attachment and dreams of marriage.

The Westons gave many reasons for rejecting individual suitors. Anne refused a Mr. Chaplin because "he is engaged in nothing special and never will be." She warned Debora that Henry B. Stanton was intellectually dull: "I do not esteem his conversational powers as very great and I doubt whether he will do for you. On the whole you may dismiss all thought of him." Anne also dismissed poet John Greenleaf Whittier, a man who spent his life in the household of his mother, Abigail Hussey Whittier, her sister Mercy Hussey, and his sister Elizabeth. Anne liked Whittier "particularly" but could not "set my cap at him with any conscience at all, for I certainly cant turn Quaker and he grows more and more Quaker-fied." She asked

Lucia what she thought of the gracious and agreeable Dr. Whipple, who, she believed, "respects me with a preference. What think you of my turning my attention that way?—He is so good, he is nearly perfect . . . I am afraid he is so *vastly* good that we should not get on well." Caroline found a Mr. Burton only "somewhat interesting," and Debora told Anne that she "must put herself to rest" about Henry Lee, as he was also courting a Miss Morton in New Bedford. Anne turned down a proposal from Mr. Bigelow, an Oberlin College professor turned land speculator, because although he was a good man and "strong" abolitionist, he was also "'new school Presbyterian' & holds to the doctrine of perfection and, I believe, thinks himself to have attained thereto."[86]

While actively exploring the emotional highs and lows of courtship, the sisters neither had their hearts set on marriage nor pursued it as life's goal. Cousin Lucretia Cowing came into Boston from Weymouth to attend Caroline's school, in hopes that, although a dull scholar, she might yet make something of herself. She complained in proper Weston fashion, "In Weymouth there is nothing but marrying and giving in marriage, they are going off by the dozen."[87] When Anne saw family friend Melania Ammidon with her new husband, she criticized Melania as "manifest[ing] so much happiness that I was ashamed of her." In Weston eyes such a change in a woman's habitual approach to life accorded marriage too great an importance, even produced a somewhat distasteful narrowness.[88]

While interested in the marriages of friends and neighbors, the Westons tended to describe their acquaintances in dry tones as "having done well for themselves" or "not as well as they might have." Such assessments they tied not primarily to economic or social status but rather to their criteria of the beau ideal. In the case of the courting Ammidon sisters (Matilda, Sylvia, Angelina, Melania, and Elizabeth), for example, the Westons could not escape hearing every detail. Following a visit to Lowell, Massachusetts, and the married Matilda, Sylvia Ammidon wrote to Debora Weston about her sisters' marital affairs. Matilda "seems well and happy[,] her good man is as brisk as a bottle of beer. I wish every lady loved their husbands as well as she does. Ange continues engaged and I wish I could say as much of some of her sisters, but I have come to the conclusion that the best people remain unengaged." With this lighthearted reference to her own state, Sylvia went on to report that Angelina had not yet set a date for her marriage to Mr. Chaplin, but she doubted it would occur earlier than the following spring. As for Eliza, she "is sobered down long since and I believe has made up her mind to a state of single blessedness and I think it is best she should, for I think she is not calculated exactly to *live double*.

Melania and I have formed no such conclusion but are going to live on till we see Mr Right." When Sylvia did marry, it was to her brother-in-law (Melania's husband's brother).[89] Anne ironically evaluated her acquisition: "Sylvia Ammidon's long agony is over; she is engaged to Parker's brother. I guess you have seen him. I think she has done quite well for her[self]; really better than Ange."[90]

Anne delighted in her niece Lizzie Chapman's 1853 engagement to Auguste Laugel of France, "thankful for any body that has such an experience even for a short time." She responded to one of Emma's heartaches with the sally, "You know most people think that the next best thing to being married is being crossed in love. There is nothing like having a varied mental experience."[91] Feeling no particular urgency about her own marital status, when she knew that a proposal was forthcoming from the admirable Mr. Bigelow, she acknowledged feeling "pretty well frightened for I knew what was coming well enough. However stand it I must. Accordingly I screwed up my courage to the sticking place and waited till the hour and the man both came."[92] At the appointed time, Anne and Mr. Bigelow spoke before he broached the "hot coal business." He "made me a downright offer and I as down rightly declined," she reported. "I never could for a minute have entertained the thought of making any other answer than I did but truth compels me to say that I think the man a very good one."[93]

Such reluctance in the face of a "very good" man suggests that marriage as a status or calling did not, in and of itself, draw Anne.[94] For the Weston sisters, the pull of sibling love countered the social, cultural, and economic push toward marriage. The overwhelming sense of grief and abandonment at the marriage of a sibling reported by many New England sisters in the first half of the nineteenth century reflects a gendered cultural expectation of sibling emotional primacy.[95] Anne Weston sympathized with Angelina Ammidon, "who seems to be still mourning for Melonia," her recently married sister.[96] Quincy's observation of this devotion to sibling society, expressed metaphorically as "marriage" to one another, was by no means unique.[97]

More important than individual marital status was the sheer number of single siblings among the Westons. Six daughters (and two brothers) ranging in age across nineteen years, six of whom never wed, gave to the Weston family a particular character and shape. A common household required less individual labor to sustain its members than did separate marital abodes. The surplus labor went into the Boston Female Anti-Slavery Society, the Weymouth and Braintree Female Anti-Slavery Society, and the abolitionist movement in general. Working collaboratively with each other in the cause gave these sisters a sense of belonging, interdependence, and mutual reliance. These qualities produced a confidence in their joint capacities that some of their peers found arrogant and many saw as unwomanly. Sharing everyday labors and concerns of both household and reform generated a complex set of reciprocal obligations that wove sisterly affection ever more tightly into "habitual sympathy." The Weymouth sisterhood sustained this course for decades of political activism. Their success had much to do with their being one another's primary emotional attachments, and with the many hands they could bend to a common purpose. So united in and to the cause were they that in 1858 the widowed Maria Weston Chapman wrote of herself and her sisters, "We look forward to a most interesting quarter of a century anniversary—our *silver wedding* to the cause."[98]

3

I MUST MAKE MONEY

The Sororal Economy

In 1836, after taking a class of thirty-seven students in New Bedford, Debora felt keenly her distance from Weymouth and her sisters. Melancholy, she tried reminding herself that she "used to long to be able to do something to help us along. My desires are now gratified and I believe I am truly thankful." Sounding somewhat ambivalent about her choice of occupation, she wrote, "What a comfort it is to me sometimes when I come tired and exhausted from school, to say to myself 'I have earned a dollar.'" So too Caroline asserted bluntly in 1841, "I *must* make money—just now." She acknowledged to Debora, "I need not tell you that I am not mercenary in my views but you are also well informed that it is very important to me just now to make my labours as profitable as possible."[1]

The four elder Weston girls taught school of necessity, a consequence of their father's alcoholism. Captain Warren Weston had difficulty recovering his personal and financial equilibrium after the War of 1812 and would owe the economic stability of his household to the domestic and farm labor of his wife and, more particularly, his elder daughters' employment. They pursued a two-pronged strategy aimed at supporting themselves and their parents. First, they invested in their own education and then passed on their learning, sharing job opportunities, professional skills, and business acumen. They also drew upon a safety net of well-off relatives and in-laws that allowed them important flexibility as they divided their time among wage-earning, domestic labor, and antislavery activism.

As eldest, Maria earned a position allowing her to prepare Caroline and Anne, who, in turn, qualified Debora "to enter upon the business of teaching." They found students through extensive social, educational, and political networks. Their joint earnings as schoolteachers and governesses provided their younger brothers with opportunities beyond farming, enabling Hervey to take advantage of new professional credentialing in medicine and Warren to make his way in Boston's commercial economy. Maria also initiated, and her siblings maintained, close ties with their uncle Joshua Bates, who provided a necessary economic stopgap in the form of annuities to his sister Ann Bates Weston, the amounts of which rose over time. Periodic donations of household goods and foodstuffs such as apples and flour from Maria's father-in-law, Henry Chapman, also augmented household resources.

The economic circumstances of the Weston household contrasted painfully with those of their near kin, who ranked among the economic elite of Norfolk and Plymouth Counties.[2] Warren Weston's father, Eliphaz, had served the community of Weymouth as a soldier in the Revolutionary War and a representative to the Massachusetts State Constitutional Convention. He died in 1792 at the age of fifty-one, leaving a pregnant, forty-two-year-old widow with four children. While Deborah Nash Weston struggled to raise their children in a "little old-fashioned cottage" on Weymouth's Front Street, some twenty-four miles to the south in Duxbury, Eliphaz Weston's brother, Ezra ("a man of large affairs and a leader among men"), was fast becoming America's foremost shipbuilder.[3]

By 1842, when Ezra's son (Warren Weston's cousin) Ezra II died, Lloyds of London acknowledged "E Weston and Son" as the leading shipbuilders in the world, doing more than $1 million worth of business a year and paying over $120,000 annual wages into the local economy. One wit opined that the directional initials EWNS on the weather vane over the shipyard stood for "Ezra Weston's New Ship."[4] Ezra II's son, Gershom B. Weston, lived "quite as magnificently in all respects as in Beacon Street," home to Boston's Brahmins and wealthiest capitalists.[5] By this time the company owned a shipyard, rope walks, a sail loft, a spar yard, and a blacksmith shop at Harden Hill in Duxbury (commonly called the "Navy Yard"), with offices on Commercial Wharf in Boston. How Warren Weston felt about his cousins' economic success is not known, although their names continued in his own line. Relations between the families were such that his sisters and daughters regularly visited these Duxbury kin and, socializing aside, solicited from them donations to the antislavery cause.[6]

The relationship between Ann Bates Weston and her brother, Joshua Bates, proved a more significant financial connection than did ties to the Duxbury Westons in providing a financial safety net and assuring the social status of Ann's children.[7] At age fifteen in 1803, one year before his father's death, Bates entered the Boston countinghouse of William R. Gray.[8] With a reputation for integrity, generosity, and moneymaking, Gray had moved to Boston from Salem, where he had lost everything in the Revolutionary War. Gray prospered in Boston, outfitting and underwriting ships in the European and Black Sea trades, and thereby garnering a fortune valued on his death at $3 million. After the War of 1812, Gray sent Bates to Europe as his shipping agent. In London, Joshua partnered with John Baring of Baring Brothers to become one of the world's leading merchant bankers. By 1835, the firm had made some £600 million. In the year 1849 alone, the partners divided a profit of £168,000. By 1854, Bates was paying £2,500 in British taxes, donating hundreds more to English charities, and contributing $50,000 to the city of Boston to build a public library.[9]

Joshua Bates tracked his sister Ann's economic situation through her eldest child, Maria.[10] "If money is wanting for her comfort or for that of her children draw on me," he invited, "enjoin[ing] secrecy in all these givings." He insisted that Maria address monetary appeals to his clerk, John Williams, Esq., care of Baring Brothers Company, so that he, Bates, would open the letter personally. "Do not," he urged, "be alarmed at a proposition for a private correspondence but I have a sort of dread of having it known that I give money to any body and further I like to discontinue giving when I like."[11] Then, too, he did not want his wife to know about his financial dealings with his sister. Careful not to appear as profligate relations, the Weston sisters sought financial aid only when their combined efforts proved insufficient for crucial needs. Yet even as she forwarded her mother's request for supplementary funds in 1831, when the Weston children remained largely too young to earn their own keep or contribute to that of the family, Maria acknowledged her discomfort in doing so. "[O]ne's heart sometimes fails on applying for pecuniary assistance," she wrote.[12]

By the 1830s, New England fathers of modest means found it increasingly difficult to bring along their sons, let alone their daughters, in a rapidly changing economy where their skills and lands were of less utility and the apprenticing of children was subject to new laws.[13] Daughters' occupations focused on outwork and domestic production.[14] Like others of their era, the Westons saw in education a resource and a strategy through which their family might secure economic stability.[15] Warren Weston lacked the moral authority, economic means, and business acumen to establish his sons or provide for his daughters, so Joshua Bates stepped in, not only offering his sister Ann an annuity[16] but also contributing lesser sums to cover the schooling of her younger children. For example, Bates helped out when, "after the utmost exertion on Caroline's part and economy in all the others," the family proved unable to meet Anne's educational expenses by some $200 and faced removing the boys from classes, even though "the cost of keeping them there is only $5 pr quarter each, and a year at [their] age [ten and twelve, respectively] is so valuable to them."[17]

In 1841, Richard Warren Weston traveled to England to consult his uncle about his future. Having worked as a clerk in Boston, he wished to move up in the world so as to afford marriage.[18] Largely because of his drinking, Warren had lacked the personal drive and economic acuity necessary for advancement. After a considerable struggle with his sisters, who sought to dry him out and change his ways, Warren turned to his uncle for help. Bates took a genuine interest in his nephew, offering him an opportunity to prove himself a sober, hard-working individual.[19] After weeks of visiting, during which Warren spent every evening with his uncle, Bates offered him the use of a ship, an introduction to his connections in merchant shipping, and advice as to which commodities offered the best return.[20] "He has *not given* Warren the ship Nestor outright," reported Caroline, "but has transferred it to him for a price very *low* at half its value, which is to be paid at leisure in long installments as the ship makes profits—it [is] the same thing as a gift—only it leaves Warren more independent"— and more responsible for his success and failure as well.[21] Warren followed his uncle's advice, hauling cargoes to and from Russia, China, and Cuba. Gradually the *Nestor* paid for itself under his management.

Warren's success benefited from the sober company in which he worked. In December 1831, Joshua Bates had observed in his New Year's resolutions, "In respect to general conduct I see much room for [self-]improvement," and pledged himself to be "hence forward abstemious." His diary suggests that he applied to this endeavor the same discipline he practiced in business.[22] Three years later Bates built a ship to be navigated only by seamen "who will consent not to use ardent spirits." He hoped this policy might "do some good by calling public attention to the subject which is one of deep [personal] interest." Bates's end-of-year ruminations included the hope that "all men will pay attention to morality and temperance as the only true source of prosperity and happiness."[23] Surely his advice to his nephew, particularly given his brother-in-law's disposition to drink, would have included at the very least an admonition, and more likely a condition, of abstinence.[24]

Despite Bates's express interest in the economic circumstances of the Weston family, Warren failed to serve the larger need of his siblings. In a burst of what Caroline believed to be juvenile male pride, he turned aside his uncle's query about how else he might aid the Weymouth household. Warren denied any need for assistance. Bates asked specifically "if the *place* had not better be enlarged at Weymouth—but Warren thought it was big enough—[Bates] seemed distressed some what and did not see he said how we lived on $500 a year—and then it was that it was not given to Warren to say that the rest of the means was raised by ourselves—and that we by no means lived on $500 per annum," the amount of the annuity Bates had settled on his sister Ann.[25] With no track record on which to stand, Warren bragged about his own ability to provide for the Weymouth household. "I am sorry to state," Caroline informed her sisters, "that no measures seem to have been taken for the benefit of the laughing group— Tho' had Warren been older and wiser—or had the grace to think of any body but himself I suppose something would have been done." Nevertheless, she conceded, "I dont blame Warren for he has not the tact and judgment necessary for such a job—and perhaps was wise not to undertake it."[26] If Caroline wished that Bates had recognized her own and her sisters' contributions to the family income and rewarded their diligence by further easing their path, she was relieved nonetheless that her uncle had both invested in Warren and provided him with an incentive for sobriety.[27]

Ultimately, Bates enabled Warren (along with Horace Gray, the son of his old friend and business partner William R. Gray) to buy into the merchant bank Goodhue & Co., Baring's agents in New York City. This step up from merchant shipper to merchant banker ultimately made Warren a wealthy man.[28] When Maria's husband and father-in-law gave up their lucrative shipping business with the American South in a principled refusal to trade with slaveholders, Bates lent the Chapmans capital and helped them refocus their business on shipping copper while developing new commercial clients.[29] The contributions of Joshua Bates to the Weymouth household allowed the Weston sisters the flexibility to temporarily leave teaching and return home to Weymouth (or to Maria's town house in Boston) when they themselves were ill or when they were needed to nurse others, to address some other personal problem or domestic duty, or to focus their efforts on antislavery activism.

Weston investment in women's education served the family well. The eldest daughter, Maria Ann, began in Weymouth under S. P. Miles, a well-regarded instructor who later taught at the English High School in Boston. In 1825, at age nineteen, Maria accompanied her uncle Joshua Bates and her aunt Lucretia Sturgis Bates to London for "finishing." This act helped open education as a source of cultural and, therefore, economic capital that enabled what their cousin Lucretia Cowing called "a large family of girls . . . to maintain themselves all their lives."[30] Perhaps Ann Bates Weston had enjoined her brother to take Maria under his wing; certainly letters among family members as well as Bates's own diaries record his sense of family duty. Perhaps, too, he admired his niece's intellect and vivacity, and sought to provide her with advantages on either the marriage or the occupational market. His wife may have wanted reliable domestic help, companionship, or a governess for their children William and Elizabeth, of an age with their Weymouth cousins Debora and Hervey Weston.

In London Maria attended Mrs. Elwell's school, which offered the usual female arts curriculum of languages, drawing and painting, dance, and amateur theatricals. Maria later characterized the school as providing an excellent "distribution of time" and enjoyable companionship.[31] After finishing her course of study, she joined her uncle's household as governess of his two children before returning with him to Massachusetts in 1828. Maria's finishing abroad provided her with such good cultural and educational credentials that, in 1829, Ebenezer Bailey appointed her preceptress of the Young Ladies' High School, a liberal experiment in women's education attached to his newly established Boston academy.[32] Maria's position gave her sisters entrée to this school, where they had the opportunity to acquire an excellent education and practice the professional skills she modeled for them.[33]

In birth order, each sister mentored the next. Caroline, two years younger than Maria, did not have her sister's European "finishing." She gained advanced knowledge and learned her profession by completing her education under the tutorship of Ebenezer Bailey himself and teaching younger girls under Maria's supervision. After Maria left Ladies' High in October 1830 to marry, Anne joined Caroline and followed the same pattern of studying while teaching.[34] In January 1834, Caroline left Bailey's employ, taking the now experienced Anne with her. The two sisters established a boarding school in Boston. To enhance their school's visibility and appeal, they counted on the glamour of Maria's European finishing, her name recognition as preceptress of Ladies' High, and their credentials as teachers in Bailey's experiment in public female education.

Caroline borrowed domestic furnishings and cutlery from friends and relatives, advertised for students in a variety of newspapers, and wrote her uncle Bates for business advice. Her aunt proved dismissive: "We think Caroline is undertaking rather too much—A boarding school in Boston never succeeds."[35] Nevertheless, the sisters established their school in brownstone buildings owned by their uncle Bates at 38 and 39 Boylston Street.[36] The two young women set out to attract students, secure domestic help, and develop a quality curriculum.[37] Debora Weston was among the first to enroll. Lucia and Emma followed after Debora expressed concern about the weakness of Weymouth schooling for girls and its provincial ways. "I think Emma had better come in from Weymouth I am afraid she will grow savage out there," she wrote her sister.[38]

By spring 1835 the school had ten scholars. The Westons built it up (and their other schools as well) through extensive networks rooted in family, community, and political connections. Ebenezer Bailey sent them his two daughters, a testament to his assessment of the Westons' teaching abilities and curriculum.[39] Antislavery connections also supported the Westons' professional labors.[40] AAS founder and MAS president Joseph Southwick and BFAS stalwart Thankful Southwick sent their daughter Sarah to the Westons.[41] An ardent abolitionist herself, Sarah later wrote of Caroline, "I look back to her as a teacher and life long friend with love and gratitude—a sensible, cultivated, unaffected, warm-hearted woman, whom everybody respected. How much I owe to her in the way of education I can never express."[42] Weymouth acquaintances also sent their daughters to the Westons. "The Groggs move to Boston in March," wrote Anne, "so we may have them as pupils." Noah Fifield, their Weymouth neighbor and the local doctor, sent his daughter Mary.[43]

Primarily in Caroline's hands, the Weston school lasted in Boston for some six years. In 1836, Anne took a prestigious position in New Bedford, Massachusetts, supervising twenty-five scholars under the highly regarded educator John F. Emerson, earning five dollars a week and board.[44] Twenty-two-year-old Debora replaced Anne when illness took her back to Weymouth. Individually and together, the Weston sisters maintained a presence in New Bedford as both teachers and abolitionists for two decades. Ultimately, Debora and Caroline attempted a second "Misses Weston's School for Young Ladies" there, offering instruction "in all the usual English Studies, Mathematics, Latin, and the modern European languages; Drawing, Painting in oil and water colors; Plain and Ornamental Needle-work."[45] They advertised "the most strenuous exertions . . . for the intellectual and moral cultivation and advancement of the pupils," indicating, as Mary Kelley has put it, a commitment to instructing young women "in the larger meanings of the knowledge they were pursuing . . . and the values and vocabularies of civil society."[46]

While neither Lucia nor Emma Forbes Weston formally taught, both completed their educations at the Boylston Street school under their sisters' tutelage. Lucia also acted as a teaching assistant for her sisters and a governess to her Chapman nieces.[47] In 1840, when the Westons' Boston school closed, Emma accompanied Caroline to Roxbury, where she, along with Elizabeth Bates Chapman and thirty-three other students, enrolled in her sister's new school.[48]

Teaching was demanding work—intellectually, personally, and physically—and not for the faint of heart.[49] It was also women's work. In 1834, some 56.3 percent of Massachusetts teachers were female; 61 percent by 1840; and 77.8 percent by 1860. Onerous working conditions resulted in considerable turnover. According to one account, one of every five Massachusetts women taught school at some point during their lives.[50] In 1840, Massachusetts school reformer and secretary of the state board of education Horace Mann encouraged resistant school committees to give women teachers a chance: they were "unaspiring, self-sacrificing, driven by a desire to mother the young"—and cheap. (In the 1840s, hired male teachers in Boston earned between $1,500 and $2,400 annually, while women earned $300 plus a $25 room allowance. As late as 1872, women teachers in Massachusetts still earned less than 40 percent of their male colleagues' pay.)[51] Like the Westons, other women teachers sought upgraded working conditions, better wages, and an opportunity for self-improvement, regularly attending public lectures on a wide variety of subjects—political, scientific, and scholarly. These turned some female schoolteachers toward abolition. As Melissa Doloff wrote in her diary on 9 September 1858, "Slavery was a very wicked thing" and "women ought to do something for the cause either by their pen or if nothing more now and then say a word in behalf of them."[52]

The Weston sisters knew all too well the rigors of educating the young. With forty-four scholars in 1837, Debora insisted that she had "never worked so hard in my life. It seems to me as if I could not stand it going on at this rate all summer. I have been so tired for the last week that I could not sleep at night, and that is something wonderful for me." After a particularly trying period, Caroline complained that "life would be to me a different thing from what it is if I could sleep as long as I like every morning—live in my own, or my father's house—and never see a *child* except when I chose. . . . If I were not obliged on account of pressing occupations to know 'what is it o'clock'—the whole day through and part of the night—and live 'up to time'—forever." Anne, too, acknowledged, "This keeping school fatigues me so." While "the salary would, of course, be an inducement," she did not pursue regular positions, disliking subordination to a (male) school administrator or the often idiosyncratic local committee.[53]

Nevertheless, Anne feared the financial risk involved in managing her own school. For a time, she taught privately the three children of Amos

Farnsworth, a Groton physician, widower, and abolitionist. She enjoyed the independence of such a position far more than the classroom, and acknowledged that "if I could be making the same money there as in N[ew] B[edford] the situation would be altogether preferable."[54] Although Caroline was offered $300 per year to act as governess to Robert Sedgwick's children in Connecticut, neither she nor Anne, nor most New England women of her generation, could make as much money teaching the children of one family as in a school of any size greater than ten where tuition was assessed per student.[55]

The business of teaching was particularly stressful when it involved responsibility for school administration as well. The Westons' correspondence iterates not only the difficulties of finding and holding positions and stretching their salaries to cover the costs of their own lodging, clothing, and laundering but also the problems of dealing with landlords, recruiting and retaining students, stretching tuition to cover instructional materials, contracting and paying for fuel to warm the classroom, and supplying wages to keep a cleaning woman. Sometimes parents or school committees paid fuel and cleaning costs, but this arrangement required considerable negotiation. Caroline reminded Debora to pay close attention to details, think carefully about contractual arrangements, and "make no fast bargain without a handsome consideration."[56]

The Westons, as did so many other teachers, found school charring a constant irritation. Caroline complained in her diary about the "cross" she bore in losing a charwoman at the beginning of a new quarter in their Boston school. "I hope she may come back *yet*," she sighed. Anne, however, was relieved to see Margaret go, because while "good in many things," she was wasteful. "We shall get along for a little while with only Sarah," she reassured. But the loss required a greater expenditure of cash to hire out the week's wash. Determined to wait until the right person became available, Caroline soon found herself "almost tired to death with sweeping and dusting."[57] She felt rewarded for both her hard work and her patience when a Miss Baker of Dorchester applied for the position. In Caroline's eyes, Baker was both beautiful and "whiter than snow," an allusion to the race and ethnicity of the women who made up the majority of housekeepers and charwomen in Boston: African Americans and Irish.[58] The Westons should have paid more attention to Miss Baker's character and less to her appearance and demeanor. Three months after her hire, this "jewel" requested leave for an evening and never came back—but continued to charge goods to the school's accounts, spreading confusion and ill will about the city.[59]

Teaching for a living required a complex process of searching and weighing positions. Selection committee criteria could prove surprising. A Mr. Kimball of Canaan, Connecticut, sought a teacher for a small school of six or seven students. He found Caroline's "tout ensemble better than any body's" because she could "knock a girl down" if necessary. "I was flattered by this last praise of course," noted Caroline archly, but despite "a very liberal" salary, she did not want to leave Boston.[60] Debora's negotiations with John Emerson dragged on for ten months in 1836–37 as she weighed her homesickness against losing a good position for the family and he sought to solidify his own situation. Caroline warned her, "Our prospects [at the Westons' Boylston school] are some what discouraging at present and if you *can* be comfortable and contented it would be well." Months later, as Debora was finding her forty-three students "pretty fatiguing" and looking to contract for a pay raise, Emerson took the headship of a new high school. The job offer included a directive from the selection committee to hire a Miss Baylis rather than Debora to head the Female Department.[61]

Valuing Debora's experience and capability, Emerson urged her to stay in place because the new master would want a female teacher to attract female pupils. In June, J. K. Lord of Weymouth hired Debora for the fall term. When he failed to garner sufficient students to ensure the success of his school, Debora considered a similar arrangement with a Mr. Carter. Anne reminded her, unnecessarily, that the Weymouth household depended upon her employment: "Only remember that if you can get a good situation we all wish you to do so." With no good options, Debora left New Bedford, only to be called back by Emerson in December 1838 when he brokered for her a short-term private tutoring position while the parents of her previous students reestablished a school for the "beloved Miss Weston."[62]

Negotiating teaching contracts required both spine and artfulness. The Westons generally regarded Debora as too trusting for success. "I must say," Anne complained, "you ought to see that proposals are more definite if you expect them to be settled at any definite time. The question of *the salary* is the thing. You are not quite apt enough to pin things." Anne carried Debora's offer to Roxbury for Caroline's perusal, as the sisters believed her to be the best negotiator. She reported back that Caroline found Debora's contract "so vague that her answer cannot be determinate, but she will write one that you *can shew* [sic] to people." Anne advised Debora to "say nothing" to her would-be employer until she had Caroline's counteroffer in hand.[63]

The Westons had numerous opportunities to upgrade their employment conditions if only they had been willing to change locales. One friend
believed Caroline would find success establishing a school in St. Louis;
the Reverend Henry Colburn wanted her to come to Philadelphia.[64] The
rejection of these and other offers arose from a sibling imperative for proximity and a sisterhood's commitment to antislavery activism. In debating
an offer from Mr. Congdon, Caroline acknowledged how difficult it would
be to leave her Roxbury position, which allowed her to "be in Boston as
much as I choose."[65] Proximity enabled her to participate fully in both the
BFAS and the MAS. Her sisters reacted negatively to a good job offer from
Providence, Rhode Island, in 1839, that would divide their efforts into
three distinct communities across two states (Boston, New Bedford, and
Providence), although the distance of Providence from Boston was negli-
gible. All agreed that if economic necessity compelled Caroline to take the
position, one or another sister would accompany her so that she would
remain emotionally connected and politically supported.

Caroline did leave Roxbury in the early 1840s, when the division between Garrisonians and anti-Garrisonians made her Roxbury position
untenable. She joined her sisters in New Bedford, the city that provided
the Westons their most sustained teaching possibilities, as a result of their
connection with John F. Emerson, principal of the New Bedford High
School and treasurer of the New Bedford Anti-Slavery Society.[66] Debora
in particular suffered from homesickness, telling Anne, "I want to come
home so much that I can hardly stay. Though every thing is so pleasant
here, the truth is I don't like the thought of coming back."[67] Anne attempted to console her saying, "One week nearly of your time is gone.
Comfort yourself with that." She confided her own struggle, writing: "To
tell the honest truth, I do not like keeping school. But if I must, why, certainly I had rather be with you than any where else."[68]

The necessity of generating income and keeping her sisters together,
along with changes in the antislavery movement that increasingly focused
on fugitive slaves and the pursuit of electoral power, provided the impetus
for Debora to establish her own school in New Bedford, one that made her
less dependent upon Emerson and provided a space to which her younger
sisters might flock and the elder ones cohere when desirable. Given that
a school of one's own was a dicey proposition economically, Debora wrote
her sisters for advice about the opportunity presented by a Miss Appleton's
decision to sell out. Anne responded positively: "If you have 20 scholars,
the profit of the school will about equal what we had from Emerson. Then
too, you may be able to do more and better with it than Miss Appleton."

Aunts Priscilla and Mary Weston gave their opinions as well. According to Anne, Mary thought Debora "had better take it." Looking for a job herself, Mary also asked Debora to look out for a position that might suit her as well. "Neither, she adds is she very particular what the place is. To double her allowance is what she aims at." Priscilla encouraged Debora to do "that which is the most comfortable to yourself—irrespective . . . of the recompense or reward."[69] Caroline warned of pitfalls: "In the first place I should *give nothing* for the *good will*. I suppose that is not expected—2d— I should ascertain whether if there would *be certainly some* scholars—for I should go against the school if it did not enable you to keep Lucia or Emma with you as I don't think you well enough to be alone. What would you do were one of your head aches to set in?" She urged Debora to "calculate the price of board—washing etc. . . . . If taking the school will mean your *credit don't* do it—if it will not—I *should take* it."[70]

Despite reservations, Debora took on the school. When students did not appear immediately, she began to lose money. Worse, she had borrowed from Caroline and could not repay her. "I wish I were at Weymouth," she mourned. "I am so vexed with myself for beginning at all that I almost hate myself." She reported symptoms of depression—sleeplessness, homesickness, and lack of appetite. "I try to mollify myself by thinking I acted for the best," she wrote. "It was as I thought in the way of duty, but thinking only seems to aggravate me. I tell myself all this is very wrong, then I betake myself to the bible and to thinking of other peoples *real* troubles, but nothing seems to bear upon me." Debora felt keenly that her situation involved significant sacrifice with little promise of "recompense" and she "resolved to give up." As she wrote, "It seems to me as if I could not live as I am now long."[71] Her sisters urged her not to retreat, assuring her that students would appear and she would clear expenses. "Doing that, I would be content," wrote Anne supportively. "Let me therefore admonish you to dismiss every anxiety connected with scholars or no scholars."[72]

Nevertheless, and using illness as her reason, Debora withdrew to Weymouth for the winter. She emerged the following spring when the Morgan School became available in New Bedford with a guaranteed student body. "I *decided*—and we *all* decided," Caroline insisted, "that the Morgan School was the thing—that you had better close with it at once. I should think $450 or even $400 very good compensation if *they* fund rent and fuel—if you have to promise these it will be little or nothing." She told Debora to contract for the first of January and to assure Mrs. Morgan that if her health continued poorly, one of her sisters would step in until she improved. "It is better than the Appleton situation could have possibly been—do not trouble yourself about any little loss that the Appleton School—rent—fires—&c may occasion—it is not worth fretting about," Caroline wrote.[73] Anne agreed to take up the position in January and hold it for Debora if she remained unwell; and so she did.[74]

Thus was established in New Bedford "The Misses Weston's School for Young Ladies," run alternately and in tandem by Caroline, Anne, and Debora. As Caroline wrote that first year, "The *School* is interesting, as what school is not? Perhaps you never knew that I am a first rate teacher boiling over with professional enthusiasm—but so it is and I am conscious now and here of a field for effort such as I never before entered upon." As so many teachers have, Caroline found, "The *hearts* of these young people are not entirely uncultivated—but their *minds*—are howling wildernesses— We cried out with the American footman in Willis's drama *'here's* an eligible missionary station'!!"[75] Aware of the mixed messages she had sent about teaching during her latter days at Roxbury, Caroline acknowledged to Ann T. G. Phillips, "I suppose you had concluded from the general tone of my remarks that I was quite ready to resign a life which brought so much trial and temptation—but you are mistaken. I should like very well to *re-form, re-organize, re-arrange* it all—but my attachment to it is intense—I should never have come here of my own accord but being here, I wish to stay."[76] The tenacity, strength, hard work, and courage required to undertake a school in antebellum New England, and the fragility of its potential for success, were revealed in Caroline's use of a southern fable. Life as a teacher was pretty "agreeable," she asserted, "if one is fairly determined to 'ride the alligator'—and continue to do it—but *this* is incentive for he stands always ready to devour one with his jaws open."[77]

The Westons viewed teaching as the family business. They substituted for one another as necessary so that one of them might take leave to heal from illness or exhaustion, attend a political meeting, help in the natal household in Weymouth, or labor in Maria's marital household in Boston. They conducted their school teaching as a common enterprise, sharing lesson plans, books, and other classroom materials. Caroline offered Debora help with mathematics problems: "If you will let me know where your classes in arithmetic are I will work out all the sums & send them to you done as the modus operandi may trouble you." Debora worked out some of the problems herself, "exonerating" her sister from that effort even as she asked for explanations on others. As she put it to Caroline, "Your explanations heave light on other dark subjects and set me straight."[78]

From her older sister Debora also sought lesson plans for classes in drawing and painting. "Do up a parcel of very easy drawings for beginners, the great difficulty being that I cant get any thing half easy enough," she wrote. There being some urgency, she begged her sister to "send them off by the stage on Monday morning, so that I can have them Monday night, Tuesday being drawing day, or rather afternoon." A week later Debora enthused, "The drawings you sent were just the thing I wanted."[79] So too the sisters exchanged language grammars and reviewed textbooks for one another.[80]

While the Weston sisters participated in a family wage economy, pooling their income so as to augment the financial resources available to the Weymouth household, they retained a sense of independent decision-making on expenditures. They chose, on their own or in consultation, how they spent their wages so as to address their individual needs while contributing to the necessities of the broader family and Weymouth household. Debora, for example, paid a week's worth of her earnings for ten riding lessons for Anne because she worried about her sister's health and believed the exercise would improve it. When she had a dressmaker cut out a new cape and gown for herself, she had one cut for Anne as well.[81] Anne, in turn, bought shoes for both herself and Lucia.[82]

Upon the elder sisters' shoulders fell much of the responsibility for maintaining the homestead. Renovations to the Weymouth house were made over the years by means of the sisters' earnings. The general process followed a consistent pattern in which they built consensus as to what improvements and purchases were required and how these would be funded. In 1840, for example, Anne, Caroline, and Debora pooled money to purchase wallpaper.[83] When Henry Chapman left a $400 bequest to the sisters, Anne and Debora combined their portions to pay off a debt to their grandmother Debora Nash Weston's estate and secure the land that their father farmed.[84] In 1850, it was Debora's turn to handle capital improvements. She went to "work upon the house with just as much spirit as if I were a great architect and knew any thing about building." She wanted to add a third story and attach it to the new parlor, although the connection with the flat roof over the rest of the house proved difficult. She also "coveted" a furnace.[85] In 1852, with the house "tumbling down about our ears," the sisters planned a new staircase, a "jog" in the new dining room wall, and "a polished parquet" floor inspired by their foreign travel.[86]

As part of their family economy, the sisters also lent money to one another to meet urgent or unexpected expenses for their cause. Debora requested two dollars of Maria to pay the stage fare should she come for an antislavery meeting, a request that presumed the money to be a loan, not a gift. Maria, short on cash, begged thirteen dollars of Debora to pay the binder's bill for the *Liberty Bell* magazine they edited, published, and sold at the BFAS fair. Here, too, the implicit expectation was for repayment when fund-raising brought in the money.[87]

On other occasions, money forwarded by the sisters formed a joint donation to abolition, which was as much the family business as teaching. The Westons tithed for antislavery, consciously earmarking some of their earnings (or in Maria's case the marital finances) for political purposes. Maria, for example, pooled Debora's money with contributions made by their mother and Anne to pay some bills for the *Liberty Bell*.[88] Debora sent five dollars of an advance on her wages to help publish the *Cradle of Liberty*; Caroline paid twenty-six dollars out of some fifty she had "scraped up" from various sources for binding the *Bell*; both Maria and Caroline pledged funds, two dollars in Maria's case and ten in Caroline's, to support publication of the *Anti-Slavery Standard*.[89] During the breakup of the BFAS in 1839–40, the "peelers" of the Massachusetts Female Emancipation Society established their own fund-raising. John E. Fuller, one of the founders of the New England Anti-Slavery Society who subsequently broke with Garrison and joined in attacking female abolitionists such as the Westons, spoke regretfully in Roxbury about the loss to the annual fair of Weston money. Said Fuller, "There was no doubt that *that family alone* would keep $300!! dollars *out of the cause* at this time."[90] Of course they would not have withheld their contributions from the cause, only from the "new organization," which they deemed responsible for undermining Garrison's influence.

A significant aspect of antebellum women's civic engagement had to do with attending reform conventions, debating and voting on resolutions, and electing officers at annual meetings. Within the Weston family, an individual's opportunity to participate in antislavery gatherings required negotiation. One of the more entertaining and representative of these exercises occurred in 1842 as Debora and Anne debated who would represent the "House of Weston" at the annual meeting of the American Anti-Slavery Society in New York City. Debora wrote to Anne with the following proposition: "A letter came from the Gibbons, with an invitation for you and Caroline to come on to them during the annual meeting. I think you had better go. *I* you know have money, and it will reconcile me very much to staying here to know that somebody is having fun through my means."[91] Anne demurred: "I should be glad to accept of your offer about going to N.Y. if I felt it right; but I do not." She worried that Debora needed her money for other things and, indeed, hoped Debora would put some of it toward a new carpet at Weymouth, as Anne did "not see how we can get along this summer without."[92]

Feeling flush, Debora countered Anne's objections with encouraging words. "As to my money, you can go to N. York and we can have the carpet too and not go into my next quarters money much—very little if any, but of course this depends upon the price of the carpet and upon 2d thoughts it will not go at all into my next quarter. My advice is that you go by all means to N. York."[93] As Anne gathered more information about the costs of the excursion, she became more and more excited about going. Ellis G. Loring and his mother were traveling from Boston, as was her friend Henrietta Sargent.[94] Antislavery agent John A. Collins had arranged for train tickets for two dollars round-trip, and "good" accommodations in the city for fifty cents a day. With such promising company and economical arrangements, Anne began to plan the excursion. Within days, Caroline too had decided to go. Anne would travel "from Northampton—via Norwich—probably with David Lee [Child]," while Caroline would join with Henrietta and Catherine Sargent in Collins's expedition.[95] She only wished she might "join them coming home, for they mean to return via Albany and Springfield— going up the Hudson from New York—but neither time or [sic] also money will allow me to do this."[96]

Meanwhile, Anne moved forward on obtaining a new carpet, spurred on by a bout of capital construction in Weymouth, the impetus for which was Henry G. Chapman's lung disease. Anne determined "to raise up a city of refuge" by raising the roof and creating a dormer in the back chamber to provide a more spacious upstairs room in which Henry might convalesce with the help of his sisters-in-law's nursing.[97] Debora sent twenty dollars for the carpet, with a promise to send five more the following month. Anne assured her, "Of course I shall do the very best I can with the money, but I suppose the carpet will cost $18. Say 25 yds at 75 cts a yard. I think it can be got good enough for that. At any rate, you may depend on it that you could do nothing more helpful with the money than to get this, for till that is got all the house is disarranged."[98]

Plans went sideways when Anne found herself strapped for funds to attend the New York convention while holding the carpet money. She had to redeem her silk dress from the dye house and purchase a stage ticket. Assuring her sister that "extravagance is not one of my vices," Anne provided Debora with a detailed accounting of her expected expenditures for the trip: $1.50 for the dye house and, for less than a dollar each, a yard of brown linen, two and a half yards of cambric for facing, new kid gloves and black worsted stockings, three yards of ribbon and silk flowers with which to trim a hat, three yards of cotton for a new petticoat, a comb and pins, and sixty-two cents to the dressmaker to make alterations. "Sorrow to say,

I had to spend more than $5 getting ready for my journies," she confided. "I dont know what I should have done had I not had the carpet money in my hands." She dipped into the carpet money for $6.15 but reassured Debora that "what is wanting Ma can supply."[99] By early June, the Weston women had purchased the carpet, claret in color. By the middle of the month, the old green carpet was set in its new location, the other chambers covered with new straw to keep down the dust, and the new carpet laid in the main rooms of the house. Only the front entry and central hall had yet to be cleaned to complete the improvements.[100]

In sum, largely because of their lack of patrimony and the dissolute condition of their father through the first decades of his marriage and family life, the economic support of the Weston household fell upon its elder four daughters. The Weston brothers benefited from, but seemingly did not contribute greatly to, the economic strategy by which their older sisters managed their earnings for not only their own good but also that of the family. With their uncle's annual assistance to their mother, Maria, Caroline, Anne, and Debora acquired an education that enabled them to pursue the uncertain and often poorly compensated profession of teaching.

The overall financial situation of the household and its members improved over time. The imperative of paid labor and significant constraint on spending that shaped the sisters' lives and reform work eased only gradually. Maria's marriage to Henry Grafton Chapman in 1830 did little to change the Weston household economy but did provide a cushion, as various siblings lived in Boston with Maria for periods of time and the elder Chapmans gifted the Weymouth household occasionally with such staples as tea, sugar, coffee, and flour.[101] The most significant changes in the sisters' finances occurred with the death, not of Maria's husband in 1842, but of her father-in-law in 1846. Henry Grafton Chapman left no will. He owned no real property, although he had some stocks and bonds and a share in the chandler's business he managed with his father. These went into a trust established for his children by his father.

By way of contrast, when Henry Chapman himself died, he left an estate of stocks and notes worth $85,100 in addition to a house at 6 Chauncy Place, Boston, appraised at $11,000 with furnishings worth approximately $1,500. In 1847, with the death of Maria's mother-in-law, Sarah Greene Chapman, these passed in undivided halves to Maria and her sole remaining sister-in-law, Mary Chapman. Mary was required by the terms of the will to pay Maria rent for her ongoing use of the house—a situation that resulted in some strained feelings on Mary's part. An investment strategy determined by Wendell Phillips, Maria's lawyer, resulted in an inheritance upon her death of more than $40,000 in stocks and bonds, in addition to this property, for Maria's sole surviving child, Elizabeth Bates Laugel.[102] The other Weston sisters had nothing like this degree of financial support at any time in their lives, including their waning years.[103] Three outlived Maria—Debora, Anne, and Emma. In addition to the real property they received from Mary Weston (the little house on Front Street) and the larger house and lands Joshua Bates provided for his sister in the early 1830s, each inherited $1,000.

Weston letters convey satisfaction with their teaching careers and their competent management of (oftentimes limited) financial resources. Their utilization of political and social networks to obtain students, their strategy of combining their individual earnings from teaching, and leaning on extended family when necessary made it possible for the Weston sisters to uphold their social status and live reasonably (if sometimes tightly) despite their father's alcoholism and their brothers' reliance on their nursing, occasional economic support, and housekeeping. Their collective decision-making spread the responsibility to spend wisely, just as shared accounting ameliorated anxiety over income variability and unexpected expenditures.[104] Intertwined with and reinforcing the sibling ties of mutual obligation and reciprocity forged by the sisters' economic practice were those of social reproduction: child-rearing, nursing, and housework—the subject of the following chapter.

4

THE CROSS OF MY LIFE

Social Reproduction in the Sororal Household

At home in Weymouth, Anne fretted, "I am naturally of so anxious a temperament that this trouble about other people's lives and health has been *the cross* of my life. I sometimes envy the people that stand alone in the world never having had any remembered ties of blood."[1] Yet while Caroline lived abroad in the late 1840s and early 1850s with Maria, her children, and sisters Lucia and Emma, Anne lobbied strenuously for her return: "I begin to feel as if I *must* see [Caroline]. When that feeling comes about an absent person it is needful."[2] Within the month, Caroline took passage for home. Her arrival eased Anne's growing fears about Lucia's consumption (for Caroline never would have left France had she thought Lucia in decline) and took up some of the nursing chores occasioned of Anne and Debora by Warren's worsening health.[3] Anne's expressions of anxiety and longing represented the opposing sides of siblicity's coin—the costs and benefits of love and loss arising from intertwined lives. The sibling affection that bound these sisters down, the worry that accompanied their devotion, and the exhaustion attached to the labor of caring for each other also buoyed them up and sustained them.[4]

More than any other sisters in the family, Caroline and Debora met the distaff requirements. "Is she not the Martha of the family, and has she not her hands full & her heart full too of the concerns of those around her?" noted one family intimate of Caroline. The refrain echoed through Weston correspondence: "How is Caroline and where is she and who is she taking care of?"[5] Debora too was "famous" for "attending to . . . the thousand little duties of a country neighborhood" with efficiency and intelligence while also acting as the family's "indispensable housekeeper and care-taker."[6] No less engaged in politics than Anne or Maria, Caroline and Debora proffered a more nurturing mien. However, given the family's means and political commitments, the size of the family Weston required each sister to give time and labor to rear the children; clothe, clean, and provision the Weymouth and Boston households; and nurse the ill.[7] Continuous engagement in domestic labor animated sibling ties, grounding the connections upon which the paid labor of teaching and voluntary engagement with politics were devised. In fulfilling their domestic roles, the Westons acknowledged the obligations of kinship and expressed their love for one another.

Just as they cooperated in educating their younger siblings, nephew, and nieces, the four eldest Westons jointly reared them. Maria bore four children: Elizabeth in 1831, Henry in 1833, Ann in 1837, and Gertrude, who died within months of her birth in 1841. The two younger Westons, Lucia and Emma, were closer in age to the Chapman children than to their older sisters, with Emma only six years older than Elizabeth and nineteen younger than Maria. These youngsters worked, played, and learned together.[8] They traveled back and forth between the Boston and Weymouth households according to convenience or necessity. Concerns about the birth of a new baby,[9] the illness of any family member,[10] the emergence of a developmental or disciplinary problem with one of the children,[11] and a variety of antislavery circumstances propelled the younger Westons and Chapman children from one household to another.[12]

The elder Weston sisters often referred to their mother's heavy child-rearing responsibilities at Weymouth, desirous of easing her labor. Debora, for example, while looking forward to the end of the 1836 school term in New Bedford, fretted about her mother's burden. "How are the children getting on?" she wrote Anne. "I feel uneasy about them at times, and as if I ought to be there to take care of them."[13] By "children" Debora meant not just her niece, age five, and her nephew, age three, but also her youngest sisters, ages fourteen and eleven.

Over the next decade the Chapman children increasingly took center stage in their aunts' concerns, particularly young Henry, who everyone agreed was "awfully troublesome." Debora admonished Lucia to "keep [Henry] off Ma if you can," and Anne noted with relief that once the Chapman children returned to Boston, Ma Weston was "not so full of constant worry and excitement."[14] On another occasion, "in the midst of [such] hurry and bustle" at Weymouth that she knew not "whether I am on my head or feet," Anne asked Debora, then at the Chapman home in Boston, to "get Lizzy ready to come out [to Weymouth] for we shall send Henry in pretty soon and take her in his room for I fear he will kill Ma."[15]

Caring for the young Chapman children exhausted both their aunts and their grandmother. While they adored the "little jewel" (Ann Greene Chapman, Annie or Handy as they called their youngest niece), they plotted to separate her from her older siblings as much as possible, unable to "bear she should get hardened by contact with other people like Henry and Lizzy."[16] So trying were the two older Chapman children that their aunts simultaneously worried about their well-being and welcomed their absence. "How does Lizzy do?" asked Debora. "Give my love to her. It seems like heaven without her." Anne anticipated that young Henry would be paying a long visit to Weymouth, "as Maria had brought his clothes." While Anne did not wish to "oppose his staying," she acknowledged her intention to send him elsewhere, "if I can, for you must remember that he has been with me ever since I came from Abington about. He accompanied me into town, and now has come out and I am pretty tired of him."[17]

Everyone involved with rearing Henry and Lizzie deemed them hellions. Their aunt Mary Chapman acknowledged, "I fear Emma to day must have sighed for the quiet of West St. [Maria's rental house in Boston] with only little Ann to caress for Elizabeth has been very teasing to her—My own patience is sometimes nearly exhausted—I hope all children do not try their friends so constantly." Anne pleaded with Debora to "get Lizzy into the way she should go." In turn, Debora sent Elizabeth to her grandmother in Weymouth, "in hopes that you [Ann Bates Weston] will reform her, for all her relatives in town pronounce her totally unbearable."[18]

Henry seemed to grow more impossible every year. Lucia described his "wickedness" and Caroline called him "by all odds the worst child I ever saw." With a dose of black humor, she recorded Henry's restlessness, poor hygiene, and labile emotions: "He cant of course help snuffin, and sneezing, and coughing—and whimpering (tho he does less and less of the latter) and snoring all night so loud that I get next to no sleep—and sob[b]ing and hurting his fingers (which of course have sores on them) and hurting his mouth—which of course has canker in it—in short every part of his body is continually in presence." She promised to "try to keep him [in Weymouth] as long as possible as he is a trial to which they seem quite unequal at home [in Boston]."[19]

A year later, Caroline traveled nightly from Roxbury, where she was keeping school, into Boston to lend her stabilizing hand and calm demeanor to the volatile Chapman household. She told Debora that "Henry is and always was the most foolish and selfish of children but he has begun to go to school [and] the whole house is filled with violence on account of his lessons." His sisters reacted to the uproar in character: "Little Ann does herself justice of course—and Lizzy is so busy making her own superiority in matters of behavior and scholarship &c felt and acknowledged as to employ her very fully." Caroline passed along an incident in which Elizabeth, "being much provoked . . . by impositions and insults from Henry . . . did then and there seize him and give him a sound *drubbing* at which," she confessed, "I rejoiced in spirit and if he was not much refreshed by it I certainly was."[20] In desperation, Henry G. Chapman offered Debora $100 if she would leave her New Bedford teaching job and come to Boston to "take charge of little Henry."[21] "He acts like sin," Anne acknowledged. "We think it is because he is in boy's clothes."[22]

The children's misbehavior became worse when one or both parents remained unavailable—away from home and seriously ill. In 1838 the children stayed with their grandmother and aunt in Boston while their mother attended the Anti-Slavery Convention of American Women in Philadelphia. When Maria fell ill and extended her absence, the children grew increasingly difficult. They moved first to New Bedford under Debora's care and then to their grandmother in Weymouth when Anne, who had accompanied Maria to the convention and remained to nurse her, called for Caroline's help with the deteriorating and potentially deadly situation. Very much worried, Anne described the children as behaving "more like evil spirits than ought else."[23] Henry started school in Boston with a Mr. Blanchard in April 1839, but as his father became more ill, his behavioral problems multiplied. In early 1841, with his father and mother in the Caribbean seeking to ease the tuberculosis that would kill the elder Henry the following year, young Henry became so difficult that the Weymouthians pulled him out. Anne reported, "On some accounts this renders him more troublesome, yet on others it is far better."[24]

Lizzy's and Henry's moody temperaments and rowdy behavior developed in a political atmosphere of anti-abolitionist violence that the children encountered both directly and vicariously. "Born on the field of battle," as their mother put it, the older Chapman children experienced a prolonged sense of endangerment when young.[25] Threats to family members, wild cries and shots fired in the street outside the house, loud banging on the door, and various kinds of vandalism occurred regularly from 1835 into the mid-1840s as the Chapman household "received many insults—and letters—the last was most alarming informing Maria in a friendly way that a plot was had to personally injure herself and her husband." When the New England Anti-Slavery Society held its quarterly meeting in Boston in 1835, Henry Grafton Chapman felt "great apprehensions" of mob violence. While Maria, Anne, and Debora attended the meeting, Caroline waited at her school, "thinking every noise I heard was the coming mob."[26]

The anxiety that roiled the Chapman household during these years could not have spared four-year-old Elizabeth or two-year-old Henry, who surely intuited their elders' fear without understanding the nature or extent of the risks involved or the plans made by adults for protecting the household and its members. In similar situations, the elder children of William Lloyd Garrison and of George Thompson suffered nightmares and acted out their fears with temper tantrums and other forms of misbehavior.[27] As armed men moved stealthily in and out of the Chapman home and urgent adult voices analyzed threats and formulated contingencies, Maria and Henry bundled up the children and carried them to the greater safety of Weymouth. With false heartiness, and only days before the Weston sisters were among the mobbed at the Boston Female Anti-Slavery Society meeting of October 1835, Anne attempted to reassure the household there: "Do not any of you be alarmed. Tell my mother to be of good cheer."[28]

These events shaped the Chapman children's psyches throughout their lives, defining one cost of the family's commitment to abolition.[29] As late as 1856, when Anne proposed a trip through the southern states so that she might see slavery at first hand, her nieces panicked: "Language seemed to fail them when they thought of it, they could not express their horror." Ann Greene Chapman wrote "a most serious remonstrance and could not believe it was Anne's duty to be lynched. The *Cause* had no right to ask it of her. She thinks apparently that it is a matter of *course*, nothing *could* be expected but lynching." Quoting poet Felicia Hemans, Maria expressed her belief that her eldest daughter had suffered greatly from the trauma of these years:

> Afar
> From the sweet home of thy young fancy,
> Whose image unto thee is a dream
> Of fire and slaughter.[30]

Henry acted out his fears and frustrations by threatening death to anyone who stymied him. "He never spoke to me except to threaten to kill or shoot me—and repeatedly assured me that he would '*did a hole in the dround and tick me in*,'" reported Caroline.[31]

In households characterized by frequent changing of the guard, even the youngest Chapman learned quickly to assert and protect her interests. With her mother in Haiti, Ann had been dispatched to Weymouth for care. When her aunts Caroline, Anne, Lucia, and Emma left Weymouth for a week to attend the Ministry Convention in Boston, she, "with her usual wisdom made her arrangements—She addressed herself formally to Debora—with 'Bella will you be my mother while Lule [Lucia] is gone'— Bella assured her of her maternal intentions and Handy [Ann] saw them depart with great composure."[32] Refusing to be lost in the shuffle, little Ann had learned to take matters into her own hands and appointed a guardian for herself.

After more than a decade and a half in the cause, and following the death of her husband, Maria focused her attention on the children's educational and social needs. As early as January 1848, Chapman discussed a "European tour" for her "children's benefit."[33] Gradually she began to think about a longer stay of perhaps two to three years' duration. Ultimately she remained abroad for seven years.[34] The timing was informed by the inheritance she received following the deaths of her husband in 1842, father-in-law in 1846, and mother-in-law in 1847, as well as the support of Eliza Cabot Follen. The two widows, their children, and their sisters—Susan Cabot and Caroline Weston—traveled together. Eliza accompanied her son Charles to London to enroll him in university.[35] Maria determined that Henry would attend the University of Heidelberg. Elizabeth and Ann would "finish" in Paris, tutored in French, Italian, art, history, and culture.[36]

Having lived solely in one another's company, the Chapman children were immature for their ages. At eighteen years old, Elizabeth Bates Chapman thought of herself as a child rather than a marriageable young woman. Not long after their arrival in Paris Maria reported, "Poor Lizzy has entirely rejected the Marquis De Tonquiere. These things [courtship and marriage proposals] disturb her childhood very much. She plays with the cat on the floor just the same, but she is startled out of her infancy; and it plagues her."[37]

Henry's erratic education and undisciplined behavior grew worse after his father's premature death. At the University of Heidelberg he ran with a rowdy crowd known for making public scenes, dueling, smoking, and drinking.[38] Chaos ruled during one reunion with his sisters and cousins, reported British abolitionist Mary Ann Estlin, who witnessed the scene. "It was a great proof of German tolerance of foreigners that we were not on that occasion one and all handed over to the police," she noted, "for the prolonged shoutings and disturbance we made resounded [in the hotel] from one end to the other of the long corridor and must have made the unfortunate occupants of all the adjacent rooms vibrate in their beds." Nor was decorum restored the following day, as "the same racket pervaded every spot that any of our party had to do with." Shrieks of laughter rang out while the children's heads and feet extruded from windows and into halls and passageways, a hindrance, an embarrassment, and an irritant to other guests.[39] Twenty-five-year-old Emma, nineteen-year-old Elizabeth, seventeen-year-old Henry, and even thirteen-year-old Ann expressed their delight in reunion through pandemonium.

When the children first arrived in France they rejoiced in their new environment. As Caroline put it, "We are *social* creatures," though the notoriety of the Westons and Chapmans in Boston had constrained their social life. In France and Great Britain the family interacted with a broad array of people who felt no need to isolate them for their politics, discriminate against them on the basis of their religious views, or seek their company for reasons of fame. Nor had they to fend off the disapproval of "the fashionables."[40] Maria described European sociability as a release from the constraints of New England conformity, noting that she had found there "a social Freedom which tempers [society] so that it is easier living here." Although "we have hardly been either to church or to the theatre . . . all our friends, who zealously go to both, find no fault with us who do neither."[41] Lectures, galleries, concerts, and opera beckoned. The girls relished opportunities to explore nature, particularly the many romantic sites associated with what they read in history and novels.

Chapman succeeded in her goal of finishing her daughters and, to a lesser extent, of educating her son abroad. "The children improve rapidly," she wrote following a few months overseas. "Paris is the place of places for good *teachers* and good cooks. Both are alike artists and both equally important to the growth of the young."[42] By 1850, British physician and abolitionist John Bishop Estlin found thirteen-year-old Ann quite "frenchified"—having nothing of the "falseness and insincere politeness" of the French but rather acquiring the "formally french manner . . . evidently caught unconsciously, and perfectly consistent with entire artlessness."[43] In January 1855, Maria contracted an eligible marriage for her eldest child. At twenty-four, Elizabeth Bates Chapman married August Laugel, secretary to the Duc D'Amale.

Henry remained incorrigible. Caroline described him as Europeanized, by which she seems to have meant that he had acquired a gloss of sophistication. But he continued to drink heavily, and his lack of discipline worried his mother and aunts. Although the record lacks detail, it seems that while in Paris, and against his mother's wishes, Henry may have become engaged to a Boston heiress, Miss Tudor. Whether Maria deemed the young woman or her family unacceptable or thought Henry not yet ready for marriage remains unclear. In any case, she sent Henry back to Boston, where he lived with his aunt, Mary Chapman, in the house left to her by his grandfather. There he sought to learn the business of brokering stocks while he continued to pursue Miss Tudor. Maria returned to Boston briefly in 1854 to deal with the situation.[44] She again removed Henry, sending him to New York, where his uncle Warren took him into business. In addition to putting some distance between Henry and Miss Tudor, Maria must have hoped that her brother could improve Henry's attitude and behavior, as his "Weymouth aunts" found his manners "by no means agreeable . . . being exclusively those of a boy 6 years old."[45] Chapman returned to France to watch over Elizabeth's courtship.

Just as educating and nurturing the Chapman children occupied the Weston sisters for many years, so too did family nursing. Nursing played a key role in the organization of household labor and, while a labor of love, was labor nonetheless. Anne, for example, described how the Weymouth household rallied during a medical crisis in November 1841. Ann Bates Weston felt ill as a "result of broiling over the fire." Lucia purchased a stove so that she and Emma might share the cooking and relieve their mother of working over an open fire. Hervey arrived, "looking rather thin and poorly" and complaining of his studies, his boarding place, and his meals. Caroline followed swiftly upon her brother. She came home "firstly because ma did not get well as fast as could be wished—and 2dly because I was sick myself." Suffering "greatly" with an "inflammatory" cataract, Caroline felt all the "worse knowing it would last at least a week—the very week [Thanksgiving vacation] when I wished to be useful at home." Maria came and went in an effort to quiet the Boston household (where her husband lay desperately ill) by passing the children off to Weymouth.[46]

Despite the crowded conditions and illness there, Anne insisted, "We get along better than you would suppose." In an effort to ease Debora's apprehension with a detailed report on the household, Anne wrote, "Fortunately I am perfectly well; so I am up before light, I never stop doing as fast as I can till 10 at night. Lucia is like wise now very well and extremely gifted with her hands. Emma has nearly failed; but her complaints require nothing but quiet. Lizzy [Bates Chapman] has been here thro' the whole scrape, but she leaves tomorrow with Caroline, that is, if Caroline be well enough to go tomorrow."[47]

For most New Englanders, care of the sick and injured took place at home, accomplished by women for whom nursing consisted largely of keeping the patient comfortable, clean, fed, hydrated, and entertained.

Mothers, daughters, and sisters dosed their kin with homemade and commercial remedies as recommended by competing authorities of family, neighbors, physicians, friends, and domestic advice books.[48] Caroline detailed how an attack of cholera galvanized professional, neighborhood, and familial resources to aid her mother. "[A]unt Mary [Weston] was with her all the time—and aunt Cynthia [Bates Cowing] and Mrs Fifield and the Dr [Fifield]—you may know how ill she was when I tell you that the Dr was there all the morning—that though the day was intensely hot—she was surrounded with hot flatirons—and rubbed with hot Brandy-Mustard poultices on the bowels & hot water at the feet—there was great difficulty in keeping any thing on the stomach tho' brandy was tried directly—finally oil, took effect—then opium—and at last she kept down soda."[49]

Not only did family and neighbors—Warren Weston's sisters and Hannah Cranch Bond Fifield, the doctor's wife—help care for Ma Weston, but also Captain Weston drove into Boston to collect Caroline. She dismissed her school and returned with her father to spend the week in Weymouth cleaning house, laundering clothing, making meals, calming her father, and nursing her mother.

In the face of their mother's fatalism, the Weston sisters clung to the belief that active nursing kept their loved ones alive.[50] As Maria put it, "There are states of health where a person, if left alone a moment free to do it, drops out of existence at once." When her brother Warren fell desperately ill, Lucia felt strongly that he "could not die if she could only get" to his side and care for him.[51] In addition to coping with the usual colds, headaches, constricted breathing, fevers, chills, boils, stomach and intestinal disorders, and the more unusual cases of smallpox and cholera, the sisters Weston arranged themselves, their time, and their labor to address five significant illnesses among the sibling band. In addition to Warren's decade-long nervous prostration, Hervey's chronic invalidism, and Lucia's consumption, the sisters grappled with Maria's acute "brain fever" and Henry G. Chapman's fatal case of tuberculosis.[52]

Henry Grafton Chapman's struggle with tuberculosis required constant oversight and active nursing. His sisters-in-law reorganized their work, residences, and activities to assist Maria with his care as well as that of her household and children.[53] In June 1840, Maria had given birth to her fourth child and third daughter, whom the parents named Gertrude.[54] Debora left New Bedford in May to attend Maria's delivery and remained with her through the fall to aid with baby care.[55] By that time, Henry's condition had visibly worsened. Anne, who replaced Debora in the Chapman household, found that "living with him gives one the settled idea that he is a short lived man." His mood swings made it difficult to entertain, distract, or placate him. Maria somehow found the discipline of mind and strength of body to manage this irritable patient, "who never having been used to sickness requires great care and patience."[56]

Henry gradually withdrew from business, and a family consensus emerged that he must seek warm air to ease his worsening cough.[57] The couple decided upon the Caribbean, as travel to warm climes had become a popular treatment for those suffering nervous disease, dyspepsia, rheumatism, scrofula, and consumption.[58] Frustrated at Henry's ongoing symptoms, the Westons tried to remain upbeat, saying, "Improvement was perhaps as much as we could have xpected [*sic*] reasonably."[59]

Driven away by island heat in July 1841, the Chapmans returned to Boston. Their baby, Gertrude, had died in June of a sudden fever, perhaps associated with teething, but Maria had little time to mourn. She, with the aid of one or another sister, washed and changed Henry's shirts and bedclothes through night after night of sweats and cleaned up and comforted after long bouts of continuous coughing that raised phlegm or blood, frightening them all. They tended to his head and muscle aches, his growing lethargy and muscular weakness. By August, Maria decided they would have to return to Haiti for the winter.[60] The Westons organized Maria's clothing so that she and Henry could leave on a moment's notice. Anne and her friend Henrietta Sargent made linen chemises for Maria, a family domestic made her a new chintz dress, and her mother repaired an old silk one.[61]

Although forced by the board to lay aside his office as treasurer of the Massachusetts Anti-Slavery Society (MAS), Henry resisted his colleagues' conclusions as to his health. He took a position with an insurance company and insisted upon remaining in Boston to meet this obligation, although he rarely felt well enough to work. Anne reported, "His mother & Maria said every thing that was in their power, but he absolutely declined [to leave the city]. I do not think he would go unless an angel should specially inform him that it would save his life."[62] By February 1842, Henry's condition had so deteriorated that his father, in panic for his son's life, literally picked him up off the bed and ran to the wharf in a frantic attempt to put him on the packet boat *Lockhill*, which had departed mere moments before for the Caribbean. Maria and Henry sailed before the end of the month with Garrison's prediction "that *he* [Henry] may never come back" ringing in their ears.[63]

The couple cut short this second Haitian convalescence when the onset of a yellow fever epidemic among the local people coincided with a bout of diarrhea in Henry. He panicked, thinking this latter a new and "alarming feature of his complaint."[64] According to Anne, her brother-in-law arrived home looking wan and thin but showing improvement. "His appetite is good, very, & he slept well. He does not cough so much. I do not know that his health will suffer by his returning in such an abrupt manner tho' I had thought at first it must. He does not complain at all of the cold as he did last year."[65] However, while Henry said that he felt better and he briefly looked it, his condition continued to deteriorate.

Having expected to stay away longer, Maria had made no living arrangements in Boston. She took a rental in Summer Street, and while Anne and Caroline supervised both the building's rehabilitation and their nieces' and nephew's behavior, the couple repaired to the Northampton, Massachusetts, water cure. Wrote Anne to Debora, "You well know that it is utterly impossible to tell *one minute* before hand what they mean to do." She blamed these vagaries on Henry, whose "spirits rise & fall just as they used to with the slightest thing."[66]

The trip from Boston to Northampton proceeded in stages: first by train to Worcester, thence to Wilbraham, and finally by coach to Northampton. Poor roads made the last fifteen miles more difficult than the previous seventy-six. Exhausted, Maria rested upon arrival. Henry's spirits revived in this new setting, and in a lightning change of mood, he set out to hunt up a bookstore and meet the neighbors. Yet he grew bored within a week, complaining that his health was not improving. He insisted on returning to Boston. The Westons began to worry less about Henry and more about Maria, who felt "beat out being with him day & night."[67]

Through the summer and early fall of 1842, Henry became "more & more discouraged daily." His breathing was "toilsome," his sleep poor, and "his appetite variable & delicate."[68] Caroline wrote Debora, "Poor Maria stands it as well as one could expect but she has not *one minute* to herself except her morning sleep." Caroline prayed for strength, feeling herself "never so hurried & deprived of leisure at any period of my life." She tried "to smooth poor Henry's painful life" and ease Maria's burden. "I look forward with anxiety inexpressible to the next six months & pray that we may be supported," she wrote, "—let us try to take care of ourselves—& bear what we must as well as possible."[69]

After June 1842, Maria rarely left the house in Summer Street. As her sisters moved in and about to read and respond to antislavery correspondence, manage the house, and care for the children, Maria concentrated on nursing Henry. Gradually the family came to grips with the irreversible nature of his condition. Anne reported that she did "not expect any thing for him now but occasional relief." She feared "he would [not live to] see the cold weather. This is a dark cloud settling down in the distance over every thing."[70]

By August, Henry's breathing was so labored and his suffering so intense that Maria accepted the advice of Dr. Charles Eliot Ware, a Cambridge physician renowned for treating lung complaints, to dose him with laudanum.[71] "He gave Henry a mixture of which opium is one of the parts, & which makes him of course much more comfortable, but which fills me with horror," she wrote. "It is awful to me, to see any one under its effect. It ought to be called 'death-in-life.' It alleviated every bad symptom[,] reduced the pulse from 125 to 90—lengthened the breathing, helped the cough, lessened the expectoration, stayed the perspiration. Yet I cant abide it."[72] By mid-September, Henry could no longer speak and barely moved. On 3 October 1842, he died.

Even as Henry declined, new fears arose as to Lucia's painful condition. Although diagnosed as rheumatism, her illness was probably tuberculosis. Like Ann Greene Chapman, Henry Grafton Chapman, and Ann T. G. Phillips, Lucia Weston had spent considerable time in the Chauncy Place home of Henry Chapman and Sarah Greene Chapman, where she may have contracted the illness.[73] In the spring of 1842, Lucia suffered a severe attack of pain in her limbs and head. Debora packed her body daily in cold compresses to help restore appetite and improve sleep. Lucia's pulse raced, her muscles stiffened, and she developed difficulty breathing.[74] A second severe attack in the fall of 1844 caused Caroline to give up her school and return home to Weymouth in order to provide Lucia with full-time nursing. The sisters maintained some optimism by viewing Lucia's symptoms as ensuing from overexertion in antislavery work or exposure to poor weather conditions.[75] Lucia proved sufficiently well to join Debora, Hervey, and Anne in New York in the summer of 1851, when an ill Warren retreated from his business to be nursed at home. By May 1853, the two invalid siblings—Lucia and Warren—left for Europe under Caroline's care in search of better health abroad.

Lucia temporarily revived. Her sisters closely watched her exposure to cold and damp air and worried about the ever-present possibility of bronchitis. Caroline took Lucia south of Paris to Pannes, hoping that the "green grass & the dandelions & marguerites growing by the road side" would improve Lucia's spirits while the warmer weather eased her lungs. After a couple of summers in Switzerland with the "French Westons"—Maria, Caroline, and the children—she was still weak but found the fortitude to ascend the Right and Wengern Alps in a chair.[76] When Switzerland proved too rainy and cool, she decamped to Italy. Anne rejoiced, believing that Paris had never suited Lucia—not because it did her "any material injury" but rather because "she languishes for a place where she can get air & exercise more regularly." Lucia remained abroad, primarily in Rome, until she died in July 1861.[77] Always a sister kept her company (usually Emma, but occasionally Caroline or Anne) to provide nursing and companionship.[78]

Lucia's sisters deemed her a model patient, unlike Hervey or Henry, with a character well matched to her condition. Maria described her as having such "a great stock of patience and good spirits" that she could not be made to "complain or seem more depressed at one time than another." Lucia "was born with an easy quietness of disposition that makes her a prey to what a fretful, uneasy, selfish disposition would find a way to get rid of. She forgets *herself* and remembers every body else."[79]

Just as they nursed the entire kinship circle and jointly undertook the arduous and energizing tasks of rearing their younger siblings, a nephew, and two nieces, the elder Weston sisters divvied up the family's housekeeping. With their mother's assistance and occasional help from their aunts and hired workers, they took up the cooking, cleaning, and sewing necessary to sustain both the Weymouth and Boston households.[80] Despite many hands, this was no easy task. Anne reported, for example, that merely cleaning out, ordering, and reducing the inventory of the cedar closet in Weymouth took an entire day, all accomplished while she "had too the whole care of Ann [Greene Chapman]." Mother Weston handled the day's cooking and routine cleaning.[81]

Domestic labor—cooking, cleaning, and mending—anchored daily life in antebellum America. Its patterns marked the seasons of the year as wardrobes were refreshed in spring and fall, and stores of staples laid in after harvest and before winter. While in the Weston households politics interrupted household labor year-round, they commanded particular attention during the quarterly and annual antislavery meetings. Having finished with the Christmas fair in January 1855, for example, Anne turned to "*Spring cleaning*," which she found "a much more charming occupation than buying and selling."[82]

Whether she spoke ironically about the commercialization of antislavery fund-raising or was simply expressing her feelings about housework, Anne's chores demanded continual attention. The much-despised laundry was passed to hired women when the family could afford them. Warren's Boston landlady refused to do his washing, although she was willing to accommodate with light housekeeping, so he sent his dirty clothes to his sisters or mother. When teaching, his sisters found it difficult to accomplish their own laundry, let alone that of their brothers. The families with whom they boarded rarely accepted teacher washables, as their status fell somewhere between that of guest and renter. Hence the Weston siblings, brothers and sisters alike, routinely sent their clothes home to Weymouth or to Maria's for cleaning.[83] For example, Anne sent "some things of mine" out from Maria's to Weymouth, for, "as Emma's things are washed here I do not like to put in any things into the wash but trifles as handkerchiefs, stockings etc." Chapman diapers were done in Weymouth. Debora sent out a few things with the request to "Ask Mama if she thinks this handkerchief will wash." Her nightgowns traveled from New Bedford to Boston to be put into Maria's laundry.[84]

What with "getting things to rights and putting things in order" and "being almost tired to death—with sweeping & dusting," the Westons occasionally hired local women to help them cook and clean.[85] Maria reputedly had both an Irish and a black domestic.[86] Such "experiments" had their challenges, as when Hervey returned to Weymouth from New York City with a young immigrant who spoke not a word of English. "Hervey has to be the spokesman and we with the aid of phrase books say what we can," wrote Anne. "Ma has wholly fled from the kitchen, and sits groaning over her hard fate in the parlour. . . . As for the girl, Annette[,] she is a very obliging, pleasant kindly creature, very reasonably neat, and thus far a very satisfactory cook." Ma Weston much preferred doing her own "chopping & fixing," but Hervey and Anne hoped Annette would prove useful. "We have not had any washing and ironing done yet but hope she may shine there. She is very quick and apt to learn."[87]

Like other nineteenth-century householders, the Westons complained that good cooks were difficult to find and to keep.[88] "Mary McIntyre, we learn, is going to strike for higher wages, a dollar a week," Anne reported to Debora. "This will give Maria a good chance to get rid of her." She wrote, "M[aria] has written to Mary Ann Knox asking her to come here. I hope exceedingly she may . . . for the house looks like distraction under Mary McIntyre's administration."[89] For their Boston boarding school Caroline looked to getting "the new cook under way—She is a good sort of woman, blind at one eye—and is, we have learned, sometimes intemperate—but she is neat—and careful—and quiet and we shall go on with her until we see some symptoms of her besetting sin."[90]

Yet despite the time invested in their occupations and social activism, the Westons accomplished themselves most of the domestic labor required by the Weymouth and Boston households. As Anne said, "It is exceedingly comfortable having every thing so 'to rights' here. We keep the house in the most perfect order. Lucia is very smart & helpful."[91] Ann Bates Weston certainly preferred to keep housework within the family, rejoicing when domestics left the field. "Ma is on the top of the highest wave, Hannah being gone and so she for a week or two alone," Anne told Emma. "Aunt Mary writes me that Ma has put the house from top to toe in the most perfect order and that it looks like a castle."[92] No Hannah or Annette, particularly one who did not speak English, would do for Ma Weston what she and hers could do for themselves. Her more urban, urbane, and frazzled daughters, however, welcomed the help.

Clothing the family remained an arduous affair requiring considerable manual labor, negotiation, and calculation about the assignment of individual tasks and the outlay of funds.[93] Historians have estimated that home production was widely abandoned for commercially produced goods in the North between 1820 and 1830; nevertheless, the sewing of clothing continued to dominate the lives of middling-class antebellum women such as the Westons well into the 1850s.[94] Even as a diverse array of commodities and specialized services became available in Boston and even Weymouth, the Westons continued to rely primarily upon their own domestic labor for the production of family clothing. The sisters used the occasional services of a modiste or local seamstress for unusual needs. But even in the more well-to-do Chapman household, the sisters did most of the routine needlework, getting "the children clothed, Henry's things made and Handy's made &c—and curtains up—and towels made."[95] The responsibility for household sewing (cutting, piecing, seaming, patching, and darning) had no regard for location. Hand sewing was portable. It fit into the interstices of other pursuits. Anne, for example, took her sewing for Lucia along on a visit to friends in Groton, while Maria took hers to MAS board meetings.[96]

Weston sewing ran the gamut from household wares to baby clothes, from workday wear for teachers, students, and young urban clerks to suitable clothing for going to church, public lectures, soirees, and antislavery conventions. The Weston brothers expected that their sisters would sew for them whether they remained at home, were visiting or working elsewhere, or were engaged in business. After helping his younger brother, Warren, settle into a Boston rooming house, for example, Hervey returned to Yale and wrote home to Weymouth with a list of their sartorial needs: Warren "wants 3 or 4 shirts right off, you must send in Monday his pantaloons—he will have to have his washing done at Weymouth—send in Monday one shirt and a bosom made like that one sent to me." He himself required a new vest, for which he sent a pattern. "[I]f you can understand how to cut one by this have one cut by it," he wrote, and if not, he would retrieve Warren's vest and have his sisters take it apart to create a pattern that worked. Even as he tried to take the sting out of his demands with self-deprecating humor—"you will think I order pretty well"—Hervey undermined his attempts at charm by insisting, "Mind send in a shirt or 2 Monday or Tuesday if you get 20 tailors to do it." Four months later he sought "2 pair of draw[er]s made as soon as possible."[97] His expectations for speedy servicing of his clothing requirements continued throughout Hervey's schooling.

The Weston sisters conducted the cutting out, sewing together, turning, and refurbishing of wardrobes as a shared and continuous occupation; that is, not only done for one another but also accomplished together.[98] It took all hands to meet the needs of such large and active households. Anne, for example, agreed to sew a dress for Elizabeth if someone else would cut it. A new nightgown for Lucia required the hands of three different Weston women for completion.[99] Caroline took on the project of reconstructing Lizzy Chapman's yellow gown, for "such a fright I never saw." Anne put the hooks and eyes on a new pink dress for Emma to go with "a most lovely bonnet [of] white watered silk" made by Caroline.[100] Even as she began a new term in her Roxbury school, Caroline sent Debora a gown she had cut out and basted for Maria because "she is in need—and you will be able to do it directly."[101]

The Westons expanded their wardrobes not only by sewing new garments but also by refreshing and exchanging them. This strategy generally met the sartorial requirements of both professional and social lives. Debora gave a pair of her gloves to Emma so that she, in turn, might give hers to Lucia. Her "free labour principles" prevented her from purchasing calico, so she sought to exchange dresses with her aunt Mary, "for I want a new blue gown."[102] Debora also solicited a cloak from Caroline and a dress from Emma to round out her professional wardrobe. Lucia notified Debora, "When Emma comes in [to Boston] she will of course bring her white gown, and then I will present the important matter to her. I presume she will let you have it, as she has a new blue muslin one. Your bonnet we will all put our wits to work about, we will *all* look round." Seeing her needs somewhat differently than Lucia did, Emma agreed to share her dress with Debora but asked of her, "When you have got through the most of your parties, if you could spare my gown as well as not that you would send it [back]. I would not say a word but I am rather poorly off having only my new muslin."[103]

Fashion vied with economy in the matter of dressing the family. Anne provided a revealing vignette in describing the manufacture of a cloak in

1842. Emma had hers cut out in Boston by Maria's professional mantua-maker, who had been hired to outfit the Chapman daughters. She sent all the pieces to Weymouth so that Lucia might copy the pattern for her own use. Seeing the "very pretty" results, Anne sought a new cloak of her own. Proud of her economy, she boasted that she had succeeded in making cotton look like cashmere, and homemade like professionally tailored, for "only $1.20": "Warren brought home two large pieces of twilled figured cotton which I cannot describe better than by saying it looked like an imitation of the cashmere cloak of Henrietta [Sargent]'s. . . . [I]t is quite likely looking stuff and as I was in a suffering state I went to work. Lucia cut the cloak out by hers, and with a little help from Ma, I made it into a short cloak and it looks very well; not like the young Misses Weston's to be sure, but very well for one *une peu passee* like me." "Une peu passee" at age thirty and as fond of fashion and fabric as her seventeen- and twenty-year-old sisters, Anne proudly reported that the cloak passed muster with the wealthy Henrietta and Catherine Sargent and Maria's equally well situated mother-in-law, Sarah Greene Chapman. The manufacturing had taken a week and the labor of six women—Anne, her mother, her sister Lucia, her cousin Lucretia Cowing, and two hired seamstresses, Martha Bond and a Miss Watson.[104]

The Westons shuffled, recalled, and remade their garments as needed. A single item might undergo multiple transformations. "Lucia is not going to have any new gowns," Debora confided sadly in the summer of 1837; "all hers are to be made over old ones." Turning an old dress back to front for even wear or inside out if the fabric permitted made it last another season. Turning her silk gown occupied Debora's "every moment . . . from Monday till Saturday," but she had to take the time as "the spots on it looked so bad." Caroline told Anne that she had returned to their Boylston Street school from Weymouth "and made an old gown of yours—your old buff—into a dress for Lucia—and very well she looks in it—then made my old green muslin into a gown for myself—a morning gown—and got it all cut and basted to take to Weymouth for ma to finish."[105]

In order to clothe Debora suitably for social life among the fashionable abolitionists of New Bedford, her sisters offered two gowns from which to choose—one Emma's and the other Caroline's. Caroline instructed her in how to refit the dress while preserving its future usefulness. "[Y]ou can take in or let out my silk one as much as you please," she wrote, "only be careful to cut off nothing and baste a strong coloured thread the underside where it is basted at present so that I may know how to fix it." Since Weston dresses had to carry on even as styles changed, Caroline suggested ways that Debora might update the dress without undermining its fundamental structure. "[I]t is fashionable to wear gowns as this is made close in the throat—but if you prefer you can open it to the waist by ripping and turning it in—I send the silk to finish with and some pieces, and you can send it as soon as your need is over."[106] Because they lacked the wherewithal to purchase new clothes each season, the Westons copied and reworked the little things that made a dress au courant: sleeve style, neckline, or trim. "This afternoon, with the aid of Mrs Beane," wrote Anne, "I altered my blue gown. I let it out under the arms, and put a piece into the belt of the skirt altering the front plaits a little."[107] In these ways the Weston sisters made the most of a clothing budget limited as to time and money.

When domestic work could not be sorted out among the sisters because they lacked sufficient skill or available hands, the Westons added to their number and resources by purchasing help or exchanging their labor within a broader kinship or neighborhood network. Whereas earlier in the century, particularly in provincial communities, women hired local girls or took in young relatives to aid with domestic labor, households in the 1830s and 1840s faced competition for New England's daughters from a beckoning wage labor market.[108] In Weymouth, where shoe manufacturing drew young female laborers, the Westons enlisted the domestic help of their cousins Hannah Nash and Lucretia Cowing and their aunts Phebe and Mary Weston.[109]

When they could afford to, the Weston women hired a seamstress to aid with cutting and sometimes with sewing.[110] "If Maria can get a dress maker to come and cut Annie's things tomorrow (Saturday) I shall stay in town for that day and hope to make them right up," promised Anne.[111] This combination of professional cutting and their own handwork addressed even the more difficult dressmaking challenges. "Lucia likes her gown much," wrote Anne, "and wants a favor of Emma; she wishes E to send out her new gown tomorrow night as a pattern for her and she will return it Tuesday if possible. Mrs Clark [a local Weymouth seamstress, not a Boston modiste] will cut Lucia's but L is afraid to trust her without a pattern." Lucia promised she would "be careful of it as of new laid eggs."[112] Anne sent pieces of Lizzy's new dress to Debora in New Bedford with Maria's injunction that she hire "somebody to make it as there is too much here to be done [for the antislavery fair] to permit of any sewing."[113]

Sewing together made of the task a social affair. Considerable laughter, teasing, and even hectoring accompanied the production of clothing in the Weston household. Anne badgered Debora about ribbon she wanted for her new bonnet: "If Aunt Mary comes in town, you can send out by her.

If not, you must send out by the stage, for I want the ribbon. You ought to have sent it by Caroline. . . . So have my bonnet ready for me to wear to the [antislavery] meeting." Emma reported: "My pink gown is not made yet[. A]s I am writing, Anne turns round to me with a look of defiance and says 'well Emma I *will* put the hooks and eyes onto your gown' as if I stopped her."[114]

In the summer of 1843, Eliza Lee Cabot Follen wrote to compliment Maria on her work as temporary editor of the *Liberator*.[115] "I like all your articles in the Liberator very much indeed," said Eliza. "But 'How do you get the apples in'[?] Alas! how useless and insignificant you make me feel—but no matter if the work is done."[116] The abolitionist productivity that Eliza envied had much to do, of course, with Maria's extraordinary energy and talents—her gifts as a writer, organizer, and inspired fund-raiser. But Maria did not bring in "the apples" alone. Together the sisters not only harvested but also made pies of Eliza's metaphorical fruit by extending the reach of their household and, thus, their collectivity.

5

AS IF I HAD NEVER BEEN ABSENT

The Household Extends Its Reach

After five months in Europe, Caroline Weston wrote to Samuel J. May, "I do not feel as if I had been at all separated from home. I have received from my sisters information so precise that I should be quite able to go on as if I had never been absent should I be suddenly set down at 25 Cornhill," where the Massachusetts Anti-Slavery Society (MAS) and the *Liberator* rented rooms.[1] By "home" Caroline meant both the natal household in Weymouth and the antislavery offices in Boston, thinking less of place and more of people. Home had to do with the affection and solidarity she felt for her sisters both of blood and of association. Caroline's assertion reflected her experience that collaboration need not require long-term physical proximity given continuous interaction—correspondence, visits, and commissions.[2] The immediacy with which Caroline felt connected to faraway people and events followed from sibling practice in the virtual "House of Weston," where she and her sisters relied upon a rigorous discipline of communication and exchange. Correspondence proved key to the construction and maintenance of the Weymouth sisterhood. Exchange maintained the ties forged in a common household through shared labor for kin and cause.

Details about the survival and archiving of the Weston correspondence, and about its material conditioning by postal practice and the availability of paper, are given in the Appendix. Here, suffice it to note that although not every sister wrote every other each week, letters traveled from location to location at least that often.[3] Many letters did not survive, but from references to others in those that did, it is clear that long breaks were rare, even after some of the sisters moved to Europe. In late October 1850, for example, Anne reported feeling "a *little* anxious, a *little* perplexed and very impatient . . . when I tell you that we have not received a line from my sisters [Maria and Caroline, in France] since the 21st of August."[4]

Writing regardless of how busy or dispersed they found themselves, the Westons nevertheless punctuated their correspondence with importunate demands for still more frequent, more detailed letters about family doings and those of the cause. As Debora in New Bedford wrote to Lucia in Boston, she would shortly receive a package. As soon as it arrived, Debora instructed, "sit down & write me a very long letter putting in every thing you can think of." She reminded her sister, "Now dear Lucia do as you would be done by—Think how we used to long for news sometimes at Weymouth—& then imagine a place 10 times more barren & where letters are all the comfort I have—Now don't let this pathetic appeal fail." Lucia did as Debora requested. She caught Maria "& put pen and paper in her hand and ma[d]e her write." Lucia, who found it difficult "to make a letter out of nothing," laid onto Anne some responsibility for the lack of correspondence to Debora: "I write long letters to Anne every week, which she said she would pick all the news out of and send it to you. I don't know what she has written to you so I hardly know what to write."[5]

So too from New Bedford Debora forwarded to Lucia (then at Maria's in Boston) a letter she had received from Anne (in New York with Caroline at the 1842 annual antislavery meetings).[6] She attached the following note: "I received this letter to-day and hasten to send it to you. Why have you not written to me you lazy things; one would think you could not write. Write *instantly* on the receipt of this." At the time, Maria was nursing her dying husband with Lucia's help. Within a week of returning from the New York meetings, Anne replied to Debora, providing details both of the convention and of Henry's condition and care.[7] The process reversed a few months later when Anne, having taken up Debora's teaching position in New Bedford, requested that her sister keep her informed of events in Boston. "Write by Hatch's express if no other way," Anne insisted, "for I cannot get *over a Sunday* without knowing how it fares with the slave."[8]

Illuminating the assumptions that undergirded Weston correspondence were these characteristic lines from Anne to Debora: "As I have not written to you since you went away I have a sense of duty that prompts me to write. As obligation to our parents involves all other duties even to the 4th & 5th generation, I begin to be afraid my days wont be long in the land unless I do."[9] In the House of Weston, the kinship contract came with a penalty clause. Debora affirmed the importance of this family responsibility: "We were sorry & grieved not to have a letter last week, for though we are all swallowed up in George [Thompson's antislavery mission to the United States] yet you *are* our sisters."[10] Communication kept family ties fresh and vital, while extending across time and space the web of social and political obligations and responsibilities that bound these sisters together in the grip of an unyielding affection.

Indeed, while teaching in Groton, Anne wrote her sisters: "I dare say that every soul of you are at Weymouth today save myself. I am bound with you, or to speak more plainly, I am writing with you in spirit."[11] Associated with ties of blood, metaphors of bonds and binding haunted Weston epistles, evoking as well the bloody chains that held captive their fictive sisters and brothers in slavery. Exhausted after traveling with Anne from New Bedford to attend a large public debate on the dissolution of the American union at Marlboro Hall in Boston, and then reporting on the meeting to Caroline, Debora sighed, "I . . . can write no more." Pleading for relief, she asked, "Haven't I remembered them in bonds as bound with them?"[12] Appropriating to herself Christ's commandment to care for the imprisoned and enslaved, Debora expressed herself as bound down by her sisters' insistence on an update about their beloved cause and bound together with them in their devotion to the slave as to each other.

As part of this devotion, and despite her feelings of isolation in her New Bedford school, Debora responded to Anne's expectation for a weekly letter. "As you wished me to write the last of the week," she wrote, "I will though I have nothing particular to say." She complained of going "on in the same sleepy way as ever, & all attempts to keep myself excited are vain." Feeling "glad to be abed most of the time," she castigated herself for "how low I must have got, to feel so." She thanked Anne for her letter, as "it was a great comfort to me," and acknowledged that she had felt cut off from "the civilized world": "The first of the week I am looking all the time for a letter, & the last for the Liberator & in that way I get through the week."[13]

Despite differences of style rooted in personality, Weston letters usually followed a format mimicking conversation through call and response, or question and answer. "Before I say aught of myself," wrote Anne, "I will proceed to comment on your letter." Or again, "I shall take up your letter paragraph for paragraph," admonishing Debora, "Whenever I ask a question, I shall expect to have it answered in your next."[14] For the most part, the answers followed apace as commanded.[15] Thus Anne gathered and exchanged information, negotiated duties, and commissioned from her sisters the tasks necessary to accomplish the work of both the antislavery Weymouth sisterhood and the House of Weston.

In this highly educated family, letters covered a broad swath of ground: politics of course, but also personal sallies about beaus and fashions, gossip about friends and acquaintances, opinions about what they read in books and newspapers or heard at church, reports on the weather and those under the weather, and humorous and sententious commentary on sights and personalities met at home and on the road in Massachusetts or abroad. The sisters enjoyed gossip, which Karen Hansen has described as "a medium for monitoring as well as negotiating community opinion."[16] As Caroline noted, "No gossip is so trifling as to be beneath *our* attention." Lucia could not wait for her sisters to decamp from Boston to Weymouth: "If you are not coming out under a week, it behooves you to *write* . . . , for we are really dying for light news." And Edmund Quincy, after thanking Anne for the "full account of the history of the West St. circle" (Maria's town address), asked that she "continue your journal of them for my benefit." As he put it, "I want to be kept *au courant du jour* as to the thousand little unnameablenesses which are continually turning up but which do not find their way into the grand folio's of the Liberator. In short I want to have the same sort of gossip with you all here at Dedham that I used to have around Henry's pleasant fireside."[17] Gossip was, indeed, the "mainstay of community discourse."[18]

Weston missives developed multiple lives as they passed through the hands of numerous readers: nominal addressees, those receiving letters forwarded to them, those who read letters out loud to others, those who listened to such readings, and those who copied portions of letters before passing them along (with or without permission) to their own circle of correspondents. Occasionally one or another Weston specified someone to whom a letter should be forwarded after it was read by its initial recipient. Debora told Anne, for example, "Send this letter to Maria, she may like to see what St Clair [a clergyman who supported the Massachusetts Abolitionist Society] is about."[19]

Unless marked otherwise, letters from any sister were deemed common rather than individual property, forwarded around the sisterhood from one to another. Lucia, for example, received from Debora a letter from Anne to which Debora attached a note: "Dear Lucia I received this letter to-day [Thursday] & haste to send it to you."[20] Wrote Anne to Debora, "I ought to begin this letter to Lucia, for she has written me one of the liveliest long newsy letters full of little interesting bits, but I bethink me the letter came through your hands. This afternoon I dispatched a letter to Caroline which will finally reach you."[21] Co-resident Westons opened and read letters addressed to one another. Anne confirmed to Debora that she had "received your letter, open of course as it came through Maria's hands." The shared nature of Weston correspondence was recognized by others, including Maria's sister-in-law Mary G. Chapman, who wrote a single letter to both Debora and Maria knowing that it would reach both recipients. "Dear friends," she wrote, "I will thank you both together for your very acceptable notes for fear I have not matter enough for two distinct ones and as your letters always seem to be common property it will make but little difference."[22]

Political correspondence passed around the sibling circle before it was delivered to abolitionist meetings, organizational boards, or movement newspapers. Anne wrote that she "employed all day Monday and Tuesday what leisure I could get in writing out my notes of the N.Y. meeting. They amounted to 23 pages, the part relating to the woman question is really very full and satisfactory." She sent these minutes "with a letter to the poor famishing Debora who has never as yet heard [a] word from one of us since the N.Y. meeting." Anne instructed her sister to send the minutes back quickly because Garrison might want them for the following week's *Liberator*. When Debora returned the notes, Anne redirected them to Weymouth, assuming she could collect them should Garrison ask for them, as he did.[23]

Letters originating outside the sisterhood also circulated freely within it. As Caroline noted to Debora, "Lucia left a letter for you that I send— I also send a letter I had from E. Quincy as it may amuse you—send it back—also James Gibbons last letter—which please to send also." Anne wrote to Caroline, "I enclose what letters I have from sundry people & that will give you such news as I cant write." Demonstrating great mutual trust, as most people would have answered a letter *before* passing it on, Anne sent Debora a letter from Elizabeth Pease with the request, "Send it back the *very first* chance as I want to answer it." Her comment reflected the sisterhood's expectation of continuous correspondence characterized by swift replies. Occasionally a Weston letter returned to the fold from the outside. Edmund Quincy, for example, enclosed in his dispatch to Maria "a good long letter from Caroline, which she requests me to forward to you & through you to [the family in] Weymouth."[24]

Movement correspondents frequently passed missives from hand to hand. Edmund Quincy sent Maria his letters to William L. Garrison and Wendell Phillips, asking her to read them first, then "seal & send." The intermediate stop provided Maria with important information and Edmund with an additional political perspective. So too Maria gave to Wendell and Ann T. G. Phillips a letter received from Richard D. Webb with instructions to pass it next to Quincy.[25] Samuel J. May Jr. forwarded to Anne a "very full, specific letter from Mr. Estlin," intending that it should begin a conversation: "I think you would enjoy it greatly; and I mean soon to send it to you, and shall be glad to know, when you return it, what you think of his views about the B[ritish] & F[oreign] A[nti-Slavery] S[ociety] Reporter, & its new Editor, &c."[26] Anne sent May letters she received from Mary Ann Estlin, Emma Michell (Estlin's aunt), and Richard D. Webb. Lucretia Mott told Webb that he would soon be hearing from Chapman via a circuitous route: Lucretia Mott had received Maria's letter and forwarded it to Sarah Pugh, who would copy and send it to him.[27] This process built and extended the conversations necessary to sustaining a constituency for abolitionist ideas and political works and identified the Weston household as a crucial support for Garrisonian abolition.

Letters were often read aloud to a group.[28] Guests and visitors were treated to oral performances in the Chapmans' Boston town house and the Weston household in Weymouth. When Caroline, for example, reported news of Maria's election to the MAS executive committee and Abigail Kelley's to the business committee at the 1840 annual meeting of the American Anti-Slavery Society, Anne acknowledged the degree of detail in the letter: "We feel as tho' we had been present." This letter was *caroused and recaroused*" as Emma carried it from household to household, reading the tale aloud at the Essex Street home of Wendell and Ann T. G. Phillips and the Chauncy Place household of Maria's in-laws. Emma decided to take it to Weymouth "tomorrow I think; indeed I am sure I shall," so that parents, siblings, and the aunts next door might hear the news.[29] On another occasion, Anne informed Debora that her bundle of letters had arrived in Boston from New Bedford. "Never was a bundle so welcome, for it was all unexpected," she enthused. "Then I ran over to Grace. Mr Emerson had gone to an A.S. meeting & Grace was delighted to hear."[30] Maria so appreciated Mary Ann Estlin's letters from Bristol, England, that she read them to Helen Benson Garrison, Wendell and Ann T. G. Phillips, Eliza Cabot Follen, Susan Cabot, Francis Jackson, and Henrietta and Catherine Sargent.[31] Richard D. Webb acknowledged the practice, saying, "I don't know which of your circle I wrote to last but it is no matter—as I understand you all reap the benefit of whatever I communicate in this way."[32]

Weston communication also involved face-to-face visits, which offered respite from solitary employment and the opportunity to exchange confidences that could not be committed to paper. Such visits occurred frequently among the geographically dispersed sisters. Meetings provided a chance to offer and receive physical affection and care, inspiration and conversation, rest and renewal. When one sister visited another she carried messages, information, and tokens of love: food, cash, books, clothing, antislavery pamphlets, and abolitionist newspapers. She brought correspondence from friends in the movement and relatives. She might also bring her own daily journals, which offered more detail than could be put into a letter and provided extended descriptions of event sequences occurring over time.[33]

Personal and family events were for letters; journals followed political events and were conducted with an awareness of the importance of maintaining a record. Written in the moment, journals also conveyed a sense of immediacy that enabled one sister to enter into another's feelings, experiences, and judgments as they occurred.

As with correspondence, journalizing met a sororal expectation. "Keep a journal *if you can* all the time of the quarterly [MAS] meeting," Debora begged Anne. While Maria and Henry were in Haiti, several sisters kept journals for one another's benefit. Maria's focused on her political observations of the new black republic, and described her interactions with Haitian politicians. These provided data for numerous writing projects after her return.[34] Meanwhile Caroline, back in Boston, commenced a diary of her own: "Tomorrow—if there is faith in woman—I will open a journal addressed to you in which I will write *every* day—& you shall have no reason to complain in future that I did not do what I could—I shall give you the annual meeting in full." When she wrote her first entry eight days later, Caroline exulted in self-mockery, mimicking those diaries kept by "great men" whose detailed observations served primarily to establish their place in history: "so here begins—Caroline Weston's—diary addressed to her well beloved brother & sister when absent from home in the first part of AD 1841—having especial relation to the Anti Slavery enterprise in the United States—in its most interesting person—& comprising many anecdotes of the most distinguished persons of that period."[35]

While this practice followed the nineteenth-century pattern of using a journal to mark an extraordinary event as it unfolded, the Westons routinely diarized when absent one from another. Caroline, for example, kept a journal during the terrifying days of October 1835.[36] So did Lucia, who refused to leave Boston during the riots following the arrest and trial of the fugitive slave George Latimer. Lucia aided Maria in raising money and producing a daily newsletter of events for abolitionists in Boston and beyond. "I have been religiously keeping a journal for you all this week," she wrote Debora, "and meant to have sent it to you today, but William Coffin and Mr Emerson called with a letter from Anne this morning, and

I felt compelled to send my journal to the poor thing."[37] At the time Anne was teaching, alone, in New Bedford.[38] Debora journalized from there during the controversial days when Texas sought to join the Union and Garrison called for disunion if it was admitted.[39] Written with humor, intelligence, and considerable political insight, these journals functioned to weave, maintain, and strengthen sibling ties by placing one sister within the thoughts, activities, and context of another. In the process, a political sisterhood was constructed, reinforced, and preserved atop the sibling foundation.

As much as shared information—personal, familial, or political—what built this sisterhood was the exchange of commissions. These were of three kinds. The first had to do with the acquiring of necessary goods, purchased or borrowed. Purchases were made in Boston with cash, while borrowed goods were obtained from one another's closets. Caroline, for example, sent Lucia a packet of needles.[40] Debora apologized to Caroline, who was temporarily in Boston at Maria's, for giving her "so much trouble, when you have cares enough on your hands"; however, she wrote, "the articles I send for I want very much." With "Anne being out of town [working in Groton as a governess]," she acknowledged, "there is no one but you to attend to it." And Debora's list was long: "In the first place I am knitting a pair of mits for Mrs [Sarah Greene] Chapman and have not silk enough to finish them into 2 skeins. Will you go up to *Millers* down in Milk St., up stairs (don't you remember the place, you went there once with me) and get 2 skeins of *Canton* sewing silk, the colour of the one I send. I cant get any here. 2nd I am in want of a pair of shoes. If you will send me $1.25 I will thank you, and what is better pay you in May. 3d I wish you would send me 6 or 5 sheets of letter paper. 4th and worst of all, for my *bones ache* with thinking of my carelessness, I was fool enough to lose out of my pocket the first vol[ume] of a book which Susan Congdon lent me; will you buy and send me another copy." Not content merely to replace the missing book, Debora sent the volume she "*did not lose*" so that Caroline might match bindings. As the Westons valued books more highly than most possessions, they took the contract implied in borrowing them quite seriously.[41]

From Weymouth, Anne asked Debora to collect fabric samples while she resided in Boston caring for Gertrude, Maria's newborn daughter. "I believe I shall be obliged to have a new gown," Anne wrote. "Will you therefore get me a number of patterns of mouseline de laine, not higher than 50 cts and send out by the basket tomorrow or if you have not time by the Liberator bundle." Anne's request sent Debora on a specific round through Boston's commercial district: "There is a pretty pattern at Hills' that I should like to see. Maria will remember it; green on a light ground. I see some advertised at Smith & McQuaids two doors below West St (to South End) which you had better look at."[42] The sisters frequently, even routinely, ran errands for one another. Yet such an undertaking was rarely taken for granted. Each recognized that the need for assistance would, necessarily, rotate. Reciprocity, then, served as the coin of the sibling realm, manufacturing affection and sustaining relationships.

Commissions involved expenditures of effort or funds, for both of which the Westons held each other accountable. They balanced accounts, itemizing encumbrances in promissory notes as necessary. For example, Debora sent Caroline funds with which to purchase a bonnet for her. Caroline obtained one and sent Debora an exact accounting of her money as well as the terms of exchange. "This bonnet costs flowers and all $3.09—the balance of your $5.00 is in my hands—a straw [bonnet] would cost $3.50 to begin with the trimming at least, .75 or a dollar more—and you would not appear to have a new bonnet after all. Maria's does not look much more expensive than this and cost nearly $9.00. I hope you will like it, if you do not, I will take it, as I got it to suit myself."[43]

On Debora's behalf, Anne searched for a new collar. This commission became awkward, eventually requiring the labor of three sisters and some borrowing from Peter to pay Paul. "I am sorry for your being in difficulty about your cape or collar," Anne grumbled to Debora, "but never set any body to buying such a thing again for it is a most vexatious piece of work to do." She, Caroline, and Lucia trekked down to Brownell's store to buy a collar and the lace with which to trim it. "I gave for the whole $1.75. I spent part of the $5 you paid Ma for my white bonnet so I took of my annuity to pay this," she reported.[44] Here was evidence of a sibling economy of effort to which all contributed and, therefore, from which all might draw. The scrupulousness with which monetary accounts were kept reflected neither a reluctance to assist one another nor a fear of being taken advantage of, but rather the reassurance that each dealt with a reliable, even scrupulous agent and that no one sister would bear too great a financial or temporal burden.

A second set of sisterly commissions had to do with domestic chores. A call for assistance went out to Debora in spring 1838: "Caroline says that she wants you to appear on parade as soon as may be, that now is the time when you can be the most useful, as she wishes to be out of school packing up," Anne wrote. "As you have been gone 9 weeks Tuesday, we think you have done pretty well."[45] In other words, it was Debora's turn to help out. When sending some of her clothing from Boston to be laundered at Weymouth, Anne sought to balance the labor pool between households by noting that she herself was "working slowly on Ma's garment."[46] So too the Boston household offered sugar from Maria's stores if those at Weymouth would do the baking.[47] When, from her school in Roxbury, Caroline commissioned Debora's sewing assistance on behalf of Maria, she not only noted her own contribution to the project but also explained that Lucia was sewing for the antislavery fair and thus could not be spared.[48] An exquisite sense of accountability sought to balance both domestic and political work among the siblings.

Requests in aid of political commitments constituted a third set of sibling commissions. Some were straightforward. Debora sought Anne's aid in New Bedford's "anti-slavery business" as the female society there struggled with the issue of African American membership. With eleven African American women poised to join, she asked Anne to use her office as corresponding secretary for the Boston Female Anti-Slavery Society (BFAS). "Suppose you write a letter to [the New Bedford Society], merely opening the correspondence & using great swelling words," she wrote.[49] For her part, Anne in Boston asked Emma in Weymouth to "go to my upper drawer and take from there two letters in Henrietta [Sargent]'s handwriting addressed to women at the South and a letter to the same effect by Debora P. Palmer. Send me these by Maria, in case I should find any chance to send them to the women's conference at Georgetown."[50] She also asked Debora for a careful reading of the content and tone established in the draft of a letter she had composed to Angelina Grimké Weld. "If . . . you see nothing to disapprove," she wrote, "seal it and carry it to the [anti-slavery] office" for publication in the *Liberator*.[51]

Other commissions commanded far greater expenditures of time and effort. Debora refused to undertake a formal role as officer in any anti-slavery association for reasons that seemed to reflect a somewhat retiring personality and a discomfort with interpersonal conflict. "I am sorry to disappoint you, but I am afraid I must bang to your glorious door again—I am never going to take upon myself the management of any society matters, such as 'passing resolutions and voting supplies'—I feel no call and certainly no ability for the thing—Indeed I have an oath in Heaven against it," she told Maria.[52] While understanding Debora's aversion to such activity, Anne nevertheless urged her to organize New Bedford women to sew goods and gather autographs of well-known local denizens for sale at the annual Boston antislavery fair. She explained that Maria feared "as to the number of articles." Additionally, Anne asked her sister to solicit funds among New Bedford abolitionists to publish the annual fair magazine, the *Liberty Bell*, "for there is only $30 collected" from among the Garrisonian faithful in this year following the BFAS division.[53]

Raising money for the cause engaged all the sisters in various schemes ranging from sales of handmade or donated goods at antislavery fairs, to the solicitation of personal contributions, to the distribution of and collection from cent boxes into which went a household's weekly mite. In 1839 and 1840 the Westons sought to counter the anti-Garrisonian public relations and organizational efforts of the new American and Foreign Anti-Slavery Association. They created a new propaganda instrument, the *Cradle of Liberty*, in which they hoped to disseminate Garrisonian ideology in less incendiary language than that expressed in the *Liberator*, and with a focus solely on the emancipation of slaves (to attract readers who resented Garrison's forays into women's rights, Native American rights, temperance, antisabbatarian practices, nonresistance, disunion, and opposition to the annexation of Texas, among other causes).[54] A subscription to the proposed *Cradle* would recognize that "the abolitionists are from all classes and conditions of men and that the opportunities of culture and the standards of taste differ in each class." Having racked their brains for ways to raise the $500 they thought necessary to establish the new paper, the sisters came up with the idea of a bazaar, the proceeds of which would go solely to its support.[55]

Anne urged Debora to organize "a pretty little Fair in N[ew] B[edford]," confident that it "would meet with good success. I think the millionaires would come." Maria added her voice, suggesting that Debora call upon New Bedford abolitionists Susan Taber, Mary Congdon, and Mary Anna Bailey for assistance in devising the sale. "Let it be a private concern," she counseled, "so that you can dispose of the money as you please. Call it 'for the cause'—make your medium of aiding the cause the *Cradle*. You may expect $100 certainly, perhaps more, from me and mine. Nothing could have so happy an effect."[56] In the face of Debora's reluctance to take on so large a task by herself, Maria insisted. "Try it—Try it," she demanded. "Let me know as soon as possible what the friends say [about a fair]—for the money must be had." She urged Debora to "consider every subscriber counts twice—a gain to us, a loss to them [the anti-Garrisonian 'new organization']. We must preachiphy," she instructed. Through Anne, Maria offered to come to New Bedford to see Andrew Robeson, "to collect pledges & set things strait [*sic*]." In seeking to motivate Debora, Anne teased, "If N.Y. [the AAS] or any body else comes on & gets a few hundreds out of Andrew Robeson we shall require it at your hands."[57]

When the women of New Bedford decided that they could not manage such a fair, Debora attempted to complete her commission. She "wrote to the Marshfield people who are getting up one to try to hook their money." She urged Maria to add her weight to the scale and encourage this small society that they might coordinate their fair work to Boston's advantage: "The person to be addressed is Miss Sarah Little. I *believe* it is south Marshfield, but you can direct I should think under cover of Louisa Phillips." In December, several months of ongoing effort by both sisters came to fruition. Debora could exult, "'Thanks be to praise,' the last fair or sale of any kind that I am to have any thing to do with for the present is over, & I feel as if the weight of mountains had been taken off."[58]

The sisters also used each other's contacts to collect and process information for the *Cradle* and the *Liberator*. After attending an antislavery meeting at Lynn, Maria asked Anne, then visiting in Milton, to solicit information from neighbors who had also attended. "Maria says that if the reports that you have of what happened before she got there are worth the trouble," Caroline told Anne, "she wishes you would write out your report and send it in town by Monday morning at farthest" so that Maria might include it in her article for the *Liberator*.[59] From Haiti, Maria sent William Lloyd Garrison petitions she had circulated there requesting American recognition of the newly independent government and seeking abrogation of discriminatory "color laws" in America. She urged Garrison to have any *Liberator* article resulting from her transmittal translated into French by her sisters and sent to her, so as to build cooperation between the two peoples and bring international weight to bear upon the issue of emancipation in the United States.[60]

Caroline took up organizing the state's abolitionists to protest against the Massachusetts legislature's "*truly infamous*" attack on the women of Lynn who had petitioned to end the state's laws prohibiting interracial marriage. She urged Debora to have "the N. Bedford men" pass resolutions condemning the legislature, for it seemed logical that elected officials would give more heed to the opinion of voters than to the unenfranchised. She suggested language for their use: "'Resolved, that the passage of so totally unworthy & base [a] report as the one on this subject which has just passed the house, indicates to us that much yet remains to be done to abolitionary Massachusetts & that we should put our souls to the work with renewed vigour.' Or something of that sort." Furthermore, she insisted that Debora "tell Mary Congdon to *see to it* that the Female Society [of New Bedford] passes resolutions also" in support of President Aroline Chase and the Lynn Female Anti-Slavery Society petition. Here too she offered a model: "Resolved That, awakened by the fidelity of the women of Lynn in the holy cause of human rights, we will not cease to use all our influence to procure the repeal of all the laws of Mass[achusetts] founded on distinctions of colour until every such disgraceful enactment shall be blotted from the statute-book."[61]

Only days later, Maria sent another long list of tasks for Debora, asking her to follow up on a package of handbills sent to John French, a local abolitionist, calling for a meeting of the New Bedford Society to address the growing division between Garrisonians and their opposition. Maria proposed a specific agenda of five "important particulars": "1st an expression of opinion against the New York brethren's course. 2nd against the[ir] new paper as part and parcel of the same movement. 3d recommendation of the newest paper [the *Cradle of Liberty*] as an auxiliary to those who cannot afford the Liberator. 4th recent proceedings of the Legislature. 5th Delegation to the quarterly M[AS] Meeting. Let it be Large—very large— Let every thing that hath breath speak. Throng up in full strength." She even proposed a resolution to "run thus. Resolved that we are surprised and pained at the raw, unkind, and unbrotherly course taken by the ex. Com. of the Am[erican Anti-Slavery] Soc[iety]. And most heartily approve and sustain the spirited and judicious course of the M[assachusetts] A[nti-]S[lavery] S[ociety]."[62]

Caroline undertook a similarly peremptory approach to commissioning her sisters' political assistance. From New Bedford, she wrote to Maria, "I will enclose a little paper containing items of business that I wish you to attend to—and hasten to give a brief sketch of the [antislavery] proceedings here since Sunday." She reported on a protest against the New Bedford Lyceum for refusing to admit a black man to membership. Insisting that her letter was "private—that is *don't leave it about*," Caroline ordered her sisters to "go to Garrison & tell him that it was a great mistake to publish any thing that Isaiah C. Ray says on the subject—& I thought he would know that—his comments on that connexion [*sic*] will do great harm—Mr R is a professed mischief-maker. . . . Tell Garrison—*never* to do any thing to identify the New Bedford abo[litionist]s with Ray—for they will not *abide* it."[63]

Caroline insisted that Maria "see that no *comment* on this New Bedford affair—gets into the *Standard*,"[64] for she feared "it would be an irreparable misfortune if Isaiah [C. Ray]'s dirty article & Garrison's more foolish remarks should get in." She asked her to write Sydney H. Gay, the editor of the *National Anti-Slavery Standard*, and "stop it out." Feeling "provoked to death by G[arrison]'s folly," she insisted that Maria convince him to reject Ray's articles for the *Liberator* and accept only those coming "through *us* [meaning herself or Debora] or Mr [Andrew] Robeson or Mr [John F.] Emerson."[65] A continual string of such political commissions passed from one sibling to another, as each sought assistance in writing antislavery letters, resolutions, and organizational constitutions,[66] calling and reporting on meetings,[67] collecting funds for one antislavery project or another,[68] contributing articles or poetry to the *Liberty Bell*,[69] petition-ing,[70] or providing a Weston presence at meetings.[71]

Crucial to understanding the workings of the Weymouth sisterhood is the way in which commissions for domestic and political labor overlapped and converged. Political consciousness, both individual and collective, emerged from and was strengthened by such mutual tasking. Anne asked Caroline to fulfill a request made of Debora by an acquaintance seeking to acquire a bonnet frame. She hoped that fulfilling this commission might reinforce the woman's interest in the cause. "Mrs. Birdley . . . is going to make herself a velvet bonnet. She wants you to buy her a frame. She wants a fashionable shape; as for its size it must fit Debora. . . . If bonnets are being worn larger, you need not get one of the largest kind, as this is to be made out of old velvet. Mrs B. did not propose for any body to get it but D., but as she has just given $5 for the Cause, I felt anxious to oblige her."[72] From New Bedford, Debora requested of Caroline a long list of purchases. She also asked her to "do up" a packet of antislavery newspapers and some letters from the Grimké sisters "when you are in town Saturday and leave with Maria—for there may be an opportunity to send Monday or Tues-day."[73] She was as impatient to acquire the newspapers and political letters as the consumer goods.

Although they preferred to go in clusters, at least one member of the Weymouth sisterhood attended state and national meetings of the various antislavery organizations to which they belonged. "Anne has concluded to go to New York—and I shall go if she does—wish you could go—can't you manage it?" Caroline appealed to Debora.[74] At any given time one or more of the Westons were likely to be serving as official delegates or association officers. Always they represented "the House of Weston," and invariably this required that attention be paid to appearance. It took the entire circle to dress their representative appropriately. Debora, for example, insisted that if she were to attend the 1840 annual antislavery meetings in New York, she would "want some sort of a gown. . . . I have just got me a dark silk, & now it is made up it looks much too dressy & hand some to wear to N Y—Has ma ever had that died plaid silk made up? I don't like to take it from her, but what can I do—If it is *not* made up & she concludes to let me have it, send it by the stage Wednesday." In 1837 Maria offered to pay Anne's expenses so that they both might attend. To do so Anne sought from Debora the return of one of her own dresses and the loan of another and "any other little thing that you think may be of use to me. I don't know that you have any thing more than I. I think however, the handkerchief that Aunt Sally gave you would be of use."[75]

Thus two lattices of social interaction overlapped and intersected. When Anne sent material and a pattern for a gown to be sewn by Debora for Maria's daughter Ann, she included some grass cloth that might be used to make a second dress for her niece "if you like or not just as you please." She noted, "Maria puts the whole at your disposal. You can make aprons for the fair or do what seems to you to be good. This is *her* commission. As I go on the ground that charity begins at home you may make *me* an apron with a pocket, and trim it with pink ribbon—if you can get it."[76] The intermingling of domestic and political commissions provides but one expression of how integrated was the House of Weston with the Weymouth sisterhood—the family circle with the political one. When Debora told Anne that "the Liberator did not come till last night, it seemed really like a letter," she reflected the family's sense that their political relations and communications mapped closely upon those of kinship, reinforcing the loyalty and cooperation of the sisters.[77]

Even as it organized exchanges of labor, goods, and information, both domestic and political, letter writing expressed and nurtured affection. In corresponding, the Westons expressed their longing for home and the familiar presence and support of the sisters with whom they scripted their days and accomplished their various tasks. As Debora returned to New Bedford from a Thanksgiving spent in the Weymouth household, her sisters traced her retreat in their imagination: "Last evening we sat in a melancholy mood saying every few minutes 'well now Debora has got to Taunton; now she is almost to N[ew] Bedford.'"[78] Emma mourned her sister's departure. "You cant think how bad I felt after you was [*sic*] gone," she wrote to Debora. "When I came home it seemed as if three or four were gone instead of one."[79]

The Weston sisters remained each other's primary emotional attachments and references. Corresponding, then, was an act of love and a means of bridging the temporary geographical distance that failed to diminish the web of affection that enveloped them all. Attending to the maintenance of that web was a duty and obligation of siblicity. Wrote Anne, "Your birthday dear Debora. I believe that you will think I can keep it in no better way than by writing to you."[80] Debora herself wrote at midnight on a Sunday evening—her appointed day, if not her usual time, for corresponding with family. "Oh how I long to be with you," she told Anne. "Your letter left something [of] the effect upon me that novel reading is said to have. Here looks gloomy."[81] And when visiting the abolitionist Sargent sisters in Boston, Anne wrote to Debora, "Henrietta & Catherine send love & wish you were to be with me to night in the trundle bed. I heartily wish it too."[82] Sisters, especially in families with so many daughters, often slept in the same bed, and Anne missed the snuggling for its familiarity, physical comfort, and emotional support. The reminder of those feelings reassured separated siblings and reaffirmed their connection.

This is not to say that there were not moments when the multiple expectations and continuous requests of this large and politically active family frustrated the individual member. Asked to do one thing too many, Debora snapped, "However strange you may think it, the reason why I have not written before, is because I have not had any time." And Caroline, while acknowledging to Debora that she would send Emma's newly made gown for her approval and lend her a watered silk dress "not yet done," added a touch astringently, "Can I do any thing else for you?" She signaled the disingenuous tone of her query by following it immediately with the reminder, "I have no time to write another word." Lucia indicated that she had reached the end of her tether in a letter from Boston, where she was supervising the education of her niece, Ann Greene Chapman. She assured Debora, "I have really done the best I could for you," though "poor's my best in regard to letter writing. I will make Caroline write very soon, but thought I would send this to tell you something was coming." Plaintively, she attempted to convince Debora that it was "a great favor" for her to have spent "as much time upon you as I have [with] my whole wardrobe to put to rights, with all the disadvantages of being here to do it[. A]t Weymouth you know I could have had some help."[83]

The occasional calling to account of one sister by another reinforced their pattern of shared responsibility. Anne pulled Debora up sharply after hearing that she had written to Caroline "about my taking the Fall R[iver] Monitor, as I call Miss Buffum's letter, to Groton, and finally that you made her answer it. I must say that I should think you would be ashamed not to write one letter in the cause." In so saying, Anne was, in the way of sisters, projecting onto Debora her own feelings of having "made so few sacrifices" and "not cast in my all" for the BFAS fair, despite the fact (or perhaps because) she had been writing antislavery letters "almost every day since I have been" in Groton, socializing.[84]

Siblicity traveled, as did political sisterhood, because it rooted itself in shared practice and mutual commitment rather than propinquity alone. Correspondence, shared journals, and fulfilled commissions reinforced the habits and refreshed the emotions rooted in extended periods of shared habitation. The knowledge that one would "have help" for the asking enabled each sister "to go on" with the full range of her commitments.

6

YOURS WITH THE
UNITED FACULTIES OF
MARTHA AND MARY

Politics and Kin-Keeping

In early 1845, Maria Weston Chapman closed a letter to her sister Debora with the words, "Yours with the united faculties of Martha and Mary."[1] In referring to the two New Testament sisters of Bethany who devoted themselves to Christ—Martha by nurturing his body and Mary by studying his words[2]—Maria represented herself as keeper of both the "House of Weston" and the house of God.[3] Indeed, she often combined her labors as both Martha and Mary by taking her sewing and mending to political meetings ("I've seen odder things by far") and contemplating the Lord's work at home of a Sunday sewing hooks and eyes.[4] The latter, she claimed, would prove in God's eyes "more acceptable as a work of maternal piety to a benevolent and wise being" than if she "had passed the time at any church in town: more especially as they had all lost sight of what they were formed for," including liberating the bound and comforting the imprisoned.[5] (She had pulled her membership from the Unitarian Church several years earlier and also given up on the nonsectarian and antislavery experiment that was Boston's Free Church.)

The combined needs of the Weston households and the antislavery movement required labor sufficient to fill the hands of every Weston woman. To accomplish the work, these siblings interwove the domestic with the political in their individual activities, divvying up and sharing both antislavery and domestic responsibilities, whether clothing the family and conducting the antislavery bazaar, or teaching school and petitioning governments to end slavery and racial discrimination. Exhausted by the strain, Debora first attributed her debility to the stress of teaching. On second thought, she wondered whether "perhaps I have been more fatigued on account of my arduous anti-slavery labours." The latter usually energized her because she believed that, in politicking, "I have not laboured in vain." She sometimes lacked similar confidence in her teaching; and, of course, the housework was never done.[6]

Caroline divided her time between the cause and her students. She left their New Bedford school in Debora's capable hands, for example, to "throw in as [George] Avery said a 'day for the Lord'" selling subscriptions to the *Anti-Slavery Standard* in Fall River, Massachusetts.[7] So too while residing at Maria's in order to tutor and clothe Elizabeth, Lucia helped Maria with her political writing by listening to and commenting on drafts while she sewed for the household. Maria "writes a great deal, and nobody will hear her read what she writes but me," she said.[8]

Caroline aided Maria in handling her voluminous antislavery correspondence.[9] In November 1841, for example, she was teaching school and boarding in Roxbury. She had both her nephew and younger brother living in her rooms as she sought to improve the temperament and discipline the behavior of the volatile Henry Chapman while overseeing Warren's recuperation from the effects of too much alcohol and too many late nights carousing in Boston. When Maria called for assistance with the cause, Caroline described for Debora the process of preparing her charges, both students and kin, for her absence. She likened the task to going into battle: "Last friday noon . . . Maria appeared to have so many important letters just ready to dispatch—& urged me so much to go in town that afternoon that I concluded to do so tho' I wished much to wait till evening to see Warren who I supposed would come by the afternoon cars—however I got ready—made my will—arranged my effects as I have done two thousand times before—took little Henry—who by the way has been sick all the week with cold—cough—sore mouth &c . . . & was set down by my *cab* at the door of Chauncy Place—leaving word for Warren to come in the morning & report of you."[10] On this as on many an occasion, Caroline put the demands of abolition before other occupations and conducted kin-keeping in tandem with both. Her concern for Warren reflected not only his sisters' view of his inadequate self-governance (at the time) and their reluctance to give him too much independence but also her desire to glean from him any information he carried about the state of abolition in New Bedford, where he had been recuperating under Debora's watchful eye.

As in Caroline's epistle, the topical sequences of Weston letters reveal the sisters' experience of antislavery politics as both central to their identity and intertwined with their daily labors. Maria, for example, organized one letter alphabetically, intermixing household chores with antislavery duties just as she did in her daily practice. No doubt this conceit reflected a sense of fun and a desire to entertain her recipient(s), yet it also bespoke a life embattled on multiple fronts. "I left off at C. so c—correspondence," she wrote. "I have written 8 pages to [Charles] Hovey & 25 to H[arriet] Martineau since I wrote last. To Jeremiah Winslow [a letter] of thanks. D.—Decorations. When we got your letter ordering curtain-stuff, I had just completed our curtains here, for one window & a bed, of a beautiful red woolen damask."[11] Maria had written multiple notes and informal letters to family and friends at this sitting. However, under "correspondence" she listed only the well-thought-out and carefully articulated communication and argumentation of formal antislavery business, not counting the informal exchanges that included details of domestic business as well as the family business of abolition.

The Westons found it challenging to manage so diverse an array of tasks through epistolary communication. Caroline reported, for example, how busy she was with her school, her preparations for the annual antislavery bazaar, and household and family matters. "You cannot comprehend how much I have to do," she wrote. "All my neglected business to bring up—the House . . . shut up—my clothes all out of order—Emma's affairs to see to—letters to write & Maria driving us all like mad about the fair." In spite of the flurry, she assured Anne, "Our preparations [for the Boston antislavery fund-raiser] go on well—Lucia [is] at work at a great rate. Emma has come in town—to Rox[bury] I mean & is boarding at Mrs Shoves. My school is fuller than I expected."[12] Having moved too quickly from antislavery activities in Boston to teaching in Roxbury, Caroline had to stop and specify Emma's destination in order to clarify that Emma had left Weymouth, not for Maria's fair headquarters in Boston but rather for Roxbury, where she was to enroll as a student in Caroline's school.

Clarity often required such backtracking. In writing Mary Weston, for example, Debora paused to more fully explain her point. "Lucia and Emma will tell you what little has been, & is going on. Lucia was at our meeting. The rooms are to be given up, that is the anti slavery rooms," not their living quarters or schoolrooms.[13] Her phrase "what little has been, & is going on" referred to developments in the cause. This verbal conflation of tasks and workplaces reflected the mind-set of women grounded in multiple spheres of labor in a variety of locales.

While Maria was known for her strategic thinking, tactical creativity, and powerful political writing, her correspondence evinced as well a mind caught up in the everyday logistics of household and movement maintenance. For example, she provided this accounting of her time over the course of one day: "Wrote to Mrs. Brooks, sending her some of the Edward Davis silks to be sold for the cause, which Marian Fuller told me she wanted. Wrote to Abby Kelley by request of E[dward] Davis, enclosing his letter. To E. Davis acknowledging the receipt of silks & assurances of gratitude & cooperation in his plans for a campaign in Penn[sylvania]. Mary Fifield called at the door to enquire for Lucia. Did not see her. Abby & Sarah Southwick called, & we planned a board meeting to be held here on Thursday, or on Friday if it rained. Searched the straw in the chamber over, preparatory to a cleaning up, & found a little perfume bottle, two covers to water bottles & a little jewel of a doll's tea pot among it."[14] Each day's labor required moving about the house on an endless round of domestic tasks, while slotting in time for movement correspondence and political calls.

Politics pervaded not only Weston domestic activities but also occupational experiences. Just as the Westons acquired students through abolitionist connections,[15] so too the Garrisonian cast of their allegiances cost them both students and positions. Even as a Mr. Kimball interviewed Caroline in Boston for a teaching job in New Canaan, Connecticut, the school committee there was dismantling his institution as a hotbed of antislavery indoctrination.[16] When student Mary Ann Davenport returned home to Pepperell, Massachusetts, refusing to eat food sweetened by slave-grown sugar, her father forbade her to return to the Weston School the following term. While Anne Warren Weston "comforted her all I could, gave her free labour black meringue and cake, and told her the storm would blow over," she recognized that her student had chosen a particularly tense time to take a political stand at home. The Grimké sisters, Sarah and Angelina, had been speaking in the area about slavery's horrors, and Weston had accompanied them to Pepperell. There the sisters were refused permission to use the meetinghouse and forced to lecture in a barn. The incident aroused considerable, and mixed, feeling among the town's population. Incensed, the local minister believed his authority had been undermined by the willingness of a congregant to offer the Grimkés a platform, however humble, in defiance of his command that the sisters should not speak in town.[17]

So too the emerging divisions within the antislavery movement between Garrisonians and anti-Garrisonians in the 1840s affected schools. Caroline remained in Roxbury until the community became openly hostile. "I am anxious to leave R[oxbury]," she wrote to Debora in late 1841 or early 1842, having "*no* acquaintance in the place & a great & intense dislike of me to make head against." She revealed that she had "only *once* in the four years [of teaching] been to church there . . . all this time Mr Kent with Mr Putnam's whole parish to back & support him & abuse me has been warring against me . . . with all Mark Anthony's Episcopalians to back them." She had grown "tired however of bearing up—& long[ed] for a little of the wind that once filled my sails."[18]

By the mid-1840s, Weston professional and social resources had been strained by the divisions that had emerged between clerical and electoral abolitionists and Garrison, the brief loss to the Massachusetts state legislature of the Westons' Whig friend and mentor John F. Emerson in 1839, and the division of New Bedford's Quakers over the use by some abolitionists of what they viewed as coercive tactics in rescuing the "fugitive" slave Lucy Faggin in 1841. The alienation of Frederick Douglass, after the Westons attacked his British speaking tour as an exercise in hubris, further affected their relationships with those in the African American community with whom they had worked to aid fugitive slaves. As a battle emerged over the admission of African Americans to membership in the New Bedford Lyceum in 1845, Caroline asserted, "Our School flourishes— as yet but the bitterest of this hatred and malice is in the families of our pupils."[19] Antislavery was not popular in New Bedford, where, as Debora put it, the "wharves and churches" were arrayed against it.[20]

Nevertheless, she and Debora, alternately and together, persisted with their political activism. Debora had not only carried out petition campaigns in New Bedford in the mid-1830s; she also modeled the use of "free" produce (as opposed to slave-grown products such as sugar—a great sacrifice for one with her sweet tooth). She complained about boarding in a "dissipated" house that failed to observe free labor practices, and the "fruitless endeavours [*sic*]" she undertook "to keep the abolitionists in the house in the right [Garrisonian] way" ideologically.[21] Despite working "in school now every moment of daylight—that is available time," Debora and Caroline attended two evening antislavery sewing meetings a week in the 1840s to prepare goods for the Boston fair, "because it is best for the cause—tho our own work could be better done at home." Their attendance encouraged others to participate and thus supported the city's female antislavery organization.[22]

No teaching job outside Boston dissipated a Weston's responsibility to the Boston Female Anti-Slavery Society (BFAS), however.[23] Caroline, for example, ran in and out of Roxbury and Anne in and out of Dorchester to attend BFAS meetings in the late 1830s. Anne arranged with her head-master, a Mr. Wilder, to take her classes in the morning so that she might go to Boston in time for afternoon sessions. "I staid at school till near 1 and then hurried home, bolted my dinner, and a little after I found myself in the Omnibus." She arrived at Maria's about 2:00 P.M. ready to accompany her sister to a meeting.[24] Early in her career Debora worried that if she established her own school in New Bedford, she would feel obliged to remain there, a situation that could diminish her usefulness to the BFAS. "It seems as if the money were not coined that could pay me for staying. Every thing here disgusts me. In short I hate it."[25] Remain she did, however, for over a decade, despite the six hours by stage up the New Bedford Turnpike that it took to get to Boston before the train arrived in the 1840s.[26]

The same rules applied for Weston participation in the Weymouth Female Anti-Slavery Society, anchored by Aunt Mary Weston. She held her nieces to account, writing in frustration, "Our Society held no quarterly meeting why?—because I was not at home to make it go"—a not particularly subtle reminder to her nieces that they, too, must take responsibility for the Weymouth association. She employed the same tactic in an effort to induce her nieces to aid the local antislavery bazaar. It was "Mary Weston's Fair," she told Anne, and she expected help. Anne apologized for her negligence. "I wish I could send you something," she wrote, then teased, "It is 'Mary Weston's Fair' true enough, but I think she was a most impudent trollop to say so in the spirit she did." So too Mary told Debora in no uncertain terms, "Perhaps you will think it hard, but you are a member of our society & must send us some article for the Fair. Send it tolerable soon, as it will encourage others."[27]

When home in Weymouth, all six sisters attended meetings for the making of fair goods.[28] Caroline came from Roxbury to join twelve women, including Aunt Mary, Maria, Lucia, and Emma, in the sewing circle. She reported, "I had much work to finish and much talking to do." Wanting more of the decorative boxes Caroline had been making for the fair, Maria urged her to take the six dollars reserved for fair goods by the Weymouth Female Emancipation Society and use the money to purchase the necessary materials.[29] On another occasion, in seeking to meet the needs of both the Weymouth and Boston societies, Maria asked, "Cant the Weymouth sewing circle get up a table [at the BFAS fair] for *Weymouth*? I will supply it with muslin enough to make a *dozen* capes & collars at 12cts a yd—From auction. Only let them meet & begin & before October. I'll warrant a hundred dollars worth of things; whatever is left can begin a fair in Weymouth itself—towards winter."[30]

Debora and Anne, who enjoyed "making W[eymouth] a hot anti slavery place" when home, took responsibility for organizing visiting speakers such as William Lloyd Garrison, Frederick Douglass, and William W.
Brown. Anne repeatedly petitioned the orthodox Congregational Meeting
House for permission to use its facilities on such occasions. She needed
that particular church building, she explained, "to make an impression on
the members of that parish . . . most of whom will not enter the Universal-
ist Meeting House," either because "they conscientiously think it wrong to
do so, or are in fear of the censure of others." Debora stirred up business
for one Weymouth meeting by repeatedly entreating her sisters to come
out from Boston to "swell" the attendance.[31]

Politics and public relations affected even family nursing, most dramatically when Maria suffered a debilitating bout of "brain fever" following
the mobbing of the second Anti-Slavery Convention of American Women
in Philadelphia in 1838. As the demoralized Boston delegation fled the
violence, Maria sought to sustain their courage. A traveler who witnessed
the scene recalled,

> How well I remember the light of her presence amid that band of fugi-
> tives; the other abolitionists were drooping, tired, despondent, while
> she stood glorified like a prophetess, triumphant in nominal defeat—
>
> "Calm and resolute and still.
> And strong and self possessed."

Having known Chapman for many years, he noted this behavior as "only
one of the many instances of the self forgetfulness with which she threw
herself into every cause she espoused." Yet even as he sought to praise,
his language, with its emphasis on "the *untiring enthusiasm and spirit
of martyrdom* which always marked her course," evoked popular beliefs
about the dangerous effects of "passion" (strong feeling) upon the female
mind and character.[32]

Rumors about her condition spread rapidly during the weeks that followed Maria's collapse in Connecticut and her physicians' diagnosis of
"brain fever." Contemporary medical authorities defined phrenitis as "an in-
flammation of the membranes surrounding the brain," which, in addition to
a pounding pulse, vomiting, fever, and pain in the scalp and neck, induced
"great anxiety and mental dejection, or . . . delirium." Acute phrenitis was
thought to result from a blow to the head, the suppression of bodily discharge (such as the early weaning of a child), or emotional excess, including
"gusts of vehement or prolonged passion" such as sorrow, pride, or mortified

ambition.[33] (Maria's family and friends thought she had weaned her daughter Ann early, and numerous antislavery advocates, male in particular, had charged female advocates with unfeminine pride and ambition.) Brain fever was said to be "often fatal from the third to the seventh day. If prolonged from this period, it is apt to terminate in mania or idiotism."[34] Insanity remained, "[e]ven when the . . . exciting cause is withdrawn . . . the extraordinary energy induced is necessarily succeeded by a state of diminished sensibility and weakness, or of collapse, subversive of the mind."[35]

As Maria lay ill in Connecticut, gossip and rumor circulated wildly in Boston. The hypochondriac William Lloyd Garrison latched onto each new detail about her condition with a fascinated horror. "Mrs. C. took a very active part in the Women's Anti-Slavery Convention in Philadelphia and was consequently in a high state of mental excitement, which has resulted in a brain fever," he wrote. "She got as far as Stonington on her return home, where she now lies—a raving maniac. There is no hope for her recovery."[36]

In an effort to contain damage to Maria's reputation, nurse Caroline withheld information about Maria's condition even from Mary Chapman, fearing her lack of political sophistication and self-control.[37] "Let them hear the exact truth at Weymouth," Caroline urged Debora, but warned her, "My letter is not designed for the public." Caroline asked Lydia Maria Child to quash any rumors of Maria's insanity.[38] Tracking Weston political alliances, she also asked her sister Lucia to "remember who inquires for us—& who is afflicted by our troubles for I shall wish to know."[39] Disputing a rumor that Maria was "so faint & exhausted as to be obliged to be supported" during her speech before the convention, Anne insisted, "Her voice was clear & firm & her manner quiet & unruffled. From a knowledge of her character, I feel sure that she was at that time entirely tranquil & self possessed." She contended that Maria's "health will be perfectly restored; her mind became so when the fever left her."[40]

As Maria's delirium continued, Caroline asked Lucia to close her school and explain Debora's absence in a way that would protect family privacy. Lucia was to announce that "we were *all* obliged to take a long journey to be with a friend we thought about to leave us—& tho' she is a little better yet D. will lose a day or two this week—& we are all so fatigued that I must shut up the school for a week & put it on at the end of the quarter—you can explain all this."[41] In such a way, Weston rumor management sought to ensure Maria's future political effectiveness.

Maria's family and friends interpreted the meaning of her illness through a lens of martyrdom, praising her capacity to rise above "persecution,

abuse, and the depression of ill health" to return to duty.[42] To her political enemies, it mattered little whether the cause of Maria's illness lay in
having "abandoned" her daughter in order to attend the convention or in
"exhibiting herself" before a public audience at Pennsylvania Hall. Each
pointed to an unwomanly nature.

Those who opposed abolition specifically, or female activism in general,
saw a woman punished by nature for overreaching her sphere. Sarah T.
Smith, who had attended the convention but preferred that women pursue abolition through private moral influence, gleefully spread the word
that "Mrs. Chapman was in the Insane Hospital, because at the convention a majority opposed certain views of hers, and she could not carry her
point."[43] Years later, Maria's British devotee Emma Mitchell overheard a
similar assessment by a Mrs. Marshall, who "informed [Mr. James] that
'Mrs Chapman left Boston for Europe because she was mad'" and wondered whether Boston intended to ship all "its mad subjects to this side
of the world." James replied that Mrs. Marshall was mistaken, that he had
seen Maria frequently, and "that there was not a trace of any thing of the
kind." When Mrs. Marshall insisted that "all Boston know it was so quite
well," James admonished, "'You know Mrs M it cannot be true'—'oh no
certainly not' was the reply 'Mrs C. *could never have found time for it.*'"[44]

Even pregnancy was viewed through a political lens. Anne, for example,
wrote to Debora about Maria's third pregnancy, "I have one fearful piece of
news to communicate. The fact that Maria is in a family way seems to be
pretty well ascertained. She is sick all the time. The thing that I care most
about is that it will break up her going to New York [for the first national
women's antislavery convention]." More circumspect with those outside
the sibling circle, Anne offered Wendell Phillips a somewhat disingenuous
response to Maria's fourth pregnancy: "Maria is as busily engaged with
the cause as ever and the children are so well and so pretty (little Ann in
especial) that we are not disquieted at the prospect of their number being
increased." Gertrude's early and unexpected death brought forth a political
bromide for public consumption. "This is the first child Maria has lost and
I know how much she will grieve over it; but it will not lead her to inac-
tion. She will only labour the more devotedly for those who mourn over
children took from them not by the providence of God but the cruelty of
man."[45]

Such public comments did not reflect indifference. Indeed, the Westons
worried over this pregnancy, in private, as they had the previous ones.
Three years earlier, when Maria became pregnant with Ann, Anne wailed
to Debora, "Did I mention to you the fears that we entertained or rather

they amount to a certainty that Maria is in a family way?" She attempted to comfort herself and her sister with religious strictures on obedience: "It is the Lord's will so we must submit."[46]

The sisters' individual reactions to Gertrude's birth were complicated. Designated "head nurse," Debora kept close watch over child and mother. Caroline admitted that some three weeks after her niece's birth she had yet to see Gertrude; she had been so "much occupied with business I entirely forgot her." So too Maria had taken the baby to Nantucket, perhaps to escape the heat in the city and recuperate by the sea, or perhaps in search of privacy. Reticence about childbirth, or a difficult recovery after delivery, would have reinforced the need for special circumspection given the previous public speculation about her maternal practices. Six months after Gertrude's birth, Henry's worsening tuberculosis encouraged Maria to leave her child in the trusted care of her sisters and in-laws in order that Henry might enjoy a warmer climate during the winter of 1840–41. Even in this personal exigency, the Chapmans chose Haiti for political reasons, hoping that they might bear witness to the transformation of slaves into self-governing citizens in the new republic.[47] The couple sailed on 28 December 1840. Three months later, Gertrude contracted a severe fever, perhaps related to teething or from her grandmother Chapman, who had been ill. She died within days.[48]

On 6 April 1841, Caroline Weston and Mary Chapman wrote Maria and Henry with "the sad tidings." Anne assured the shocked and grief-stricken parents "that every thing that care & tenderness could do for her relief was done and that her suffering did not appear to be great." She hoped that the news would not injure Henry's health and suggested, as no parent would, "that pretty and dear as Gertrude might be, the loss of her, in the very nature of the case must be less than that of either of the others" because they had spent so little time with her. She also piously hoped that Maria's "views both of this life & the other are such that you will feel there remains to you abundant consolations."[49] The Chapmans returned home immediately. Neither participated in the August 1841 Massachusetts Anti-Slavery Society (MAS) quarterly meeting, as Henry had begun bleeding from his lungs.

Amid these personal tragedies, Maria and Henry found themselves objects of character assassination. Following the 25 May 1841 meeting at the Tremont Chapel, Boston, the Massachusetts Abolition Society published its Second Annual Report. Titled *The True History of the Late Division in the Anti-Slavery Societies, Being Part of the Second Annual Report of the Executive Committee of the Massachusetts Abolition Society*, it contrasted Maria's language and demeanor with the more ladylike behavior and character of Mary S. Parker, the former president of the BFAS, "now just going to her grave, a *real* martyr to her efforts for the slave during this period. When the *true* 'Martyr Age' comes to be written, her name will occupy a conspicuous position in it." Alluding to Harriet Martineau's *The Martyr Age*, a history of the anti-abolitionist mob of 1835 in which Martineau had written admiringly of Maria's courage, the authors sneered, "It is not the wont of real martyrs to chronicle their own deeds while living, or to get their friends to do it for them, and then reprint it themselves for general circulation!"[50] The report not only betrayed the authors' anger at Maria's attack on the "new organization" in her report on the division of the anti-slavery societies but also revealed their own appetite for celebrity even as they targeted Maria's unfeminine ambition.

Political work incurred a physical cost requiring the Westons to juggle it with nursing care. Anne confided in Debora, for example, that she had lived in "one unmitigated fog since you took your departure. First the Bazaar Report kept me at it all day and every day for a week, poor Lucia down all the time and putting herself back as I believe by copying it for Sydney [H. Gay]. I just got it off in time to get a little readied up for the Annual Meeting." Having "mend[ed] the most pronounced holes," Anne "was seized with sudden chills . . . , took right to my bed and had every prospect of a fever. My pulse was at 125 and I could not sleep a wink." When able, Anne returned to Weymouth to care for Lucia, who was left briefly in Hervey's and her mother's hands while she politicked in Boston. She confessed she was as poor a nurse as patient, acknowledging, "Sickness even when not dangerous annoys and troubles me terribly." She wished for Debora's "quiet and patient endurance," confessing that she feared it "the last grace to which I shall ever attain."[51]

Usually, Maria exhibited a sense of humor about her various ills. In 1843, as she lay sick with influenza, she followed Hervey's prescription to drink hot pennyroyal.[52] It reduced the "violent pain" in her hands but did not improve "the chest-soreness & *stuffedness.*" With a wit honed by abolition, Maria urged her brother to "administer such antidotes as the books tell of:—always remembering that *whipping*, which was one of them, would probably have no effect on my constitution, & therefore he must catch a running slave, & whip *him*, outside my chamber-door which would probably be a successful irritant" and so purge her system.[53]

From experience the sisters knew that heightened political tension first revived and then debilitated them. Anne suffered eyestrain for decades. Worried about potentially permanent blindness, she abstained from reading for almost a year in the mid-1850s before once again succumbing to a temptation "not in human nature to resist." Despite the poor light of dusk, an unexpected arrival of some New York newspapers led Anne to do herself "a great mischief by my eagerness to find out how much had been done to Mr Sumner," the senator from Massachusetts beaten unconscious on the floor of the Capitol by a fellow legislator.[54] "I only write now to warn you against letting Lucia read the whole account of the [Anthony Burns] slave case," wrote Debora to the "dear folks" in Paris, where Lucia convalesced from what the Westons thought was a rheumatic attack but presaged her decline into consumption. "If my blood rises with such fury I am sure hers will too. Tell her that I say I cant hardly stand it, & I *know* she cant, for it takes the best of health. I am not so much exhausted however with my emotions as you might suppose, for I be awake planning vengeance upon [Benjamin Franklin] Hallet & his crew."[55]

The kind of determination Lucia showed while ill to finish copying an antislavery report for publication was commonplace among Weston women. With rare exception, political work continued despite private considerations, including one's own illness or that of a family member. Having come from political meetings "with a cold" and being "poorly one way or another ever since," Anne nevertheless wrote out the minutes she had taken because "Garrison might wish to see them" for the *Liberator*.[56] Maria took advantage of being "sickbed" to write Caroline about "some matters [relating to the] necessary to be settled," which included finding a machine to emboss stationery with an antislavery seal to sell at the fair.[57]

When too ill or harried to accomplish the political labor they expected of themselves and each other, the sisters evidenced considerable frustration. The anxiety-prone Anne, for example, spent a difficult summer nursing her brother Warren, caring for his pregnant wife (who gave birth in the Weymouth home), worrying about her mother's fragility in the "distressingly warm" weather, and fearing that her aunt Priscilla's decades-long struggle with physical paralysis and mental "imbecility" had come to a fatal crisis. She found that the experience of nursing others changed her, "not outwardly perhaps but very consciously to myself. I live very much in the present and little circumstances do not annoy or distress me, the little daily routine I mean that goes on around me." She felt "all the time that if people are only alive and in tolerable health, and not left to the commission of any shocking crime, they should overflow with content and thankfulness." Yet when autumn came her thoughts returned to her political responsibilities, and her new philosophy bowed to the urgency of preparing the Weymouth and Boston fairs. "I hope to have strength sufficient for the demands of the bazaar, the *Liberty Bell* etc.," she wrote, knowing that, in the absence of her sisters (Maria, Caroline, and Emma in Paris supervising the Chapman children; Debora nursing Warren; and Lucia nursing Priscilla Weston), the fairs' success depended upon her.[58] Worried though she was about her aunt, Anne left Weymouth after their local fair to spend a month in Boston "as the bazaar and its preparations necessitated." The November Weymouth fair earned about $170 ("our aims are not very high"), but December's Boston bazaar returned some $3,000 despite an inauspicious change of setting, intensely cold weather, a poor economic outlook, "and pro slavery people quite as bitter as ever."[59] Priscilla Weston died 24 January 1852 after fifteen years of dementia. Anne, convinced that ultimately she died of exhaustion, wrote that Priscilla suffered greatly and that she herself and Lucia "thanked God very truly when the scene closed. She had great original strength of constitution and this so prolonged the last struggle that it seemed as if it would *never* end. She was more than 30 hours in that state which it is so terrible to witness and where human help is so entirely unavailing."[60] Anne and Lucia remained at her bedside throughout.

If illness and nursing took place in and around political activity, so too did child care. Anne wrote in frustration to Debora that Maria was "over run with business. The baby [Ann] is not so good as she might be. She begins to *meander*," thus disrupting Maria's concentration on "business."[61] On another occasion, Debora fretted, "What Maria will do with those three children I know not." At the time, with Anne's and Caroline's help, Maria was actively working on the annual fair, the *Liberty Bell*, and *Right and Wrong in Massachusetts*, her history of the conflict dividing the BFAS in 1839. Anne's strategy was to ask Debora to invite their niece Elizabeth to visit Weymouth so as to reduce the chaos in the Boston household. She chose Elizabeth because she "cannot be so troublesome as Henry."[62]

Because they bound themselves to one another in a common labor pool committed to accomplishing their domestic and political responsibilities, individual Westons felt free to devote themselves, on a temporary and even idiosyncratic basis, to abolition as an individual priority. While attending meetings in Boston, for example, Anne was called home to Weymouth to care for her parents. She refused to go, saying that she would come when the nonresistance meeting was finished and not before. Exercising seniority, she insisted that Emma put off her own plans to come into town for a (merely) social visit so that she might help out in Weymouth until Anne returned.

With excitement building in Boston over the pending trial of fugitive slave George Latimer, Lucia similarly rejected a summons to Weymouth. "I dont think I shall come out without you want me very much, till after the trial," she wrote, "and upon the whole I think I shall accomplish just as much in here as I should there, where you have two children and are painting [the house], and besides I want very much to hear the rest of [Theodore] Parker's lectures." So too, when faced with the return from Europe of her invalid brother Warren, her sister Anne, and her son, Henry, Maria scurried to "get my affairs, *causeward*, in such a train as that the inroad shall not interfere with them."[63]

On the occasion of the 1841 "Church, Ministry, and Sabbath" convention called by Garrison to explore issues related to the contemporary practices of all three,[64] the sisters debated which among them would attend the convention and who would stay at home with the Chapman children and their grandparents. On another occasion when Maria accompanied Henry to Haiti for his health, the four Chapman children were divided among their aunts and grandparents. Anne anchored Maria's Poplar Street household, attended to her correspondence, and cared for Lizzie. Debora (to the dismay of New Bedford's Susan Tabor) handled matters at Weymouth, tutoring Henry (who "at present . . . shows more genius in any direction than in the literary corner"), minding little Ann (who "bears away the bell at Weymouth . . . the most gifted *I* think of any of them"), and managing Pa Weston's volatility. The Chapman grandparents kept baby Gertrude (the "pride of the family") with them at Chauncy Place, Boston. Caroline moved between her school in Roxbury and these various households as needed. "I shall be [at Weymouth] the whole of the latter part of the week to keep fast at home," she assured Maria.[65]

In determining who would stay with whom and conduct which responsibilities during the 1841 Chardon Street convention, Lucia rooted her claim to freedom in an invitation extended by the Southwicks to stay with them. Anne also had an invitation, to visit her beloved Boston friends Henrietta and Catherine Sargent.[66] When Mary Chapman invited Debora to stay with her at Chauncy Place, the Westons found themselves understaffed in Weymouth. The elder sisters decided they could not spare both Debora and Lucia, so Debora would remain in Weymouth attending to the press of household and family responsibilities. When Debora declined Mary Chapman's invitation, Mary "kindly sent for Emma to come up—& as she [had been] deprived of the Annual meeting [of the MAS]—we *treated* her to the ministry convention & let her come."[67] Such negotiations recurred regularly as the Weymouth sisterhood organized their combined resources to meet their diverse workloads and tend to one another's social needs.

The Westons continually weighed competing obligations. Anne, in the midst of a flurry of abolitionist controversy in Boston, pointedly informed Debora that she could make no specific commitment as to when she would return to Weymouth, where the family needed her: "It will depend on where the fun is for my coming or going."[68] (The Westons frequently used the word "fun," as both a noun and a verb, in describing antislavery work.) A few months later, in July 1839, she explained to Debora, "Of course, I can make no plans about coming out [to Weymouth] just now. If John Quincy [Adams, representative from Massachusetts] does not speak here [in Boston], I shall, of course, want to be at Weymouth on the 1st" of August, the anniversary of the British emancipation of slaves in the West Indies and a day celebrated by American abolitionists and free blacks with picnics, parades, and speeches.[69] Anne would decide when to return home to help with family matters if and when Adams announced whether he would attend the celebration or not.

In 1839, the growing conflict between Garrisonians (who relied upon moral suasion) and political abolitionists (who relied upon elections and party politics) put new demands on the Westons, who helped anchor Garrisonian efforts by supporting antislavery organizations and holding office in these societies at the city, state, and national levels. Wrote Anne to her aunt Mary, "I shall come to Weymouth next Monday. I long to be there now, but Maria is trying to get up a meeting of the Boston Female on Saturday next, & wishes me to stay for that." Every vote counted in the struggle waged by anti-Garrisonians to dissolve the association. A week later, Anne reported new developments to Debora and begged her to come to Boston from New Bedford: "A meeting of the Mass[achusetts Anti-Slavery Society] is to be called for the 26th of this month to settle all the whole row. Great efforts will be made to have it a full meeting. How can you manage? Cant you come for a day or two?" Debora herself had written to Caroline, "Write me word when the N[ew] E[ngland] Convention is to be for I want to arrange my vacation accordingly—How is the cause getting on I am so worried about it, that I cant tell what to think."[70]

The process varied by which the Weston sisters negotiated their individual responsibilities to the corporate sisterhood. Some provided details of their reasoning; some took a no-holds-barred affirmative stand on their own ground; and others stated their intent or preference while leaving room for compromise as new information emerged. Caroline, for example, acknowledged her appreciation of family needs and her concern for the individuals she loved before rejecting both the need and the love as a sufficient basis for taking action adjudicated by her sisters. "I am quite distressed at Ma's ill turns," she wrote, "& should come right home were it not for a desire I have to be in town over Sunday. Would you think it, [William L.] Garrison & [Francis] Jackson are such fools that they have got [Henry B.] *Stanton* & [Joshua] *Leavitt* with others to speak at the Faneuil Hall meeting [about the incarceration of the fugitive slave George Latimer] which comes off Sunday night."[71] Lucia took a more direct approach with her mother. "I hear papa is going to take one of us out to Weymouth when he comes in. I should be happy to go out with him, provided he comes in after Monday. I want to stay Monday to go to [Theodore] Parker's lecture." Worried that she had not been sufficiently assertive, she restated her position firmly. "Papa better not come till Wednesday, if he comes Monday I shant come out with him."[72]

In departing Boston for Europe in 1848, the widowed Maria changed the dynamic of the sisters' political engagement. For various periods, as a result of Lucia's and Warren's health, the sisters stood divided by the time it took to cross an ocean rather than to travel down a turnpike. Their abolitionist sisterhood stretched to meet their commitments to the cause, but their personal and political resources were strained. Caroline traveled to France with Maria and the children, Debora held down the school in New Bedford, Anne managed the Boston fair and Weymouth homestead, and Emma nursed Lucia in Weymouth and Italy as her consumption worsened.

Maria had in mind her children's social and educational needs, although her own desire for a change of scene, of task, and of pace may have entered into her decision.[73] She had driven herself to maintain the *Liberator*, had undertaken editorship of the *Anti-Slavery Standard*, had written the annual histories of the year in abolition, maintained an enormous political correspondence, and continued to produce and manage the annual Boston antislavery bazaar. As she wrote to Mary Ann Estlin, "When I felt it wearing upon my own iron nerves and strong organization, to write much, and to one point, I *changed works*, and went to Europe. 'Consequence is' . . . I'm alive yet."[74] Denying that she was retreating from activism, Maria insisted that she merely wanted a new vineyard to cultivate and a new mode of operation: "I change my hand not because it is tired, but because I get at my work sometimes best with one, and sometimes with the other."[75]

Precisely why she chose Paris is difficult to say, particularly given what others saw as the Westons' "prejudices a *l'Anglais*" arising from Maria's education in England, her close friendship with Harriet Martineau, the abode there of her uncle and his family, and her personal associations with various British abolitionists.[76] The Weston papers provide no explicit rationale for the selection. However, Britain would have provided less of the "butterfly life" they enjoyed in France.[77] Residing there would have expanded rather than lessened their political labors. So well known had the family become that even in France they were swamped with invitations to speak at antislavery gatherings. The many requests of Maria and her sisters contradicted reassurances that "your position and your welfare is the constant theme of those who know you, and of some who know you not."[78] For some time British abolitionists had urged one or another Weston to conduct an antislavery mission to the women of Great Britain, and their insistence increased in both urgency and volume once the sisters crossed the Atlantic.[79]

After Caroline and Maria visited London in 1851, the Estlins urgently strove to draw them to Bristol.[80] "I do believe if your sisters could have spent as many months with us as they were able to spare weeks and had bestowed an equal time on a few other abolitionist strong holds, such as Glasgow, Leeds, &c we should have accomplished the victory," wrote Mary Ann to Anne. Eight days later, she again raised the issue of a visit by Maria, Caroline, and Emma, insisting, "I am using no figurative language but very much understating the way in which these sentiments [of British abolitionists] are expressed." She pressured Anne, back home in Weymouth, to weigh in on the side of such a mission. The Weston admiration society's "loving thoughts are following them to their distant abode [in Paris], and hoping the day may come when [we] shall see them again," she wrote. Four days later, Estlin entreated Maria: "I cant think how those sisters of yours could be so cruel as to desert us in our extremity, and *it appears to me*, that as you get so many compliments for the 'sacrifices' in which you were a somewhat involuntary participant you could not more appropriately prove that they were deserved than by earning the title and relinquishing the attractions of Paris winter for the sake of coming back here to take part in our work!"[81] A year later, when the Westons took a Swiss holiday to provide the Chapman children with a break from urban life, and in hopes that clean mountain air would aid Lucia's breathing, Estlin huffed disapprovingly, "Our mission is not as yet that of personal amusement."[82]

Refusing the "rule" of others, however synchronous their Garrisonian agendas, the Westons conducted antislavery business by their own lights while abroad. During the seven years she lived in France, Maria carried out three antislavery assignments in Britain: two in 1851 and another in 1853.[83]

Caroline and Maria hosted informal visits to Paris by such British abolitionists as George Thompson of Manchester, William Ashurst of London, Charles Wicksteed of Leeds, and Richard D. Webb of Dublin. Their hospitality helped lubricate communication and coordinate strategy among Garrisonians on both sides of the ocean. In 1854, a more or less formal consultation occurred among Maria, Caroline, and Louis Alexis Chamerovzow, the newly appointed president of the British and Foreign Anti-Slavery Society.[84] Maria had earlier acknowledged only "the friendliest and most indulgent feelings" toward the man, in contrast to Weston dislike of the previous leader, John Scoble. She remained skeptical of Chamerovzow's character, fearing that a paid position with the British organization would undermine true independence: "I can feel no such security in him as I should do if *we* had a £600 secretaryship to offer him."[85]

The family also hosted a number of American abolitionists. Some, such as Parker Pillsbury, came to Europe on antislavery missions; others, such as Harriet Beecher Stowe, traveled with mixed agendas, professional and personal.[86] The Westons wove these consultations in and around the private agendas that inspired their European stay.

The sisters Weston decamped to France in part for social reasons—their own as well as those of the children. As Anne explained, "We are so *dis*liked by most people for our Anti Slavery position that we do not in general have fair play. This is not a very comfortable situation to occupy and I am particularly glad that Emma and the Chapman children should make friends, and mix with society under the natural circumstances that surround other young people."[87] Edmund Quincy acknowledged that the Chapman girls and younger Westons had been "thrown upon the Abolitionists mainly for companionship." The sisters, he noted, had "great contempt for Society in this country; but then they have never been in it."[88]

Quincy expected his friends would be admitted to more sophisticated levels of society in Paris than they had been in Boston because many Americans traveling abroad carried with them the romantic ideal of a democratic society without social distinctions and, therefore, felt no inferiority regarding the well-to-do, famous, and aristocratic Europeans with whom they interacted.[89] In Paris the Westons mixed with a liberal, multinational society of political, literary, and artistic men and women. Their circle included Alphonse de Lamartine, Victor Hugo, Juliette Récamier, Hilaire Belloc, Alexis de Tocqueville, and Ivan Turgenev. In several cases, saloniere Mary Clarke Mohl, the British-born wife of a German scholar, facilitated introductions. British literati visited, including George Eliot, Ruth Gaskell, William Makepeace Thackeray and his wife Isabella Shaw Thackerary, Robert and Elizabeth Barrett Browning, and the Trollopes, Anthony and Rose Heseltine. George Thompson reported that the Westons enjoyed a "choice circle for they are careful and select.[90]

When in England, the family interacted with acquaintances of their uncle Joshua Bates, who socialized with the British upper crust, although not, he felt, on equal terms.[91] The result of mixing with both literary and political notables and British aristocracy was such that, after a separation of several years, young Henry Chapman wrote his uncle Warren Weston to say that "he had an entire new acquaintance in [his sister] Ann. He should never have thought he had seen the girl" who had polished up so well during her Parisian habitation.[92]

Of their European sojourn Maria concluded, "My objects in coming [to Europe] are completely answered as far as regards my children. They have made great progress in all they have undertaken," particularly their social and educational affairs. So too both the Chapman children and the younger Westons gained a broader political perspective on the difference between subjects and citizens. They had a front row seat to the revolution of 1848 and its aftermath. They came to understand the place of their nation and its institutions, including slavery, in the broader community of Western nations. "Aside from success in particular branches of education," Maria believed, "it is good to become cosmopolitan early in life, & to be able to say with an experiential feeling, 'My country is the world my countrymen are all mankind.'"[93] She thought "foolish pride & patriotism . . . does more to sustain slavery than any thing else, except the love of power & of money," and concluded, "'Our country right or wrong' is very apt to be the war-cry of those who have seen no country but their own."[94]

While traveling abroad had primarily to do with expanding her children's social contacts and intellectual horizons, Maria also measured the success of the family's European stay in terms of their continued antislavery activities abroad. As she put it to Ann and Wendell Phillips, "I hope to be more useful here than at home to our cause, for I can do more financially, at least I hope to be able to do so." To British Quaker and abolitionist Elizabeth Pease she insisted that while her children's education commanded the bulk of her attention, "my thoughts are at the same time devising plans for the cause."[95]

Caroline and Anne (who managed a trip abroad to visit her sisters Debora and Emma in 1856) both took seriously their responsibilities to educate Europeans as to the nature of slavery and abolition in the United

States. Caroline rejoiced in extended visits with British abolitionists, many of whom spent extended periods with them in France, as well as their own visits to England. As Caroline wrote of a month-long trip across France, Switzerland, and Germany with the Estlins, "We enjoyed this companionship & opportunity to be useful to the cause—greatly—for we found them begging for facts & arguments which we could supply. You would laugh could you know how thoroughly we have been examined how carefully we have been sifted until as [George] Thompson you remember used to say we sieve very fine indeed." Anne lamented her inadequate French, a hindrance in her efforts to persuade European women to support American abolition. "I have been able to do nothing for the Cause here in Swi[t]ze[rland]," she groused to Wendell and Ann T. G. Phillips. "Difference of language is an immense barrier in the way of any success." Told of "two saints at Lausanne whom we might propitiate," she took Emma along as translator. Too often, however, she was unable to "arrange it so that the French [speaking] Westons could accompany me."[96]

Maria and Caroline solicited articles for the *Liberty Bell* from those they met at Mme Mohl's Parisian salon and collected letters of introduction to notable and sympathetic French men and women of whom they might ask the same. With a flair for public relations, Maria used copies of Frederick Douglass's slave narrative to approach various French republicans with whom she hoped to establish "a hint of Anti-slavery communication between the United States and France, and of obtaining the testimony of the celebrities of the other country against slavery. De Tocqueville, De Beaumont, Victor Schoeler, Lamartine and many others have a name and a fame in the United States which will make their words tell, and I trust soon to find means to condense and conduct the anti-slavery feeling latent here aright."[97] With the aid of their new acquaintances, the Weston party organized a Parisian society to cooperate with the American Anti-Slavery Association and carry on the work of the Société pour l'Abolition de l'Esclavage, a group active before the 7 April 1848 emancipation of slaves in French colonies. The Parisian political and social elite who sympathized with abolition represented a mixed group of republicans and evangelicals.[98] They never really gelled as a working society but, in response to Weston influence, contributed richly to the annual Boston fair.[99]

While in Europe, the Weston sisters focused much of their political activity on aiding that antislavery bazaar, management of which had devolved primarily upon Anne in their absence. Almost as soon as they arrived in Paris, Maria and Caroline began searching for unusual and tasteful goods to freshen the fair's appeal. By 1846, British donations had begun to outnumber American contributions, lending it a European cachet and transforming it into the commercial highlight of Boston's Christmas season.[100] Yet by 1847, the quality and quantity of these goods had begun to decline as British unemployment worsened and famine stalked Ireland. Among the British contributors there arose "the very general feeling . . . that all the time & money they c[oul]d spare should be devoted to our own, now, afflicted country."[101] Thus Caroline and Maria raided Parisian department stores and small shops to find unusual items that would retain a fair audience that had developed a taste for European goods.[102] The sisters chased "from the Arc De Triumphe to the Bastille, and from the Barriere de Chily to the Observatoir, to find things costing 25 sous which will sell in the U.S. for 125 sous and be at the same time useful and ornamental works of art."[103]

Three boxes of goods worth approximately $150 (over $4,500 in 2012) were sent to Boston from Paris that first November and three "immense cases" the following year, "so selected that they will not be duplicates of the contributions of English friends."[104] With the aid of Mary Clarke Mohl's niece Selina Martin, a strongly evangelical woman married to a protestant minister and active in missionary charities, the Westons produced in Paris a miniature version of the Boston fair, exhibiting their items so as to draw continental attention to the cause and stimulate Parisian giving. A success among the fashionably benevolent, the exposition drew the praise of Mme Coquerel, a conservative evangelical who conducted an annual fair to benefit the protestant schools of Paris and who "pronounced the articles beautiful even for Paris, and took note of them for her own future guidance."[105]

Of course it was not always possible to meet the diverse responsibilities of both Mary and Martha despite the good-faith efforts of six women. Nevertheless, while historians maintain that the demands of household and family pulled married women away from activism in the public sphere, the Westons' example suggests that with sufficient numbers of unwed sisters, both sets of tasks could largely be accomplished. Individual sisters maintained a balance between antislavery and household labor by negotiating specific tasks within the combined resource base of the collective.

Yet life and labor were more complicated than a computation of available hands and bodies.[106] An undated and unsatisfactorily vague letter from Maria to Wendell Phillips intimates the difficulty. Maria informed Phillips that she could not attend a MAS board meeting because her mother was ill and Debora remained in New York nursing their brother Warren.[107] Caught between political duty and family obligation without her sisters to back her up, Maria chose to attend to her mother's need.

When Caroline left Paris in 1852 to nurse Warren, Maria wrote that she began to understand "why women have never produced so many works of art or systems of philosophy as men in the fact that they do not pass their lives producing works of art." She attributed this insight to "the maternal duties I have been fulfilling so zealously the last few days, of conducting . . . my children to their professors, to their soirees, to their riding school."[108] In the shuffling of sibling employment, the widow Chapman faced these tasks without the aid of her sisters for the first time. In so doing she discovered just how demanding the household labor of one lone woman and mother of three could be.

7

ROCKING THE NATION
LIKE A CRADLE

The Political Import of Households

In describing Boston's response to the passage of the Fugitive Slave Act in 1850, Debora wrote to Caroline, "Every decent person reprobates [this bill]. The country is very much stirred up—never more so. It only wants an attempt to seize a slave in Mass[achusetts] to make an outbreak. It is a very interesting time. People behave better than you would suppose." And to her sister Maria, then in Paris, Debora asserted, "If you were at home with a house in town, this nation would have been rocking like a cradle."[1]

However promiscuous Debora's metaphor might have seemed to some of her contemporaries, it worked well for the Weymouth sisterhood, who knew intimately both wakeful nights tending crying or restless children and nights of dread awaiting marauding anti-abolitionist mobs. The Westons frequently utilized domestic metaphors in discussing political activity.[2] For example, Anne described preparing an antislavery article for publication as "Diffikult cooking," and Maria wrote of political correspondence as "a mere repetition of facts & principles—a preparation of milk for babies."[3] Yet the critical aspect of Debora's metaphor was not so much the metaphorical adjectival phrase as the subjunctive clause: "if you were at home with a house in town." The Westons found that conducting social revolution in antebellum Massachusetts required an urban base, a household in town.[4]

This is not to downplay the political role played by the Weymouth household. The Weymouth sisterhood conducted the entire range of antislavery work from their natal home: writing political correspondence, sewing goods for the annual bazaars (in Weymouth and Boston), organizing and carrying out local petition campaigns, and providing hospitality to peripatetic antislavery agents and lecturers. The Weymouth household offered food, drink, and a bed to those lecturing or organizing south of Boston, including Samuel J. May Jr., Edmund Quincy, Wendell Phillips, William L. Garrison, Henry C. Wright, George Bradburn, Nathaniel P. Rogers, Frederick Douglass, and John A. Collins. On occasion the household served multiple constituencies and purposes, as when the sewing circle met in one room of the house while Massachusetts Anti-Slavery Society (MAS) agent George Bradburn ate and relaxed in another, "seem[ing], shy of seeing the sisters."[5] Uncomfortable with the "uproarious time" accompanying a Weymouth revival, the rather imperious Bradburn preferred keeping his distance from locals who mixed handwork for the cause with gossip about who had been saved, who remained beyond God's grace, and why.[6]

The proffer of antislavery hospitality at Weymouth sometimes ran up against the resistance of Pa Weston, who thought primarily of his own comfort and tended to throw temper tantrums when his daughters' politics infringed upon it. Anne's frustration with him produced *"that letter . . . to Pa,"* aimed at laying down his daughters' requirements in hopes of eliciting his acquiescence if not his extension of a warm welcome to antislavery activists.[7] On occasion, Captain Weston's general disapprobation dissipated in the face of his appreciation of a particular visitor. That he enjoyed certain individuals certainly "made matters easier" for his daughters. Weston enjoyed the company of Frederick Douglass, for example, thinking him "the smartest fellow that had been along yet." He also "took a great liking" to George Bradburn, whom he permitted to stay two days and nights. On the other hand, bringing Henry C. Wright home to dine was tantamount to a declaration of rebellion. As Debora confessed, "I have fought so many battles with [Pa] I am tired out."[8]

The worst skirmish over his daughters' use of the natal home for abolitionist activities may have come in 1851, when a restless Massachusetts pitted slave hunters with warrants for the repatriation of fugitive slaves against abolitionists swearing to protect the freedom of runaways. Jane Richardson, a New Bedford acquaintance, asked the Westons to keep a fugitive overnight while an escape to Canada could be arranged. Debora readily agreed yet felt she must at least consult her parents. She described having "found pa and ma at breakfast and rush[ed] into the hot coal business at once." "You may imagine," she wrote her sisters, "the scene which followed. . . . [Pa Weston] vowed the man should not come, and told me to go back and tell Jane we could not take him. This of course I declined to do, and after a short and very severe conflict, I shall say we will take him gladly." Her father continued to agitate the issue, however, "ke[eping] up with spirit all day, so that by night or not," Debora felt, "a rescue or a mob seemed a very small matter."[9]

More of an impediment to the Westons' antislavery business than frayed tempers and fraught emotions was the natal home's distance from the front lines in Boston. "At Weymouth I trouble myself sometimes by watching the length of my inspiration," complained Anne. She "burned" to be "as near the scene of action as possible."[10] Caroline, too, spoke of "being quite out of the world" when not in the city.[11] Debora complained from New Bedford, "My suffering has been intolerable during the last week. I always thought the story of the two Foscari rather unnatural, but upon my word I begin to think it exact to life. I am almost ready to do anything for the sake of getting home" (by which she could have meant either Weymouth or Maria's Boston town house, where political intrigue rivaled that of the Foscaris' Venetian city-state).[12] "I knew in reason that there was a posse of brethren at Maria's," she wrote. "When Wendell Phillips left [New Bedford], I burst into tears, speaking metaphorically, not from grief at his departure, but from desire to go with him."[13]

Whether in West Street, Poplar Street, Summer Street, or Federal Place, the Chapman abode drew abolitionist men and women as a magnet to discuss, strategize, and labor for the cause. When Maria closed her Boston household to go to Europe in 1848, Quincy wrote: "The Weston's are all at Weymouth, and it is but seldom that I see them, now. You can hardly imagine what a difference the closing of Mrs. Chapman's home makes to me. Boston is a different place to me. Any of my blood relations might go away and not make such a change. For I love not only the society of herself and her family, but in a great degree all of her sisters, too."[14] The town house provided a base for organizing the annual fair that funded much antislavery activity—not only for producing the correspondence necessary to its organization and administration but also for generating and storing goods, and providing overnight hospitality for staff and participants. The Chapman house also provided a base for Weston petitioning, a predominantly female activity that politicized household space as signatures were collected from women gathered in their homes and open to discussion of the issues.[15] The loss of this center undermined Boston's antislavery movement as much as its availability had energized it.[16]

One Weston letter suggests the myriad purposes of Maria's town house and how her household drew in those committed to the cause, family and nonfamily alike. In May 1846, the widow Chapman resided with her children at 53 Federal Street. She hosted an afternoon's "full sewing meeting" in preparation for the annual bazaar. Garrison arrived to share information and stayed to read aloud letters from George Thompson urging him to sail for England on 16 July. As Debora explained, Thompson wanted Garrison to hold a great rally in London with additional meetings in Glasgow and Dublin. Debora reported from Weymouth to Caroline in New Bedford that Anne had joined Garrison, Maria, and the various Boston Female Anti-Slavery Society (BFAS) needleworkers present in discussing Thompson's request, made in what she called his "palmist" manner "in full feather rending & tearing."[17] Thus the gathering represented both a formal meeting of the BFAS Sewing Circle and an informal gathering with one of the antislavery brethren who had brought to Maria, and those of her fictive sisters ensconced in her parlor, a matter of some strategic concern. Was this the time for Garrison to leave the country? Was his presence in Britain of sufficient benefit to the cause for his colleagues to raise the funds necessary to support his mission abroad? The debate flowed outward from the Chapman household to the extended Weymouth and abolitionist sisterhoods for further commentary and the refinement of a plan, as their support and action would be required for any such plan to succeed.

The Chapmans' Boston household provided a highly visible headquarters for Garrisonians and, as such, a flash point for public resistance to abolition. Edmund Quincy teased Maria that a Mrs. Godfries of Milford "desired her respects to you and said she rec.d your letter and would have answered it, had it had any address—but did not know that 'Boston' was enough."[18] Standing open to antislavery business, the Chapman abode offered no closed-off, private, domestic retreat. Although the MAS and BFAS had rented rooms (first in Washington Street and then in Cornhill), the committees conducting antislavery business frequently met in the homes of members.[19]

In April 1836, for example, Maria invited Samuel J. May to tea, and "he told her that he, with her permission would invite *the Board of the Mass[achusetts] Society* to her house, that they might have the benefit of the Ladies advice." The entirely male board agreed. "The party accordingly consisted of Mr [Joseph] Southwick, Mr Sam[uel] Sewall, Mr [Ellis Gray] Loring, [William L.] Garrison, [Isaac] Knapp and [Samuel J.] May, Messrs [Drury] Fairbanks and [John S.] Kimball, two of the brethren that we dont know much, and Dr [Charles] Follen. The Ladies were Mrs [Lydia Maria] Child, [Louisa Gilman] Loring and [Eliza Lee Cabot] Follen, Ann and Mary [Chapman], Ange Ammidon, Caroline, Debora and I [Anne Weston]."[20]

At Maria's, "the business was carried on regularly, every thing being moved, voted, and all in order. Mr May recording. At the same time, all talked freely; the Ladies giving their opinion." In 1836 the "woman question" had yet to emerge as an organizational issue, and such interaction, though subject to note, was not subject to objection.[21] The boards of the Boston Female Anti-Slavery and Non-Resistance Societies also met at the Chapman house on occasion, perhaps because of its central location, or to accommodate a young mother serving as an officer of each society and one of their most visible and valued members.[22]

The "Boston clique" of Garrisonians gathered at Maria's for informal political discussions. The Chapman home provided a space in which Garrison tried out his speeches, addresses, and editorials before an intelligent, critical, and politically savvy audience.[23] Crafting strategy in times of political conflict within the movement or of urban unrest by anti-abolitionists frequently involved small meetings at the Chapman home. "Garrison spent the evening at Maria's and we had much important talk," Anne reported. Urging her sister to "breathe not its name," she informed Debora that the "Pastoral Letter" attacking female antislavery activism and the Garrisonian strategy of holding church denominations responsible for supporting slavery if they did not take a public stand against it, had so shaken the New York offices of the American Anti-Slavery Society (AAS) as to cause "the very elect" to "deny the faith." Indeed, she asserted, the executive committee were "all shivering in the wind."[24]

Ultimately the committee would fold and then peel away from the AAS to form the new American and Foreign Anti-Slavery Society, but in the meantime Maria sought to caulk the holes in the walls. She wrote to Elizur Wright and Theodore Weld, "giving it to them about right," and to William Goodell "signifying her approbation, for he alone has borne himself valiantly."[25] As Anne explained, "The National seems to consider the appeal as a quarrel between brethren, as if [the Reverend Charles] Fitch was about as right as the others &c. [The] Mass[achusetts Anti-Slavery Society] itself seems to stand pretty strong, and we hope to win through this, but it is considered a dark hour. Mary Parker [president of the BFAS] waxes valiant in fight and it is to be hoped that the Female Society will stand to their colours."[26] They did not entirely, and it was to the Chapman abode that the female Garrisonians retreated following the stormy session of the BFAS at the 1839 annual meeting, where the legitimacy of women voting in convention was put forward as a test of MAS organizational membership. Anne, so tired that she "could hardly sit up," poured tea for forty as they assessed the day's developments.[27]

The Chapman town house provided a forum for informal political education and organizational maneuvering as well. Maria noted, for example, that Laura and James Boyle, to whom she had given "a roving commission to a tea-fight," were scheduled to "come up to the assault on [T]hursday evening." The Boyles "wanted to talk over all about the cause."[28] Maria arranged for agent John A. Collins and his wife to join them, ensuring that the tea party would not only address the Massachusetts "colored laws" that were of immediate interest to the Boyles but also provide an opportunity to assess whether James Boyle could be persuaded to fill Collins's position as general agent of the MAS.[29] Maria wanted to broach the idea informally and gauge Boyle's reaction before the board addressed the appointment formally.

Caroline offered a glimpse into the nature of these "tea-fights." As she reported to Anne, "The Alcotts have invited M[aria] to go there Saturday night as they think that she may do Mrs M[orrison] great good—and as to use Mrs A's own reason 'Mrs M is good at description'—so I suppose Maria is considered quite a shew—Mrs M is to come to Maria Sunday evening." She then provided a detailed account of the Alcotts' return visit. "In the evening went to Maria's. Mrs Morrison, Ann Terry [Greene] and the Chapmans and the Alcotts there. Mrs M was brought by Mrs Alcott to be convinced that Mrs Furness and her abolitionism was not the real article. Mrs Alcott having tried in vain to enlighten her ignorance, Maria succeeded in opening her eyes, though she did not say much, and what she did say not very strong."[30] Thus these social occasions served as community opinion-shapers and opportunities for the political education of potential female recruits to the cause.

So too the household served as a communications center for political news and information. One or another sister routinely checked the antislavery rooms in Washington Street for newspapers and letters from agents in the field or associates abroad.[31] They interrogated visitors who called frequently to dispense whatever intelligence they might add to the common fund.[32] Anne reported, for example, "Mary [Chapman] called in the afternoon and in the evening [Stephen] Foster and [Francis] Jackson. Foster has got 100 subscribers for the *Liberator*. Jackson seemed in good spirits, said he was going to Barnstable with [John A.] Collins. . . . E[dmund] Quincy called here a moment to day. He goes to Hartford at the meeting of the 19th."[33] Thus, within two days, three prominent male leaders of the Garrisonian movement dropped in on the Chapman household with no specific agenda other than to share and gather the latest news, engage in political conversation, and enjoy abolitionist fellowship with these sisters.

On returning to Boston from his in-laws' home in Connecticut, Garrison called immediately at Maria's, staying to tea in the evening and returning later to spend the night. After time away from the Boston abolitionist scene, he sought to catch up on both formal business and informal gossip. Such behavior was usual practice for Garrison. So too Lydia Maria Child, John Greenleaf Whittier, and Samuel J. May routinely dropped in when business or pleasure took them into the city. Publisher Oliver Johnson brought letters for the *Liberator*, which he and Maria edited in Garrison's absence. Whenever possible, both he and Dr. Amos Farnsworth of Groton brought newspapers from around the state to update the Westons with the most recent movement lore.[34] Such gatherings provided almost daily intercourse during which members of the Boston clique heard "fresh afresh [*sic*] the daily occurrences & even the flying rumors" that shaped the broader social and political context in which they acted.[35]

So well established a center of sociability, congeniality, and progressive fellowship was Maria's salon that Edmund Quincy called it his "other home." It was at Maria's town house that he enjoyed "the true society" of "educated accomplished minds informed and elevated by devotion to great and sublime principles." He told her that while he had "seen much of society in various parts of the country and [had] been familiar with fashionable literary and religious circles," he had "never found what satisfied my heart till I became intimate with your family and the circle of friends which gather around it—for I never before found genius and talent without vanity and the thirst for display, literature without a slight tinge of pedantry or strong, pervading religious feeling without some admixture of cant."[36] Fulsome as it was, the sentiment reflected the viewpoint of many Garrisonians.

The Chapman home provided not only an afternoon's or evening's social and intellectual exchange but also a night's hospitality. Lucretia Mott and J. Miller McKim from Philadelphia, the Tappan sisters from New York City, George Thompson from Great Britain, and many activists and curiosity-seekers from around provincial Massachusetts stayed at the Chapmans' on their occasional visits to Boston.[37] Along with Henry, Maria arranged the sleeping arrangements when a Deacon Tarbell and his companion Miss Sessions were put off the Weymouth stage and sought refuge for the night. "Which will be the best arrangements? to put Deacon Tarbell in the Lower chamber, & Miss Sessions in the Dressing-room, or Deacon Tarbell in the Dressing Room, Miss Sessions in our chamber; & we in the Lower chamber? It is all the abolition there is in the Western Counties, and 'by coarse' as the dustman says, deserves a nights lodging of us."[38]

Bazaar and convention time packed the house with saleswomen coming into Boston to assist at tables sponsored by their local societies. So too conference-goers sought to ease expenses while expanding their acquaintance in the movement by staying at the Chapmans'.[39] Caroline, when teaching in New Bedford, knew to put her bid in early at such times, particularly during the years when her brother Hervey lived with the Chapmans while trying to establish his medical practice in Boston. "Tell Hervey that I shall expect him to give up his chamber to me for the time of the fair & I will take in any body that may be offered me—he can sleep somewhere else or be hung on a peg."[40] A few years later she apologized to Lucia for entirely forgetting to save room for her, although, she wrote, "Maria said and *I* suppose you would come all the same." She determined to "put the precise Emma in *garret*—large bed—Debora in *cot*—and the others in large bed—below—so if you bring bed clothes all shall be taken care of, and returned, all can be accommodated."[41] Despite the gaggle of Westons at fair time, other close friends and allies expected to be made welcome, among them Evelina A. S. Smith, who assured Caroline that she would be very happy to accept their invitation, despite knowing "you have a great many to accommodate and to look after at that time." She assured her cousin, "I can put up with very few accommodations and shall give my friends, I hope, very little trouble."[42] Typically, the women slept several to a bed during fair or meeting times.

The Chapman household offered a space as well for the intellectual work necessary in bringing about political change. In April of 1836, Maria came before the public as an author for the first time when the *Liberator* printed a hymn she had written for the MAS quarterly meeting. And when *Songs of the Free*, a collection of antislavery hymns gathered with the help of Eliza Cabot Follen, came out in June, an advertisement in the *Liberator* read: "When we mention, that it has been published under the critical and exclusive superintendance of the talented authoress of 'RIGHT AND WRONG IN BOSTON,' the announcement alone will be sufficient to draw general attention to it, and to insure for it a wide-spread circulation." The advertisement also included names of various "female writers" who had contributed poems to the collection, including her sisters Anne and Caroline Weston and her sister-in-law Ann Greene Chapman.[43] For a quarter century, antislavery conventions and society meetings routinely used the hymnal.

Each year for ten years, Maria wrote at home the BFAS published annual reports. She transformed the traditional format used by charitable female organizations that recorded a list of officers and members and provided an accounting of funds acquired, materials distributed, and projects undertaken. Maria added a partisan and provocative history of the year-in-abolition through Garrisonian eyes. Her annual histories met with both acclaim and denunciation, the latter growing stronger as Garrisonians battled first the orthodox clergy who wished to keep abolition from their houses of worship and then those in search of electoral success who sought to build an antislavery coalition to compete for electoral supremacy. From 1835 to 1840, Maria's reports were undertaken as formal documents written for and sanctioned by the BFAS.

Although Maria authored these annual histories, production was a sibling enterprise in which the Westons debated ideas and language, conducted research, and helped organize material before proofreading the final document. In 1839, for example, Debora anxiously reminded Anne, who, because of her teaching commitments, could "only act in a Boston capacity Saturday and Sunday," to ensure that Caroline had the proof sheets "thoroughly scrutinized, in respect to accuracy."[44] In New Bedford, Debora obtained at Maria's request a letter written by Rev. Amos A. Phelps to Joseph Emerson, her academic mentor and friend. This letter provided evidence of public duplicity among key figures in the anti-Garrisonian "new organization."[45]

From 1840 to 1848, the Chapman abode served as the editorial office of the *Liberty Bell*, an annual magazine of essays, poetry, and biography.[46] Sold to fair visitors and distributed without charge to fair workers, it served as acknowledgment of an individual's contribution to the cause and a memento of the occasion.[47] One idea for the publication originated with Ann Greene Chapman, who spoke of filling an album with contributions from antislavery friends.[48] She had made a beginning on such a project for herself and, on her deathbed in 1837, gave the scrapbook to Anne Warren Weston, urging her to finish the effort. Maria described the process of obtaining contributions to Wendell and Ann T. G. Phillips in hope of eliciting their assistance. She and her sisters had solicited work from such celebrated Europeans as the Irish M.P. Daniel O'Connell, British authors Harriet Martineau and William and Mary Howitt, philosopher George Combe, and actress and antislavery memoirist Fanny Butler. "Now we want you to do your possibles with whatever writers you fall in with," she wrote the Phillipses. "There are the French deputies. St Anthoine, Dumas, La Martine—Do attack them ferociously with a troop of horse shod with felt. Combine urgency and suavity to that degree that they cannot refuse. But above all remember to write yourself. We could not as you see, send our 1st number to press without Wendell's name."[49]

It was in the Chapman town home, surrounded by her sisters' sharp-witted conversation and a library of religious scholarship, political theory, and abolitionist tracts, that Anne drafted, and her sisters vetted, the BFAS response to the General Association of Congregational Ministers' "Pasto-ral Letter" of 1837 critiquing female public activism.[50] Working side by side, discussing language and strategy, the sisters-in-residence continued on many an occasion to spend "most of the day in writing protests." Anne described one such day taken up by writing letters to Ohio, fielding anx-ious local calls, then writing more letters to Ohio.[51]

Letter writing occupied many hours in all Weston abodes and both Weston households, but particularly Maria's.[52] Considerable correspon-dence involved formal antislavery business, as Maria, Caroline, and Anne served, at various times, as recording, domestic corresponding, or foreign corresponding secretaries of the Boston Female.[53] No matter who bore the title, the work was largely accomplished in the Boston town house, whose location facilitated access to Maria's collection of newspapers and docu-ments, the antislavery offices and library, and key individuals in the BFAS and MAS with whom the writers might choose to consult. From these spaces the sisterhood sent out letters of support to the newly converted and offered advice to new societies on model constitutions and resolu-tions, information on current events roiling the movement, explanations of tactics and strategy, and responses to queries both sophisticated and naive about doctrine, petitioning, and fund-raising. They supplied tracts, newspapers, and suggestions for itinerant or local speakers. As strains within the movement in general, and the BFAS in particular, grew more divisive, Anne reported that she and Maria "spent most of the day in di-recting protests, writing as little in them as circumstances seemed to di-rect. We have written to many people and to all the female Societies."[54]

In addition to the work of educating the public, petitioning Congress, and organizing women to stand up and speak for their beliefs in their churches and communities, the Westons expanded and formalized fund-raising to pay the salaries and expenses of professional agents, the pub-lication costs of newspapers and tracts, and the operating costs of local, regional, and national associations. In their capacity as organizers and managers, the Westons corresponded with a vast array of individuals across the Northeast and abroad, soliciting contributions and volunteers year after year.

Caroline, for example, assured her siblings that she was "looking out for the Fair" and, "in the midst and multiplicity" of her engagements was writing "to all whom I know to help."[55] A letter from Harriet Miller of

Milton attests to the Westons' continuous priming of the pump. In response to Maria's request, Miller provided a list of five women who might contribute. All were solicited. A note from S. Lincoln Gardner replied to a similar query, identifying potential contributors from Warren, New Braintree, Hubbardston, South Orange, Athol, Westminster, Fitchburg, Bolton, Leominster, Boylston, Upton, Royalton, and Ashburnham.[56]

The Chapman town house served as the epicenter of fair organizing and management.[57] In addition to hosting the volunteer sales force that came to Boston for the duration of the annual bazaar, Maria's household provided a meeting space for committees of arrangement and for the BFAS sewing circle that met regularly to produce items for sale.[58]

Early on, the Weston sisters set up a lighthearted competition with their in-laws (the Chapmans living in Boston's Chauncy Place), pitting the two households against each other in the production of fair goods. Maria's mother-in-law, Sarah Greene Chapman, and her daughters Ann and Mary were "at work furiously for the fair, and *there's no telling* what they will have done," Caroline informed Anne as she wrote from Maria's in 1836. "I mean to do a good deal in the shape of work—and we shall try to beat them." Even Lucia and Emma, the youngest sisters, joined in fair work. In 1839, for example, sixteen-year-old Lucia apologized for neglecting Debora, explaining that after coming to town a week previously she had simply been too "engaged in working for the fair [to have] written." Fourteen-year-old Emma and Aunt Mary Weston had accompanied her to Maria's, "so that we had quite a 'bee.'"[59]

Maria's town house provided a place to receive, store, sort, and price goods, mail out thank-you notes to contributors (with their copies of the *Liberty Bell*), and write the fair report for the *Liberator*. Anne noted the household's practical necessity during those years of having to manage the fair from Weymouth after Maria left for Europe and closed her town house. "A person occupying my position should *live* in Boston," she explained. "Not living in Boston, we do our work there at a great disadvantage. I make arrangements to be there a few days, perhaps, then new work comes up, or new delays arise & I have to hurry my affairs & crowd into those few days what really might fill a week."[60]

Without the house in town, Anne felt obliged to leave much of her work "undone till the fortnight that precedes the opening of the bazaar." She found it almost impossible to do all that was required in so short a time: "Every foreign box has to be unpacked, marked & noted, & the requests therein contained, observed & complied with as far as may be in our power. Supplies for the refreshment table obtained. Door keeper &

other officials engaged, letters from sundry friends in the country to be answered, some proposing to come as helpers (& many of these are really hindrances). Advertisements to be drawn up. 1000 notes to the gentility of Boston folded, sealed & directed, & all this devolves on my sister [Debora], myself & Mr May together with a multitude of other details to which I dont refer." Numerous women could be counted upon for aid. Anne reported, "Mrs May (Mr May's *mother*,) Mrs [William L.] Garrison, Mrs [Theodore] Parker, Mrs [Ellis Gray] Loring, & Anna L[oring, their daughter] & several others extremely useful," but she found nonetheless that "it is we three [Debora, Anne, and Caroline] who are the people on whom the responsibility rests."[61]

To organize this logistical nightmare, she would "need twice the time" that had been necessary before her sisters went abroad, even after turning over some responsibilities associated with the fair to antislavery men: production of the *Liberty Bell* to Edmund Quincy, for example, and a variety of organizational details to Samuel J. May.[62] When Maria returned from abroad in 1855, she, like Anne before her, organized the fair from Weymouth with Debora's help. "I have been very busy, Maria and I, for the last three days over the fair things," Debora wrote. They had stored the goods in a coach house and, with the fair upon them, had to quickly unpack, mark, and repack the goods for transport to the Boston hall reserved for the fair. There the goods could be prepared for presentation and sale. "It is a dreadful work and disturbs my sleep," she confessed. She suffered nightmares in which she went into the garden to water newly planted flowers only to find, "as the water washed away the earth . . . a whole crop of worsted mats, bugles, beads, cushions, &c 'protruding their noses' like the ghouls in 'Natheds.'"[63] The difficulty of carrying on the fair after 1848 was not simply the lack of a house in Boston but the loss of the household there. It had less to do with the lack of a convenient space in which to work than with the absence of sibling labor and colleageiality to accomplish it.

The 1854 report of the twentieth annual bazaar reflected Anne's exhaustion with the task and, even more telling, her feelings of isolation in the face of a geographically spread out sibling band and declining participation among Boston's reform women. As she wrote, "The interest afforded by novelty and the spirit of adventure has long since died away. The number of abolitionists in the city . . . is necessarily small, and of that small number, only a few are so situated as to give to the bazaar much earnest and effective labor. Many of the committee do not reside in Boston, and several of its most efficient members [such as her sisters] are absent from the country." She utilized the familiar language of Christian "suffering"—of acts "ennobled and sanctified" by sacrifices "cast upon the altar of our faith"—to express her struggle to keep the fund-raiser afloat.[64]

Then, too, while innovation and commercialization had expanded consumer interest in the fair, they had also alienated some longtime supporters. Abby Kelley Foster, for example, refused to append her name to the bazaar announcement (the "call") in 1851 because she disapproved of raffles, an innovation proposed to enliven attendance that year. In the West, Garrisonian Sarah Otis Ernst objected that "it *is* gambling the best we can make of it and it seems to me the high toned principle which characterizes the Old Society ought to shun *all sin*."[65] Maria herself feared that moral influence had been sacrificed to crass profiteering, and the fair had lost its ability to move hearts as well as pocketbooks. Where once the production of wares for the fair had caused women to identify with the slave as they crafted goods, by the 1850s the best-selling items were foreign or factory made. Indeed, the Weymouth sisterhood had so tastefully selected European goods on their travels throughout France, England, Italy, and Germany that the fair advertisements for 1855 to 1857 enumerated only these.[66]

The depression of 1857 reduced the production of bazaar goods and proceeds. Gross profits of $5,250 for 1856 fell to a net gain of $3,800 for the 1857–58 fair.[67] According to Chapman's analysis, the "great cotton manufactures, who have been so long in alliance with the plantations that they can hardly conceive of any other mode of existence," had been "our best customers heretofore—they and their parasites—out of a sort of expiatory politeness at the thought of their mobocratic violence of past times. This year their bankruptcy prevented their coming to buy." In consequence, the fair directors retained fully half of the contributions sent them for sale and faced a massive effort to dispose of these over the course of the succeeding year. Indeed, the Westons estimated that "the price of every thing is so much reduced, that, taken together—with the diminished resources of buyers it will prevent a market, not only this year but for two years to come."[68]

There was also increasing competition for volunteer production of bazaar goods. Many sewing circles found aiding fugitive slaves and ameliorating the condition of poor blacks a more compelling project for their sewing circles than contributing to the fairs that supported AAS agitation.[69] The Boston fair announcement for 1856 explicitly spoke to them: "Let all who pity fugitives help us; for our funds go directly to awaken that public sympathy which gives the slave a refuge on every threshold."[70] In an oblique attack on Frederick Douglass, whose Rochester newspaper competed with MAS priorities for contributions, Chapman deprecated the idea that "assistance, given to the men freed by their own heroism can be accepted as an equivalent for direct, positive Anti-Slavery action."[71] Competing demands on British reformers for charitable contributions to numerous local and colonial causes made it ever more difficult to sustain support abroad for the AAS.[72] Chapman foresaw the falling away of French contributions as well once she left Paris.[73]

Given all these factors, the Westons decided to do away with the bazaar and to replace it with a more direct means of soliciting the money needed to sustain the various projects of the AAS. Maria tried to sell the idea as a matter of abhorring the effects of routine on human consciousness and spirit: "We ought not to settle down into trade," she argued.[74] But in fact, without her town house and the full complement of her sibling cohort, it was simply impractical to continue. The labor could not be accomplished by only one or two Westons based solely in Weymouth.[75]

The key to Weston productivity and impact during four decades from the 1830s to the early 1860s was sorority. Shared beliefs and shared labor in a common household sped hands and minds. Workloads diminished, both literally and figuratively, when undertaken together. Collaboration built affection and inspired a high degree of productivity. The sisters looked after each other and, in so doing, looked after the cause of slavery's abolition. "I should feel much easier if you were in Boston," wrote Debora to Anne, "and I wish you would stay there, not altogether on my own account, but on Maria's for it must be a great help to her to have you."[76] Commitment to the work kept their spirits high and reinforced their engagement with the cause and one another. Wrote Anne from Italy, where she had repaired to visit the invalided Lucia in the aftermath of several difficult years on both family and antislavery fronts, "Looking at matters from this distance I feel very hopeless. Perhaps the very sad condition of things immediately around me, the oppression, the superstition, the terrible condition of the masses of the people . . . tend to dispiriting reflections, for I really feel less encouraged about Abolition than when at home. It may be because I am sitting still. People find their best encouragement in feeling that they themselves are hard at work."[77] The lack of work, not a heavy workload, and the loss of collegiality in that work produced both languor and hopelessness among siblings who thrived on both.

So too working alone sapped the fun from the enterprise. Debora suffered particularly when she first went to New Bedford, as the townsite did not permit nightly commuting to Boston as had Weymouth or Roxbury. Without her sisters for much of her time there, she found that her ardor in organizing abolition in New Bedford left her "more fatigued" than energized. "The Anti-slavery business here is rather dull," she reported. "The Female Society here is struggling on and will I hope come to something."[78] Returning after the 1840 Boston fair, she found herself feeling "so miserably" that she "had no heart for any thing." She brought work with her, but without her sisters to share the responsibility and the effort or enliven her spirits, she found "those *fair articles* that I brought with me to sell, rested on my mind like a dead weight." She felt "not a minutes comfort till they were sold, think[ing] perhaps that Maria was suffering for the money and depending upon me for it." Debora retired briefly into illness—a "face ache"—then rallied, feeling "that I must do or die, so rushed out and *peddled* my goods from house to house, that is to say I took them to those houses where I thought they would be likely to see" and managed to sell most of her load. "I got $28.00 for Maria, don't you think I did very well?" she asked.[79] That she did the job primarily for Maria, and worried she would have let Maria down had she failed, was telling. Debora worked alone and in pain for her sister rather than the cause; it was Maria, not the slave, who put her back on her feet and selling.

8

IMPUDENT PUPPIES

Sisters in the Household of the Faith

In 1852 Anne Warren Weston wrote Wendell Phillips asking him to address the annual Weymouth antislavery fund-raising fair. She informed him of "the bold step we have taken in announcing dancing in the last evening." "This is our last card," she wrote, "& I hope by playing it we may make $50. In this trust, I lend the influence of my respectability to what Mr Perkins & all his church have laboured very successfully for the last 40 years to stigmatize as the great sin of the age."[1] Weymouth's Rev. Jonas Perkins was antislavery but also anti-Garrisonian; Anne implied that churchmen who policed dancing more stringently than slavery were irrelevant at best and complicit at worst. She teased Phillips, inciting him to share her ignominy: "Now I think that you had better come down from Northampton with the intention of staying over the dance. You can . . . pirouette to the admiration of the whole household of faith. It is not every day that people get a chance to *dance for the Cause*."[2]

This was vintage Anne—witty with a touch of the minx, flaunting her lack of respectability before one of the brethren and daring him to join her in shocking the more pious sisters and brothers of antislavery's house.[3] She was well aware that many critics in Weymouth and beyond had questioned her good repute and that of her sisters. Dancing was hardly the Westons' most scandalous act, not even their first "disreputable" contribution to antislavery fund-raising. However, she implied, the sisters and brothers who peopled the Garrisonian "household of faith" shared a sense of proportion, caring little for what commonly passed as propriety and greatly about enslavement as a sin against God and mankind.

The Westons took every opportunity to poke fun at Weymouth clergy, particularly Perkins, the 1813 graduate of Brown University who ministered to the Weymouth Union Church from 1815 to 1860 and helped author the anti-Garrisonian "Appeal of Clerical Abolitionists on Anti-slavery Measures." Caroline, in describing the "Appeal" as his "first disaffection" from abolition, implied that affection grew among those bound to the cause and working together in its traces. She challenged Perkins's gravitas by labeling the "Appeal" "a curious document signed by three or five very insignificant orthodox ministers who were collectively used as cat's-paw by much more important men."[4]

Debora expressed the family's dim view of Perkins when reflecting ironically on a sermon delivered in New Bedford by a visiting clergyman, Reverend Gould of Fairhaven, Connecticut. "I enjoyed it very much it seemed so like Weymouth," she wrote. "He is a real *Perkinsite.*" In her opinion, Gould was a self-important man who lacked subtlety and opportunistically suited his antislavery rhetoric to his audience.[5] Mary Weston agreed. She reported to her nieces that, at a joint meeting of the two Weymouth female antislavery societies, the Weymouth and Braintree Female Emancipation Society and the South Weymouth Female Anti-Slavery Society, Perkins "walked in [with his wife and mother] as if it had been a meeting of his own, & proceeded to read a chapt[er] from James, 'Go the[e] now ye rich men,' then made some observations on the chapt[er] which was strong meat, much as to say that Emancipation must come. Some contended it could not without bloodshed—'we are not of that number, we have proof that it can—but what if it cannot—why let it come, emancipation must take place.'" Of the abolition prayer Perkins then offered, Mary Weston wrote, "If he only would make such an one in his pulpit I would ask no more of him."[6]

In their antislavery labors the Westons frequently ran afoul of "cocky Perkins," making no secret of their distaste for his pretentiousness and utter conviction that women required the governance of men.[7] His modus operandi was to insert himself into the workings of the Weymouth Female by using his wife, Rhoda Keith Perkins, in ways the Westons found demeaning to her, insulting to the membership, and inappropriate for a self-governing woman's organization.[8] At the annual meeting in September 1837, for example, Hannah Cranch Bond Fifield, the Westons' friend, moved that Rev. Amos Phelps, a Massachusetts Anti-Slavery Society (MAS) general agent and, at the time, a Garrisonian immediatist, be invited to address the group. "It was opposed in small measure, but passed," and the society directed Fifield, as corresponding secretary, to extend the invitation. Rhoda Perkins asked that the matter not be put to a vote, but Mary Weston, as president, ruled that parliamentary order required it. The motion passed after several recounts necessitated by timid members who spoke in low voices and refused, in the face of the minister's wife, to stand and be counted when the voice vote proved inconclusive.

Later that evening, Hannah Fifield received a visit at home from the Reverend and Rhoda Perkins, "telling [Fifield] *he* wished her not to write to Mr. Phelps at present, as he had more questions to ask Mr. Phelps, which if [Phelps] answered to Mr. P[erkin]s satisfaction, he might come, if not [Phelps] should not be admitted to his pulpit." Perkins insisted on calling another meeting of the Weymouth Female to reconsider its vote, and Fifield questioned whether "*he* could call a meeting of the female society." Perkins replied that his wife would front the request. Hannah hurried across the back field to warn the Westons of impending trouble. Mary coolly announced that she had already written up the minutes for the *Liberator* and would send them immediately to Maria in Boston for proofing and transmission to the antislavery office. "Now say what you think of all these proceedings," she told Debora, "I call it 'high-handed.'"[9] Two years later Amos Phelps rejected the MAS and its policies, joined the anti-Garrisonian Massachusetts Abolition Society, and supported the Liberty Party. Only then did Perkins extend to Phelps an invitation to speak from his pulpit at morning services.[10]

Perkins was not the only Weymouth minister to clash with the Westons over their gender insubordination and antislavery politics. The Reverend Wales Lewis, minister of Weymouth's Second Parish, found the sisters insolent and their politics dangerous.[11] After Garrison gave an October 1836 address in Weymouth, Lewis joined Perkins in publicly denouncing the doctrine of immediate abolition. Eliza S. Loud, a member of both Lewis's congregation and the South Weymouth Female Anti-Slavery Society (which, in Weston opinion, lacked the reformist stuff of "our part of the town"),[12] expressed her pastor's views to Mary Weston, who had called to request her help with the upcoming Boston antislavery bazaar. The South Weymouth Female society happened to meet at the Loud home the same afternoon, so Mary remained. She reported to her nieces that Rev. Wales Lewis "was there *nearly* all the time," and, of the six or eight women who appeared, his presence seemed to encourage three to "peel" away from Garrison. "I was prepared to *fight* and *vote* him," she wrote, "but he was quite straight. This time we did not come to the real screws, but I sat without *fear* and said Garrison, Liberator and other obnoxious words with utmost calmness."[13]

Mary's behavior surely irritated both Lewis and Loud. A "beloved friend" to Phebe Nash Weston, Eliza Loud often visited her for tea and conversation. On one such visit she expressed unease over Weymouth gossip. "[Y]ou mustn't mind that," said Mary Weston. "People will talk, there's your minister [Lewis] who says that we are all infidels. Indeed, said Mrs. Loud with a good deal of spite, 'I never heard that, I know he says that the Westons are all impudent puppies.'"[14]

The charge of "impudence" often attached to the Westons as it did to other abolitionist women, Garrisonians in particular. The local Weymouth clergy objected to their public independent-mindedness, self-assurance, and sense of gender equality. Other male activists, political allies and foes alike, believed that their authority and status were undermined by these women. Particularly in the 1830s, ministers, deacons, and other pastoral officers of Boston's churches accused antislavery women of impudence when they insisted upon inserting notices of BFAS meetings among the announcements of charitable association gatherings and reform lectures routinely read to the city's congregations by sextons or deacons before the worship service.[15] Deeming antislavery gatherings to be political rather than benevolent in intent, these men objected to lending the church's imprimatur to so radical a movement. The Westons carried their notices to as many churches as possible of a Sunday only to find themselves abused by pulpit and congregation as arrogant, high-handed, and presumptuous, motivated by an impertinent (because female), unfeminine, and unchristian contempt for (male) clerical authority.[16]

One Sunday in 1836, for example, many of Boston's elite watched Maria "standing quietly in the Chapman pew" belonging to her father-in-law at the Federal Street Unitarian church.[17] On this occasion, Maria had put forward the announcement of a BFAS meeting despite a policy decision by church elders dictating an end to such publicity. Although angry at the hapless sexton, a Mr. Brown, who read the BFAS announcement, parishioners correctly assumed that Chapman had intentionally violated church policy. One congregant leaned forward to ask another in the adjacent pew whether he did not feel insulted by her act. Samuel E. Sewall later remarked, "Never was such a stir" as he witnessed that day.[18]

On the first Sunday of June 1836, Maria further inflamed the congregation's ire by calmly walking to the vestibule of the church, as usual after the service, and mixing with other worshipers in casual conversation. This act struck her Christian brethren and fellow congregants as dismissive of their disapproval, an attempt to "brazen out" her bad behavior in submitting the BFAS notice of meeting. Their use of the term "brazen" may have been intended to slander Maria as sexually provocative, or perhaps they lacked language to express the idea of an offensive, gendered arrogance in other than sexual terms.

Abigail May Alcott, who had been wandering "unsuspectingly on the porch to look up a missing child, heard loud declamation against Mrs. Chapman's *impudence* and declared determination to *insult* her." The brethren may have meant they would physically attack her person, verbally smear her reputation, cut her acquaintance on the street, call her before the church's ruling body to answer for her actions, or refuse her admission to communion—all consequences that were meted out to her at one time or another. One complained that Maria dared look at him, a charge that Lydia Maria Child likened to "the child's complaint of the boy 'Boos 'ooked at me.'" Boston newspapers played up the incident. The *Commercial Gazette*, for example, describing the controversy as "done by the tinkery of a prominent member of the Abolition society."[19] To label Maria's actions "tinkery" was, of course, to diminish the substance of the notice as well as to undermine the sincerity of its proffer while promoting a perception that her purpose had been to make fools of those who governed the congregation and legislated church policy.

In the 1840s, George Bradburn, a prominent Bostonian, one-time state legislator, and recipient of Weston hospitality on several occasions, leveled the slur of impudence at Maria when she admonished his "conduct in relation to the Liberty Party." She implied that Bradburn stood to gain personally from raising up a political party to counter "slave power" in Congress, a strategy opposed by the very organization that paid his salary and "cloth[ed him]" with their credit and commission." Infuriated by her temerity in questioning his character, Bradburn expressed disgust with Maria's "impertinent, impudent, insolent" manner.[20]

So too, David L. Child and Frederick Douglass objected to the directness of her language and her authoritative manner in asserting her viewpoint. Her temerity in critiquing their work or questioning their politics caused considerable ill feeling. Gender, as much as or more than the substance of their disagreement, caused these abolitionists to dismiss intellectual or operational critiques they might have considered seriously from a man. While they took her flattery as a given, they objected to her exertion of political discipline over them, even as she spoke with the authority of the MAS board behind her. When Child complained about her oversight to the MAS board that had assigned her to deal with him on matters relating to his editorship of the *National Anti-Slavery Standard*, Maria asked him directly, "Is it, in your view or to your feelings uncomfortable or unjustifiable that I should speak thus?"[21] Douglass accused her of "driving" him, a form of mastery he rejected from a man yet found even more insulting from a woman.[22] Edmund Quincy teased Caroline about Maria's having been chosen to sift the wheat from the chaff for the MAS executive committee, saying, "If great things be done by this corps [the board], the Lord has again chosen the weak things of the earth to confound the things that are mighty."[23]

Thus spread the Weston reputation for "impudence," a term signifying contumacy more than mere impropriety. Gendered female, impudence connoted shameless effrontery, insolent disrespect, obstinate disobedience, unabashed presumption, insubordination, and a contemptuous disregard for male authority, all of which challenged the habits of superordination and deference constituting gender differentiation in the American church and social order. "Impudence" was also the term antebellum slave owners attached to slaves whom they identified as failing to show proper obeisance as well as obedience, and arbiters of class and taste used the term to describe those of lower social status who exhibited a lack of proper respect for their "betters" by ignoring upper-class sensibilities. To be challenged by the daughter-in-law and wife of two of Boston's merchant princes in one of the city's leading churches constituted a deliberate flouting of male authority in the eyes of the clergy and those conservative men of standing who made up the congregation's leadership.

One critic penned an abusive letter explicitly identifying the source of Maria's insolence as the ineffective governance of her "head" or husband. Calvin Allen told Maria she had made herself "ridiculously conspicuous" in "pursuing a course which God and nature never intended to be pursued by [her] sex." He charged her with operating out of "infatuation" with her prominence (by which he meant an inappropriate and unfeminine interest in renown) and urged her, "for sake of the honour of [your] sex, to . . . strive to put on the garb of modesty, which you are at present so totally destitute of, do this . . . for the sake of that respect which you ought to cherish for your husband."[24]

In custom as well as law, Henry G. Chapman, like Warren Weston, was expected to govern his household and was held responsible for the behavior of his dependents. The communities of abolition and anti-abolition alike assumed that Maria and her sisters would never have pursued so inappropriate and public a course of action had her husband or their father asserted proper authority. One New Bedford abolitionist expressed this view of Henry's role and the costs of rejecting it, even as she praised his submission to what she assumed was Maria's intent: "How happy I am that *Mr* Chapman cooperates so well in his wife's plans. It must require great independence to do it in the midst of so much opposition on the wharf and on charge."[25] Ambiguous at best, this correspondent's praise of Henry's willing acquiescence to his wife's political views, despite the resulting pressure on his and his father's business, suggested not manly independence but rather emasculation. The writer seemed oblivious to the possibility that Henry's own commitment to the cause drove his actions.

Henry's seeming inability or refusal to curb the behavior of his wife and sisters-in-law raised questions in the minds of many, abolitionists and anti-abolitionists alike, as to whether he was capable of carrying out his proper social role as head of household. If not man enough to govern his dependents, how could he be trusted with civic or business responsibility? In the early to mid-1830s, when women were just beginning to attend public lectures, court trials, and political debates, when they sat silently in the churches and men presided over female antislavery society meetings, Maria's willingness to face down the mayor of Boston during a mob, Henry's business colleagues in her living room, Boston's editors in their newspapers, and the city's clergy in their churches left those same men wondering who wore the pants in the household, Henry G. Chapman or "Mrs. Chapman and sisters."[26]

The "and sisters" suggested that the Westons, lacking husbands of their own and adequate paternal or fraternal governors, ought to have been more closely supervised by Henry because they spent so much time under his roof.[27] While the Westons viewed Henry as a good husband and brother-in-law for respecting their sisterhood, their reputations for independence and gender-inappropriate behavior branded him an ineffectual head of household among many of his fellow pew-holders, householders, and customers, particularly those who feared that abolitionist publicity would undermine the considerable economic business Massachusetts did with southern states.

In the second quarter of the nineteenth century, growing scrutiny of household relations, and of the prerogatives and obligations of heads of household, magnified the importance of perceived challenges to male rule by political sisters and wives.[28] Issues of governance—the proper subordination of dependents, the diminishing power of fathers to organize their daughters' marriages and their sons' labor, and the growing independence of women—roiled antislavery politics.[29] In the summer of 1837, for example, the *Liberator* reported an incident in which one local head of household confronted a group of young, presumably unwed women on his doorstep seeking any ladies within who might be interested in signing an antislavery petition. He "answered in a very decided, contemptuous manner, 'NO'—without even so much as asking them." The petitioners concluded that he "belonged to that class of men who claim the right to 'possess exclusive jurisdiction in all cases whatsoever' over their wives' consciences."[30]

The signature gatherers left and walked to another house, where they were met at the door by a father who declared that he hoped no one in his house would sign their petitions, proclaiming it "an insult to the public to send such papers to congress, and a very great imposition, altogether too bad, to send young people about in that manner, on such despicable business." When the petition carrier explained that she and her companions engaged in their task "because we thought it our duty to do what was in our power for the oppressed," the head of household ordered her "to be gone and to mind and never bring *such a thing to his house again*." When she refused to leave, saying that she wished to give the women of the house a chance to do their duty, the man sent the canvassers on their way with, "It's none of your business, *gals*, and you'd better go *right straight home*." He assumed that there a worthy head of household would assert his proper authority over their too-great liberty of thought and action.[31]

That the Weston sisters, married and single, might operate independently of husband, father, or brothers posed a challenge to the strength and security of the boundaries believed to separate the male domain from the female. Thus newspaper articles and sermons said of abolitionist women, "They had better go home & take care of their [no doubt] ragged children." Such criticism assumed that all women had supervisory heads, homes, and children and these women were either unwilling to care for them or inadequate to the task.[32]

By ignoring or openly rejecting male privilege in household, church, and civic society, women such as the Westons undermined the political and social rule of the brother.[33] Many a Boston householder rightly feared that when Maria and her sisters, of blood and association, left their homes for the streets, courthouses, and meetinghouses of the city, they brought contagion with them. One prominent abolitionist expressed "horror of the Gyneocracy which would be constituted by having Miss [Abigail] Kelley in the field and Mrs. Chapman in the council" of the American Anti-Slavery Society (AAS). This sense of a world turned upside down was manifest explicitly in the widely held view "that Garrison was entirely ruled by Maria W. Chapman."[34]

Weston critics were not wrong in their assessment that the sisters lacked due deference to men. But the roots of their independent-mindedness and irrepressible behavior lay not in the absence or weak governance of a husband. Weston autonomy emerged from the household organization and family relations into which they were born and those they manufactured. As Michael Roper and John Tosh have argued, the family offers a crucial site for exploring social relations of power because it is in the family that gender definitions are first taught and gender identity initially formed. In the family, a child discovers her or his gender identity, encounters inequalities of treatment based on sex, and learns what behavior is expected of adult men and women.[35] In contrast to the Republican ideal of the early nineteenth century, the Weston sisters (and particularly those born between 1806 and 1814) experienced freedom of expression and action in one another's company, the weak governance of a debilitated father, and the dependency of their damaged, younger brothers. Their views of the antislavery brethren were informed by these family relationships and the subjectivity of competence and independence they crafted in the Weymouth households of their mother and aunts.

When, in 1837, Maria Weston Chapman assessed her fifty-six-year-old father as "now a temperate man," the evidence of his ineffectual governance remained.[36] The chaos surrounding his erratic moods was such that Anne noted upon arriving home one evening that she found the family "all well & beautifully quiet," an indication that even in 1845 such was not the usual state of the household.[37] The sisters' interest in Weymouth's temperance activity also suggested their ongoing concern for father and brothers. Lucia regularly attended the meetings of various Weymouth and Braintree temperance societies. Her older sisters came out from Boston to attend these gatherings, as when William L. Garrison and Nathanial P. Rogers debated the efficacy of moral suasion as opposed to prohibition for reducing alcoholism. It must have galled the sisters that meetings of the Weymouth temperance society were held every evening in the vestry of Rev. Jonas Perkins's Union Religious Society church.[38]

The Westons grew up with a failed patriarch in a household organized to cope with male frailty and disorderliness. As Maria wrote to Joshua Bates of the experience, "I am now 31 years of age: I feel much older. But you know my dear uncle, I never was young."[39] She and her sisters devised "tactics of habitat" that not only supported the household economically and met its members' needs for emotional support, nursing, child-rearing, clothing, cooking, and cleaning, but also sustained a thoroughly conjoined and mutually supportive female social activism. Valuing the female strength of character that enabled the household to prosper despite their father's and brothers' struggles, they came to believe that women generally held up better than men, learning lessons in the family about female fortitude, women's ingenuity, and the dependability of sisters. They brought this sororal confidence into the political arena, acting upon it in the face of "weak sisters" (male and female) whose imagination, courage, and constancy they viewed as unequal to their own.

The Weymouth sisterhood experienced their fictive brothers in the antislavery family as disappointing. Overdetermined as their expectations may have been given their experiences with the Weston men, these women vividly expressed their frustration with male backsliding, poor judgment, incompetence, selfishness, and laziness as much if not more so with their male allies as with their detractors in the cause and their opposition in the broader society. Maria, for example, spoke of "Wobble Garrison," indicating her frustration with his impulsivity—his tendency to rush into connection or confrontation and then retreat from the consequences by leaving town, taking to his bed, or pushing others forward to take the heat and ease relations. She thought Quaker poet John Greenleaf Whittier "that kind of man who was hardly competent to grasp any very enlarged ideas, or able to comprehend the true sublimity and beauty of the toleration that forgets creeds in its zeal for Human Rights." She despaired of Samuel J. May Jr.'s credulity, calling him "shilly shally" and a "wonderful blunderer."[40]

Similarly, Caroline complained that Boston lawyer Ellis Gray Loring's "heart would fail him when it became necessary to fight out the battle." She grieved that "Dear George [Thompson] has not found strength to stand," and regretted her vote "to place [David L.] Child in a position [as editor of the *Anti-Slavery Standard*] where he can do so much mischief—I *hope* it is *mere* folly & stupidity—but it looks much like *perversity*." With regard to Henry B. Stanton, of whom Mary G. Chapman was quite enamored, Caroline wrote, "I hope he is going to have a good wife—If he were married to a woman of fine taste & some talent it would do him great good for he needs constant polishing."[41]

Anne too turned a critical eye on the brethren. She bemoaned the inability of Massachusetts state legislator Dr. Henry Ingersall Bowditch to obtain a political appointment deemed valuable to the cause. "I think it might have been done had a quicker person been present but you know what he is," she wrote her sisters. She worried about Nathaniel P. Rogers's refusal to vacate his proprietorship of the antislavery newspaper, the *Herald of Freedom*, when asked: "He is ill & nervous & we are all grieved at our hearts; but he has disappointed me. I did not think that illness or any thing else could have made him so unmindful of Garrison, or so thoughtless of the magnanimity shown by all his best friends. . . . I have loved him so well that I cannot bear to think of his last six months' developments," she wrote. "It is a severe ordeal through which reformers pass. Their temptation is great to confound Liberty & License." Anne also thought Sydney H. Gay, editor of the *Anti-Slavery Standard*, too "frightened" to arrange for an annual antislavery meeting during a period of anti-abolitionist public opinion. "I conferred a little with Sydney, but it is no more use to talk with him than with a very fractious & unhappy child," she reported. "His own *troubles* are the first thing & his own *associations* the second, & the Cause as a *duty* I dare say comes next, & as a *pleasure* I don't think it comes at all. This is not the state of mind the controlling agency of the A[merican] A[nti-Slavery] Soc'y should be in just now."[42]

Indeed, the subject of male character and its weakness evoked powerful emotional responses within the Weymouth sisterhood. Maria denounced Edward Mathews, an English-born Free Baptist missionary and peddler of devotional literature to the American South. She objected to what she saw as his misrepresentation of Garrisonian ideology to British audiences in an effort to curry favor with the anti-Garrisonian British and Foreign Anti-Slavery Society as he sought economic support from the pro-Garrison *Anti-Slavery Advocate*. She compared Mathews to Louis Napoleon: "If Louis Napoleon could have got [Czar] Nicholas . . . to embrace him as an Imperial brother, he would have gone to war with England. If Matthews could have got the welcome of [John] Scoble [leader of the British and Foreign Anti-Slavery Society] he would not have gone farther for one. Character is one in Emperor or baptist colporteur. . . . It is the same low type in both, that seeks first, *itself*."[43] Maria saw such men as driven less by a moral compass and more by their pocketbooks and reputations.[44] She valued best those who served abolition at whatever cost to their reputations, incomes, and physical or emotional well-being.[45]

Perhaps Richard D. Webb was on to something when he commented to Maria that "much which your sister [Anne] attributes to baseness, meanness, treachery and hostility to the cause" in the conduct of those who had peeled away from Garrison or withdrawn from the antislavery fight "resulted from inability to follow the path of duty . . . and at the same time maintain their allegiance to their creed and escape its terrors." He related his own sense of caution when facing such Weston certainty: "It takes great nerve—at least I think it does—to conquer the terrors of the nursery. I never knew a strong woman yet who was able to make sufficient allowance for the weaknesses of weak men."[46]

Among the failings for which the Westons had little patience was sexism. Debora complained of MAS agent Amos Phelps, "If he were to save his life he cant write in any way but a very dictatorial one, when it comes to addressing women."[47] Evasion of responsibility constituted another flaw. The sisters found Garrison avoidant of interpersonal conflict, behavior that evoked considerable irritation when they saw it affect his business dealings and those of the cause. Garrison struggled, for example, to face up to the problems of Isaac Knapp, his childhood friend, printer, and partner in the *Liberator*. Knapp's drinking undermined his reliability. His marriage to a thirteen-year-old girl scandalized his friends and confirmed his enemies' worst notions of his character. Gambling increased Knapp's indebtedness and led to a significant quarrel among the MAS board members over the terms on which they bought out his debt.[48]

A disagreement arising between Garrison and the two booksellers, Dow and Jackson, who rented half of the antislavery building at 25 Cornhill, Boston, caused Maria to attack his vacillation. Within days of opening their business, these partners vacated their lease, having failed to sell any product. Maria and Garrison debated how the MAS board should handle the transaction. Garrison recommended leaving the matter entirely up to the partners, but Maria disagreed: "'The business of the world is conducted on rascally principles': argued Garrison! Ay, said I 'but who does the Lord receive to his holy hill?' 'We must do as we would be done by' said Garrison. 'I would scorn to *wish in my heart* that any body should do by me as Dow & Jackson are asking me to do by them.' 'But we may rely upon their *generosity*.' 'I cant rely *at all* upon the man that fails to keep his word. But its a bad bargain for them.' 'Had it been so for us, should *we* have been justified in breaking it?'"[49] Such acerbic dialogue characterized many of Maria's interactions.[50] And while her assertiveness entertained some, Edmund Quincy for example, it earned Maria a broader reputation for despotic arrogance—what her good friend Anne Whitney called her "rhadamanthine eyes."[51]

The Westons littered their correspondence with both lighthearted and sharp-edged humor, poking fun at male puffery, preening, and presumption. Anne commented snidely of George Thompson "placing his glories in a high point of view." The sisterhood doubted not the necessity of "constantly polish[ing]" the rough edges of their male colleagues and ensuring that the brethren "hold fast their integrity" and not "flinch" in critical moments. For, as Caroline observed, "You see how for good or ill women invariably carry on their principles better than men do."[52]

When those of the MAS sought to limit the Grimké sisters' lectures to afternoons and exclude evening gatherings during their 1837 Massachusetts tour, Anne and Maria, as the BFAS arrangements committee, "informed them that we should transact this business and they finding we were not to be guided by their superior wisdom, gave in. They [their male colleagues] declared however that they were afraid of a mob not exactly of men but of *boys*. We really felt as if we could not succumb to the boys." So too Anne derided Garrison for "making a fool of himself" about a forthcoming meeting in Syracuse. "It is a Gospel truth that in deciding on holding a meeting, which meeting may break up in a riot, I do not wish for his opinion. His nerves get flurried & he loses his head & yet undertakes to manage." She insisted that in like circumstances, and despite her own fearful nature, she might find it desirable to hold a meeting, for "my nerves never influence my judgment." She believed Garrison "really not the man for such an emergency." Debora agreed that he was "timid and fearful to a degree."[53]

Anne complained of having to negotiate language and tactics with brethren whose egos required that they have a say about everything within abolition's sphere. "[W]e are worn to 'skilintons'—keeping our troops in order—'fitting' the protest to suit all comers," she wrote, finding it a "wearisome job to run from man to man as alteration & amendment has been proposed." Caroline observed ironically that Garrison continually "[gave] these men just countenance enough to have the fighting of his battles use up all *our* strength."[54] Hence, when Samuel J. May described the women of the BFAS as antislavery's "most efficient brethren and the men their weak and less efficient sisters," the Westons recognized the accolade not as gallantry but rather as simple truth.[55]

The Westons' jaundiced view of male privilege and self-indulgence appears also in their later objections to laws that ascribed solely to women responsibility for the spread of sexual disease. After abolition, the woman's cause that engaged them most was the repeal of the Contagious Diseases Acts in both Britain and the United States.[56] Discussions with British feminists and abolitionists—Harriet Martineau, Elizabeth Reid, Anne Knight, Emma Mitchell, Mary Ann Estlin, Elizabeth Pease Nichol, and Jane and Eliza Wigham, all of whom had worked with the Westons over the years on the Boston antislavery bazaar, informed their understanding of the issues and engaged their sympathy.

Upon publication of her 1876 article on the Contagious Diseases Acts in the *Westminster Review*, Harriet Martineau wrote to Maria of her feelings, as "an old woman, dying and in seclusion," in taking up "this question of national purity," which "plunges us into the most fearful moral crisis the country was ever in, involving our primary personal liberties, and the very existence, except in name, of the home and family."[57] These were some of the same issues drawing the Westons into the battle against slavery—an individual's right to bodily integrity, equal treatment under the law, and work that enabled one to support one's family and enhanced rather than demeaned the soul. In the "Memorials of Harriet Martineau," Maria described these "d—d laws" as "the most oppressive, insulting, and outrageous in their application to women, while men in the same conditions were wholly exempt from their penalties."[58]

While the Westons, Anne in particular, contributed funds, signed and passed petitions, and supported the efforts of their abolitionist coworkers with encouraging letters, it was Sydney H. Gay and Elizabeth Neall Gay who led the charge against these laws in the United States.[59] The modesty of Weston activism had largely to do with the breaking up of a common home as the sisters cared for family (nieces, grand-nieces, and grand-nephews) abroad; nursed one brother in New York and cared for his entire family when they relocated to Weymouth; and continued to sustain a second brother who languished alongside an aging mother in the family home.

Almost forty years earlier, Maria had written in *Right and Wrong in Massachusetts*, "Women are so accustomed to suffering under the many indignities which men unconsciously inflict, that in this instance they felt less keenly for themselves than did their [Garrisonian] brethren for them, the tyrannical attempt to assume their responsibilities." The "false brethren" of "new organization," she wrote, lived "in horror [and] great darkness on the subject of '*woman's* rights,'" willing to deny "the fundamental principle that brought them together." Thus the brethren "trampled on *human* rights, and the rights of *membership*, in the persons of those women whom they labored to exclude."[60]

Chapman refused to separate women out as a special category of members with limited, gender-specific, and therefore lesser or different rights.[61] "I cannot but hope that the whole Mass[achusetts] Delegation [to the AAS national convention] will see clearly that neither they nor any other persons have authority to prevent women since they *are* persons" and therefore under the society's constitution held all the rights and duties of membership. Even a hypothetical delegation entirely "composed of *coloured women under 21*" would be competent to vote as members on matters before the national society, she wrote. "If a word is said about womans rights &c I hope the party uttering it will be called to order, this being not the question of *womans rights . . .* but *members* and persons rights."[62]

Similarly, Anne agreed with Paulina Gerry, who stood upon the principle, "If Women are persons the constitution [of the AAS] surely entitles them to the right to act in any of the antislavery deliberations & no man conscious of possessing the superiority his sex claim would fear any diminution of his rights by permitting Women to cooperate with him." Gerry attacked the conservative argument from precedent that because women had not from the organization's founding had the explicit right to vote in convention or hold membership on associational committees, they therefore were forever disqualified from equal participation. She offered an analogy that appealed to Anne. When passed, the Massachusetts state bill of rights declared all men free and equal. However, she wrote, "slavery existed in the state and the coloured man continued in bondage for a time unconscious that he was legally entitled to himself but when one more sagacious than the rest filed into a court of judicature a bill of habeas corpus it was decided that he was a free citizen and a precedent established for the Liberty of all. This I consider a parallel case to Womens [*sic*] acting in the business meetings of the MAS." In the same way, Gerry insisted, referring to Abigail Kelley's appointment to the AAS business committee in 1839, women "always possessed the constitutional right [to full and equal participation] but did not improve it [take it up] for some years."[63] This stance echoed that of the Westons, who insisted that membership and willingness to serve provided all the grounds necessary for women to vote in AAS meetings and serve on its committees and those of its associated organizations.

Fully engaged in the debates as to woman's role and rights, the Westons read volumes on the subject from authors such as Mary Wollstonecraft, John Stuart Mill, Sarah Grimké, Harriet Martineau, and Wendell Phillips. They corresponded and visited with British feminists Elizabeth Reid, who founded Bedford College for women in 1848 and published the *English Woman's Journal*, and Anne Knight, an English Quaker, suffragist, and leader of the Sheffield Woman's Political Association.[64] However, as abolitionist Sarah Otis Ernst remarked to Anne, though "[t]he subject of the burdened and crushed life of woman, claims my most ardent sympathy . . . if I remember right, *you* do not view it as I do." Neither Maria, Caroline, Anne, nor Debora saw herself as did Knight, who was "evidently a *woman* before she was any thing else."[65] In Weston eyes, free women were persons born with the inalienable rights of all human beings and the responsibility to act for themselves and for the enslaved in any arena that called to them, utilizing their individual capacities for the expansion of human freedom.

Rejecting fraternal despotism, the Westons and other like-minded women insisted upon their rights and responsibilities as equal laborers in the cause. But as activists, the Westons had little patience with discussing those rights and focused instead on their responsibilities to the slave. They went where conscience, and a view to the necessary, took them. Weston activism emerged from a bone-deep rejection of the imposition on women of false limitations.

As matters of competence and self-respect, the sisters' pragmatic feminism was nurtured in the family dynamics of the Weston household,[66] emerging to become a tool in the battle to end slavery. They frequently asserted their social independence and gender equality and praised that of other women. Debora wrote to her nephew, for example, about the mastery of a female whaler: "There is a lady of the name of Howland here, who has gone a whaling with her husband & the people think she exerts a good influence for the vessel has made $1,000 per month ever since she has been gone."[67] The Weston women—independent aunts, a competent and determined mother, and assertive sisters—demonstrated a temperament that resisted dependency and male domination.

The Westons conducted the antislavery movement with a confidence born of their belief in themselves and in other women. But in neither their language nor their actions did they permit a mixing of woman's rights with antislavery. Maria wrote in 1843, "We have a letter from [Stephen A. Foster] saying that since the lib[erty] par[ty] let women vote & do Sabbath lecturing, all[']s right. . . . Just as if to secure the rights of women or the making of the Sabbath common & unclean had been any object of ours!"[68] In 1852 Anne wished the proponents of a Boston woman's rights convention were far away "at California." She called them Satan's "devils, to draw away the time (& money & worse than that, the fervour and enthusiasm) of Abolitionists from the Cause." She did not "*blame* folks if their *consciences* tell them to get up these things . . . I'm only sorry people *have* such consciences *just now*." The following year she forbade Lucy Stone to speak at the Boston antislavery fair because Stone was a "bloomer" (or so the story went, as Anne loathed the dress). Said Anne of her actions, "A little despotism is exceedingly wholesome at times." After Emancipation, in 1866, she wrote, "I do not think the suffrage question is to be *settled* at all after the Anti Slavery method. I did not tolerate any difference of opinion as to slavery. I tolerate very wide differences as to negro suffrage, or indeed the question of suffrage generally," meaning woman's as well. Abolition of slavery was a moral imperative, whereas in her mind, full political rights for African Americans and women of all races was a question about which ethical people of good character and goodwill might differ.[69]

The focus on woman's responsibilities as human being and citizen was also evident in a rare article on woman's rights written by Maria from France in 1848 for publication in the *Liberator*. "I was astonished on my first arrival . . . to find how deep and general an interest was taken throughout the various circles with which I came in contact, in the question of the rights and duties of women," she wrote. "The laws are less favorable here to that oppressed portion of the human family, than with us in the United States, while the customs are more so. They are here allowed to fill many more positions, and act in many more capacities, than with us." Maria noted women who held positions in hospital administration; who worked as artists, mathematicians, and scientists; who served in the military: "in fine, transacting business in almost every department of business life, and doing what the despotic spirit of Bonaparte caused him to declare to be the *'une chose qui n'etait pas Francaise; c'est qui un femme prisse faire ce qui lui plait.'"* This, she insisted, "is the very root of the 'woman question;' why should *not* a woman do what it pleases her to do, as well as another?"[70]

Maria "regretted to see men depriving [the human] race of the benefit of [woman's] services, for the mere gratification of narrow-minded and inherited prejudices—prejudices as unreasonable and absurd as those against Jews and negroes." She struck at the crux of her viewpoint in referring to a book by Ernest Legouvé titled *The Moral History of Women* that, while "producing a profound impression, and preparing the way for a better state of things," did not in her opinion "build on the only true and logical foundation—that a woman, being a human soul, having a moral nature identical with that of man, has, equally with him, a right to life, liberty, and the pursuit of happiness." While she thought Legouvé had "excellent ideas, and abundance of illustrative historical facts," she found his book lacking in that "it never occurs to him in speaking of woman's duties and functions, to say, 'It is for *her* to decide what she will be and do, exactly as it is for me, a man, to determine what I will be and do.' He always takes it for granted, that man's duty is to mark out woman's course."[71] Maria and her sisters had long rejected any such assumption out of hand. Weston feminism, as did their abolition, rooted in their determination to choose their own duties.

In describing French feminism, Maria noted the monthly magazine *L'Opinion des Femmes*, edited by Jeanne Deroin. The bulk of her epistle focused on Deroin's candidacy for legislative office.[72] In an April 1849 letter, Caroline also rejoiced in Deroin's candidacy, eagerly describing the moment when the president of the General Assembly dismissed Deroin's request to speak before a meeting, saying, "'We do not doubt but that there might be great force in her views but why urge them *now*? They were uncalled for & *other* & pressing interests claimed consideration. There was no urgency in this.' Ah '*But there is*,' cried Madame Deroin—'Moi, *je suis* l'emergence.'" Caroline insisted that the "lady had the best of it," and reveled in the popular response to Deroin the following day as she walked the streets of Paris. "I should not be surprised if she had a huge number of votes," crowed Caroline. Indeed, she believed Deroin "would look quite as well in the assembly as does the Lady [Queen Victoria] who sometimes meets the Lords & Commons of England—& there is little doubt of her having more ability."[73]

Maria's article noted that Deroin had established her candidacy on the principles of equality and fraternity, asserting the value to society of selecting its legislators from among the "superior talents" in an open field of aspirants. She praised Deroin's "high moral character and intelligence" as the basis for a conscientious advocacy of female representation in France's legislative assembly. Maria approved the notion that a body "composed entirely of men" was "incompetent to make the laws which regulate a society composed of both men and women." And Maria assessed Deroin's candidacy as "taking the most direct way to agitate the public mind" on the question of woman's public role and responsibilities—given that "she has no non-resistance principles to prevent her from participating in governments as at present constituted."[74]

Maria and her sisters, however, followed their own conscientious commitment to nonresistance principles of noncooperation with governments dependent upon the threat of physical force to uphold their practices and laws. When faced with a petition demanding woman's right to the suffrage, Caroline responded, "I wish I *could* ask it—No one ever submitted to civil death with a worse grace than did I consent to the Non-resistance principles."[75] Thus the Westons, while deeply interested in woman's rights, acted as their beliefs dictated and took little formal part in the movement to expand women's civil equality.

They rejected the electoral franchise as disunionists and nonresistants.[76] Both political philosophies caused the Westons to view voting as an act of collusion with an illegitimate and unjust government that harbored the institution of slavery and empowered slave owners through the constitutional advantage of enumerating slaves for the purpose of establishing congressional representation, legitimating the use of police and juridical powers to return fugitive slaves to their masters, and prohibiting consideration of antislavery petitions on the floor of Congress. So too the Westons dismissed the idea that men, as fathers, husbands, brothers, and heads of household, could or would adequately represent the interests of women. Until Americans reconstituted the social compact, the Westons dismissed the franchise in an act of political dissent and a conscientious moral strategy for improving a society characterized by inequality and a political system dominated by sexism and racism.

The accusations of female impudence that followed the Westons, and many of their fictive sisters in the antislavery movement, suggests the importance of the household and its relationships for female public activism and returns us to the social categories of single and sibling. How did sibling relations shape gendered relations of power in the first half of the nineteenth century? What were the implications of that process for political identity and the political activism of women? While historians have argued that families played a role in socializing women to subordination, siblicity also may have enabled sisters, especially unwed sisters, to imagine an equality not evident or encouraged outside their circle yet enacted and sustained through their shared commitment to a defining and overarching political labor.

As siblings coming of age in a particular household and family arrangement, the Westons developed ways of living and working that encouraged their independence rather than their subordination or dependency. Acting accordingly, and together, the Westons formulated a critique of patriarchal authority and fraternal order that informed their relations with the fictive siblings within abolition's house. As Emma Michell put it to Anne, "Are not abolitionists all brethren? And there are no Misses or Masters among them, either with the seen or unseen, they are truly a household band . . . linked together one family in Heaven."[77] The "anti-patriarchal, egalitarian, reciprocal, and interdependent reign of siblings" in the fictive Garrisonian household encouraged among some of the sororal bands that emerged within the antislavery movement a feminist critique of gender relations in American society, its churches, and its reform movements.[78] Even for those sisterhoods that did not embrace the Westons' independence, their commitment to singlehood, a common household, and a practice of shared labor provided the makings of an affectionate and productive model of female social activism in nineteenth-century New England. Within the horizontal structures of their sibling families, the female governance of their households, and their lateral ties to voluntary associations, they constructed a sorority of overlapping blood and fictive kin that helped bring slavery to its knees.

Acknowledgments

This book had its roots in a study on the transatlantic Garrisonian community undertaken many years ago at the University of Michigan. The questions raised by professors James O. Horton, Kenneth Lockridge, and Harold C. Livesay helped me refocus this inquiry into antebellum women's public activism on the Weston family. I wish to thank them and the many historians of eighteenth- and nineteenth-century women who have commented on my work over the years and shared their own. Special thanks are extended to Clare Taylor and Anne F. Scott for encouragement, and to Anne M. Boylan, Jean Fagan Yellin, Lorri Glover, Katherine Holden, Leonore Davidoff, and Barbara Engel for reading parts of this manuscript. I offer my great appreciation to Nancy Mann for her extraordinary skills in sorting wheat from chaff, to Chuck Grench, who has worked patiently with me on two projects, to two anonymous readers who provided me with deeply informed comments on the manuscript, and to Mary Carley Caviness for her intelligent and careful editing of my manuscript. They gave me much to consider and have made this a better book.

My thanks as well to the many archivists and librarians who have aided my research, particularly those at Tufts Library in Weymouth, Massachusetts, the Rare Books and Manuscripts Department of the Boston Public Library, the Boston Athenaeum, the Massachusetts Historical Society, the Smith College Library, the American Antiquarian Society, the Schlesinger Library of Radcliffe College, the Houghton Library of Harvard University, the Essex Institute/Peabody Essex Museum, the Concord Historical Society, the Rare Book and Manuscript Library of Columbia University, the Clements Library of the University of Michigan, the Cornell University Library, Dr. Williams's Library of London, the John Rylands Library of the University of Manchester, and the Baring Archive. I am grateful for the courtesy of the personnel at these institutions and the permission of their trustees to quote from select manuscript letters, diaries, and organizational papers in their collections. No words can express my gratitude for the love and support of my parents. My mother, Marjorie Bell Chambers, did not live to see this book published, but she would have appreciated a story about women who stood up for and acted upon their beliefs. My father, William Hyland Chambers, knows a thing or two about courage, sacrifice, and commitment. His example and understanding have helped me stay the course.

Appendix

To Be Left at Capt Weston's Near Wales' Tavern

On Correspondence

While other primary sources—newspapers, organizational records, legal and property records, pamphlets, songbooks, and memoirs—have contributed, this study has been made possible by the extraordinary substance and frequency of written communication among the Weston sisters. Their correspondence offers an intimate view of sibling relations, culture, and work habits. Chapter 5 discusses Weston letter writing as crucial to the construction of the Weymouth sisterhood and to kinkeeping; this appendix asks how this archival collection was formed and what an understanding of epistolary practices and the material aspects of correspondence offer the historian.

The largest collection of Weston correspondence resides in the Anti-Slavery Collection of the Boston Public Library, with additional letters scattered throughout the holdings of their colleagues and correspondents. The Westons retained their letters for their own reference, and that of Garrisonian colleagues who spoke and wrote, privately or publicly, in furtherance of abolition. Prolific correspondents, the sisters wrote to one another, others of their immediate and extended family, and a wide circle of friends and colleagues. As domestic and foreign corresponding secretaries of the Boston Female Anti-Slavery Society (BFAS), organizers of the annual Boston antislavery fair, members of various organizational boards (the Massachusetts Anti-Slavery Society [MAS], American Anti-Slavery Society [AAS], and Anti-Slavery Convention of American Women), participants in and delegates to meetings of these societies, and authors of reports and histories of the BFAS, they also corresponded with abolitionists around the United States and across the Atlantic. Much of this correspondence remains.[1] Less of their personal correspondence with other family members (father, mother, brothers, uncles, aunts, and cousins) and friends has survived.[2] What has been lost is almost as compelling to the historian as what remains, for our histories are "embedded in what has survived."[3]

John Randolph has suggested that archives and archival collections have a "biography."[4] That of the Weston Papers raises epistemological issues concerning what we know about the Westons and how we know it. Who gathered and saved these letters and for what purpose? What was left out of the collection and why? Additional questions address how scholars evaluate and utilize correspondence as a historical source. What was the epistolary practice of these correspondents? What do we learn from the material state of the letters?

Antislavery activists, Garrisonians in particular, relied upon the Weston penchant for retaining correspondence. Colleagues drew upon the family archive for their own political projects. In 1844, Edmund Quincy, for example, borrowed Maria's 1840–42 letters to her sisters from Haiti for a piece he was writing on the Haitian revolution for the *Liberty Bell*. He resisted returning these missives when finished with his article. "I will send them to you, but only upon one condition," Quincy stipulated, "and that is, that you will keep them carefully and never let Maria lay her eyes or hands upon them. . . . She is a perfect Medea to her literary offspring." He offered instead to get a blank book and have Elizabeth Bates Chapman copy the letters out "for the benefit of family and of her own calligraphy."[5]

On another occasion, Caroline wrote Wendell Phillips, "While examining the piles of papers & documents among which I sought for what you wanted" (documentation of growing strain among the original founders of the AAS), she realized "the importance of preserving these things for I was amazed to find how much of their villainy I had forgotten."[6] She also exchanged a number of letters with Phillips discussing the revisionist story of the 1835 Boston mob offered in 1870 by Col. Theodore Lyman, the son of Boston's mayor at the time of the riot. Outraged over young Lyman's "imperfect and one sided" account, Caroline provided material that Phillips used in "The Lyman Mob," a public lecture given at the Music Hall on 17 November 1870. City newspapers covered the talk, and for weeks, the *Daily Advertiser* published a furious exchange of letters between the two men regarding their different interpretations of the event.[7]

Most consequentially, Wendell Phillips Garrison and his brother Francis Jackson Garrison sought access to Weston correspondence as an aid in writing the biography of their deceased father, William Lloyd Garrison. They published their work in four volumes between 1885 (the year Maria died) and 1889 (when Debora's death left her sister Anne the sole surviving sibling).[8] Thus, though much of a domestic, familial, and personal nature remains in the Weston collection, it was assembled in the first instance because these men wished to define their father's legacy. What shaped the Westons' antislavery archive was a desire to preserve the antislavery works of the movement's "great men" and not, necessarily, to focus on the Westons themselves. Thus no personal correspondence with their father (who lacked a strong abolitionist sympathy and belonged to no antislavery society) remains, and little with their mother.[9] Among aunts, uncles, and cousins, only Aunt Mary Weston is represented to any significant degree in the collection, perhaps because her role in the Weymouth and Braintree Female Emancipation Society and her Garrisonian leanings and works rivaled those of her nieces.[10] Few letters exist in the Boston Public Library collection from Weston brothers Hervey and Richard Warren.[11] Emma, the youngest Weston sister, is least represented as both letter recipient and writer.[12] Her limited presence is lamentable in that she might have offered a different perspective on the dynamics of the Weston household and the family business of abolition.

CENSORSHIP

After their deaths, letters to and from the Weston sisters were gathered together by Richard Warren Weston's two daughters, Rosamond Weston Meigs and Helen Weston.

Both lived in Weymouth, with or near the aunts who had nursed their father through various illnesses, and neither had much firsthand experience of the antislavery movement. The process necessarily reflected the nieces' own concerns for gender propriety and family reputation, as well as their post-emancipation understanding of antislavery politics.

Obliterated passages, cut-out paragraphs, and missing pages provide evidence of culling, editing, and censorship. Some small deletions were identified as such. For example, the name of a woman (perhaps Abigail Kelley Foster) described as "truly kindhearted" yet also "injudicious," "officious," and impractical was inked out to prevent identification. In another instance, Anne had written to inform her sisters that Wendell Phillips was not available to speak in New Bedford as they had hoped: "Let me say in a few brief words that all idea of your convention must be up for the present" as "Wendell *cannot* come." Although someone crossed out the explanation for his absence, the vaguely legible wording suggests that Ann T. G. Phillips did not want her husband leaving home for so long as six to eight weeks. Perhaps a Weston sister or niece quashed the hint of disapproval at her attitude because Ann was Henry G. Chapman's first cousin, or out of deference to the Phillipses' legacy.[13]

When Helen Weston excised material, she noted the fact, using the same dark ink with which she crossed out words and sentences, and made the notation "marked out by me (H Weston) strictly personal nothing about the A. S. Cause."[14] On another letter she noted, "page 7 & 8 private cut out."[15] Helen also extracted material she deemed important and acceptable, copied it in her own hand, and included the extract rather than the problematic original in the collection.[16] Her statement as to motive ("private" or "strictly personal") does little to illuminate the standards guiding these editorial decisions, as the confidential and controversial remains alongside excised and crossed-out material. Perhaps the inconsistencies emerged from the piecemeal gathering of correspondence over time and the lack of a single sensibility overseeing the selection.[17] Given the evidence of censorship, the likelihood remains that some material disappeared entirely from public view.

The Westons themselves censored their correspondence while preparing letters for public circulation among abolitionists. A letter from Debora to Caroline about events surrounding the Boston trial of fugitive slave Anthony Burns, for example, contains so many scratched-out words as to make it unintelligible: "In the midst of this matter [Theodore Parker's speech at the Music Hall—six words crossed out] suddenly—She [two words inked out] terrible [four or five words blotted out] & it is privately announced with [one word scratched out]. Her disorder is *called heart complaint*."[18] The context surrounding this excision suggests that a pregnant woman may have collapsed in a public meeting. The controversy over women's appearing in places of public debate, reticence about the female body, and an intent to mask the woman's identity and preserve her privacy explain the censorship.

We cannot know all that was culled from Weston correspondence in the creation of their archive. Caroline Weston exchanged daily letters with Edmund Quincy, yet only six remain among the Quincy Family Papers in the Massachusetts Historical Society, and nothing like a daily correspondence persisting over thirty years resides in the antislavery collection of the Boston Public Library. Evidence supports the view that the sisters destroyed some correspondence as it was received. Caroline commanded Debora, *"Pray burn this letter as soon as you have read it"* in reference to an explicit description of her brother-in-law's medical condition.[19] Anne asked that a letter from Debora be kept from Maria because it reported a decision by the MAS to release Henry from his position of treasurer, after fifteen years of service, due to his illness; Anne feared that knowledge of the action would further undermine his health. After attacking Garrison for allowing the termination ("I begin to think what I did not before that he is a vile bad man"), Anne informed Debora that she would tell no one but Emma that she had received the letter: "We could not well account for its not coming through Henry's hands and M[aria] might insist on *seeing* the letter or suspect some thing, so when you write again, you need make no allusion to having written & if you have any thing to say about this, a line darkly expressed may be safely trusted."[20] This particular expression of family feeling and pique at Garrison survived the editorial eye, suggesting the informality and inconsistency of the censorship.

In addition to the excised "personal" material, censorship also reflected politics. Over time, the Westons (particularly Maria) came to view Frederick Douglass as having betrayed the Garrisonian wing of the movement. They disapproved of his character, specifically the means by which he conducted his search for financial independence and his scandalous relationships with women other than his wife. A letter from Maria in spring 1858, for example, assessed the British and Foreign Anti-Slavery Society as having lost influence within the cause, "when its only pretense of work—the only thing it can *venture* to do, is to support the poor knave Douglass;—simply because he is a selfish, knavish, tricky shifty fellow, who discerned by his cleverness that the Antislavery cause would never enrich him, while opposition to it, might."[21] The first page of this letter has gone missing—censored, misplaced, accidentally damaged, or intentionally destroyed—and the beginning of the third page has been excised without explanation.[22]

Perhaps, given Douglass's statesmanlike postemancipation reputation, someone worried about purveying gossip about his private life but wanted to save Maria's general rant about his character. Evidence of such consideration, and of its irregular application, is revealed in a note Helen Weston attached to a letter from Richard D. Webb to Maria: "On the 10 & 11th pages of this letter there is a good deal about Douglass which was not at the time to be made public. [T]old in confidence I have hesitated about cutting it out, but thought on the whole I had better send it."[23] The questionable material related to the effect of Douglass's relationship with Julia Griffith on his reputation, domestic relations, and finances.[24]

Diaries also are missing. Both Caroline and Anne mention the journals they routinely kept and shared with one another. Caroline promised Debora, "I am truly going now to write a journal addressed to you which shall be D'Arblay'an in its character but cannot say one word more to'night." On another occasion she noted having "discontinued" the diary she kept primarily for Maria, then in Haiti: "You will laugh at me when you find that . . . for the last few weeks I must rely upon my memory for all the news you can get by me on this present occasion." Commenting on her poor eyesight, Anne noted, "I write a good deal because I keep a regular journal for Emma," who was living abroad at the time. Anne also kept a "daily journal" to keep Caroline apprised of domestic and antislavery matters when she left the country to accompany Maria and the children to

Europe in 1848.²⁵ These documents have largely disappeared, along with Maria's journals of her Haitian visits in the early 1840s, which contained her observations of life and
politics in the new black republic. Quincy, Phillips, and Garrison all drew upon these
journals for newspaper articles and speeches on Haitian independence.

Despite references to diaries kept by Caroline, Anne, and Debora during the 1835
anti-abolitionist violence in and around Boston, only a few pages remain in the Boston
Public Library from Caroline's descriptions. These provide a play-by-play of the events
leading up to and following the mobbing of George Thompson in Abington, Massachusetts, but also include oblique references to distressing familial and personal matters.
"I am not so comfortable in many respects as I wish I were just now—but I hope that
all inconveniences may be disposed of before long," she wrote. "[I]n not remarkably
good spirits—I hope that a few weeks will relieve me of some uneasiness." She fretted
over "embarrassments that seem to be springing up." She worried about her brother
("My mind is disturbed about H[ervey]'s plans but hope it is all for the best"), sister
("Anne in a quandary"), George Thompson ("our friend was mobbed . . . just grazed by
a stone"), and everyone's physical safety ("We felt great apprehensions of a mob"),²⁶ but
it remains unclear whether these stated concerns covered all her "uneasiness." There
is some suggestion in her letters that her "embarrassments" may have involved gossip
about Anne and the married George Thompson, or about Anne and her employer Dr.
Amos Farnsworth.²⁷ The survival of these few pages of Caroline's diary may have resulted from a niece's judgment that the political material was worth salvaging, while the
personal notes were so "darkly expressed" as to safeguard the privacy of those involved.

EPISTOLARY PRACTICE

Beyond the problems common to using personal letters as historical sources,²⁸ Weston
epistolary practice had two characteristics that importantly affect interpretation. Journals provided an individual's first draft, and the expectation of multiple readers (even
stronger for the Westons than for other nineteenth-century letter writers) may have
censored content.

The "journal letters" sent by the Weston sisters were based on their personal journals that served as a first, unpolished, and highly individual record of events and their
thoughts about themselves, people, and politics. These journals no longer exist, although we know they did.²⁹ Anne, for example, explained how she mined her journals
to inform her correspondents. She began these letters with "a concise account of the
state of things," and would "then look over my journal . . . and omitting the weighty
matters pick up the fragments of news, the *on dits* so unimportant that nobody else
will remember them."³⁰ The letters based on these personal documents offered the sisters' insights into antislavery people and events, personal opinions, and political assessments including organizational details.

One example from Anne's hand resembled organizational minutes but demonstrates the balance of "weighty matters" and "on dits":³¹ "In the afternoon we went to
the meeting of the Boston Female. Only about 15 or 16 were there. A number of people
were gone out of town or were tired with the Fair. The Sargents, the Lorings, Mary Robbins (others were absent who are generally there). Even Lucia & Emma wouldn't go. We

passed resolutions of thanks to various friends abroad and voted to take 50 copies of the Liberator, also we voted to send or rather pledge £10 to the Herald of Freedom—as we had no money in the treasury." Along with information, Anne recorded her emotional reactions to the individuals present at and absent from the meeting, to the discussion, and to the decisions made. Such matters would not generally be put into formal organizational minutes and conveyed not only a sense of a meeting or interaction but also its dynamics. "Anna Southwick spoke against [the pledge] & Sarah spoke for it which [*sic*] shows the difference between the two," she wrote. "There was a little talk about the Herald in which Maria spoke with rather more warmth than was necessary but still she said nothing amiss. She spoke handsomely of Rogers.[32] I was sorry to do a thing which [*sic*] might hurt R's feelings."[33]

The tone of these journal letters lacked the humor ("Nothing was heard from the people in Paris by the last boat; I have therefore altered my will & cut off each & all with a shilling") or informality ("I am quite on the qui vive about the elections & am glad not to be looking out for them any longer") of prose in her usual correspondence with close friends and family.[34]

Thus the journal letters were a genre that did not so much leave out "weighty matters" of ideological import, organizational development, or political conflict as surround these with human interest, first impressions, personal insights, interpersonal dynamics, and political commentary of a highly individual, even idiosyncratic nature. Journal letters were more self-conscious, more apt to be given an overall shape than ordinary notes. Such missives suggested a greater awareness of audience. The sisters took time to write these: the time required to cull material from personal documents and to compose. Thus, journal letters were less marked by signs of interruption (see below, *discours décousu*) than other, ordinary Weston letters.

Chapter 5 discusses how forwarding and reading letters aloud helped tie together both the sisters and their larger abolitionist circle. But the expectation of these practices may have limited what writers were willing to risk saying. Privacy in such circumstances was an illusion. Maria in particular had few scruples about opening any and all letters that came to hand, regardless of addressee,[35] and she had a habit of leaving letters about the house where they could be and were handled by visitors.[36] The sisters used various devices to restrict their readership. Optimistically choosing to assume Maria's acquiescence, Anne proscribed her reading one page of a multipage letter: "I will privately address my other sheet to Caroline."[37] In one instance, when conveying information about well-known persons that might, if published, have caused controversy among abolitionists, Debora somewhat disingenuously attempted to circumscribe readership with, "I think my letter had better be marked *private & family letter*."[38] Anne, who valued such circumspection, cautioned Wendell and Ann Phillips, "I have not written this letter as you will perceive by the freedom of its style, for any body but your two selves. If Debora Weston should chance to call in, as she is a person of immense prudence & discretion, you may show it to her, other-wise, I have given my pen such boundless liberties that I do not think it will edify any other reader than your two selves."[39] In like vein, conveying information on President Tyler's household arrangements, Anne urged, "now comes privacy" in identifying her source: a visit from Tyler's "black servant (a free man, a Virginian)" to the antislavery rooms in Boston. "You may state these facts," she told her sisters, "but not our informant's authority as his visit to the Liberator Office is private. Only tell Edmund." The Westons trusted Quincy, as much as anyone outside the sisterhood, with their gossip and views. But even with him they practiced evasion: "I read your letters to Edmund who was here when they arrived. Of course I left out & altered a little but otherwise it was all well enough for him."[40]

In extreme cases the sisters resorted to the dramatic instruction "burn this letter." Lucia, for example, repeated a story about Oliver Johnson reproving Martha Ball for "pretending to be in favour of the Liberator and Garrison, and then doing every thing she could to put them down." She begged Debora to "burn this letter"; indeed, she went on, "I hope you commit all my letters to the flames. If I thought you did not I would not write any more." So too Debora insisted that Maria "burn this letter, as I don't want it to get into the 'Mass[achusetts] Ab[olitionist]' & you are very careless of letters." Caroline wrote Maria, "Be sure to burn this letter, for I don't intend my cautions or my solicitude for your beauty & goodness for the Benefit of either Catherine Parker [president of the BFAS], the cabal clique [Boston Garrisonians] or the public gener- ally."[41] Yet these particular letters survived not only the burn bag but also the Weston nieces' censorship.

Caroline asked other correspondents for such action but of course could not ensure their compliance. "I have not burned your letter," Evelina A. S. Smith reassured her, "but I have done better, I have forgotten what you wrote that did not relate to yourself."[42] Mary Ann Estlin replied to such a request that she found "many portions of [Caroline's correspondence] too valuable just at this moment to be able to commit it to the flames in the precipitate manner you request, tho' I will promise to protect your reputation for composition, or forbearance or anything else that you may consider endangered by its style."[43]

The sisters also adapted their correspondence to their various constituencies by reading letters aloud selectively rather than passing along entire epistles for audience consumption. This process changed both the mode of communication and what was communicated. Anne acknowledged to Debora that she had read aloud to the Beanes "about the mob, & they listened with interest." When she read the same letter to Grace Emerson, she indicated, "I read more to her than I did to them for I had to furbish it up in reading to the Beanes lest it might be to their injury."[44] Thus Anne massaged the text according to what she saw as her audience's political or social needs, while accom- modating her own privacy and sororal propriety.

Perhaps most importantly from a historiographical point of view, Anne may also have censored what she herself wrote, as on at least one occasion she attempted to per- suade her sisters, then in Europe, to do so: "Above all be careful what either Maria or yourself write, for I really don't think any body but myself can be trusted with a private letter."[45] Evidence for the Westons' avoidance of writing on certain subjects, of refusing to say all they knew on paper, is difficult to ascertain, but there are allusions to such behavior and concerns. Hibernian abolitionist Richard D. Webb apologized to Maria for publishing a letter she had written to him in the British abolitionist newspaper, the *Antislavery Advocate*. Despite having suppressed her signature, he knew that astute readers would attribute the letter to Chapman, thus infusing it with greater interest as well as augmenting his standing in the movement as recipient.[46]

On occasion the Westons sought to direct one another as to what could be read aloud and to whom. "I think my letter had better be marked *private & family letter* but I trust it will reach you safely & you will profit by it," wrote Debora to Caroline. The letter had largely to do with antislavery matters. She labeled it "private and family" because its contents involved controversial topics about well-known individuals, the dissemination of which among French sympathizers with little knowledge of the American scene, or the British partisans then visiting, might have produced embarrassment or political upset. By labeling as private and family that which was public but confidential, Debora underscored the sensitivity of her comments and dictated the recipients not the contents of the letter.[47]

Copying of letters or selections from letters served to entertain, disseminate information, and edify family, friends, and activists. Mary Ann Estlin reported to Anne, "Mrs Steinthal has copied all Mrs Chapman's letters (I believe) to her husband & given [abolitionists in Bristol] & Leeds, & Edinburgh & Manchester the benefit." Thus began "a regular interchange of correspondence between these Societies who cooperate with the American AAS for the sake of keeping each 'posted up' [up to the mark] & to strengthen each other's hands in readings for any concerted action that may be called for."[48] In achieving public standing (and sometimes that of policy) by circulating specific letters, these individuals might effect a purpose other than that originally intended. The process of selection, editing, and copying, whether oral or written, was guided by the consciousness, purpose, and politics of the recipient, or someone else other than the author. This transformed the meaning of documents along their route.

Anne expressed some doubts about such sharing of correspondence. In a letter to Wendell Phillips, she wrote: "Here is dear George [Thompson]'s letter. Ann [Phillips] can keep as long as she likes & then return to me by mail." With an utter lack of irony she insisted, "I don't wish it shown, as a matter of principle; for this easy handing about of letters that is the present fashion I am opposed to *as* a matter of principle. A letter, if worth any thing is most generally intended for very few persons, & sometimes only for the one person to whom it is addressed."[49]

Correspondents differed in their sensibilities regarding the circulation of letters, but all recognized that the recipient determined dissemination. And many recipients acted according to their own devices, viewing the letters they received as theirs to do with as they pleased. Decisions as to handling correspondence, and the debate over who had the right to make such decisions, remained an ongoing source of conflict among Weston correspondents. Miscalculations occurred, particularly when letters were written in haste or influenced by strong feeling. For example, Maria wrote fellow member of the AAS executive committee James Gibbons, "This letter is of course private; but I never write any anti slavery letters that I am not willing should be published upon the housetops. One that I wrote you contains so painful a truth that I would willingly see it destroyed."[50] The contradiction suggests that Maria hoped Gibbons would destroy her previous letter before its contents leaked; but in case he had already shared it, she positioned herself as having the courage of her convictions and indifferent to what others might think.

When combined with her publication of others' private communications, Maria's attempts to recall her own correspondence angered many. Mary Ann Estlin lost her temper with the Westons' exquisite sensibilities as to their own privacy. She asserted that it had never entered her head that any of them might object to her granting their friend, newspaper editor Richard D. Webb, permission to extract "from your narrative of a peculiarly interesting state of things in Boston, such parts as he thought suited to awaken sympathy for the Cause amongst the readers of the *Advocate*."[51] She reminded the Westons that the first letter she ever wrote Maria, "a most uninforming juvenile effusion," had been published in both the *Liberator* and the *National Anti-Slavery Standard* with her name and address attached. "And when I ventured to express my astonishment & dismay Mrs C. seemed to think me very fastidious, & said the Abol[itionist]s were themselves so accustomed to that sort of notoriety & so willing to endure it when any good was likely to result to the Cause that they were unable to estimate properly the [reaction] English people might have to seeing themselves named & reproduced in print." Impatient with what she saw as the Westons' self-importance, Estlin nevertheless managed to flatter them even as she expressed her annoyance. "It was far from my thoughts that *you* would be adverse to our availing ourselves of one of the few vehicles we possess for binding other hearts to your cause by sharing with them some of the light & warmth you impart to ourselves." While reassuring the Weston sisters that she would give "no ground to complain of a similar offence in future," Estlin insisted that if the British Garrisonians were to be deprived "of so important a resource for rendering the *Advocate* useful & attractive you will I trust feel induced to supply it with the substitute of *original communications*." Mary Ann believed, as did Maria, that "a private letter from the field of action often effects what hours of argument or of statistical details fail to touch."[52]

Chapman continued to maintain that her letters ought to remain private, for "they are so seldom written with an eye to their possible effect. (Providence forbid they should be!—they would cease to be letters & become diplomatic protocols.)"[53] She blamed her own unfiltered communication and careless wording on the material conditions in which she wrote: "What one writes in a room full of persons, & in the midst of conversation, (the only way in which I can write letters at present) must be read only by the very loving & indulgent personal friends to whom it is addressed."[54] The lack of privacy, the distraction of conversation and noise, the expectations of social interaction with visitors, the competing demands of children and household, and the lack of a dedicated time and place to write (a room of her own) combined to undermine professional deliberation in writing for publication as well as in letters.

MATERIALITY

The constant flow of information, query, and debate within the Weymouth sisterhood produced not only a large correspondence but also graphic strategies with which to prioritize business (both antislavery and domestic) over gossip in their letters to one another. In addition to the penned sketch of a hand pointing a finger to draw her reader's attention, Maria also enumerated her action items (1st, 2nd, etc.).[55] Anne confided to Caroline, "As I wish having a good deal to say to make the best use of my paper, I will take up business matters first."[56] In a letter to Anne, Debora arranged "all my *commands* in one corner by themselves that you may not forget any of them." Maria wrote from Paris to Anne in Weymouth, "I suppose Caroline has written so fully, that I '*need*' only reply to your business questions, which she has sorted out for me."[57] The playful underscoring of "need" and "commands" signaled the sisters' view of sibling dynamics as give-and-take among equals.

The Westons' correspondence also revealed signs of continual interruption. They overwrote their initial text, added second thoughts in margins and postscripts, and inserted material between existing lines. They drew attention to certain content by underscoring it or adding multiple question marks or exclamation points. The multiplicity of demands—household, family, occupational and political—that pressured their time and disrupted their labor also marked their prose style. As Anne wrote to Caroline from the Chapman home in Boston, where she was helping Maria while attending a Marlboro Hall meeting on the dissolution of the Union, "I will try to do a little something for you but you know the difficulty of writing in such a flurry as it is here."[58] In considering the circumstances under which nineteenth-century women wrote, literary critic Sharon M. Harris has argued that the interruptible nature of women's domestic labor shaped the production, content, and style of their writing. Harris has found that women writers turned this problem of disruption into an "intellectual and philosophical aesthetic," a discursive pattern or poetics of interruptibility that she called *discours décousu*.[59]

Such writing bore a visible mark. "You see by this letter's looks," wrote Maria to Mary A. Estlin, "that *nobody* but your father, & your dear Aunt Emma [Michell] are to see it."[60] What was it about one letter's "look" that invited publication while that of another prompted concealment from the public eye? *Discours décousu* contained abrupt sentence endings, run-on sentences, paragraphs that alternated writing implements or hands, evidence of lost concentration in dangling sentences or incomplete paragraphs, repetition, winding or inconclusive trails of thought. A letter written by Debora, for example, offered a stream of associational thinking that few but her sisters might make sense of: "Write me a word when the N. E. Convention is to be for I want to arrange my vacation accordingly—How is the cause getting on, I am so worried bot [*sic*] it, that I cant tell what to think—The American Soc acknowledge the receipt of $350 from Mass by H. B. Stanton, 'terms to be given hereafter'—."[61]

Caroline's correspondence similarly reflected the aesthetic of *discours décousu* in hurtling along before backtracking to explain, incorporating parentheses, underscoring key elements, and using dashes and lists rather than complete sentences. For example, in 1834, Caroline wrote to Debora about her Boston boarding school: "Got Henry to go & chinck the house which is done—& Henry has behaved in the kindest & handsomest manner about it—by the way I have another scholar—Miss Easton—& all things look bright—the pigs are all quiet. Mr Chubsen says he has a pair of candlesticks—some spoons & 12 plates for me—every little helps—you know—I shall make some purchases & come to Weymouth—Saturday if I can get there—if you can send for me by *any body* do."[62]

In a more political letter, Caroline wrote Ann and Wendell Phillips, "I have just read the last [*National Anti-Slavery*] Standard with great horror—I have a feeling nearly akin to remorse for the vote I gave in New York—to place Child in a position where he can do so much mischief—I *hope* it is *mere* folly & stupidity—but it looks much like *perversity*."[63] Caroline's mind simply moved faster than her pen. Snatching time when she could, she offered mere glimpses of feeling rather than full explanations of her thinking.

Caroline's correspondence was not alone in reflecting the "look" of *discours décousu*. Maria, for example, in seeking to disarm Mary Ann Estlin, excused the "want of polish" in her correspondence saying, "It is not to *every body* that I write in short saxon sentences."[64] In fact, Maria rarely wrote such sentences. More often she piled independent and dependent clauses one upon another until the meaning was all but lost. Her style reflected less the leisure to elaborate than an adaptation to the likelihood of imminent interruption. Even the practice of forwarding other peoples' letters revealed, on occasion, the lack of time for assimilation, reflection, and writing. As Anne explained in a hurried note, "I enclose what letters I have from sundry people & that will give you such news as I cant write."[65]

Interruptions characterized Weston labor whether the sisters engaged in child-rearing, teaching school, antislavery activism, or visiting. Journal-keeping helped them to impose continuity and maintain consistency in their correspondence. Debora, for example, wrote to Anne (who had replaced her as a teacher in New Bedford), "Though I intended to have kept a journal for your particular benefit yet I have not written a word since last Monday, therefore I will go back and remember what I can, & be more particular in future. Last tuesday morning I believe was where I left off." Not six months later, having returned to Boston from New Bedford, Anne responded to her sister in kind: "I will begin methodically or otherwise I shall omit some things that you would wish to hear. I have not written since last Wednesday week. That day. . . ." She then proceeded to report on each day's activities.[66]

Caroline struggled to order her letters and remember what she had written to whom. "I must keep a regular journal for I have so much to do & think of that I cant tell to save my life *what* I have written to you *what* to Anne & *what* to Weymouth—but I'll keep a journal—& see if I wont know," she insisted.[67] All four elder sisters kept daily journals out of necessity—for their own edification and as grist for their published writings and their personal and political correspondence.

Other factors shaping their writing included the scarcity of paper, the cost of postage, the delay and unpredictable delivery of letters sent by hand, and the possibility of misdirection. Letters frequently began with a reference to paper shortage.[68] As Lucia wrote to Debora, "I had intended to write to you [but] we had not an atom of paper in the house." Again she wrote, "You may perceive by my writing on [the back of a printed fair announcement], that we have no paper in this house you have no idea how much paper is used here it is impossible to keep any in the house."[69] On one occasion, "to save paper," Anne wrote Debora on the back of a document titled "ADDRESS OF THE BOSTON FEMALE ANTI-SLAVERY SOCIETY TO THE WOMEN OF NEW ENGLAND." On another she wrote on a petition form with the header, "To the Women of the United States." She offered the rationale, "I have only gilt edged paper & that I will not take." So too she informed her sister of the engagement of Martha Pickens on the back of a 4x6 typeset card calling "the attention of the Ladies of Boston to the District of Columbia" to a forthcoming petition seeking to end slavery in the District and "earnestly implor[ing]" them "not to refuse" their signatures. Maria wrote to her mother from New York with the details of her return to Weymouth by train on the back of a typeset antislavery hymn composed for the annual fund-raising bazaar. Anne, caught in her schoolroom by a hard rain and desperate "to improve all my time," decided to make do with the paper at hand. She took up a piece of waste and apologized for utilizing "this awful crumpled sheet . . . to write to you."[70]

Such a shortage encouraged the use of every inch of any paper at hand. Sheets were filled left to right across the paper, then turned ninety degrees and written over.[71] Small print filled margins and the spaces that traditionally surrounded the heading, greeting, or signature areas of a missive. Notes were even written under the closing flaps of envelopes and around the wax that sealed a letter when folded in upon itself to make a space for the address. When such letters were opened, seals often tore the paper, destroying readability.[72]

An additional factor influencing letter size was the way in which the postal system assessed payment. The Postal Act of 1792 (extended through the 1830s) calculated postage according to the number of sheets of paper used.[73] Page length and postage, therefore, affected style and substance. Anne wrote to Mary Ann Estlin that she was allowed only one sheet of paper because Caroline wanted the second and the limit for overseas mailing was two sheets. "My space is so confined," she acknowledged, "that all I can do is to state a few facts very abruptly a few important ones that is for much must be omitted." A year earlier, under similar constraints, Anne allowed that Estlin had "been so good in the way of writing to me of late that I feel as if I might well occupy a whole sheet in thanking you. But I cannot really spare the room," given the considerable antislavery material to be imparted.[74]

Mail delivery practices also influenced writing and reading. Debora decided to write every night, "for if I do not there is frequently an opportunity to send and I have no letter ready, besides forgetting much that I wish to say."[75] To avoid postage or embrace a delivery opportunity, the Westons often sent correspondence by hand. Debora, for example, asked Anne to forward from Boston some letters to Weymouth because she had a "direct opportunity to Boston" that would be "a pity to lose." Debora also sent letters to Anne through Ann Maria Bailey, Mr. Charles, Mr. Clark, Mr. Appleton, and Mrs. Hastings.[76] Letters also went by Hatch's Express, a stage that ran from New Bedford to Boston.[77] Consigning letters to individuals meant that delivery depended upon convenience. The stage left mail at regular stops, such as a tavern or store where it could be held until called for or sent on with a friend or neighbor.[78] Letters were also held for pickup at the post office. On occasion, abolitionists suspected postal workers of retaining rather than delivering their mail. Betsy Newton of Worcester wrote Maria that while she had received the petition forms sent on 27 June, they had "lain in the post office a month, as I suppose, I was a little apprehensive this was intentional as we often send to the office for papers."[79] Perhaps for assured delivery, much of the Weston correspondence that had to do with antislavery business was sent "care of HC & Co, Boston," Henry Chapman's ship chandlery.[80]

Until 1847, recipients paid postage.[81] Scholar Rebecca Earle has suggested that this arrangement "endowed correspondence with distinctive social and monetary obligations," placing one writer in another's "debt" and creating expectations for reciprocity.[82] For the Westons, the obligation to maintain a continuous correspondence was overt as well as implied. They accepted the responsibility of paying postage as they did that of writing, sure in the knowledge that the favor would be returned. None counted the cost or tallied the equity of outlay. Anne assured Debora that, while she had written "rather more than a week ago," she thought "by this time you will be glad to hear again. To say the truth, I have such a vivid recollection of my own lonely situation in N[ew] B[edford] that I feel as if you would think that ten cents could be in no way so well paid out as in the payment of postage."[83]

Weston Genealogy

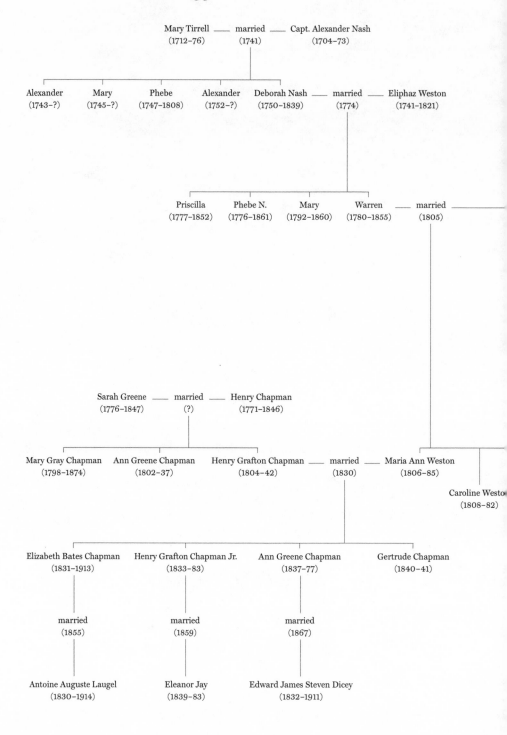

Mary Tirrell —— married —— Capt. Alexander Nash
(1712–76) (1741) (1704–73)

Alexander | Mary | Phebe | Alexander | Deborah Nash —— married —— Eliphaz Weston
(1743–?) | (1745–?) | (1747–1808) | (1752–?) | (1750–1839) (1774) (1741–1821)

Priscilla | Phebe N. | Mary | Warren —— married
(1777–1852) | (1776–1861) | (1792–1860) | (1780–1855) (1805)

Sarah Greene —— married —— Henry Chapman
(1776–1847) (?) (1771–1846)

Mary Gray Chapman | Ann Greene Chapman | Henry Grafton Chapman —— married —— Maria Ann Weston
(1798–1874) | (1802–37) | (1804–42) (1830) (1806–85)

Caroline Weston
(1808–82)

Elizabeth Bates Chapman | Henry Grafton Chapman Jr. | Ann Greene Chapman | Gertrude Chapman
(1831–1913) | (1833–83) | (1837–77) | (1840–41)

married | married | married
(1855) | (1859) | (1867)

Antoine Auguste Laugel | Eleanor Jay | Edward James Steven Dicey
(1830–1914) | (1839–83) | (1832–1911)

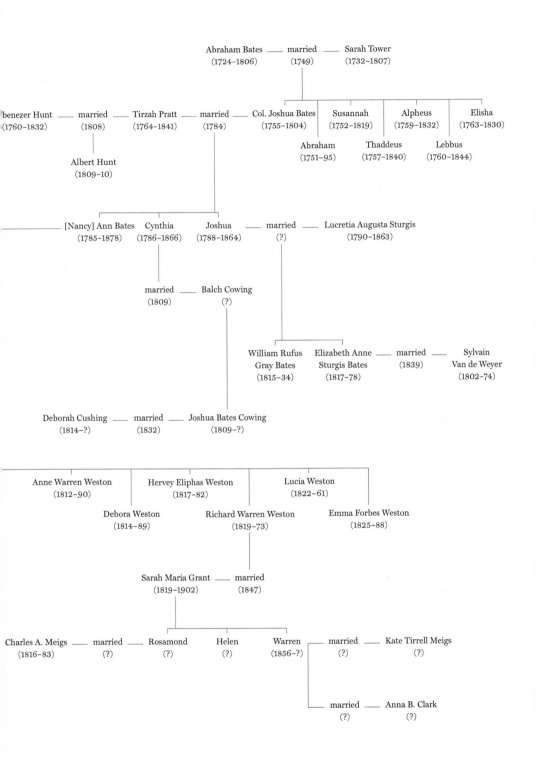

Antislavery Chronology

1829   *Walker's Appeal, In Four Articles; Together with a Preamble, to the Coloured Citizens of the World, but in Particular and Very Expressly, to Those of the United States of America* published in Boston.

1831   First issue of the *Liberator* published in Boston.

Mrs. Maria W. Stewart, *Religion and the Pure Principles of Morality*, published in Boston.

1832   New England Anti-Slavery Society (NEAS) founded.

Maria W. Stewart lectures at the Franklin Hall, Boston.

1833   Maria W. Stewart gives lecture in Boston, *An Address Delivered at the African Masonic Hall.*

Slavery abolished in the British colonies.

Boston Female Anti-Slavery Society (BFAS) founded.

Massachusetts Anti-Slavery Society (MAS) founded.

First convention of the American Anti-Slavery Society (AAS) held in Philadelphia.

1834   First fair of the BFAS held.

1835   American lecture tour of George Thompson.

Charlotte Phelps, first president of the BFAS, dies.

Weymouth and Braintree Female Emancipation Society founded.

Boston mob attacks BFAS and William Lloyd Garrison.

Harriet Martineau visits Boston.

South Weymouth Female Anti-Slavery Society founded.

1836   Congress imposes a "gag" on antislavery petitions.

Speaking tour of Massachusetts by Sarah and Angelina Grimké.

1837   First Anti-Slavery Convention of American Women held in New York City.

Angelina Grimké publishes *An Appeal to the Women of the Nominally Free States by an Anti-Slavery Convention of American Women.*

"Pastoral Letter" sent to Congregational churches.

1838   Angelina Grimké publishes *Letters to Catharine E. Beecher in Reply to an Essay on Slavery and Abolition.*

Sarah Grimké publishes *Letters on the Equality of the Sexes and Condition of Women.*

Angelina Grimké addresses the Massachusetts legislature.

Second Anti-Slavery Convention of American Women held in Philadelphia; Maria Weston Chapman and Anne Warren Weston elected vice presidents; speech by Maria Weston Chapman.

Mob burns Pennsylvania Hall in Philadelphia.

Maria Weston Chapman appointed to rules committee, New England Non-Resistance Society.

1839   Third Woman's Anti-Slavery Convention held in Philadelphia.

Female delegates at the annual meeting of the AAS granted the vote.

Contested election of BFAS officers.

Massachusetts Female Emancipation Society founded.

Maria Weston Chapman publishes *Right and Wrong in Massachusetts*.

Westons publish the *Liberty Bell*, an antislavery annual.

1840   Maria Weston Chapman publishes *Right and Wrong in the Anti-Slavery Societies*.

Maria Weston Chapman elected to the AAS executive committee.

American and Foreign Anti-Slavery Society founded in New York City.

Anne Warren Weston elected as secretary of NEAS.

World Anti-Slavery Convention held in London.

1842   Washington Total Abstinence Society of Weymouth and Braintree founded.

Fugitive slave George Latimer arrested; Westons publish the *Latimer Journal* (to May 1843) in Boston.

1844   Sydney H. Gay, Maria Weston Chapman, and Edmund Quincy edit the *National Anti-Slavery Standard*.

"Gag rule" repealed by Congress.

1845   Law office of Wendell Phillips closes; Francis Jackson resigns as justice of the peace, Boston.

1846   Maria Weston Chapman edits the *Liberator*.

1847   Maria Weston Chapman elected as BFAS foreign corresponding secretary and Anne Warren Weston and Mary Chapman as counsellors.

1849   Peace Conference held in Versailles; Westons host British and American delegates.

Maria Weston Chapman conducts antislavery mission to England.

1850   Congress passes Fugitive Slave Law.

Women's Rights Convention held in Worcester, Mass.

Vigilance Committee founded in Boston with Hervey Weston.

1851   Boston Vigilance Committee fails to prevent rendition of fugitive slave Thomas Sims.

Maria Weston Chapman, Ann B. Chapman, and Caroline and Emma Weston attend Peace Conference in London.

Maria Weston Chapman conducts antislavery mission to England.

1853   Maria Weston Chapman conducts antislavery mission to England and Ireland.

1855   Maria Weston Chapman conducts two antislavery missions to England.

1858   Maria Weston Chapman rejects editorship of the *National Anti-Slavery Standard*.

1859   Maria Weston Chapman replaces Boston Anti-Slavery Fair with Subscription Anniversary.

Attack on Harpers Ferry by John Brown and company.

1863   Thirtieth anniversary meeting of the AAS held in Philadelphia.

1865   Abby Kelley and Caroline Remond Putnam replace Maria Weston Chapman
          and Anne Warren Weston on MAS executive committee.
       Congress passes Thirteenth Amendment to U.S. Constitution; the *Liberator* is
          discontinued.
1869   Congress passes the Fifteenth Amendment to U.S. Constitution.
1870   Final meeting of the AAS held.

Notes

ABBREVIATIONS

ASC   Anti-Slavery Collection, Boston Public Library, Boston, Mass.
BA   The Baring Archive, London, UK
BPL   Boston Public Library, Boston, Mass.
EP   Estlin Papers, Dr. Williams's Library, London, UK
HL   Houghton Library, Harvard University, Cambridge, Mass.
JBEP   John Bishop Estlin Papers, Boston Public Library, Boston, Mass.
MHS   Massachusetts Historical Society, Boston, Mass.
WP   Weston Papers, Boston Public Library, Boston, Mass.

INTRODUCTION

1. Debra Gold Hansen interpreted the BFAS division to be the result of diverse approaches to female activism caused by class and religious differences among the membership. She identified the Westons as Unitarians who, along with Quakers, Universalists, and Episcopalians, became wary of their Congregational and Baptist sisters after the General Association of the Massachusetts Congregational Churches published a pastoral letter denouncing women's public activism. Mary Parker (president of the BFAS), Lucy and Martha Ball, and their allies split from the BFAS and founded the Massachusetts Female Emancipation Society (MFES). Hansen argued that the Weston faction attracted privileged women from old or well-to-do Massachusetts families (Southwick, Cabot, Sargent, Loring, and Shaw, for example) while the MFES women came from middling backgrounds as single women schoolteachers, milliners, and boardinghouse proprietors or married to small businessmen, artisans, and evangelical ministers. Hanson viewed these "conservative" women as retreating from abolition to engage in "moral reform and missionary causes." See Hansen, *Strained Sisterhood*, 97–105, and "Boston Female Anti-Slavery Society," esp. 61. In a new interpretation, Julie Roy Jeffrey finds that such religious and class differences did not cause the split. She rejects the view that those who left the BFAS to form the MFES were under the thumb of evangelical clergy who opposed female activism, as Maria Weston Chapman charged, or that these women reduced their antislavery activism. See Jeffrey, "Liberty Women of Boston," esp. 42–43. My study of the Weymouth Sisterhood complicates Hansen's characterization of the Westons' religious affiliation and economic status. Jeffrey's scholarship on the women of the MFES offers new insight into the division of the BFAS and the ongoing activities of the "Liberty [Party] Women," but agrees that the Westons viewed the problem as resulting from an anti-Garrisonian clerical plot. See Chapman, *Right and Wrong in Massachusetts*.

2. In the nineteenth century the term "promiscuous" (meaning of diverse and disorderly composition) was attached to a mixed-sex or multiracial group. Today's sexual connotations emerged later, although considerable concern developed in the 1830s that black men and white women meeting together in abolitionist conventions would lead to transgressive sexual relations. The word also carried a connotation of intersexed bodies and identities, a charge of manliness deployed against women who were active in politics. For discussion of how antebellum politics utilized the idea and attached it to political women, see Isenberg, *Sex and Citizenship*, and Ginzberg, "Pernicious Heresies."

3. After 1840, Garrisonians used the term "new organization" to characterize those who broke away from the Massachusetts and the Boston Female Anti-Slavery Societies to form the Massachusetts Abolition Society, the Massachusetts Female Emancipation Society, and, on the national scene, the American and Foreign Anti-Slavery Society. The members of these organizations opposed Garrisonian views on civil nonresistance, the necessity of disunion, and the impact of conservative clergy on antislavery tactics and organizational structure, including the role of women in mixed-sex organizations, particularly with regard to holding leadership positions. The "new" organization supported an electoral strategy as the primary means of ending slavery and built a political party to fulfill this goal. The Liberty Party nominated James G. Birney as its first presidential candidate in 1840 and dissolved in 1848 when many joined the Free-Soil Party.

4. *Formation of the Massachusetts Abolition Society*, 7; Chapman, *Right and Wrong in the Anti-Slavery Societies*, 27.

5. Caroline Weston to [Maria Weston Chapman and Henry Grafton Chapman], Boston, n.d., A.9.2.6.70, WP.

6. Oliver Johnson (1809–89) edited two abolitionist papers, the *Anti-Slavery Bugle* of Salem, Ohio, and the *Pennsylvania Freeman* of Philadelphia. His wife, Mary Ann Johnson (1808–72), was assistant matron of the female state prison in Sing Sing, New York. Both participated in the women's rights movement.

7. A lawyer, Sydney H. Gay (1814–88) began lecturing on behalf of the AAS in 1842. In 1844 he joined the *National Anti-Slavery Standard* as editor and, with the assistance of Edmund Quincy (1808–77) and Maria Weston Chapman, continued in that position for thirteen years. He married Elizabeth Johns Neall (1819–1907), a Philadelphia Quaker, in 1845. They moved to New York City, where, in the 1850s, he worked for the *Tribune* and the *Evening Post*.

8. Maria Weston Chapman journal, 20 November 1855, A.9.2.6.29, WP.

9. Southwick, *Reminiscences*, 35. Southwick was a year younger than Lucia Weston, and the two spent considerable time together. Her father participated in founding the AAS in December 1833, and her mother supported the Garrisonian wing of the BFAS.

10. Lydia Maria Child to Lucretia Mott, Northampton, 5 March 1839, in Meltzer and Holland, *Lydia Maria Child, Selected Letters*, 107. Child (1802–80) wrote extensively on the subject of abolition, publishing her most important work, *An Appeal in Favor of that Class of Americans Called Africans*, in 1833. Both she and her husband, David Lee Child, also edited the *National Anti-Slavery Standard*, the official organ of the AAS, a position for which Maria recruited them, although she did not always approve of what they published. For Child's response to such criticism, see Lydia Maria Child to Maria

Weston Chapman, New York, 11 May 1842, A.5.1.28, ASC. For criticism by the Westons, see Caroline Weston to Wendell and Ann Phillips, [New Bedford], n.d., Phillips Collection, HL; and Maria Weston Chapman to David L. Child, Boston, 29 December 1842, A.4.1.60, ASC.

11. Harriet Martineau (1802–76), a British political economist and author, toured the United States from 1834 to 1836. She befriended Chapman, staunchly supported Garrison, and published *The Martyr Age in America* to celebrate their activism and promote their cause. Martineau and Chapman remained close friends, writing each other weekly. Martineau lived as an invalid, but Chapman visited her often while in Europe and edited her autobiography. Jeremiah Winslow was brother to Isaac and Nathan, the latter two among the earliest supporters of Garrison and the *Liberator*. They participated in founding the AAS.

12. Harriet Martineau to Crabbe Robinson, 6 July 1850, quoted in Webb, *Harriet Martineau*, 25. For a similar perspective, see Mary A. Estlin to Caroline Weston, Bristol, 15 October 1855, A.7.2.75, JBEP. Other women emphasized Maria's tender side as well. Emma Michell, for example, thanked Maria for two notes, saying, "I send you for them, the reward you desire in telling you that I am not pained at our separation beyond that sense of sorrow that all must feel who truly love. . . . When recalling . . . how far removed from me in moral and intellectual attainments I am lost in astonishment at the result which followed our meeting, but it is a blessed one to me, and gratefully do I thank you for the rich gift of your affection—knowing it to be mine, I am at rest. I want to clasp my new found treasure it is true, but dearest love we are very near to each other" (Emma Michell to Maria Weston Chapman, Bristol, 30 September 1851, A.9.2.25.122, WP). Anne commented on such tenderness in Maria's relationship with Elizabeth Cabot Follen: "She and Maria have got up a friendship of the most enthusiastic cast. It is nothing but 'dearest' & 'sweetest' & they behave like girls of 16 when together. No matter, it is perfectly innocent" (Anne Warren Weston to Caroline Weston and Debora Weston, Boston [April 1840], A.9.2.16.13, WP).

13. Richard D. Webb to Miss Weston, Dublin, 28 November 1858, A.9.2.29.60; Edmund Quincy to Caroline Weston, Boston, 23 March 1846, A.9.2.22.34, WP. See also Edmund Quincy to Maria Weston Chapman, Dedham, 15 November 1842, A.9.2.17.111; William L. Garrison to Dr. Hodgson, Boston, 17 July 1848, A.9.2.24.17, WP; William Garrison Jr. to Helen Benson Garrison, Boston, 21 November 1864, Sophia Smith Collection, Smith College; Parker Pillsbury to John A. Collins, London, 1 November 1839, A.9.2.12.73, WP; Thomas Wentworth Higginson, "Anti-Slavery Days," *Outlook* 9 (3 September 1898): 47, 52, 54; and Martineau, *Martyr Age of the United States*, 18. Even opponents applied to Chapman terms signifying unusual female power, such as "Amazon," "ye Captain," and "Lady Macbeth," for her influence over William Lloyd Garrison and the MAS, on whose executive board she sat. See Epes Sargent Dixwell to John James Dixwell, Boston, 28 May 1838, Wigglesworth Family Papers, MHS; and Sydney H. Gay to Richard D. Webb, New York, 19 July 1848, A.1.2.18.27; and Richard D. Webb to Maria Weston Chapman, Dublin, 30 September 1845, A.1.2.15.63, ASC. Sculptress Anne Whitney spoke of Maria's "radamanthine eyes" through which she saw justly, if strictly. See Anne Whitney to Maria Weston Chapman, [Boston], [6 or 13] October [1880], Whitney Collection, Wellesley College.

14. Richard D. Webb to Elizabeth Pease, Dublin, 28 March 1849, A.1.2.18.54, ASC; Richard D. Webb to Edmund Quincy, Dublin, 11 August 1851, Quincy, Wendell, Holmes, and Upham Family Papers, MHS; M. A. W. Johnson to Maria Weston Chapman, Sing Sing, 24 November 1844, A.9.2.20.103, WP; Evelina A. S. Smith to Caroline Weston, Dorchester, 8 December 1844, A.9.2.20.118, WP; Richard D. Webb to Anne W. Weston, n.p., 8 February 1858, A.9.2.29.36, WP; Edmund Quincy to Richard D. Webb, Dedham, 13 January 1853, Quincy, Wendell, Holmes, and Upham Family Papers, MHS; William L. Garrison to Dr. Hodgson, Boston, 17 July 1848, A.9.2.24.17, WP.

15. Upon graduation from Oberlin College in 1851, Sally Holley (1818–93) became an agent of the AAS and wrote columns for the *Liberator*. After the Civil War, she and Caroline Putnam established a school for African Americans in Lottsburg, Virginia.

16. Sarah Pugh to Mary A. Estlin, 18 December 1853, 24.232.52, EP; Edmund Quincy to Richard D. Webb, 13 January 1853, Quincy, Wendell, Holmes, and Upham Family Papers, MHS; Chadwick, *Life for Liberty*, 114; Samuel J. May Jr. to Richard D. Webb, Leicester, 30 June 1857, B.1.6.6.57, May Papers, BPL; William Garrison Jr. to Helen B. Garrison, Boston, 21 November 1864, Sophia Smith Collection, Smith College. An advocate of woman's rights, Unitarian minister Samuel J. May (1797–1871) helped found the NEAS in 1832 and the AAS in 1833. He served as general agent and secretary of the MAS in 1835–36 before taking a pastorate in South Scituate, Massachusetts.

17. Debora Weston to Mary Weston, New Bedford, 6 November 1836, A.9.2.8.68; Anne Warren Weston to Debora Weston, n.p., n.d., A.9.2.3.51; Anne Warren Weston to Debora Weston, Boston, 15 January 1842, A.9.2.17.24, WP; Samuel J. May Jr. to Richard D. Webb, Leicester, 30 June 1857, B.1.6.6.57, May Papers, BPL; Caroline Weston to Debora Weston, Boston, [1841], A.9.2.5.22, WP; Southwick, *Reminiscences*, 38.

18. Lucia's attitude differed dramatically from that of Ann Terry Greene Phillips, Maria's cousin by marriage and the wife of abolitionist Wendell Phillips. Ann's illness led her to retire to her Exeter Street bedroom for much of her married life. Clare Taylor has speculated that both Lucia and Ann suffered from tuberculosis (variously diagnosed as rheumatism, fever, and consumption) picked up from the drains at Chauncy Place, the home of Henry and Sarah Greene Chapman, where they spent considerable time. Henry Grafton Chapman and Ann Greene Chapman may have died of an acute form of the disease. See Taylor, *Women of the Anti-Slavery Movement*, 5.

19. Richard D. Webb to Edmund Quincy, Dublin, 17 September 1857, Quincy, Wendell, Holmes, and Upham Family Papers, MHS; Maria Weston Chapman to Mary A. Estlin, Paris, May 1854, A.7.2.10, JBEP; Southwick, *Reminiscences*, 38. Attended by Emma, Lucia died in Rome in 1861.

20. Sarah Pugh to Maria Weston Chapman and Caroline Weston, London, 11 June 1853, A.8.3.70, ASC; John B. Estlin to Anne Warren Weston, Bristol, 10 October 1851, A.9.2.25.125, WP; Anne Warren Weston to Wendell Phillips, Weymouth, 22 November 1852, 1289, folio 4, Blagden Collection, HL; Edmund Quincy to Richard D. Webb, Dedham, 1 February 1849, Quincy, Wendell, Holmes, and Upham Family Papers, MHS.

21. William Garrison Jr. to Helen B. Garrison, Boston, 21 November 1864, Sophia Smith Collection, Smith College; Edmund Quincy to Richard D. Webb, Dedham, 13 January 1853, Quincy, Wendell, Holmes and Upham Family Papers, MHS.

22. See, for example, Emma Weston to Debora Weston, Weymouth, 18 April 1839, A.9.2.11.86; Anne Warren Weston to Debora Weston, Weymouth, 10 March 1842, A.9.2.17.40; and Debora Weston to Emma Weston, Weymouth, 16 March 1842, A.9.2.17.43, WP.

23. Lucia was nine and Emma six years older than Maria's eldest daughter, Elizabeth Bates Chapman. They were eight and eleven years younger than Debora, the sister nearest their ages.

24. Maria Weston Chapman to David L. Child, Boston, 24 August 1843, A.4.1.77, ASC.

25. Ann "Nancy" Bates Weston's signature appeared on the Weymouth women's petition of 1836. She appears to have been sympathetic to the cause, but there is little in the record of her activism on behalf of the slave. The signatures of the Weston women (Debora, Nancy, Priscilla, Phebe, and Mary) on the petition were all written in the same hand, likely Debora's. Warren Weston's name appeared on no petition.

26. Hunt, *Weymouth Ways*, 220.

27. The collection of Weston correspondence on which this study is based contains relatively few letters originating from or written to the Weston brothers, a factor that limits a full picture of their beliefs and activities. A variety of sources (such as organizational and newspaper records) suggest they (Warren in particular) played a more limited role than their sisters.

28. He was present at a crucial meeting on 22 October 1839 when the association passed four resolutions in disapprobation of sectarianism and support of William Lloyd Garrison, the MAS, and the AAS at a time when all had come under fire. See Concord Book Transcription, Weymouth Anti-Slavery Society, Tufts Public Library, Weymouth, Mass.

29. H. E. Weston to Anne Warren Weston, c/o Henry G. Chapman, New Haven, 10 December 1835, A.9.2.7.47; Anne Warren Weston to Debora Weston, Boston, 26 September 1837, A.9.2.9.72; Anne Warren Weston to Debora Weston, Weymouth, 15 November 1840, A.9.2.14.57, WP; Caroline Weston to Maria Weston Chapman and Henry Chapman, Roxbury, 21 January 1841, A.1.2.11.33, ASC; Anne Warren Weston to Debora Weston, Weymouth, 27 October 1841, A.9.2.15.83; Anne Warren Weston to Debora Weston, Boston, 30 March 1839, A.9.2.11.71, WP.

30. The black New England Freedom Association was founded in July 1842, preceding the formation of the Boston Vigilance Committee (BVC). It provided food, clothing, and shelter to fugitive slaves. Black women such as the daughters of Rev. Samuel Snowdon, the wife of Boston clothier Charles D. Williams, and Jane Putnam, wife of Boston's premier black hairdresser, all helped with fund-raising. The Latimer case (see Chapter 1) added members, white and black, to the BVC. It raised new interest in the aftermath of the Fugitive Slave Laws at a Faneuil Hall meeting held in October 1850. A relief organization, the committee provided aid (legal representation, medical treatment, food, clothing, shelter, and transportation) for some 430 fugitives. See Collison, "Boston Vigilance Committee." See also Still, *Underground Railroad*, and Foner, *History of Black Americans*.

31. Although she served as an editor for the *Non-Resistant*, a journal addressing the relationship of nonresistance to citizenship, the Texas Revolution, Indian warfare,

and the Civil War, Anne Warren Weston expressed conflicted feelings about the use of force against slave hunting in the North. As she wrote, "The excitement on the Fugitive Slave Bill is very great & it is very hard for me *to feel* as a professed Non Resistant ought." Or again, "I am apt to *believe* in peace & sympathize with fighting" (Anne Warren Weston to Mary A. Estlin, Weymouth, 2 November 1850, A.7.2.7, February 1855, A.7.2.28, JBEP). See also Anne Warren Weston to Wendell Phillips, New York, 22 April 1851, 1289, folio 3, Blagden Collection, HL. With regard to her feelings about Hervey's role, Anne wrote of the attempted rescue of fugitive slave Anthony Burns in Boston, "All that time I was not willing to see my brother. I was so afraid I might say something to urge him on or restrain him and I was equally unwilling to do either." She did not say of Hervey what she did of Wendell Phillips and Theodore Parker, who, in trying to save Burns, "entered so gallantly and readily into plans & arrangements for which their whole previous life had operated in some respects as disqualification. It is a very hard & strange duty for gentlemen, clergymen &c." Seemingly, it was easier to see in Hervey the potential for reckless, if not necessarily violent acts. See Anne Warren Weston to Mary A. Estlin, Weymouth, 30 July 1854, B.1.6.13.75, May Papers, BPL. See also Anne Warren Weston to "Dear Folks," Boston, 30 May 1854, A.9.2.28.13, WP.

32. Anne Warren Weston to Wendell and Ann Phillips, Weymouth, 25 July 1852, Blagden Collection, HL; Maria Weston Chapman to David L. Child, Boston, 24 August 1843, A.4.1.77, ASC.

33. The "Petition from 168 men of Weymouth" included the signatures of Hervey E. Weston and R. W. Weston but not that of the paterfamilias Captain Warren Weston. See Antislavery petitions, HR24A-H1.3, National Archives. The population of Weymouth in 1836 was approximately 3,300 (the U.S. census puts it at 2,837 in 1830 and 3,738 in 1840), so the brothers joined a small minority in doing even so much.

34. The underlining of Warren's name in the original spoke volumes about the sisters' surprise at his role. See Caroline Weston to Anne Warren Weston, Boston, 9 December 1842, A.9.2.17.134, WP.

35. David L. Child to Maria Weston Chapman, Northampton, 12 December 1842, A.4.1.59, ASC.

36. For reference to "House of Weston," see Maria Weston Chapman to Elizabeth Chapman Laugel, Weymouth, 18 August 1862, A.9.2.6.39, WP; and Anne Warren Weston to Mary A. Estlin, Weymouth, 5 February 1853, A.7.2.21, JBEP.

37. Lucia Weston to Debora Weston, Boston, 22 January 1837, A.9.2.3.90, WP.

38. For use of this nomenclature, see Debora Weston to Anne Warren Weston, n.p., 10 June 1836, A.9.2.8.31; Edmund Quincy to Henry Chapman and Maria Weston Chapman, Dedham, 18 May 1841, A.9.2.13.71-72; Edmund Quincy to Maria Weston Chapman, Dedham, 4 November 1844, A.9.2.20.87; and Edmund Quincy to Caroline Weston, Dedham, 2 July 1847, A.9.2.23.32-33, WP.

39. Nancy F. Cott (*Bonds of Womanhood*) has described gender consciousness and a sense of "sisterhood" as emerging in female academies, church groups, and voluntary associations during this period, encouraging some women to view themselves as having a shared experience as a sex. Historians disagree as to when "sisterhood" in the feminist sense developed. Cott has argued that gender consciousness is a necessary prerequisite for feminism.

40. For a discussion of family cultures, see Atkins, *We Grew Up Together*.

41. Maria Weston Chapman to Joshua Bates, Boston, 28 June 1836, HC 5.1.17, BA.

42. Caroline Weston to Maria Weston Chapman, n.p., [1841], A.9.2.15.37, WP; Maria Weston Chapman to Mary A. Estlin, Paris, 20 September [1852], A.7.2.49b, JBEP; Anne Warren Weston to Debora Weston, Groton, 17 September 1836, A.9.2.8.52, WP.

43. Oliver Johnson to Maria Weston Chapman, New York City, 26 July 1845, A.9.2.21.33, WP.

44. George Foster to Maria Weston Chapman, Haverhill, [1840], A.9.2.14.90; Edmund Quincy to Maria Weston Chapman, n.p., [1840], A.9.2.14.93; Lydia H. Jones to Anne Warren Weston, Holliston, 11 May 1841, A.9.2.15.44; John A. Collins to Anne Warren Weston, Gaston, 28 March 1842, A.9.2.17.44; Harriet W. Hayden to Maria Weston Chapman, New York, 27 November 1843, A.9.2.19.80, WP. See also J. Miller McKim to Maria Weston Chapman, Philadelphia, 26 August 1846, A.9.2.22.83; and Samuel S. May Jr. to Anne Warren Weston, Boston, 17 January 1851, A.9.2.25.61, WP.

45. This cultural view of the interchangeability of sisters infused nineteenth-century literature and art. Michael Cohen has argued that Victorian artists used resemblance, especially twinning, tempered with difference (for example, a white outfit with black trim on one sister and a black dress with white trim on another) to define sisterhood as "a kind of relationship that can be exclusive, reflexive, self-regarding, and self-sufficient." While such exclusivity occasionally was perceived as producing emotional exploitation, envy, and rivalry within the band, or a sense of betrayal if a sister turned outside the circle to meet individual needs (a common plot in nineteenth-century fiction), it also encouraged sibling unity and supported female empowerment. Sisters united to become stronger, their "near identity of appearance signaling unity of purpose," according to Valerie Sanders. Figuratively, then, sisterhood offered "a way of depicting equality in a society that [found] the idea difficult to embody in any other way." See Cohen, *Sisters*, 22, 23, 36; Sanders, *Brother-Sister Culture*, 5–6; and May, *Disorderly Sisters*, 13.

46. Caroline Weston to Maria Weston Chapman, New Bedford, [December 1843], A.9.2.20.137, WP; Edmund Quincy to Richard D. Webb, [Dedham], 22 November 1863, Quincy, Wendell, Holmes, and Upham Family Papers, MHS. One disagreement had to do with religion. Anne was more orthodox than her older sisters. She wrote to Debora seeking advice about selecting a Boston church with which to align. She felt she could not ask Maria or Caroline for help: "I wish you would write to me & tell me what you think it my duty to do about joining some church. I cannot with all my heart subscribe to all the articles of the Free church neither do I feel as if either Mr Fitch or most of the Free church people were my sort of people, as for Mr Winslow, his wickedness on the Slavery matter stares me in the face, and probably his whole church are as bad. . . . I do not think Maria and Caroline any persons to advise me for they are rather prejudiced & at the same time are altogether opposed to every thing that looks like churchdom." Yet she also wrote a poem, "The Come-Outer," that became famous as a statement of individual conscience over denominational hesitancy in the battle against slavery. See Anne Warren Weston to Debora Weston, Boston, 22 October 1836, A.9.2.8.63, WP.

47. Broadening the scope to benevolent women generally reveals others whose circumstances mirror the Weston experience to one degree or another. For example,

Harriet and Mary Otis devoted themselves to the Boston Female Asylum, Hannah and Caline Chamberlin to the Worcester Children's Friend Society, and Rebecca and Sarah Waldo to First Church, Worcester. Clementine and Harriet Smith sustained the nonsectarian Calvary Sunday School in the Brandywine Valley. The labor of Eliza, Margaret, and Mary Telfair of Savannah and Hannah, Sarah, and Hester Tidyman of Charleston suggests that southern benevolence also benefited from sororal relations. See Lawes, *Women and Reform*; Wallace, *Rockdale*; Carter, *Southern Single Blessedness*; and Lockley, *Welfare and Charity*, chap. 2.

48. Henry G. Chapman's deep involvement in the antislavery movement meant that wifehood did not curb Maria's activism, although his illness and subsequent death took a significant toll from 1840 to 1842. See Chapter 4. Motherhood influenced her course, the most significant example being her seven-year absence from the United States while she (and Caroline) took the children to Europe for the sake of their educations and marital prospects.

49. See the Appendix for a discussion of the size, shape, and significance of Weston correspondence; its construction as an archival collection; and its utility and limitations for this study.

50. Epes Sargent (1748–1822) married Dorcas Babson (1749–1836) in 1772 and had nine children, of whom Catherine (1774–1852) was the oldest and Henrietta (1785–1871) among the younger. Quaker Joseph Southwick (1791–1866) was a founder of the AAS and served as MAS president in 1835 and 1836. He withdrew over Garrison's view that free states should separate from those harboring slavery. He married Thankful Southwick (1792–1867), who served as BFAS president in the early 1840s and was active with the Westons in the nonresistance movement as well.

51. Among the BFAS sisterhood there were other sisters who married and yet may be seen to have followed a sororal model similar to that of the Westons by combining the singlehood of one with marriage of another and sharing child-rearing. Examples included white and African American sisters Mary Ann Allen and Catharine Spear, Lavina Ames Hilton and Eunice Ames Davis, and Susan Jackson and Eliza Jackson Merriam. For more on these women, see Hansen, *Strained Sisterhood*, 67.

52. The Thurber and Pratt sisters grew impatient with the slow development of a female society in Providence, a city that Helen Benson, later wife of William Lloyd Garrison, described as having an informal ban on antislavery talk. They signed the roll book of the male auxiliary to the NEAS. When agent Wyllys Ames proposed that the society admit female members in January 1834, however, the debate proved inconclusive and he withdrew the motion. See William L. Garrison to Helen Benson, 18 January and 18 February 1834, in Merrill, *I Will Be Heard!*, 280, 283–85; and Van Broekhoven, *Devotion of These Women*, 84–85.

53. For discussions of this aspect of the BFAS demographic, see Hansen, *Strained Sisterhood*, chap. 4. On Concord and the Thoreaus, see Petrulionis, *To Set This World Right*; on Rhode Island, see Van Broekhoven, *Devotion of These Women*.

54. For more information on the Grimkés, see Birney, *Grimké Sisters*; Barnes and Dumond, *Letters*; Lumpkin, *Emancipation of Angelina Grimké*; Ceplair, *Public Years of Sarah and Angelina Grimké*; Lerner, *Grimké Sisters of North Carolina*; Lerner, *Feminist Thought of Sarah Grimké*; and Sklar, *Women's Rights Emerges*.

55. Kinship provided the vocabulary upon which antebellum Americans drew to understand political, social, and economic relationships and practices. C. Dallett Hemphill has argued that the increasing use of the sibling relationship as a metaphor for other relations in the antebellum period resulted from the "heightened importance of sibling relations among Americans" (*Siblings*, 130). Family metaphors accomplished considerable political work, there being the "family of man" that abolitionists cited as the goal and significance of emancipation; the "family of God" in which brothers and sisters in Christ and his church found inspiration for their activism; and the nation as family that bound together inhabitants and citizens, defining their relative duties and obligations while aiding in the construction of a national identity. Jeffrey Weeks has suggested that Victorians described every tie "within the language of family relationships." Other historians have noted that while kinship usually signified relations of blood and marriage, "it is possible to feel a sense of kinship with those to whom we are emotionally and intellectually attached but not necessarily related." See Weeks, "Pretended Family Relationships," 228; and Davidoff et al., *Family Story*, 54.

56. Maria Weston Chapman to Mary A. Estlin, Paris, 12 December 1852, A.7.2.61, JBEP. Mary Ann Estlin was the daughter of John Bishop Estlin, an ophthalmologist of Bristol, England, and a strong supporter of Garrisonian antislavery, temperance, and other reforms. Born in 1820, she was two years older than Lucia Weston. Much enamored of Maria and particularly close to Anne Warren Weston, Estlin was a frequent correspondent of the Westons and visited them in the 1840s while they resided in Europe and on a return visit to the United States in 1868. She was a leader of the Garrisonian Bristol and Clifton Ladies Anti-Slavery Society.

57. In an ongoing debate about the relationship between the terms "sisters" and "friends" as used by nineteenth-century women, Naomi Tadmor (*Family and Friends*) has shown that, in the eighteenth century, friendship was a social category signifying relations to which the obligations of blood extended. Nancy Cott has argued that the use of the term "friend" changed in the early nineteenth century so that friendship became distinguished from kinship as an elective relationship and thus "subject to idealization"; see *Bonds of Womanhood,* 186. Carol Lasser ("'Let Us Be Sisters Forever'") has concluded that sibship provided an important model for building other female relationships in the nineteenth century and uses the term "elective sisters" to describe female friends. Julie Roy Jeffrey has asserted, and certainly the Weston correspondence demonstrates, that abolitionist women "freely adopted the conventions of friendship with those who were technically strangers" and quotes the phrase Anne Warren Weston used when writing to members of the New York Female Anti-Slavery Society: "we are yet made friends and sisters." See Anne Warren Weston to New York Female Anti-Slavery Society, 21 July 1835, BFAS Letterbooks, MHS; and Jeffrey, *Great Silent Army*, 61.

58. See Smith, *Theory of Moral Sentiments*, 220, 223; and Smith, "'All in Some Degree Related to Each Other.'"

59. Smith, "'All in Some Degree Related to Each Other,'" also shows that, in the late eighteenth and early nineteenth centuries, such clustering was more characteristic of New England families than of families in the American South or in Great Britain.

60. See Kelly, *In the New England Fashion*. Kelly focuses on parochial rather than urban women and emphasizes as causal the household manufacturing that women did

in small-town New England. Weymouth, with a population between 3,000 and 3,200 in 1835, was somewhat larger than the towns that Kelly studied. Nevertheless, along with their mother, the Weston sisters did considerable domestic manufacturing, particularly the sewing of clothing, well into the 1850s. They made their own clothes, as well as those of their brothers and nieces and nephew, despite the greater economic resources available to their urban (and urbane) elder sister Maria. But their antislavery labors were as significant as their domestic manufacturing in crafting affection and sisterhood.

61. Motz, *True Sisterhood*; Hartigan-O'Connor, "Abigail's Accounts"; Cashin, "Structure of Antebellum Planter Families"; Kierner, "Hospitality, Sociability, and Gender"; Kierner, *Beyond the Household.*

62. C. Dallett Hemphill (*Siblings*, 154) has argued that American brothers undertook the majority of kin-keeping activities in the Early Republic but in the antebellum period gave these over to their sisters in New England. Brothers retained these responsibilities in the American West and South.

63. Smith, "'All in Some Degree Related to Each Other,'" 47.

64. There is no commonly agreed upon term for the sibling relationship as a collective social entity beyond the biological connection. "Sibship" and "siblicity" have been suggested. See, for example, the discussion in Bodle, "Littlest Commonwealth?"; Davidoff, "Where the Stranger Begins"; and O'Day, *Family and Family Relationships*, 93. Two important new books on the subject are Hemphill, *Siblings*, and Davidoff, *Thicker than Water.*

65. Gittins, "Marital Status"; Ryan, *Cradle of the Middle Class.* Economic and business historians have explored kinship networks extensively in studies of capital accumulation and investment. Sibling exchange marriage played an important role in capital accumulation and business recruitment in the seventeenth and eighteenth centuries and in the economy's transition to commercial and industrial capitalism in the nineteenth. Cooperative investment strategies based upon siblicity and marriage within a broader circle served to consolidate financial power and transform an economic elite into an upper class. See Farber, *Guardians of Virtue*; Hall, "Marital Selection"; Hall, "Family Structure"; Gough, "Close-Kin Marriage"; Farrell, *Elite Families.*

66. See Cashin, *Family Venture*; Dublin, *Transforming Women's Work*; Smith, *Family Connections*; and Billingsley, *Communities of Kinship.* Sally Oliver, for example, wrote to her brother Hubbard that their sibling, Stephen, was looking for work in Boston. He knew of a job, but, of course, she wrote, he "would be more pleased still if you could employ him. But let who will employ him it will be quite agreeable to him to board with you. If it is so to you and your wife" (Sally S. Oliver to Hubbard Oliver, n.p., n.d., Elizabeth Ann Oliver Papers, 1806–70, Ms. N-400, MHS).

67. Davidoff, "Where the Stranger Begins," 206. See also Davidoff, *Thicker than Water*; Alexander, *Ambiguous Lives*; Motz, *True Sisterhood*, chap. 2; and Carter, *Southern Single Blessedness*, chap. 3.

68. More work needs to be done with a critical eye to how scholars have gendered kin-keeping female. See Hemphill, "Fun with Ben and Jane.

69. Hemphill, *Siblings*, 89, 118, 126.

70. Ibid., 130–31, 141, 144.

71. Such "ladies first" rituals provided sisters with best seats in the house, first service at social gatherings, and their choice of amusements. See ibid., 149. This new cultural "reign of sisters" offered a new system of family authority for a more democratic age, providing social order while masking the broader social inequalities of race and class with gender difference. See ibid., 148, 149, 153.

72. Hemphill insists the relationship between brothers and sisters was not necessarily unequal. See Hemphill, *Siblings*, 129–30, 141–46. This view contradicts that of historians E. Anthony Rotundo and Leonore Davidoff, who have characterized the sibling relationship, in Davidoff's words, as "neatly reciprocal and distinctly unequal." While acknowledging the greater opportunity brothers found in the wider society, Hemphill finds it "exaggerated." She argues that because emotional closeness was critical to sisters' ability to influence their brothers, siblings "continued to offer each other a refuge of equality" that was "acknowledged in different but complimentary duties they owed each other" (ibid., 148). See Rotundo, *American Manhood*, 95; and Davidoff, "Kinship as a Categorical Concept" (quote on 414). The historiography of the relation between middle-class sibling culture and female equality and independence has addressed the norms or definitions of "independence" and has focused on three issues: the identity of single women in family and society, the social and economic relations of unwed sisters to their brothers, and the situations of adult sisters living in their brothers' households in nineteenth-century Britain and America. See the following on both Victorian Britain and America: Howe, *Cotton Masters*; Vicinus, *Independent Women*; Smith, "Meanings of Family"; Davidoff and Hall, *Family Fortunes*; Jabour, "'It Will Never Do'"; Miller, "'My Part Alone'"; Gordon and Nair, "Myth of the Victorian Patriarchal Family"; and Chambers-Schiller, "Married to Each Other."

73. Ryan, *Cradle of the Middle Class*. Fictive kin may include individuals taken in by the family who come to function as family members, or people who identify as kin as members of a religious, communitarian, or educational institution. The South used such terms as "kissing cousin" and "shirttail cousin" to denote a familial relationship in which the exact nature of the kinship was too distant to reconstruct but was acknowledged, or a relationship in which there was no actual relationship of blood or marriage but where a warm familiarity existed and the boundary between friendship and kinship had diminished over time. See Billingsley, *Communities of Kinship*, 19.

74. A survey of Weymouth genealogy reveals all three marital forms between 1700 and 1850, with sibling exchange marriages the most common and first-cousin marriages the least. See Chamberlain's *Genealogies*. American Supreme Court justice Joseph Story insisted that marriages between in-laws were "the very best sort," and that "nothing is more common in almost all the states of America than second marriages of this sort" (quoted in Trinterud, *Forming of an American Tradition*, 275, and Bullette, "Puzzling Case"). Among Weston acquaintances in Boston were examples of such marriages. Abolitionist Samuel E. Sewall married BFAS member Louisa M. Winslow in 1836. Following her death in 1850, Sewall married Louisa's sister, Harriet. The Dixwell brothers, nephews of BFAS members Catherine and Henrietta Sargent, married sisters in 1839. John James Dixwell married Elizabeth Boardman Ingersol Bowditch, even as his brother, Epse Sargent Dixwell, married her sister, Mary Ingersol Bowditch. For discussion of such marriages among eighteenth-century southerners, see Glover, *All*

Our Relations, 9–10, 47–49. For those among the nineteenth-century planter class, see Clinton, *Plantation Mistress*, 78–79. See also Billingsley, *Communities of Kinship*, 12–20. On cousin marriage, see Bardaglio, *Reconstructing the Household*. For a discussion of American law and ideology, see Connolly, "Domestic Intercourse."

75. In *Cradle of the Middle Class*, Mary Ryan suggests that by the 1840s, more than one-fifth of all family businesses were managed by brothers (138). Betty Farrell has mapped sibling ties onto a newly developing financial structure of interlocking directorships, banks, and insurance companies in nineteenth-century Boston, arguing that sibling connections provided a source of economic innovation and entrepreneurship as family capitalism gave way to more bureaucratic structures in New England's new market economy. See Farrell, *Elite Families*.

76. Allgor, "'A Lady will Have More Influence'"; Allgor, *Parlor Politics*, 206. For studies that explore the political uses of kinship, see Glover, *All Our Relations*; Kierner, *Beyond the Household*; Billingsley, *Communities of Kinship*; Baptist, "Migration of Planters"; Kurtz, *Kinship and Politics*; and Pease and Pease, *Family of Women*.

77. Hansen, *Strained Sisterhood*, 67; Jeffrey, *Great Silent Army*, 45–46.

78. Among the Weston aunts, single women who, like their nieces, shared a household had differing degrees of abolitionist feeling. Mary, the youngest, proved herself a mainstay of the Weymouth and Braintree Female Emancipation Society, but little evidence exists of any active engagement of the elder sisters. So too the children of abolitionists both sympathized with the cause and distanced themselves from it. Henry G. Chapman Jr. had nightmares of mobs and acted out his fears, as did some of the Garrison children.

79. Henrietta Sargent to George B. Dixwell, Boston, 24 April 1842, Wigglesworth Family Papers, MHS. Anna Sargent (1782–1873) married John Parker (1783–1844). While Catherine was the eldest child of eight siblings, and eight years older than Anna, Henrietta was three years younger. Many letters written by their nephew Epse Sargent Dixwell and their sister Esther (who married Dr. John Dixwell in 1805) expressed feelings ranging from ridicule to disdain for his aunts over their abolitionist beliefs and activities.

80. Jeffrey, *Great Silent Army*, 46–47; Boylan, "Timid Girls."

81. This view contrasts with that of Anne M. Boylan, whose work on female reform and benevolent societies covers far more than antislavery societies. The Female Moral Reform Society, for example, focused on "rescuing" prostitutes and affirmed the "duty" and *"privilege"* of "unmarried ladies . . . to labor perseveringly to promote the cause." Boylan nevertheless asserts that an "effacement of single women" in the leadership of these associations reflected deference to married colleagues despite the latter's disadvantages under common law. She found that "unmarried women's common law independence did not necessarily go hand-in-hand with economic freedom. Even well-off single adults lived as sisters or daughters in married-couple households and faced both constant demands on their time and the expectation that they would behave as dependent daughters" (Boylan, "Timid Girls," 58–59). However, correspondence and diaries of single women have shown that many did not live as dependents but rather themselves supported dependents—widowed mothers and younger siblings—as did the Westons.

82. Eliza Lee Cabot Follen (1787–1860) was very close to Maria Weston Chapman despite their disparity in age. Her husband, Charles Follen (1796–1840), was a German refugee and professor of German literature at Harvard College. He also taught ethics at the Divinity School. He joined the NEAS in 1834 and was fired from Harvard for his antislavery "Address to the People of the United States," written for the 1834 NEAS Convention and published in the *Liberator*, 6 September 1834. Follen served on the Board of Managers of the MAS and chaired numerous committees for the New England society. The Massachusetts state legislature called upon him to testify in 1835 when, in response to Gov. Edward Everett's declaration that all citizens should abstain from discussing the subject, he asserted that if slavery did not end, "we shall all be slaves, or little better than slaves"; see *Account of the Interviews*, 3–4; and Stange, *Patterns of Antislavery*, 70. Thereafter Follen became a minister but lost his position at the First Unitarian Church in New York City when his congregation objected to his abolitionist sermons and writings. After Charles died in 1840 in a fire aboard the steamer *Lexington*, Eliza settled in West Roxbury, Massachusetts. In addition to numerous children's books, she published a biography of her husband (1842) and a collection of his sermons. She also published a number of antislavery tracts, including *To the Mothers of the Free States* (1855) and *Anti-Slavery Hymns and Songs* (1836), a book she and Maria worked on together. Like Chapman, Follen joined Boston's Federal Street Unitarian Church because of its minister, William E. Channing. Her sister Susan came with her when she married in 1828, a month after her forty-first birthday.

83. Chambers-Schiller, *Liberty, a Better Husband*, chap. 7.

84. Hansen, *Strained Sisterhood*, 69. Boylan notes that never-married "women filled few positions as directors, managers, trustees, or officers. Typically, married women constituted between three-quarters and nine-tenths of leadership lists, and in some cases, *all* of a society's officers were married or widowed." Her study of the BFAS "officer corps" showed that 47.6 percent married and 45.2 percent remained single. She could not determine the marital status or history of 7.1 percent. Boylan found that single women predominated among the leadership in only three of thirty-seven benevolent organizations, although there were organizations with significant proportions of single leaders (for example, Boston's Female Anti-Slavery Society, Widows' Society, Fragment Society, and Society for the Promotion of Christianity among the Jews). See Boylan, *Origins of Women's Activism*, 55, 57, and table A. 5.

85. For work in the field not yet cited, see O'Brien, *An Evening When Alone*; Wulf, *Not All Wives*; and Beattie, *Obligation and Opportunity*. For a comparative view of widows and never-married women, see Bell and Yans-McLaughlin, *Women on Their Own*. For studies of European ever-single women, see Vicinus, *Independent Women*; Bennett and Froide, *Singlewomen in the European Past*; Hill, *Women Alone*; Beattie, *Medieval Single Women*; Froide, *Never Married*; and Holden, *Shadow of Marriage*.

86. The demographic evidence for female heads of households is addressed in Anderson, *Family Structure*, and Carr, "Change 'as Remarkable as the Revolution Itself.'" See also Withey, "Household Structure"; Ruggles, *Prolonged Connections*; Smith, "Female Householding"; and Dillon, "Women and the Dynamics of Marriage." Although focused on Victorian Glasgow, the work of Eleanor Gordon and Gwyneth Nair is also suggestive. See "Middle Class Family Structure."

87. Shammas, *History of Household Government*, 19–20.

88. Maria Weston Chapman to Elizabeth Pease Nichol, Weymouth, 20 September 1858, A.1.2.28.133, ASC. Historians of women and families, too, have foregone making marriage a category of analysis and largely assumed that the institution organized women's lives, although Nancy Cott has pushed historians to recognize the implications of marriage for both women's and men's public as well as private lives. See Cott, "Marriage and Women's Citizenship," "Giving Character to Our Whole Civil Polity," and *Public Vows*.

89. Edmund Quincy to Caroline Weston, Dedham, 27 February 1841, A.9.2.15.28; Anne Warren Weston to Henry G. Chapman and Maria Weston Chapman, Boston, 15 January 1841, A.9.2.15.10, WP.

90. For discussion of such centers, see Friedman, *Gregarious Saints*, and Chambers-Schiller, "The Cab."

91. Foucault, "Eye of Power," 149.

92. This helps explain why these sisters, among the many sibling groups in the BFAS and antislavery movement, rejected male leadership and asserted women's right to determine their own mode of activism; but I do not assume that all who joined the Westons had inadequate fathers or debilitated brothers. The sororal model of female activism emerged from sibship and was enhanced by singlehood and shared living arrangements.

CHAPTER 1

1. Amos Dresser (1813–1904) left the Presbyterian Lane Theological Seminary after officials forbid students from discussing abolition. In 1837 he, like Henry B. Stanton (1805–87), became an AAS agent.

2. Lucia Weston to Debora Weston, Boston, 22 January 1837, A.9.2.3.90, WP.

3. See Frances Drake's report of the value placed on the *Bell* and the competition that emerged among contributors for complimentary copies: Frances H. Drake to Maria Weston Chapman, 18 January 1846, A.9.2.22.8, WP; see also Maria Weston Chapman to Mary A. Estlin, Boston, 27 January 1846, A.7.2.32, JBEP.

4. Nancy Gardner Prince approached the BFAS for help establishing a black orphanage. While the BFAS did not allocate organizational funds, individual members supported four children. See M. V. Ball, Rec. Sec., FIRST ANNUAL REPORT OF THE BOSTON FEMALE ANTI-SLAVERY SOCIETY, 8 October 1834, in the *Liberator*, 3 January 1835. In 1836, Maria raised funds for the new Samaritan Asylum. Refused help on the grounds that there was no need for a separate black institution, she proved that there was, by trying unsuccessfully to get a black child in whom she was interested into the segregated orphanage on Essex Street. When Phoebe died in the Samaritan Asylum, Maria arranged and paid for her funeral. Ann G. Chapman left the asylum $100 in her will; the Westons also donated. See Debora Weston to Mary Weston, Weymouth, 23 February 1835, A.9.2.7.58; Debora Weston to Anne Warren Weston, Boston, 10 June 1836, A.9.2.8.31, WP. The issue of whether the BFAS should formally sustain the orphanage contributed to the division of the association in 1839; at issue was whether it should commit monies to ameliorate the condition of Boston blacks or focus solely

on the freedom of slaves. See Hansen, *Strained Sisterhood*, 14; and Boylan, *Origins of Women's Activism*, 32, 37.

5. Crandall (1803–90) opened her academy in 1831. In the fall of 1832, African American Sarah Harris sought admission. Protests by parents and community members caused Crandall to close the school and reopen it as an all-black female academy. She recruited students with an advertisement in the *Liberator* on 2 March 1833. Local authorities in Connecticut arrested her for violating a newly minted Connecticut law prohibiting the teaching of out-of-state black students or boarding them for purposes of instruction. Convicted although not incarcerated, Crandall experienced ongoing harassment and closed the school in the summer of 1834. A letter to "Miss Weston" acknowledged receipt of a fund-raising request with the response, "I am always glad of any opportunity of aiming a blow at slavery and as this affords me one I avail myself of the opportunity and enclose you the small sum of five dollars." See B. B. Mussey to Miss Weston, Boston, 10 September 1832, A.9.2.7.24, WP. Mussey's note did not identify the beneficiary of this solicitation. His publishing business was located at No. 29 Cornhill, just down the street from the antislavery reading room. Known for publishing Jacob Abbott's *Rollo* and *Lucy* books, Mussey also published works on slavery and abolition.

6. As was the case with Garrison, who paid considerable attention to temperance reform in *The Genius of Universal Emancipation*, coedited with Benjamin Lundy from 1828 to 1830, and in the *Liberator*. The American temperance movement emerged in Massachusetts when reform-minded ministers of Andover Seminary established the Massachusetts Society for the Suppression of Intemperance in 1813. By 1834, the society boasted 7,000 local affiliates with over 1,250,000 members. See Rorabaugh, *Alcoholic Republic*, 191, 202.

7. Anne Warren Weston to Debora Weston, Boston, 23 March 1838, A.9.2.10.15; Anne Warren Weston to Debora Weston, Weymouth, 19 June 1842, A.9.2.17.73; [Debora Weston] to Caroline Weston, Weymouth, May 1846, A.9.2.22.41, WP.

8. See Hampel, *Temperance and Prohibition*, 67–68.

9. See Anne Warren Weston to Debora Weston, Weymouth, 9 November 1838, A.9.2.10.68, WP.

10. Debora was sorry the Whigs won the 1839 election because Democrats Rodney French and John Bailey, both staunch abolitionists, had been put up for election in New Bedford. About "5 of the democratic rum drinkers refused to vote for temperance men, at least so the story goes," she wrote. See Debora Weston to Anne Warren Weston, New Bedford, 1 December 1839, A.9.2.12.101, WP. A large temperance meeting in Weymouth in November 1843 drew all the sisters, as well as abolitionists William L. Garrison, Nathaniel P. Rogers, and Edmund Quincy. See Anne Warren Weston to Caroline and Debora Weston, Boston, 10 November 1843, A.9.2.19.75, WP.

11. That same year, Gershom B. Weston, a cousin, helped found the Duxbury, Massachusetts, Martha Washington Relief Society promoting charity and temperance. He lectured on temperance frequently. See Weston, *In Memoriam*, 29.

12. Hunt, *Weymouth Ways*, 67–68.

13. Maria Weston Chapman to Joshua Bates, Boston, 29 March 1837, HC 5.1.17, BA.

14. Ibid. Despite her claims of a cure, ample evidence exists of ongoing family concern about Warren Weston's erratic behavior, impulse control, and what may have been

dry rages. See, for example, [Debora Weston] to Caroline Weston, Weymouth, May 1846, A.9.2.22.41, WP.

15. Heman Humphrey, president of Amherst College, drew a direct comparison between the slave trade and intemperance in an address to undergraduates in which he concluded, "A sober people may possibly be enslaved; but an intemperate people cannot long remain free" (Humphrey, *Parallel Between Intemperance and the Slave Trade*, 4–5). Many abolitionists came to the cause through temperance. William Lloyd Garrison, for example, linked the two slaveries during his apprenticeship at a leading temperance journal, the *National Philanthropist*, and took as one of his subjects "the suppression of Intemperance" as editor of the *Journal of the Times*. His brother James Holley Garrison (1801–42) suffered from alcoholism. This experience with a family member was one he shared with the Westons. See Rorabaugh, *Alcoholic Republic*, 194–95, 200–201, for discussion of how Americans linked intemperance with abolition.

16. Joyce Appleby has found that men born between 1776 and 1800 construed their decision to quit drinking as an event in which they confronted and defeated the temptation of self-indulgence. Their autobiographies offered "sequences of events that led up to their temperance vows as unique experiences, deeply meaningful to themselves personally and to their connection with their communities." This new masculine ethic provided a "psychological mechanism [for] stifling impulses and restraining passions" (Appleby, "Personal Roots," 142). For Joshua Bates's narrative and his relations with his tippling nephew Richard Warren Weston, see Chapter 3. On Warren Weston's death, Bates described his brother-in-law as "a very strong-minded man" who had "cured himself." Admiring Weston's predilection for reading, Bates framed the story of Weston's return to sobriety as one of self-mastery through intellectual application. See Diary of Joshua Bates, 11 and 23 November 1855, Baring Brothers DEP 74, BA.

17. She was married to Wendell Phillips from there in 1837. Ann Greene Chapman, Henry's younger sister, was a fervent abolitionist and a Weston favorite. Her death in 1837 drove Anne Warren Weston to despair.

18. Anne Warren Weston to Debora Weston, Groton, 21 January 1834, A.9.2.7.34, WP. By July, her brother was teasing her about becoming so vehement an advocate that she should "be careful what she says or she will have her furniture burnt" (Robert Warren Weston to Debora Weston, Boston, 14 July 1834, A.9.2.7.35, WP). That same fall, the NEAS established its offices at 46 Washington Street, a building also housing those of lawyer and board member Samuel Sewall. The *Liberator* moved in around the corner at 25 Cornhill.

19. Corresponding secretary Mary Grew wrote of the society as "containing not quite fifty members" in May 1834. See Mary Grew to Mrs. Reid, President of the Reading Female Anti-Slavery Society, Boston, 17 May 1834, BFAS Letterbooks, MHS.

20. Anne Warren Weston's first letter as secretary was dated 21 July 1835. See BFAS Letterbooks, MHS.

21. Debora Weston to Mary Weston, Boston, 23 February 1835, A.9.2.7.58; Debora Weston to Mrs. Warren Weston, Boston, n.p., 8 May 1835, A.9.2.7.45, WP. See also Lydia Maria Child to Mrs. Chapman and other ladies, Boston, 1 June 1834, A.5.1.26, ASC.

22. Among the founders of the AAS was Sarah's father, Quaker Joseph Southwick (1791–1866). He served as president of the MAS in 1835–36 and as vice president for several additional years.

23. Southwick, *Reminiscences*, 8. Mrs. Sarah Greene Chapman ("the old lady," as Anne called her) joined her nieces, daughters, daughter-in-law, and her sisters as a member of the BFAS in April 1836. Thereafter, the Chapman family met in common council once a year to determine the amount and nature of their financial contributions to the cause. See Anne Warren Weston, n.p., 15 April 1836, A.9.2.8.19, WP.

24. Notice was given in the *Liberator*, 22 November 1834: "ANTI-SLAVERY LADIES—ATTENTION! The philanthropic ladies belonging to the Anti-Slavery Societies in Portland, Concord (N.H.), Newburyport, Amesbury, Reading, &c. &c. are respectfully informed than an Exhibition is shortly to be opened in this city, under the direction of Mrs. CHILD and other ladies, for the sale of useful articles voluntarily contributed, the proceeds to be given in aid of the funds of the NEAS; and they are invited to assist by their skill and liberality in preparing the necessary materials."

25. Caroline Weston remembered the first fair as a production in which "Mrs. [Louisa] Loring furnished the money, [with] Mrs. [Lydia Maria] Child doing most of the hard work" to earn $360. See Caroline Weston to Samuel J. May, Weymouth, 24 October 1871, B.1.13.94, May Papers, BPL. For histories of the BFAS fair, see Hansen, *Strained Sisterhood*, 124–39, and Chambers-Schiller, "'Good Work among the People.'"

26. Caroline Weston diary, 26 September 1835, A.9.2.7.65–66, WP.

27. Mary Weston to Debora Weston, Weymouth, 24 October 1836, A.9.2.8.65, WP. Mary Weston told her nieces that the quarterly meeting did not take place because she was "not home to make it go" (Mary Weston to Debora Weston, n.p., 22 January 1837, A.9.2.5.82, WP). Several Weymouth women, including some Westons, formed an antislavery sewing circle, however, and contributed the results of their labors to the 1836 BFAS fair, the first organized by Maria.

28. So virulent had the opposition to the women's meeting become that a group of rowdy men, having difficulty finding the Washington Street building, scattered a meeting of some forty women gathered to discuss prostitution and moral reform. See Chapman, *Right and Wrong in Boston . . . 1836*, 9–18.

29. Fearing a mob, Caroline missed the NEAS quarterly meeting in September. While Anne and Debora Weston attended, she "staid at home in great trepidation thinking every noise I heard was the coming mob" (Caroline Weston diary, 28 September 1835, A.9.2.7.65–66, WP). On the day of the BFAS mob, she was late arriving, having been dispatched to ask Francis Jackson whether the women would be welcome to retreat to his home in the event of trouble. When she returned to the antislavery offices, "though I was in good time and when I first got sight of the door the way *was* clear the sudden rush of all sorts of people from every street and avenue in sight was so sudden and over powering that I, with the greatest difficulty made my way to the foot of the staircase and never succeeded in mounting it. It was so crowded with men all the way that I thought *them* in danger" (Caroline Weston to Wendell Phillips, Weymouth, 27 October [1870], Blagden Collection, HL).

30. Three accounts of this event were published by the mayor's friends and family: Lyman, *Memoir*; Lyman, *Papers Relating to the Garrison Mob*, which includes excerpts

from a number of newspaper articles; and Eliot, *Theodore Lyman*. These offer a more neutral and heroic version of Mayor Lyman's role in the Boston riot of 1835 than what appeared in the BFAS's *Report of the Boston Female Anti-Slavery Society* or Martineau, *Martyr Age of the United States*.

31. A well-to-do supporter of abolition, Francis Jackson (1789–1861) served as justice of the peace in Boston until 1844, when he resigned, saying that he could not return fugitive slaves to the South. He served as president of the MAS and the New England Anti-Slavery Conventions and as vice president of the AAS.

32. Harassment of the Chapmans continued for over a year. Caroline acknowledged that "Henry has received many insults—& letters, the last was most alarming informing Maria in a friendly way that a plot was had to personally injure herself & her husband and to beware of G or look [to] the 3d—Henry was somewhat impressed that there might be some danger" (Caroline Weston to Anne Warren Weston, [1836], A.9.2.4.85, WP).

33. An early supporter of Garrison and abolition, Joseph Southwick signed the AAS "Declaration of Sentiments." His wife, Thankful Hussey Southwick, supported the BFAS and was beloved by the Westons.

34. Maria Weston Chapman to Wendell and Ann Terry Greene Phillips, n.p., 16 August 1842, Blagden Collection, HL; Maria Weston Chapman, n.p., n.d., A.9.2.4.16, WP. See also Caroline's snide reference to "Dr. Channing," who "thought I ought to *cherish* my Anti-Slavery principles—within my own bosom" (Caroline Weston to Ann Terry Greene Phillips, New Bedford, 23 June 1844, 1483, Blagden Collection, HL). Anne reported a visit to Mary Gray Chapman by Channing "in his *pastoral* capacity" in which "Maria uttered some thorough testimonies & excommunicated his church" (Anne Warren Weston to Debora Weston, Boston, 15 January 1842, A.9.2.17.24, WP).

35. Caroline Weston to Anne Warren Weston, n.p., 1836, A.9.2.4.55; Debora Weston to Caroline Weston, New Bedford, 1836, A.9.2.8.1; Debora Weston to Mary Weston, New Bedford, 20 October 1836, A.9.2.8.62; Anne Warren Weston to Debora Weston, Boston, 19 November 1836, A.9.2.8.73; Debora Weston to Mary Weston, New Bedford, 6 November 1836, A.9.2.8.68, WP.

36. Mary Weston to Debora Weston, n.p., 22 January [1837], A.9.2.5.82; Anne Warren Weston to Debora Weston, n.p., 19 September 1837, A.9.2.9.71, WP.

37. Debora Weston to Anne Warren Weston, New Bedford, 25 November 1839, A.9.2.12.94, WP.

38. For an analysis of Adams's rhetorical strategy in attacking the gag rule and taking on the congressional defense of slavery led by John C. Calhoun and Henry Clay, see Zaeske, "'The South Arose as One Man.'" For a larger study of female antislavery petitioning and a discussion of how free black women, in petitioning against slavery, asserted "substantial political authority," see Zaeske, *Signatures of Citizenship*. See also Portnoy, *Their Right to Speak*, chap. 2; and Van Broekhoven, "'Let Your Names Be Enrolled.'"

39. The establishment of the Free Church generated considerable conflict among abolitionists, and, ultimately, both the Chapmans and the Westons withdrew their support.

40. Meanwhile the women had been smuggled from court by members of Boston's free black community who feared they would be jailed awaiting their hearing. See *Liberator*, 6 August 1836.

41. Ellis Gray Loring (1803–58) entered the bar in 1827. He became a leading Garrisonian and a founder of the New England Anti-Slavery Association. According to Caroline, the asylum renamed the child "Maria" because it was Chapman's plan that freed her. See Caroline Weston to Debora Weston, Boston, [1836], A.9.2.3.30, WP.

42. Admitted to the Massachusetts Bar in 1823, Rufus Choate (1799–1859) served terms in the Massachusetts House (1825–26) and Senate (1827) and the U.S. Congress (1830–34). He would be elected to the U.S. Senate in 1841, retiring in 1845. He served as the Massachusetts attorney general from 1853 to 1854.

43. *Liberator*, 24 September 1836, 9 October 1836, 22 October 1836. Debra Gold Hansen (*Strained Sisterhood*) writes that Mary Chapman paid the lawyers' fees, but see Anne Warren Weston to Debora Weston, Boston, 19 October 1836, A.9.2.8.74, WP, for Maria's role. So public did Maria's role become that Sophia Ammidon heard as far away as Missouri that she had been accused of doing something untoward in the case. See Sophia Ammidon to Caroline Weston, St. Louis, 10 November 1836, A.9.2.8.70, WP. Chapman's role in freeing and placing another child in a New Bedford poorhouse added to her public mystique. The press called her "Lady Macbeth." "The Thacker girl is here in town," Anne reported. She "is known as 'Mrs Chapman's protégé.'" Acknowledging Maria's high public profile, Anne teased, "Nothing can happen but you contrive to get the credit" (Anne Warren Weston to Maria Weston Chapman, New Bedford, 1 August 1836, A.9.2.8.39, WP). See the BFAS annual report for 1836. Med died in 1838. See also *Case of the Slave-Child*.

44. The *Commercial Gazette* of Boston lamented that the decision, "though unquestionably according to law, is much to be regretted; for such cases cannot but injure the custom of our hotels, now so liberally patronized by gentlemen from the South." See Lydia Maria Child to Esther Carpenter, South Natick, 4 September 1836, in Meltzer and Holland, *Lydia Maria Child, Selected Letters*, 53.

45. A professor of natural philosophy at Western Reserve College, Elizur J. Wright Jr. (1804–85) resigned to help found the AAS in 1833 and become its domestic corresponding secretary. He left in 1839 to edit the *Massachusetts Abolitionist*, an anti-Garrisonian newspaper advocating an electoral solution to the problem of slavery.

46. Mary Clark to the Philadelphia Female Anti-Slavery Society, 20 April 1836, PFAS Papers, Historical Society of Pennsylvania.

47. At this time, men commonly attended female society meetings and opened them for business; indeed, it was worthy of comment when there was "not a *man* to be seen" (Debora Weston to Anne Warren Weston, Boston, June 1836, A.9.2.8.4; Caroline Weston to Anne Warren Weston, n.p., [1836], A.9.2.4.55, WP). May was the only man "on the ground" for the 22 October 1836 meeting. At the first BFAS meeting of 1837, Catherine Sullivan presided and Maria read the convocation, a biblical passage from Hebrews that, as Anne put it, "speaks of the triumphs of faith and of the women who 'wrought righteousness'" (Anne Warren Weston to Debora Weston, Boston, 16 January 1837, A.9.2.9.7, WP).

48. Anniversary Week was that time in spring when philanthropic organizations of various kinds came together in national convention. Hence the first women's antislavery convention took place 9–11 May 1837, at the same time as benevolent reformers, including many ministers representing the American Bible Society, the American Tract Society, and the AAS, gathered. For a full account of this meeting, see Sterling, *Ahead of Her Time*, 38–44.

49. Anne Warren Weston to Debora Weston, Boston, 18 April 1837, A.9.2.9.28, WP. Anne served as one of the secretaries for the convention, as did cousins Mary Grew and Sarah Pugh, and Angelina Grimké. Mary Parker, president of the BFAS, served in the same role in the women's convention. Maria, having just given birth, did not attend.

50. Sterling, *Ahead of Her Time*, 48–49. A debate also emerged as to whether women should use their marital names (e.g., Mrs. Henry G. Chapman) in signing convention or society documents. More than four-fifths of the delegates chose not to do so; the majority of those who insisted on indicating their marital status hailed from the New York society.

51. "TO FEMALE ANTI-SLAVERY SOCIETIES THROUGHOUT NEW ENGLAND," 7 June 1837, in Chapman, *Right and Wrong in Boston . . . 1837*, 42–44.

52. Anne Warren Weston to Caroline Weston, Groton, 7 August 1837, A.9.2.9.59; Anne Warren Weston to Debora Weston, Boston, 25 August 1837 and 23 March 1838, A.9.2.10.15, WP. The Grimkés spoke to over 13,000 people between June and September, offering twenty-eight lectures in twenty-three communities.

53. Chapman, *Right and Wrong in Boston . . . 1837*, 46–47.

54. See Hemphill, *Siblings*, 153–85.

55. Sterling, *Ahead of Her Time*, 47–48.

56. Chapman, *Right and Wrong in Boston . . . 1837*, 51–52, 53.

57. Ibid., 57.

58. Juliana A. Tappan to Anne Warren Weston, New York, 21 July 1837, A.9.2.9.49, WP.

59. Anne Warren Weston to Caroline Weston, Groton, 7 August 1837, A.9.2.9.59, WP. The Westons lost a student to the Grimkés when Mary Ann Davenport's father pulled her from their school when she asked to attend a meeting where Angelina Grimké spoke.

60. Anne Warren Weston "To the Female A. S. Society," Boston, 21 August 1837, A.9.2.9.62, WP.

61. Anne Warren Weston to Debora Weston, Boston, 3 September 1837, A.9.2.3.69; Anne Warren Weston to Debora Weston, Boston, 4 September 1837, A.9.2.3.72, WP.

62. *Liberator*, 11 August 1837.

63. Ibid.

64. Published in the *New England Spectator*, 2 August 1837, and reprinted in *Liberator*, 11 August 1837, the "Appeal" was signed by five clergymen: in addition to Perkins, Charles Fitch of Boston, David Sanford of Dorchester, William M. Cornell of Quincy, and Joseph H. Towne of Boston. Only Towne and Fitch had any association with the antislavery movement. Fitch ministered to the Free Church of Boston, an abolitionist venture that turned divisive when Fitch agreed not to overtly support abolition in order to get denominational recognition. He authored a pamphlet titled

"Slaveholding Weighed in the Balance of Truth." Towne held a brief antislavery agency in Essex County, Massachusetts.

65. Garrison and Garrison, *William Lloyd Garrison*, 2:137–38.

66. Maria Weston Chapman to Elizur Wright, n.p., n.d., A.9.2.9.69, WP. This letter was written before 15 September 1837, the date of Wright's response. See Elizur Wright to Maria W. Chapman, New York, 15 September 1837, A.9.2.9.68, WP. For an extended analysis of the language and strategy of this exchange, see the Appendix.

67. Anne Warren Weston to Debora Weston, Boston, 26 September 1837, A.9.2.9.72, WP.

68. Caroline Weston to Debora Weston, Worcester, [27 September 1837], A.9.2.5.79, WP. The Reverend Luther Lee (1800–1889) "did the speaking," according to Caroline's account. He was an itinerant minister for the Methodist Episcopal Church who organized antislavery societies within his denomination. He settled in Lowell, Massachusetts, where, in 1841, he edited the *New England Christian Advocate*, an antislavery journal. He participated in founding the Liberty Party in 1840.

69. Caroline Weston to Debora Weston, Worcester, [27 September 1837], A.9.2.5.79; Anne Warren Weston to Debora Weston, Boston, 9 October 1837, A.9.2.9.78, WP. Garrison, feeling buoyed by the support of the Worcester convention, went after the AAS Executive Committee in the next *Liberator*, attacking the "most injurious silence respecting the Clerical Protests, and the movements of the anti-slavery societies in reference to them" (Caroline Weston to Debora Weston, Worcester, [27 September 1837], A.9.2.5.79).

70. *Liberator*, 11 August 1837.

71. Mary Weston to Debora Weston, Weymouth, 17 September 1837, A.9.2.3.71, WP. One consequence of the controversy was the growing reluctance of churches to allow the use of their buildings for antislavery meetings, and particularly those of women's societies. This pushed abolition further into the public arena as male and female societies sought out commercial buildings and public halls instead. In Weymouth, the female antislavery sewing circle, for example, began to meet on Sunday afternoons in a room above Merit's store and then, with the support of a Mr. Nunson, in the directors' room over the local bank. See early discussions of this shift in Lucia Weston to Debora Weston, Boston, December 1836, A.9.2.8.76; and Mary Weston to Debora Weston, n.p., 19 July 1836, A.9.2.4.94, WP.

72. Southwick, *Reminiscences*, 20–21. Among those attending were Thankful Southwick, her two sisters, Mary Ann W. Johnson, Ann G. Chapman, and Mrs. Hannah Tufts.

73. In marrying Ann Terry Greene, daughter of Benjamin Greene of Salem and niece of Maria's mother-in-law, Sarah Greene Chapman, in 1837, Phillips had entered into both the Weston and the Chapman families. Although he largely gave up his private practice to serve the cause, he conducted Maria's legal business.

74. Chapman, *Pinda*. For more on *Pinda*, see Glover, *Fugitive's Gibraltar*, 159–60, 312 n. 7.

75. For comparison, the U.S. census for 1830 recorded a resident population of 12,866,020, of whom 2,487,355 were slaves. By 1840, the U.S. population was 17,069,453.

76. On this subject see, Zaeske, *Signatures of Citizenship*. 49. She identifies a petition from 218 women in Jamaica, Massachusetts, early in 1834 as the first woman's antislavery petition. It sought legislation to cease the slave trade and educate black children in the District of Columbia. Months later, women in New York City, Boston, and Philadelphia circulated their own petitions seeking emancipation for all slaves brought into the District.

77. Of the 30,449 petitions presented to Congress, 9,112 were men's and 21,214 women's, with an additional 123 containing the names of both sexes. In 1838, James Freeman Clark reported that the AAS had sent 400,000 names to Congress, two million within two years. See Clarke, *Anti-Slavery Days*, 37. Gerda Lerner has estimated that women's names composed 70 percent of these in 1838. See Lerner, *Majority Finds Its Past*, 126. For the Weston role in petitioning, see Caroline Weston to Anne Warren Weston, n.p., [1836], A.9.2.4.55; Anne Warren Weston to Debora Weston, Boston, 22 October 1836, A.9.2.8.63; Anne Warren Weston to Debora Weston, Boston, 19 November 1836, A.9.2.8.73, WP. For more on the experiences of the Westons while petitioning, see Debora Weston to Caroline Weston, New Bedford, 1836, A.9.2.8.1; Caroline Weston to Debora Weston, Boston, 12 October 1836, A.9.2.8.60; Debora Weston to Mary Weston, New Bedford, 20 October 1836, A.9.2.8.62; Anne Warren Weston to Debora Weston, Boston, 11 December 1839, A.9.2.12.114; Anne Warren Weston to Debora Weston, Boston, 15 December 1839, A.9.2.12.118; Debora Weston to Anne Warren Weston, New Bedford, 10 February 1840, A.9.2.13.21; Debora Weston to Anne Warren Weston, New Bedford, 1 March 1840, A.9.2.13.33; Anne Warren Weston to Henry G. Chapman and Maria Weston Chapman, Boston, 15 January 1841, A.9.2.15.10; Caroline Weston to Maria Weston Chapman and Henry G. Chapman, Roxbury, 15 January 1841, A.9.2.15.11-14; Anne Warren Weston to Emma Weston, Boston, 19 October 1841, A.9.2.15.81; Anne Warren Weston to Caroline Weston, Boston, 22 May 1849, A.9.2.24.122, WP. See also Anne Warren Weston to Ann T. G. Phillips, Weymouth, 3 August [1854], Blagden Collection, HL; and Anne Warren Weston to Samuel J. May, Weymouth, 2 March [1852], B.1.6.3.44, May Papers, BPL. For the experience of other women, see Mary P. Cook to Maria Weston Chapman, Hadley, 25 December 1839, A.9.2.12.125; and Betsy Newton to Maria Weston Chapman, Worcester, January 1840, A.9.2.14.105, WP.

78. James Mott to Anne Warren Weston, Philadelphia, 7 June 1838, A.9.2.10.29, WP. Anne later described a ferocious fall windstorm by telling her sisters that "she had not passed such a night since Penn Hall was burnt" (Caroline Weston to Debora Weston, Roxbury, 5 October 1841, A.9.2.15.7, WP).

79. Abby Kelley (1811–87) was secretary of the Lynn Female Anti-Slavery Society before she took to the lecture platform on behalf of the MAS and AAS. She later supported the campaign for women's suffrage. She married Stephen S. Foster, an abolitionist agent, in 1845.

80. See Anne Warren Weston to Debora Weston, Boston, 8 March 1839, A.9.2.11.53; Anne Warren Weston to Mary Weston, 18 May [1839], A.9.2.16.11; Edmund Quincy to Maria Weston Chapman, Quincy, 12 August 1839, A.9.2.12.13; Edmund Quincy to Maria Weston Chapman, Quincy, 26 July 1839, A.9.2.12.5; Edmund Quincy to Maria Weston Chapman, Quincy, 23 August 1839, A.9.2.12.17; Edmund Quincy to

Maria Weston Chapman, Quincy, 7 September 1839, A.9.2.12.27; Edmund Quincy to Maria Weston Chapman, Dedham, 28 April 1840, A.9.2.13.59; Edmund Quincy to Maria Weston Chapman, Dedham, 2 August 1840, A.9.2.14.5; Anne Warren Weston to Lucia Weston, Boston, 21 September 1840, A.9.2.13.23-24; Edmund Quincy to Caroline Weston, Dedham, 3 April 1841, A.9.2.15.33; Edmund Quincy to Maria Weston Chapman, Dedham, 6 August 1841, A.9.2.15.54; Edmund Quincy to Caroline Weston, Dedham, 14 December 1841, A.9.2.15.111; Anne Warren Weston to Debora Weston, Boston, 11 February 1842, A.9.2.17.33; and Edmund Quincy to Caroline Weston, Dedham, 14 August 1842, A.9.2.17.88-89, WP.

81. Anne Warren Weston to William Lloyd Garrison, Weymouth, 11 November 1838, A.1.2.7.73, ASC.

82. Weston principles were strained but not broken during the Boston incarceration of fugitive slaves George Latimer, Anthony Burns, and Thomas Simms, when the sisters considered the use of violence to free the men. See Anne Warren Weston to Mary A. Estlin, Weymouth, 2 November 1850, A.7.2.7; Anne Warren Weston to Mary A. Estlin, 5 February 1855, A.7.2.28, JBEP; and Anne Warren Weston to Caroline Weston, Hazelwood, 13 November 1842, A.9.2.17.113, WP.

83. Chapman, *Right and Wrong in Massachusetts*, 102–3.

84. James G. Birney (1792–1857), a Kentucky lawyer and Presbyterian, became an agent of the AAS in Ohio in 1834 and corresponding secretary of the AAS in 1837. In 1840 he resigned from the AAS with other anti-Garrisonians. The Liberty Party nominated him for president of the United States in both 1840 and 1844. Arthur Tappan (1786–1865) and his brother Lewis (1788–1873) were businessmen and philanthropists who provided considerable financial support to several religious organizations and benevolent groups, including the American Tract Society, the Sunday School Union, and Sabbath observance and temperance movements. They helped establish the *Emancipator*, the organ of the AAS, and participated actively for many years in the New York and American Anti-Slavery Societies. Early on they supported Garrison and provided funding for the *Liberator* but broke with him in 1840 over women's role in the antislavery movement. Arthur Tappan was elected president of the American and Foreign Anti-Slavery Society and Lewis became treasurer. Both men supported the Liberty Party in 1840.

85. Kelley resigned from her Meeting in 1841 because some members objected to allowing antislavery speakers.

86. Both Garrisonians and anti-Garrisonians in Massachusetts viewed the division as the result of the other's plotting. For the Garrisonians, including the Westons, the division resulted from a clerical plot by spiritual "despots," both abolitionist (such as Amos Phelps, Charles Torrey, and Jonas Perkins) and anti-abolitionist (George W. Blagden), who opposed Garrison and women's rights. For the "new organization" it was a plot by Chapman and Garrison to incorporate abolition into a broader reform agenda. Published in 1841, the Massachusetts Abolition Society report on the division stated, "The design thus deliberately conceived has been steadily and perseveringly carried out by the two leading minds in the case, (Mr. Garrison and Mrs. Chapman,) through their subordinate agents and friends." Harping upon this plot to replace antislavery with "universal reform," the authors described Chapman's *Right and Wrong in Massachusetts* as a "work

of perversion" intended "to crush the clergy." They castigated three individuals in highly personal terms: Garrison, Maria Weston Chapman, and Henry G. Chapman. See *True History*, 15, 18, 32, 35, 36.

87. Edmund Quincy to Caroline Weston, Dedham, 9 July 1840, A.9.2.13.97-98, WP. A close friend of the Westons, Quincy was identified as part of the Garrison-Chapman conspiracy (along with such family members as George W. Benson, Garrison's father-in-law, and Wendell Phillips, married to Sarah G. Chapman's niece). While family were deemed guilty by association of introducing "extraneous" matters into the antislavery movement, Quincy was damned as a "hypocrite in regard to his religious opinions" (*Formation of the Massachusetts Abolition Society*, 29).

88. That is, the organization would return to work before the Phillipses returned from France. See Caroline Weston to Wendell and Ann Terry Greene Phillips, Boston, 25 January 1840, 1290, Blagden Collection, HL.

89. The newly elected board of officers denied the dissolution of the society. Thankful Southwick served as president, Mary A. W. Johnson as vice president, Henrietta Sargent as corresponding secretary, Caroline Weston as counsellor, and Louisa M. Sewall as recording secretary.

90. Anne Warren Weston to Maria Weston Chapman, New York, 13 May 1840, A.9.2.13.74, WP. She and Caroline traded off taking notes.

91. Although Elizabeth Cady Stanton was one of the organizers of the convention, her husband, Henry B. Stanton, insisted that his wife remove her signature from its resolutions.

92. Charles Lenox Remond, an African American born in Salem, Massachusetts, and, in 1838, a secretary of the AAS and vice president of the NEAS, insisted that he owed a debt to the women of Portland and Bangor, Maine, and Newport, Rhode Island, who had raised funds for his expenses so that he would not sit where their sisters might not. He sat with Mott in the gallery.

93. Officers of the Boston Female Anti-Slavery Association to Luther Myrick, editor of the *Union Herald*, Boston, 1 May 1840, A.9.2.13.63, WP.

94. Maria Weston Chapman to Sarah Pugh, 14 January 1840, A.9.2.13.11, WP. The quotation is from a "rough draft" of the letter.

95. Maria Weston Chapman to Mrs. Elis Gray Loring, Boston, 23 May 1840, A.1.2.9.47, ASC.

96. Maria Weston Chapman to Friends, n.p., 1840, A.9.2.14.98, WP.

97. Debora Weston to Mary Weston, New Bedford, 5 January 1840, A.9.2.13.5, WP.

98. See discussion in Varon, *Disunion!*, 154–64; and Mayer, *All on Fire*, 307–9.

99. *Prigg v. Pennsylvania* established slaveholders' right to recapture their escaped slaves. It provided the legal basis for the 1857 ruling in the *Dred Scott* case.

100. For more information on George Latimer and his wife, Rebecca, see Davis, "Two Autobiographical Fragments." For additional research on the case, see Levy, "'Abolition Riot'"; Newmyer, *Supreme Court Justice Joseph Story*, 370–78; Cover, *Justice Accused*, 169–71; and Wiecek, "Latimer." See also Asa J. David, "The George Latimer Case: A Benchmark in the Struggle for Freedom," http://edison.rutgers.edu/latimer /glatcase.htm.

101. Anne Warren Weston to Caroline Weston, Hazlewood, 13 November 1842, A.9.2.17.113, WP. She worried that her own nonresistance had "injured my spunk, or something for I cannot think of a riot without such a tremor as would amaze you. But of course, my horror of a riot is much less than my terror at Latimer's going back." She wondered, "Is there no way of breaking the jail?" (Anne Warren Weston to Debora Weston, New Bedford, 8 November 1842, A.9.2.17.106, WP).

102. *Annual Report Presented to the Massachusetts Anti-Slavery Society*, 1843, 74, Bowditch Papers, MHS.

103. Six issues were published between 11 November 1842 and 16 May 1843. For Weston work on the *Latimer Journal*, see Emma Weston to Anne Warren Weston, n.p., 31 October [1842], A.9.2.6.63; Maria Weston Chapman, n.p., n.d., A.9.2.5.102; Eliza C. Follen to Maria Weston Chapman, n.p., [November 1842], A.9.2.17.7; Samuel May Jr. to Maria Weston Chapman, [Boston], 5 November [1842], A.9.2.20.90; Edmund Quincy to Maria Weston Chapman, Dedham, 15 November 1842, A.9.2.17.111; Susan Cabot to Maria Weston Chapman, West Roxbury, 17 November 1842, A.9.2.17.114; Charles Storry Jr. to Caroline Weston, Boston, [18 November 1842], A.9.2.17.3; Fred S. Cabot M.S.C. to Anne Warren Weston, Boston, 30 November 1842, A.9.2.17.17; Caroline Weston to Anne Warren Weston, Boston, 9 December 1842, A.9.2.17.134; Rachel W. Stearns to Maria Weston Chapman, Spring[field], 18 December 1842, A.9.2.17.148, WP; David L. Child to Maria Weston Chapman, Northampton, 12 December 1842, A.4.1.59, ASC.

104. The headquarters of the Latimer Committee was in Chauncey Place. Frederick S. Cabot welcomed Anne Warren Weston to a meeting there with a request for names of other women who might also wish to attend and support the committee's actions. See Fred S. Cabot to Anne Warren Weston, Boston, 30 November 1842, A.9.2.17.17, WP.

105. Edmund Quincy to Maria Weston Chapman, Dedham, 15 November 1842, A.9.2.17.112; Lucia Weston to Debora Weston, Boston, n.p., [November 1842], A.9.2.3.107, WP. In commenting on the distinctions between the readers of the two papers, Quincy told Maria that any articles he sent her deemed insufficiently "judicious & suitable" for the *Journal* should be passed along to the *Liberator*, where "they will answer . . . well enough."

106. Maria Weston Chapman, n.p., n.d. [after November 1842], A.9.2.5.102, WP. Elizabeth Cabot Follen devised her own plan to save Latimer: "I want all the colored men, women & children & all the abolitionists from Boston & the vicinity with their women and children to fill the streets that day when he is to be tried—all without arms and to take him off. No one will fire upon them—no one will hurt them—They could do it so I believe; hundreds—nay thousands would join them, and they could not carry the poor creature away without running over his friends—if women are in the crowd there will be no violence—am I crazy? I think not—" (Elizabeth Cabot Follen to Maria Weston Chapman, 13 November [1842], A.4.6A.2.54, ASC).

107. Anne had never approved of Lydia Maria Child as editor of the *Anti-Slavery Standard*, believing her incapable of taking unpopular stands. See Anne Warren Weston to Debora Weston, Boston, 29 March 1841, A.9.2.15.32, WP. Child had edited the *Standard* from April 1841. She found it lonely living in New York and "felt the weight of the paper severely." She once "let out her heart to Mr. Loring," only to

receive letters of support and encouragement from Maria, Caroline, Wendell Phillips, Henrietta Sargent, J. G. King, and James R. Lowell. Yet she swore "by the helmeted Minerva, fresh from her father's brain," that the *Standard* would continue. See Lydia Maria Child to Maria Weston Chapman, New York, 26 April 1841, A.5.1.27, Child Papers, ASC. The gradual distancing of the Westons from Child over the means of conducting antislavery politics and the tone of the *Standard* may be followed in their correspondence. See Caroline Weston to Debora Weston, Roxbury, [June 1841], A.9.2.3.77; Lydia Maria Child to Debora Weston, New York, 25 August 1841, A.9.2.15.58; Oliver Johnson to Maria Weston Chapman, New York, 3 September 1841, A.9.2.15.6; and Lydia Maria Child to Maria Weston Chapman, New York, 1 December 1841, A.9.2.17.129, WP; Caroline Weston to Wendell and Ann T. G. Phillips, n.d., New Bedford, 1290, folio 6, Blagden Collection, HL; Lydia Maria Child to Maria Weston Chapman, New York, 11 May 1842, A.5.1.28; Lydia Maria Child to Maria Weston Chapman, n.p., [June 1842], A.5.1.33, Child Papers, ASC; Maria Weston Chapman to Anne Warren Weston, n.p., [1843], A.9.2.4.14, WP; David L. Child to Maria Weston Chapman, Washington, 11 January 1843, A.5.1.32, Child Papers, ASC; and extracts from Anne Warren Weston to Caroline and Debora Weston, Boston, 22 May 1843, A.9.2.18.40, WP.

108. Edmund Quincy to Maria Weston Chapman, Dedham, 15 November 1842, A.9.2.17.112, WP.

109. Caroline Weston to Anne Warren Weston, Boston, 9 December 1842, A.9.2.17.134, WP; David L. Child to Maria Weston Chapman, Northampton, 12 December 1842, A.4.1.59, ASC. Maria sent him $65 (contributed by Francis Jackson, Edmund Quincy, and herself, among others) to add to the $25 donated by Wendell Phillips and $25 by Bowditch to help support him "till," she told him, "I can raise something further. Pray write to me a dunning letter, before borrowing of any one at Washington. I fear that the coffers of our national Society are not in a state to put Mrs Child & yourself in funds from that source, whence they are your due as editors" (Maria Weston Chapman to David L. Child, Boston, 29 December 1842, A.4.1.79, ASC).

110. It did not take Maria long to express dissatisfaction with Child's editorial stance either. Although she defended his "independence and true heartedness" to Francis Jackson, by September she was writing Child in response to an article, "I hardly know how to express myself. Nothing but my reliance on your friendship enables me to conquer the unwillingness I feel to write at all; but this, added to my recollection of your last words to us when you left Boston—'let me have your ideas about the affairs of the cause,' does finally overcome my reluctance." Her concern had to do with what she considered an insufficiently critical article on Lewis Tappan in England. See Maria Weston Chapman to David L. Child, Weymouth, 2 September 1843, A.4.1.79, ASC.

111. Garrison spent the summer and fall of 1843 at the Northampton, Massachusetts, water cure.

112. Anne Warren Weston to Mary Weston, New Bedford, 29 October 1842, A.9.2.17.102, WP.

113. Frederick Douglass to Maria Weston Chapman, Cambridge, Ind., 10 September 1843, A.9.2.19.35, WP.

114. Abby Kelley to Maria Weston Chapman, Seneca Falls, 12 August 1843, A.9.2.19.16, and 28 August 1843, A.9.2.19.24, WP; Maria Weston Chapman to Francis Jackson, Weymouth, 31 August 1843, A.1.2.13.50, ASC.

115. George Bradburn to Maria Weston Chapman, Green Plain, Ohio, 31 August 1843, A.9.2.19.25; Oakland, 1 September 1843, A.9.2.19.25; Frederick Douglass to Maria Weston Chapman, Cambridge, 10 September 1843, A.9.2.19.35, WP.

116. Frederick Douglass to Maria Weston Chapman, Kilmarnock, Scotland, 29 March 1846, A.9.2.22.35a, WP; Maria Weston Chapman to Richard D. Webb, 29 June 1845 and 23 January 1846, A.1.2.1.41, ASC; Maria Weston Chapman to Richard D. Webb, 1 May 1846, A.1.2.1.41, ASC; Richard D. Webb to Maria Weston Chapman, Dublin, 16 May 1846, A.9.2.22.51, 22 January 1854, A.9.2.28.4, WP. Webb showed Douglass the letter revealing Chapman's efforts to control Douglass.

117. Anne Warren Weston to Caroline, Boston, 12 November 1848, A.9.2.24.43; Anne Warren Weston to Maria Weston Chapman, Weymouth, 5 June 1849, A.9.2.24.77, WP. The Westons had thought highly of Douglass early in his career as an antislavery agent, but adjectives such as "glorious" and "remarkable" gradually turned to "sordid and low minded" as the sisters came to see him as lacking in personal character and professional integrity. See Anne Warren Weston to Debora Weston, Weymouth, 1 April 1842, A.9.2.17.50, WP; Anne Warren Weston to Elizabeth Pease, Weymouth, 14 October 1845, A.1.2.15.72, ASC; and Anne Warren Weston to John B. Estlin, New York, 20 December 1853, A.7.2.24, JBEP. On the eve of her departure for Europe in 1848, Maria wrote to London literary personality Mary Howitt that Douglass was "a selfish person fighting only for his own hand" and regretted "that he should have so many personal presents from England, as it was so much taken from the Cause" (Anne Weston to Caroline Weston, Boston, 12 November 1848, A.9.2.24.43, WP). Howitt discussed the letter with Julia Griffiths (1812–95), her guest at the time, who communicated its contents to Douglass. Anne was in the Boston antislavery office when Griffith's letter arrived to inform Douglass of Maria's words. She had to suffer through Douglass's public reading of it. When Douglass began traveling with Griffiths, Maria wrote to her British contacts to embellish her charges of his poor character. She warned Elizabeth Gaskell to "abjure clever black men who wish to make money out of their colour" and prided herself on having thereby "blacked out" Griffiths' influence. See Maria Weston Chapman to Mary A. Estlin, Leeds, 15 October 1855, A.7.2.75, JBEP. See also Maria Weston Chapman to Harriet Beecher Stowe, Weymouth, 5 February [1858], Schlesinger Library.

118. The fair brought $2,082.79 into the MAS in 1842 and $1,827.96 the following year. In 1846 the women of Massachusetts brought $3,902.11.

119. For descriptions of these visits, see Elizabeth Ashurst Bardonneau to Elizabeth Neall Gay, 25 November 1848 and 19 September 1849, Gay Papers, Rare Book and Manuscript Library; Richard D. Webb to Edmund Quincy, n.p., September 1849, Quincy, Wendell, Holmes, and Upham Family Papers, MHS; Mary A. Estlin to Maria Weston Chapman, Beibrick, August 1850, A.9.2.25.17; Mary A. Estlin to Anne Warren Weston, Bristol, 19 September 1851, A.9.2.25.124; Richard D. Webb to Anne Warren Weston, n.p., 12 August 1851, A.9.2.25.108; Sarah Pugh to Maria Weston Chapman, Bristol, 31 August 1852, A.9.2.26.52; Mary A. Estlin to Anne Warren Weston, Bristol, 19 September 1851, A.9.2.25.124, WP; and Mary A. Estlin to Maria Weston

Chapman, Edinburgh, 13 October 1855, A.7.3.91; Maria Weston Chapman to Mary A. Estlin, Leeds, 15 October 1855, A.7.2.75, JBEP. See also Stoddart, *Elizabeth Pease Nichol*, 175.

CHAPTER 2

1. Edmund Quincy and his sisters were the children of Josiah Quincy (1772–1864) and Eliza Susan Morton (1773–1850), who married in 1797. Of Edmund's sisters, Anna Cabot Lowell Quincy married Robert Waterston and Margaret Morton Quincy married Benjamin Greene, a cousin of Ann Terry Greene Phillips and nephew to Sarah Greene Chapman. The relationship made Edmund a member of the extended families of abolitionists Wendell Phillips, Henry Grafton Chapman, and Maria Weston Chapman. Edmund married Lucilla Pinckney Parker (1810–60) in 1833.

2. Edmund Quincy to Richard D. Webb, n.p., 3 October 1848; Edmund Quincy to Richard D. Webb, n.p., 24 November 1857, Quincy, Wendell, Holmes, and Upham Family Papers, MHS. At the time, Caroline Weston, the eldest unwed sister, was forty-nine and the youngest, Emma Forbes Weston, was thirty-two—both well past the average age of marriage for the period.

3. The 1845 state census revealed that single women made up more than one-third of all women in the city. Barely half of Bostonians over twenty years of age were married. Even among those in their early thirties, the age when females were most likely to be married, a quarter of Boston women remained unwed. Twenty percent of those in their late forties maintained their single status. Singlehood characterized the society in which the Westons shopped, visited, perambulated, and politicked. This environment may well have reinforced the sisters' personal inclinations. See Shattuck, *Report to the Committee*, 61. Of 33,916 women over twenty, 18,324 were married, 11,879 single, and 3,804 widows. See Pease and Pease, *Ladies, Women, and Wenches*, 10. Singlehood in Massachusetts was double the national average. In the 1830s, 14.6 percent of women remained unwed in Massachusetts compared to 7.3 percent nationally, and in the 1850s, 16.9 percent in Massachusetts compared to 7.7 percent nationally. See Yasuba, "Birth Rates of the White Population," and Uhlenberg, "Study of Cohort Life Cycles."

4. This idea was abroad in antebellum New England culture. Zsuzsa Berend has argued that singlehood in this era was often a consequence of women taking seriously new ideals of marriage, love, and "religiously-grounded morality" that emphasized the importance of "moral excellence" in one's own character and that of one's spouse. "High ideals of love and marriage came together with high standards of character, and it became socially and personally acceptable not to marry if marriage involved compromising one's moral standards." A new understanding of women's social and cultural usefulness beyond the home and family further reinforced the view of the single woman as a "highly moral and fully womanly creature" (Berend, "'Best or None!,'" 936). Unitarian Artemus B. Muzzey, a founding member of the Cambridge, Massachusetts, Anti-Slavery Society in 1834, articulated this view: "Woman was not made for marriage but marriage for woman. If in any instance it shall appear that her improvement will probably be retarded by her entering the state, or her usefulness less extensive, or her happiness evidently sacrificed, then . . . it is her duty to continue unmarried." God designed "some

of this sex to remain single," yet he also "made all for the sake of character, usefulness, and happiness" (*Young Maiden*, 148).

5. See Rotundo, *American Manhood*; Frank, *Life with Father*; and Johansen, *Family Men*.

6. Mary Ann Estlin to Anne Warren Weston, Bristol, 13 February 1851, A.9.2.25.63, WP.

7. Debora Weston to Ann Phillips, Weymouth, 29 September 1857, 1291 Blagden Collection, HL.

8. Osterud and Fulton, "Family Limitation," 484.

9. Eliphaz Weston was born in Duxbury, Massachusetts, on 7 July 1741, and died in Weymouth sometime before 11 November 1792. He married Debora Nash in Weymouth on 18 September 1774.

10. Debora Nash, daughter of Captain Alexander Nash (1704–73) and Mary Tirrell Nash (d. 1776) of Weymouth, was born at Weymouth on 7 January 1750 and died in Weymouth on 4 November 1839. Her daughter Priscilla Weston was born 4 April 1777. Daughter Phebe Nash Weston came along two or three years later, while her sister Mary Weston was born 11 November 1792, after her father's death.

11. The youngest, Mary Weston, was a mainstay of the Weymouth and Braintree Female Emancipation Society.

12. Hunt, *Weymouth Ways*, 28. Ann Bates, nicknamed "Nancy," was born in Weymouth on 17 February 1785 and died there in 1878. Colonel Joshua Bates was born on 27 January 1755. He married Tirzah Pratt (1764–1841) on 7 October 1784 and died 3 February 1804.

13. Ibid., 70.

14. Browne, *King Caesar of Duxbury*, 41–48. For maritime culture and craft at this time, see Vickers, *Farmers and Fishermen*; Gilje, *Liberty on the Waterfront*; and Vickers and Walsh, *Young Men and the Sea*.

15. Captain Weston's history was not unusual. Alcohol lubricated sailors' labor and shore life, causing many to sink into acute alcoholism during the economic downturn that followed the war. See Glenn, "Troubled Manhood." Much reform and autobiographical literature of antebellum America used sailors' stories to moralize about alcohol's power to unman and enslave seamen, thwart their quest for independence and dignity, and limit their ability to marry and support a family. See Parsons, *Manhood Lost*; Dorsey, *Reforming Men and Women*, 113–31; and Murphy, *Ten Hours' Labor*, 101–30.

16. See Norfolk County Deeds, 45/128. At her death in 1839, the widow Deborah Nash Weston left her estate to her three unwed daughters, explicitly stating that she intended no "legacy or devise for my son Warren Weston." His daughters settled the debt owed their grandmother's estate for this property in 1842 with a legacy from Maria's father-in-law, Henry Chapman. See Anne Warren Weston to Debora Weston, Weymouth, 16 January 1842, A.9.2.17.25, WP.

17. While the scholarly literature emphasizes the durability of conjugal households in North America and Europe, in the United States these proved sufficiently flexible to accommodate and expand as parents aged, adult children came and went, and grandchildren were born and nurtured. Steven Ruggles has shown the stem household to be

the usual form in nineteenth-century America. See *Prolonged Connections* and "Transformation of the American Family Structure."

18. Full term is difficult to assess without knowledge of a woman's menstrual cycle but is usually regarded as thirty-seven to forty weeks from conception.

19. Smith and Hindus, "Premarital Pregnancy in America"; see also Smith, "American Illegitimacy," 370, table 17.4.

20. The widowed Tirzah Pratt Bates, aged forty-five, married the widowed Ebenezer Hunt in January of 1808, a little over two years after Ann married Warren and a year and a half before her younger daughter Cynthia married on 2 August 1809. She and Cynthia Bates Cowing, aged twenty-three, both gave birth within a year of each other. Tirzah's baby, Albert Hunt, born 6 May 1809, lived only a year, dying 1 July 1810. Debora Nash Weston did not remarry. See Chamberlain, *Genealogies of the Early Families*, 30, 177–78, 729.

21. Smith, "American Illegitimacy," 375. Historians have viewed declining numbers of such pregnancies in the mid-nineteenth century as resulting from more decorous courtship rituals, an end to bundling, a greater involvement of age-eligible young women in church activities, and the linkage of economic progress to sexual restraint. Robert V. Wells, however, has argued that prenuptial pregnancy was not viewed as sexual promiscuity until the second quarter of the nineteenth century, when personal behavior came to be understood as reflecting an individual's character. See Wells, "Illegitimacy and Bridal Pregnancy."

22. By the 1840s, premarital pregnancy carried a greater burden of moral and social disapprobation. Anne Warren Weston was "shocked and sorry to hear that Ellen Gibson has been married to Shadrech Howard about a month, and has just had a baby. I am ready to annihilate her." Her language suggests concern about the cost to her young friend as well as disapproval of Ellen's behavior. See Anne Warren Weston to Debora Weston, New Bedford, 26 October 1842, A.9.2.17.100, WP.

23. Smith, "Family Limitation," 44. Average children per American family totaled 7 in 1800 and 6.92 in 1810. Northern native-born women led the way in fertility decline. Those who married in the 1810s and 1820s bore an average of 5 to 5.5 children, 2 fewer than the national average. Scholars have proposed various causes for the decline: diminishing land availability, rising land prices, industrialization and/or the market revolution, the growing costs of child-rearing, decreasing contributions of child labor to the household, increasing literacy, new social identities and class formation, increased female participation in the labor force, domestic feminism, both religious influence and secularization, and the introduction of more reliable birth control. In her study of the Middle Atlantic region, Susan Klepp has linked fertility limitation to the revolutionary ideas emerging in the 1770s that inspired American women to assert greater control over their bodies, marriages, and daughters' opportunities. She argues that northern women chose to limit their procreation as they embodied the ideals of virtuous, rational womanhood and responsible parenthood. Ann Bates Weston followed the colonial pattern of early marriage and the bearing of children every two years until menopause. She bore at least eight children, the last in 1825, when she was forty, by which age women commonly stopped their childbearing. See Main, "Rocking the Cradle," and personal communication. Ann's daughter Maria bore half her mother's number of children, a

factor shaped in part by her later age of marriage (at twenty-four) and early widowhood (at thirty-six). While she bore her first child a year after marriage and her second two years later, Maria's third child was born four years along and her last after three more years. The lengthening time between her children's births may indicate a desire to govern her fertility, resulting from her immersion in abolition and a desire to combine her reform activism with childbearing and -rearing. While Susan Klepp (*Revolutionary Conceptions*, 267) has provided support for the idea that women chose to reduce their family size and confine it to a particular stage in life, it is important to note that Henry G. Chapman (1804–42) was one of only three children. He came to marriage without the expectation of a large family and with understanding some benefits of smaller ones.

24. These deaths occurred in 1855, 1861, and 1873, respectively.

25. The house in which Ann Bates Weston and her children died was not that purchased in the "Landing" by Captain Warren Weston in 1813 but rather a house in town arranged with the aid of Ann's brother, Joshua Bates. On this land now stands the Tufts Public Library of Weymouth.

26. To do so he sought economic advice and financial assistance from his uncle, Joshua Bates. As a young man Bates had been attracted to one of Sarah's aunts, perhaps even asked her to marry him. He recalled the attraction when he and Warren conversed. The memory may have played a part in his decision to aid his nephew, given that he proved less inclined to aid the children of his sister Cynthia Bates Cowing. See Diary of Joshua Bates, 13 May 1837, Baring Brothers DEP 74, BA.

27. Richard Warren Weston ended his career as president of the New York Stock Exchange.

28. *Stimpson's Boston Directory*, 320, 129.

29. Anne Warren Weston to Debora Weston, Boston, 24 July [1837], A.9.2.3.40, WP.

30. Anne Warren Weston to Debora Weston, Boston, 26 September 1837, A.9.2.9.72, WP. The term refers to the faithful Achates, who, in Greek mythology, was the friend of Aeneas.

31. Anne Warren Weston to Debora Weston, Boston, 19 September 1837, A.9.2.9.71; Anne Warren Weston to Mary Weston, Boston, 25 July 1838, A.9.2.3.38; Debora Weston to Anne Warren Weston, New Bedford, 1 December 1839, A.9.2.12.101, WP.

32. Anne Warren Weston to Debora Weston, Boston, [1836], A.9.2.3.39, WP.

33. Anne Warren Weston to Mary Weston, Boston, 25 July 1838, A.9.2.3.38, WP.

34. Emma Weston to Debora Weston, Weymouth, 18 April 1839, A.9.2.11.86; Anne Warren Weston to Debora Weston, Weymouth, 1 May 1839, A.9.2.11.93, WP.

35. *Quarter-Century Record*, 54.

36. Anne Warren Weston to Debora Weston, Boston, 13 February 1837, A.9.2.9.14, WP.

37. Anne Warren Weston to Debora Weston, Boston, 21 December 1836, A.9.2.8.79–80, 11 March 1839, A.9.2.1.55, WP.

38. H. E. Weston to Caroline Weston, New Haven, 16 July [1838], A.9.2.3.65; Anne Warren Weston to Debora Weston, Boston, 7 July 1839, A.9.2.11.133, WP.

39. Anne Warren Weston to Debora Weston, Weymouth, 1 May 1839, A.9.2.11.93, WP.

40. Anne Warren Weston to Debora Weston, Weymouth, 19 June 1842, A.9.2.17.73, WP; Hunt, *Weymouth Ways*, 97.

41. Anne Warren Weston to Ann Terry Greene Phillips, Weymouth, 30 September 1866, Phillips Collection, HL.

42. Maria Frawley's description of the self-conscious nineteenth-century invalid who developed a convalescent identity, growing neither better nor worse and devising a condition of "stagnation, immobility, and in a broader sense, all that could be considered inconclusive," does not quite fit the portrait of Hervey offered in the Weston Papers. She has argued that British middle-class invalidism epitomized inertia, expressing "the culture's profound skepticism not simply about the inability of scientific medicine to cure, but also about other social movements, institutions, and ideologies premised on the notion of progress." See Frawley, *Invalidism and Identity*, 12–13. However, Hervey pursued his study of numismatics with considerable discipline and pleasure and participated in abolition. Both seem to have interested him more than the pursuit of his profession or making a living. Remnants of Hervey's numismatic collection are in the Boston Museum of Fine Arts, donated by his nephew Henry G. Chapman Jr.

43. Some viewed Henry G. Chapman as having just such a temperament. In their account of the 1839–40 division of the antislavery movement, anti-Garrisonian members of the MAS attacked Chapman for a volatile temperament characterized by cursing. "The use of profane language is not unfrequent [*sic*] with that individual. . . . Yet . . . he has been put in nomination year after year, and elected to the office of treasurer of an institution that asks the co-operation and the charities of Christians, and has been heralded . . . as 'an excellent man,' with a 'spirit of self-denial' worthy of all praise!" Specific examples were given. The document concluded with a disingenuous claim to reluctance in laying out these character flaws, which "have been withheld from the public generally . . . [and] are now given in sheer justice to those most implicated, to the anti-slavery public, and to posterity." See *True History*, 36, 45.

44. Emma Forbes Weston to Debora Weston, Boston, 9 July 1842, A.9.2.17.80; [Debora] Weston to Caroline Weston, Weymouth, May 1846, A.9.2.22.41; Anne Warren Weston to Debora Weston, Weymouth, 19 June 1842, A.9.2.17.73, WP.

45. Anne Warren Weston to Debora Weston, Weymouth, 18 April 1839, A.9.2.11.85, WP.

46. [Debora] Weston to Caroline Weston, Weymouth, May 1846, A.9.2.22.41, WP.

47. See Hartog, *Man and Wife in America*, 108–44.

48. Debora Weston to Mary Weston, New Bedford, 20 October 1836, A.9.2.8.63; Anne Warren Weston to Debora Weston, Boston, 17 October 1837, A.9.2.5.80b, WP.

49. Anne Warren Weston to Debora Weston, Boston, 1 January 1837, A.9.2.9.2; Anne Warren Weston to Debora Weston, n.p., 9 January 1837, A.9.2.9.6; Caroline Weston to Debora Weston, n.p., n.d. [not later than 1855], A.9.2.3.70, WP. See also Anne Warren Weston to Debora Weston, Boston, 23 March 1838, A.9.2.10.15, WP.

50. Mary Weston to Debora Weston, Weymouth, 24 October 1836, A.9.2.8.65, WP.

51. William Shakespeare, *A Midsummer Night's Dream*, I.i.78.

52. Henry G. Chapman was the son of a noted Boston ship chandler. Despite early interest in the ministry, he joined his father in business. They ended their shipping contracts with the South as a protest against slavery, a business decision with deleterious

effects on their profits. Like Richard Warren Weston, Henry utilized Maria's relationship with Joshua Bates to become a general agent for Baring Brothers of Liverpool in the 1830s and to counter the decline in his American business. See Forbes and Greene, *Rich Men of Massachusetts*, 21; and Wilson, *Aristocracy of Boston*, 11.

53. Howe, *John Jay Chapman*, 15. Caroline quoted her sister as saying that Chapman was "the handsomest man that '*ever the Lord let Live*'" (Caroline Weston to Phebe Weston, Boston, n.d., A.9.2.3.73, WP).

54. See, for example, Debora Weston to Anne Warren Weston, New Bedford, 15 January 1836, A.9.2.8.6; Debora Weston to Anne Warren Weston, Boston, 6 June 1836, A.9.2.8.4; Mary Weston to Debora Weston, Weymouth, 11 September 1836, A.9.2.3.24; Anne Warren Weston to Debora Weston, Boston, 22 October 1836, A.9.2.8.63; Debora Weston to Anne Warren Weston, New Bedford, n.d., A.9.2.16.5, WP. Maria Weston Chapman to Mr. & Mrs. Garrison, Boston, 30 August 1838, ASC. Anne Warren Weston to Maria Weston Chapman, Weymouth, 5 November 1838, A.9.2.10.67; Anne Warren Weston to Mary Weston, [Boston], 13 January 1839, A.9.2.11.24; Debora Weston to Anne Warren Weston, New Bedford, 1 March 1840, A.9.2.13.33; Anne Warren Weston to Lucia Weston, Boston, 28 September 1840, A.9.2.14.31; Anne Warren Weston to Debora Weston, New Bedford, 22 October 1842, A.2.17.99, WP; Anne Warren Weston to John B. Estlin, Weymouth, 9 February 1851, A.7.2.3, JBEP. Anne Warren Weston to Ann T. G. Phillips, Weymouth, 26 July 1855, 1482, folio 2, Blagden Collection, HL. The Westons frequently expressed the value of an antislavery clergyman or congregation in their choice of church. See Caroline Weston diary, 13 September 1835 and 11 October 1835, A.9.2.7.65–66; Anne Warren Weston to Mary Weston, n.p., 27 October 1835, A.9.2.7.71; Anne Warren Weston to Debora Weston, Boston, 15 December 1836, A.9.2.8.87; Anne Warren Weston to Debora Weston, Boston, 22 January 1837, A.9.2.9.8; Anne Warren Weston to Debora Weston, Boston, 13 February 1837, A.9.2.9.14; Debora Weston to Anne Warren Weston, [Groton], 12 March 1838, A.9.2.10.10; Maria Weston Chapman to Anne Warren Weston, Boston, 22 September 1839, A.9.2.6.30; William Tillman to Maria Weston Chapman, Westerly, 29 November 1840, A.9.2.14.66; Anne Warren Weston to Maria Weston Chapman, Weymouth, 25 February 1841, A.9.2.15.27, WP; Rev. Samuel May to Maria Weston Chapman, Leicester, 23 July 1844, B.1.6.1.59, May Papers, BPL; and Maria Weston Chapman to Samuel E. Sewall, Weymouth, 8 August 1857, Robie-Sewall Papers, MHS.

55. For a discussion of the beau ideal and the cult of single blessedness in antebellum New England, see Chambers-Schiller, *Liberty, a Better Husband*, 10–28. On the importance of abolitionist sympathies in marriage, see Emma Michell to Maria Weston Chapman, Bristol, 30 August 1852, A.9.2.26.51, WP.

56. Anne Warren Weston to Debora Weston, Concord, 16 September 1841, A.9.2.15.67, WP. Mary's one fault in Anne's eyes was her parochialism: "She has but one want: she is no farther literary than a thorough knowledge of every thing connected with Anti Slavery or Non Resistance makes her so and as she is so companionable in every thing else, I miss this knowledge of books." This interest in all things literary, cultural, and political was what the Westons offered in abundance, and what they sought in a spouse. That Brooks was no intellectual did not undermine his marriage. As a congressman, Brooks voted for the annexation of Texas and was vehemently attacked by

Garrison for doing so. The abolitionists also disliked his opponent, William Parmenter, and campaigned against both candidates. Brooks lost the election. See Petrulionis, *To Set This World Right*, 14.

57. Debora Weston to Caroline Weston, Weymouth, 21 October 1850, A.9.2.25.33, WP. Maria's daughters both married Europeans. Elizabeth Bates Chapman, aged twenty-four, married Auguste Laugel in London in January 1855. An aide to Msr. Else de Beaumont of the French Geological Survey, Laugel was a "Scientific man." Living in Paris for the purpose of educating her daughters, Maria hosted "dancing soirees" to introduce them into society. She reported her amusement at seeing "the youth of Paris passing before me in review" and contemplated the fun of writing a novel, "which shall be at the same time a Book on France. 'My daughter's lovers' for the title." In 1867, at age thirty, Ann Greene Chapman married Edward James Steven Dicey, a British journalist. The wedding took place at her cousin Elizabeth Van der Weyer's home in Richmond-upon-Thames outside London and was attended by her aunts Caroline, Anne, and Emma, but not her mother, who never returned to Europe after her sojourn of 1848–55. Anne reported that she stood in for Maria and Laugel for Henry, who had died in 1842. Said Anne, "Our only draw back was the absence of her American family & friends. It seemed particularly annoying to us that my brother Warren who is always coming & going should have been prevented [by business] from running over. . . . We had hoped that Maria & Mary [Chapman] might come, but their first letters obliged us to give it up, and Henry [G. Chapman Jr., Ann's brother] the same. But with these drawbacks her wedding left nothing to be desired." Among the guests were Ann's cousins the Van der Weyers and the Duke de Chartre, "to whose own wedding all our family then in Europe had been invited." See Maria Weston Chapman to Mary A. Estlin, Paris, 12 December 1852, A.7.2.60, JBEP; Maria Weston Chapman to Elizabeth Pease Nichol, Paris, [1855], A.1.2.25.23, ASC; Maria Weston Chapman to Wendell Phillips, Paris, 25 April [n.y.], 394, folio 2, Blagden Collection, HL; Anne Warren Weston to Ann T. G. Phillips and Wendell Phillips, Richmond, 19 August 1867, 394, folio 2, Blagden Collection, HL.

58. Edmund Quincy to Maria Weston Chapman, Dedham, 5 April 1844, A.9.2.20.24; Samuel May Jr. to Caroline Weston, Boston, 17 October 1848, A.9.2.24.40, WP; Edmund Quincy to Richard D. Webb, Dedham, 13 January 1853, Quincy, Wendell, Holmes, and Upham Family Papers, MHS.

59. Diary of Joshua Bates, 22 November 1837, 26 November 1837, 30 January 1838, 8 April 1838, 26 May 1838, 3 June 1838, 10 January 1854, Baring Brothers DEP 74, BA; Maria Weston Chapman to Mary G. Chapman, Boston, 25 September 1842, 1407, folio 1, Blagden Collection, HL. Victoria would later stand as godmother to Elizabeth Bates Van der Weyer's children.

60. Edmund Quincy to Richard D. Webb, Dedham, 13 January 1853, Quincy, Wendell, Holmes, and Upham Family Papers, MHS.

61. Sara Pugh to Maria Weston Chapman and Caroline Weston, London, 11 June 1853, A.8.3.70, WP.

62. Edmund Quincy to Richard D. Webb, Dedham, 13 January 1853, Quincy, Wendell, Holmes, and Upham Family Papers, MHS.

63. Anne Warren Weston to Mary A. Estlin, Weymouth, 14 January 1851, A.7.2.8, JBEP.

64. Edmund Quincy to Richard D. Webb, Dedham, 13 January 1853, 12 February 1856, 24 November 1857, Quincy, Wendell, Holmes, and Upham Family Papers, MHS.

65. Debora Weston to Anne Warren Weston, New Bedford, 1 April 1839, A.9.2.11.74, and 26 April 1839, A.9.2.11.89, WP.

66. Maria Weston Chapman to Wendell and Ann Phillips, 21 April 1840, 394, Blagden Collection, HL. The reference to a mob had to do with the attack on the convention and the burning of Pennsylvania Hall, where it was held. The allusion to "beef steaks" came from Oliver Goldsmith's play *The Good-Natured Man*, first published in 1768.

67. Maria Weston Chapman to Wendell and Ann Phillips, 21 April 1840, 394, Blagden Collection, HL. Anne, too, called Chace "excellent and conscientious" (Anne Warren Weston to Wendell and Ann Phillips, Boston, 15 October 1840, Blagden Collection, HL). The Westons tried to keep the engagement secret, but the news spread, perhaps through the Chace family. Lydia Maria Child told Maria, "I heard of Mary's engagement before I left the city, notwithstanding your secrecsy [*sic*]. I could congratulate *him* in good earnest, because I know what a treasure he has found; but I am too little acquainted with him to judge whether she is fortunate or not. The chosen friend of Garrison and Benson *could* scarcely be otherwise than worthy of the best of wives, and therefore I believe he is" (Lydia M. Child to Maria Weston Chapman, Northampton, 23 August 1840, A.9.2.13.11, WP).

68. Caroline Weston to Henry G. Chapman and Maria Weston Chapman, n.p., 12 February 1841, A.9.2.15.24; Caroline Weston to Henry and Maria Weston Chapman, Roxbury, 3 March 1841, A.9.2.6.58, WP. About the same time as William broke his engagement, he lost his beloved sister, Eliza J. Chace (Mrs. Thomas Davis of Providence, Rhode Island), who had contracted quinsy (a severe infection of the throat) in the spring of 1839 but lingered into December 1840. Eliza was five years older than her brother and an ardent Garrisonian. She believed in gender-segregated societies as a bulwark strengthening women in an unpopular cause. See William L. Garrison to Helen E. Garrison, Providence, 5 May 1839; William L. Garrison to George W. Benson, Boston, 1 November 1840; and William L. Garrison to John A. Collins, Boston, 1 December 1840, in Ruchames, *House Dividing*, 456, 722, 724; and Van Broekhoven, *Devotion of These Women*, 84, 247 n. 1.

69. Chace joined a utopian community shortly after breaking off the engagement. He later became active in the Republican Party. See William Lloyd Garrison to George W. Benson, Boston, 7 January 1841, in Merrill, *No Union with Slaveholders*, 8, 10 n. 3.

70. Edmund Quincy to Friends [Henry and Maria Weston Chapman], Dedham to Cape Haitien, 18 May 1841, A.9.2.13.71-72, WP. This letter shows the censorship employed throughout the Weston letters; see the Appendix. One can only assume in context that the letter included information about Chace or a discussion of the broken engagement and the rumors that were swirling about it.

71. Maria Weston Chapman to "friends" [Ann and Wendell Phillips], Weymouth, 27 August 1841, Blagden Collection, HL; Anne Warren Weston to Debora Weston, Weymouth, 27 October 1841, A.9.2.15.83, WP.

72. On her father's death, the house in Chauncy Place, Boston, was left to Mary and Maria equally. Mary felt slighted by the arrangement. Having never lived there, Maria

grew angry when the city of Boston tried to recoup from her the taxes it levied on the property. The two women, never close and of quite different temperaments, grew apart.

73. This view of marriage, of course, overlooks the possibility that a brother—no less than a husband—might be economically dependent upon his sister, or a threat to her as sexual predator or physical abuser.

74. Henrietta Sargent to George B. Dixwell, Boston, 9 June 1843, Wigglesworth Family Papers, MHS. Henrietta and Catherine Sargent were two of four surviving siblings from among the nine sons and daughters of Epes and Esther Dorcas Babson Sargent. They occupied their natal home, which stood just southeast of the Boston Common and close to the abodes of their two remaining siblings, the widowed Esther Sargent Dixwell (to whose son Henrietta wrote) and the recently married Anna Sargent Parker. Unlike Esther, Anna limited her contact with Henrietta and Catherine because of scruples about abolition. Despite personality and political differences, however, these sisters—single, married, and widowed—traveled together for pleasure and purpose, shared social activities, celebrated holidays together, and nurtured their nephews, the widow Esther's three sons. See, for example, Epes Sargent Dixwell to George B. Dixwell, Dorchester, 13 August 1842; Esther Sargent Dixwell to George B. Dixwell, Northampton, 7 July 1843, Wigglesworth Family Papers, MHS.

75. Anne Warren Weston to Debora Weston, Dorchester, 11 July 1839, A.9.2.11.134; Debora Weston to Anne Warren Weston, New Bedford, 10 February 1840, A.9.2.13.21, WP.

76. A Mr. Sanborn, the uncle of Dr. Noah Fifield, who lived on property adjoining the Westons' in Weymouth, reportedly told his nephew that "he had better marry one of them." He had known the three sisters "when they were very young, and more lovely, beautiful, blooming girls, he never saw." Their reasons for remaining single are lost to time, as none of the family remarked upon the subject. See Lucia Weston to Debora Weston, Boston, 7 July 1839, A.9.2.11.132, WP.

77. Their mother, Deborah Nash Weston, had left the sisters an estate worth some $4,000 on her death on 4 November 1839. See Norfolk County Probate Record 19674. The will of Mary Weston was dated 1856 and probated 1861 with that of Phebe Weston. See Norfolk County Probate Court Records 19677 and 19680. Priscilla died intestate. These sisters lived frugally but not in poverty; Mary's estate was worth some $2,300 in real and personal property when she died.

78. Similar arrangements were stipulated in Ann Bates Weston's will. She left both her real and personal property to her unmarried daughters "as joint tenants," not tenants in common, "as I wish all said residue to be owned and managed jointly by them, and in case of the death of either of them her right and estate in said residue to pass to the others or other and so on to the last survivor, with whom the final disposal of all said residue shall remain." Ann [Nancy] Weston's will, dated 1873, had an 1877 codicil disinheriting her son Hervey Eliphas of the real property she had previously given him and returning it to her unmarried daughters. No reason was given for the change. Perhaps the codicil recognized his lack of heirs, the likelihood that some of his sisters would outlive him, a reward for his sisters' care for their brother for many years, or an expression of disappointment in or anger with him. See Norfolk County Probate Records 19674 and 21118.

79. Caroline Weston to Debora Weston, Boston, 14 January 1834, A.9.2.7.33; Caroline Weston to Debora Weston, Boston, 12 October 1836, WP.

80. Anne Warren Weston to Lucia Weston, New Bedford, 10 November 1842, A.9.2.17.107, WP.

81. Anne Warren Weston to Lucia Weston, Boston, 21 September 1840, A.9.2.14.23–24, WP. John A. Collins (1810–79) was a student at the Andover Theological Seminary and served as the general agent of the MAS. He played an important role in defining the "clerical plot" against Garrison in 1837–39 and toured Great Britain in 1840 on a major fund-raising tour. He turned to Fourierism in the early 1840s and resigned as agent of the NEAS to help establish a commune at Skaneateles, New York.

82. For Caroline's views of Thompson, see her Austen reference in Caroline Weston to Anne Warren Weston, Boston, 13 August 1835, A.9.2.7.63; and Caroline Weston diary, 16, 17, 18 September 1835, A.9.2.7.65–66, WP.

83. Anne Warren Weston to Mary A. Estlin, Weymouth, 2 November 1850, A.7.2.7, 15 February 1852, A.7.2.14, JBEP; George Thompson to Anne Warren Weston, n.p., 25 November 1835, A.1.3.1.2, ASC. Caroline's diary for 1835 described a discomfort so personal she could not put it to paper. Perhaps this was Anne's growing infatuation with the married Thompson. See Caroline Weston diary, 16 and 19 September 1835, A.9.2.7.65–66, WP. So too, Anne spent time at the Groton home of widower Amos Farnsworth (1788–1861, a graduate of Harvard medical school and practicing physician), tutoring his daughter Mary. Gossip about their relationship bothered Anne for years and caused a breach with Mary Farnsworth. See Anne Warren Weston to Debora Weston, Groton, 21 January 1834, A.9.2.7.34; Caroline Weston diary, 22 September 1835, A.9.2.7.65–66; and Sophia [unknown] to Caroline Weston, St. Louis, 10 November 1836, A.9.2.8.70, WP. In the face of both gossip and breach, Anne determined, "I have cast off all fear about all such matters & mean to drive round with so many men as to make all individual scandal impossible" (Anne Warren Weston to Debora Weston, Brush Hill, 11 June 1846, A.9.2.22.60, WP).

84. Anne Warren Weston to Ann T. G. Phillips, Weymouth, 15 February 1864, Blagden Collection, HL.

85. Elizur Wright came up with the term "Boston clique" as a term of opprobrium and exclusion. However, it also implied inclusion, and the circle around Chapman embraced the sobriquet. See Edmund Quincy to Richard D. Webb, 23 May 1843, Quincy, Wendell, Holmes, and Upham Family Papers, MHS; and Anne Warren Weston to Caroline and Debora Weston, Boston, [April 1840], A.9.2.16.13, WP.

86. Anne Warren Weston to Debora Weston, Boston, 8 March 1839, A.9.2.11.53; Anne Warren Weston to Debora Weston, Boston, 4 October 1836, A.9.2.8.56; Anne Warren Weston to Debora Weston, Boston, 22 October 1836, A.9.2.8.63; Anne Warren Weston to Debora Weston, Groton, 8 September 1836, A.9.2.8.47, WP. On Whittier's lifelong relationship with his sister, see his friend Thomas Wentworth Higginson's biography, *John Greenleaf Whittier*, 78–79, 107–8. See also Woodwell, *John Greenleaf Whittier*, 17, 31, 126–27; and Anne Warren Weston to Lucia Weston, Boston, 28 September 1840, A.9.2.14.32; Caroline Weston diary, 3 October 1835, A.9.2.7.65–66; Debora Weston to Caroline Weston, New Bedford, September 1836, A.9.2.8.44; Anne Warren Weston to Debora Weston, Boston, 4 October 1836, A.9.2.8.56, WP.

87. Lucretia Cowing to Debora Weston, Boston, 30 September 1836, A.9.2.8.53, WP.

88. Anne Warren Weston to Debora Weston, Boston, 1 January 1837, A.9.2.9.2, WP.

89. Sibling-exchange marriages were commonplace in late eighteenth- and early nineteenth-century Massachusetts. In Weymouth, for example, among the Bates clan alone, Levi Bates married Lucinda Rice in 1810. Three years after she died in 1813, Levi married her sister Abigail. His sister, Mary Bates, had married Lucinda and Abigail's brother Josiah Rice in 1809. Brothers John Ward Bates and Jacob Porter Bates married sisters Betsey Vinson Thayer and Susanna Thayer in 1820 and 1824, respectively. Siblings Warren and Jane Bates married siblings Harriet and Allen Vining in 1834 and 1846, respectively. Boston merchant John James Dixwell, nephew of BFAS members Henrietta and Catherine Sargent, married Eliza Ingersoll, the younger sister of his younger brother Epse Dixwell's wife Mary. Wrote Epse, "By the way—I have some scruples about this new match which I expressed last night to the parties. I told them that I did not know but what we should be deemed to be about committing *bigamy*. This double marriage is as near that as any thing can be." Henrietta tried matchmaking among her nephews, hoping to match John James Dixwell and George Dixwell with Hannah and Phebe Adams. See Chamberlain, *Genealogies*, 32, 35, 38, 39, 587, 712, 714; Epse Sargent Dixwell to George B. Dixwell, Cambridge, 25 January 1846, Wigglesworth Family Papers, MHS; and Henrietta Sargent to George B. Dixwell, Boston, 20 September 1841, Wigglesworth Family Papers, MHS. For other such marriages among the Boston elite, and a discussion of the role of such marriages in class formation, see Farrell, *Elite Families*, chaps. 3 and 4. Farrell suggests that "proximity—particularly among kin—was an important consideration for an appropriate marriage in this period" (88).

90. Sylvia Ammidon to Debora Weston, Groton, 10 September 1833, A.9.2.7.27; Anne Warren Weston to Debora Weston, Dorchester, 11 July 1839, A.9.2.11.134, WP.

91. Anne Warren Weston to Caroline Weston, Boston, 30 May 1844, A.9.2.20.33, WP; Anne Warren Weston to Ann Phillips and Wendell Phillips, 17 August 1848, 1289, folio 1, Blagden Collection, HL. In reading the Westons' comments on marriage, one is often reminded of attitudes conveyed by Jane Austen's heroines in books of which the sisters were very fond, as they were of Elizabeth Barrett Browning's ode to female singlehood, "Aurora Leigh," published in 1856.

92. The use of the phrase "the hour and the man" is one of many examples in which the Westons utilized abolitionist sayings to illuminate a private context. Harriet Martineau, for example, had applied this phrase to Toussaint-Louverture. Thereafter it was widely applied to William L. Garrison and other heroes of the antislavery movement.

93. Anne wrote that she "took a very civil leave of him however and told him that I wished to retain him as a friend &c. I have heard that every body has one chance. I am fearful that this is mine" (Anne Warren Weston to Debora Weston, Boston, 4 October 1836, A.9.2.8.56, WP).

94. Zsuzsa Berend has argued that nineteenth-century ideals of love and marriage (and, I would suggest, sibship) involved not just fancy but the "ultimate measure of existing things." Women took these ideals to be "an ultimate, unchanging, God-ordained reality," so that "self-development was not antagonistic to marriage but, in their view a necessary preparation for it." Remaining single was not the result of individual

shortcomings but rather the evolution of a process of trial and error, of individual assessment that failed to produce the one suitor who could "mean all things to the heart." Singlehood, she has argued, was viewed "as an outcome of intricate choices and spinsters champions of uncompromising morality" (Berend, "'Best or None!'" 936).

95. Many single women in New England lived in households with sisters who played crucial roles for one another as nurturers, teachers, confidants, and disciplinarians. Maiden aunts tutored the Blackwell sisters. Catharine Sedgwick and Harriet Adams found solace with older sisters. Alice Cary acted as guardian for her younger sister, Phoebe. For discussions of grief at the loss of a sibling to marriage, see Chambers-Schiller, *Liberty, a Better Husband*, 129–32; Kelley, "Negotiating a Self"; and Marshall, *Peabody Sisters*.

96. Anne Warren Weston to Ann T. G. and Wendell Phillips, April 1854, Blagden Collection, HL.

97. A growing scholarship has looked at single women and their decisions to remain unwed as well as the cultural and social contexts in which they made these decisions. For each there were trade-offs, compromises influenced by factors such as quality and situation of potential suitors, needs for female labor in the natal family, timing of proposals, and emotional attachment. See, for example, Joan E. Cashin, "'Decidedly Opposed to *the Union*'"; Anya Jabour, "'It Will Never Do for Me to Be Married'"; Miller, "'My Part Alone'"; Wulf, *Not All Wives*; and Carter, *Southern Single Blessedness*.

98. Maria Weston Chapman to Elizabeth Pease Nichol, Weymouth, 20 September 1858, WP.

CHAPTER 3

1. Debora Weston to Anne Warren Weston, New Bedford, 15 January 1836, A.9.2.8.6, 17 September 1836, A.9.2.8.52; Caroline Weston to Debora Weston, Boston, n.d., A.9.2.6.69, WP.

2. It is difficult to know how Warren Weston felt about his situation relative to his well-to-do kin. He appears in the historical record at second hand, through the words of his daughters and brother-in-law. A small but growing body of historical literature addressing failure in antebellum America provides some context for his experience, however. See Balleisen, *Navigating Failure*, and Ditz, "Shipwrecked." A valuable resource on the late nineteenth century is Sandage, *Born Losers*.

3. Hunt, *Weymouth Ways*, 28; Weston, *In Memoriam*, 3–6. Debora Nash Weston's daughters would continue to live in that house and leave it to their remaining nieces on Mary's death in 1860. Eliphaz Weston was one of eight sons of shipwright Eliphaz Weston and Priscilla Peterson of Duxbury, Massachusetts. Of these sons, four drowned at sea: Joshua with his father and within sight of home; Daniel as captain of a ship bound for Bristol, Maine, that went down off Duxbury Beach; Timothy, who commanded a privateer during the Revolution and drowned in the Bay of Fundy; and Eliphaz himself when the vessel on which he traveled went down en route to Boston from Baltimore. Warren Weston of Weymouth was named for Warren Weston of Duxbury, his father's eldest brother, who lived in his father's house and worked as a shipwright in his brother Ezra's shipyard. See Weston, "Weston Family of Duxbury, Mass.," 124,

146; Weston, *Descendants of Edmund Weston of Duxbury*; and Browne, *King Caesar of Duxbury*, 10–11.

4. *Other Merchants and Sea Captains of Old Boston*, 62; Weston, *In Memoriam*, 13–15, 19–27. The 2010 equivalent of the wages paid by E. Weston and Son was $2,892,575. The price for Ezra Weston II's success may have been high. Nathaniel Winsor (1831–83) wrote when a sophomore at Harvard about his father, Justin Winsor, a West Roxbury, Massachusetts, shipbroker and Duxbury historian, "I have hopes to get father into better ways. He generally comes home at night, gets a cigar, sits and thinks, thinks, and thinks of his business without relaxation, and allows it even to disturb his nights; it is business, business, business. The human mind cannot endure without a change; relaxation is necessary. The late Ezra Weston of Duxbury, at the same time he was amassing a large fortune, lost a measure of his mind, which was worn out by a constant exercise in the same way" (Scudder, *Justin Winsor*, 4).

5. Anne Warren Weston to Maria Weston Chapman, Boston, 15 April 1841, A.9.2.15.42, WP. Gershom (1799–1869) built a beautiful estate of some thirty acres and a mansion that was valued at about $50,000 when destroyed by fire in 1850. In 1851 his fortune was estimated at approximately $200,000. He turned to politics in the 1820s, serving as a member of the state legislature for twelve years and a state justice for seventeen years. He stood as the Free-Soil candidate for the U.S. Congress and lost by fewer than 150 votes. Thereafter, Gershom experienced significant financial reverses. In 1868, friends from the Massachusetts Senate purchased for him the small house he was then renting. See Forbes and Greene, *Rich Men of Massachusetts*, and Weston, *In Memoriam*, 31–32.

6. Caroline Weston to Henry Chapman and Maria Weston Chapman, Boston, 5 April 1841, A.9.2.15.36, WP. Ezra and Gershom B. Weston as well as Joshua Bates all saw temperance as an important element in their success.

7. Born in Weymouth in 1788, Joshua Bates died in London in 1864.

8. William Rufus Gray (1750–1825) was said to own the largest shipping fleet in America prior to the War of 1812. In 1782 he married Elizabeth Chipman (1756–1823). He went on to a political career as a state senator and lieutenant governor of Massachusetts.

9. Diary of Joshua Bates, 2 October 1835, 4 August 1849, 1 January 1854, Baring Brothers DEP 74, BA.

10. In Maria's hands too he placed the power to provide as she deemed fit for the needs of his sister-in-law, Elizabeth [Betsy] Sturgis. "I am sorry to hear that Mrs. B[ates]'s sister has been thrown on the world," he wrote, "but what can be made of her. Mrs. B is pretty shrewd in such matters, and thinks it is difficult to do any thing, but I do things even when they do not promise immediate good, and if you think good may come out of it advance her a little cash and place it to my account" (Joshua Bates to Maria Weston, London, 18 July 1829, A.9.2.7.17, WP). Elizabeth [Betsy] Sturgis and Harriet Sturgis received regular financial support from Joshua Bates. See, for example, Diary of Joshua Bates diary, 1 May 1832, Baring Brothers DEP 74, BA. So too did John Sturgis, their brother, who became a partner in the firm Sturgis and Perkins, merchants, in New York City. John lacked competence in business and, when his firm failed in 1829, entered a mental asylum. See William Sturgis to Joshua Bates, Boston, 11 June 1832,

Baring Brothers, HC5.1.5, BA. William Sturgis, the elder, was cousin to John and Lucretia Sturgis and a successful partner in Bryant and Sturgis, Boston merchants. Bates also provided his mother, Tirzah Bates Hunt, with $500 a year. See Diary of Joshua Bates, 5 October 1833, Baring Brothers DEP 74, BA.

11. Joshua Bates to Maria Weston, London, 18 July 1829, A.9.2.1.17, WP.

12. Maria Weston Chapman to Joshua Bates, 13 June 1831, HC 5.1.17, BA. It is not clear whether the statement was genuine or calculated, nor why Bates assigned Maria as go-between rather than dealing directly with his sister. His genuine affection for and trust in Maria was surely a factor. Her pride and bluntness appealed to his dislike of importuning individuals. His sister's pride may have been a factor, or her literacy. Although there are references to Ann writing her brother with explanations of financial matters, few letters of any kind exist from her hand. The marked shakiness of the signature on her will and its two codicils may have resulted from old age or ill health, yet, despite being separated by several years, all three match closely. So perhaps the obvious effort involved had more to do with lack of practice.

13. Shammas, *History of Household Government*, 108–44.

14. Weymouth did have a small shoe manufacturing business by the 1830s, but the Westons showed no inclination to work there. Deacon Hunt, who married their widowed grandmother Tirzah Pratt Bates, owned one such factory. In 1837, the industry employed 828 men and 510 women, producing $428,000 worth of goods. See Barber, *Historical Collection*, 490; and Hunt, *Weymouth Ways*, 30–31. In the 1830s, Joshua Bates was providing $500 annually to his mother's support, from which she allocated a sum to her grandson, Henry Cowing, son of her youngest daughter, Cynthia Bates Cowing, with which to begin a second shoe factory. See Maria Weston Chapman to Joshua Bates, Boston, 29 March 1837, HC5.1.17, BA.

15. See Ryan, *Cradle of the Middle Class*; Farrell, *Elite Families*; and Heffernan and Stecker, *Sisters of Fortune*. The Francis Elizabeth Gray Papers at the Massachusetts Historical Society offer the story of the dispossessed spinster granddaughter of merchant William R. Gray. Well-known but economically strapped New England reformer families whose daughters supported themselves and/or siblings as teachers include the Alcotts, Thoreaus, and Peabodys.

16. The annuities that began in the 1830s at $500 per annum had increased by 1854 to $1,000. By comparison, Bates settled £1,500 a year, about $7,380, on his daughter, Elizabeth, when she married in January 1839. See Diary of Joshua Bates, 1 January 1854, Baring Brothers DEP 74, BA; and Henry G. Chapman to Joshua Bates, 31 December 1834, 29 March 1837, 3 June 1838, 2 December 1839, HC 5.1.17, BA.

17. Joshua Bates to Maria Weston, London, 18 July 1829, A.9.2.7.17, WP. At the time, Anne was living in Boston with her married sister and attending Ebenezer Bailey's Boston High School, where her sister Caroline taught. She served as a teaching assistant to help pay her fees. As to Hervey, Bates paid school fees of $260.67, which included board and tuition at Hingham Secondary School, his tailor's bill, a doctor's bill for setting a broken arm, and his laundress bill. Bates also paid tuition for Hervey's first term at Harvard. See Henry G. Chapman to Joshua Bates, 31 December 1834, HC 5.1.17, BA.

18. For a view of this world and the importance of literacy in it, see August, *Clerk's Tale*. Caroline was thrilled to find Warren, who had spent little time on self-improvement,

reading during the voyages he undertook as a merchant shipper in the years follow-ing his clerkship: "I forgot to tell you that the ship Grafton wh[ich] arrived last week bro[ugh]t letters from Warren to the Grants & Warren's journal of his passage—quite good about 30 pages & my soul rejoiced over the books that he has recorded having read—I think it must have done him great good" (Caroline Weston to Debora Weston, Roxbury, 5 October 1841, A.9.2.15.7, WP).

19. Bates had lost his much-loved son, William, to a hunting accident seven years earlier (21 December 1834). Perhaps he saw the possibility of a paternal relationship with his nephew.

20. See Anne Warren Weston to Debora Weston, Boston, 15 January 1842, A.9.2.17.24, WP, for a description of Warren carrying a letter from Bates to Daniel Web-ster in Washington, D.C., and receiving from Webster a letter of introduction to Walter Forward, secretary of the treasury. A transaction involving Forward's aid resulted in a £1,000 profit for Warren.

21. Caroline Weston to Debora Weston, Roxbury, 10 November 1841, A.9.2.15.92, WP. The course is interesting given Bates's reaction four years earlier to another nephew, Henry Cowing, the son of his wife's sister Cynthia: "One of my nephews ar-rived today from America. Mr. Henry B. Cowing whose face I have no recollection of and think the object of his visit is to get some of my money. He seems a sound good-tempered man, has been in the shoes trade in America. I shall treat him civilly and send him home with empty pockets or I shall have all my nephews and nieces out. It is better to aid them on the other side of the water" (Diary of Joshua Bates, 13 May 1837, Baring Brothers DEP 74, BA). Both Bates and his wife, Lucretia Sturgis, believed that Cynthia Bates Cowing and her husband lacked fiscal discipline; the couple for some years lived with her mother, Tirzah Bates Hunt. See Hunt, *Weymouth Ways*, 31.

22. Bates noted with pleasure that "the Great House of B[aring] B[rothers] & Co are building a ship that's to be navigated by seamen who will consent not to use ardent spirits[;] this is true and may do some good by calling public attention to the subject which is one of deep interest" (Diary of Joshua Bates, 31 December 1831, 24 October 1833, Baring Brothers DEP 74, BA). In 1842, Gershom B. Weston founded the Duxbury Martha Washington Relief Society, which promoted temperance, and he frequently lec-tured on the subject. See Weston, *In Memoriam*, 29.

23. Diary of Joshua Bates, 24 October 1833 and 5 January 1834, Baring Brothers DEP 74, BA. When the ship sailed in early May 1834, he expressed his satisfaction: "Our ship was manned last week on the temperance plan and has sailed today without a drop of spiritous [*sic*] liquor on board. In our instructions to the Captain we have forbid the practice of profane swearing and I hope that by setting a good example to influence others and thus improve the general state of morals in the seamen and offi-cers of the merchant service" (ibid., 13 May 1834). For the story of an early temperance ship, the *Empress* out of New Bedford in 1827, see Anderson, "Captain Lays Down the Law." Throughout the 1830s, the annual reports of the American Temperance Society discussed this phenomenon and its importance for the health and safety of mariners as well as the profitability of the merchant trade.

24. Bates "beg[ged] W[arren] not to trust himself on board a sugar ship," reported Caroline, and in so saying she quipped, "So you see he is worth more than he was last

year" (Caroline Weston to Debora Weston, Boston, [1841 or 1842], A.9.2.5.22, WP). Making a trip to Havana as supercargo, Warren contracted with "the pious" (meaning temperate) Captain Rogers of the *Charles Carroll*. See Caroline Weston to Debora Weston, n.p., 3 May [1842], A.9.2.3.99, WP.

25. By way of perspective, Jeanne Boydston has shown that Massachusetts laboring men rarely earned more than $1 a day and did not work year-round. She calculated their annual income at midcentury at approximately $156. Sean Wilentz found that in 1850 in New York City, tradesmen earned on average about $300 a year, half the amount estimated by the *New York Times* as minimal subsistence for a family of four. Shipbuilding paid higher wages, on average about $579. Alan Dawley reported that Massachusetts shoemakers made about $20 a month or $240 a year. Middle-class men—clerks, accountants, bank tellers—might bring in $600-$700 a year, and the professions, $1,000. All coped with rising prices of corn and wood and urban housing rents during the period. Women's domestic labor raised household resources to the level of maintenance, as "this surplus allowed families to survive on $300 or $400 annually at a time when observers calculated $600 as the minimal threshold of subsistence." See Boydston, *Home and Work*, 61–62, 64, 69–70, 133, 136; Wilentz, *Chants Democratic*, 117, 405; Dawley, *Class and Community*, 53–54; and Ryan, *Cradle of the Middle Class*, 108, 254.

26. Caroline Weston to Debora Weston, Roxbury, 10 November 1841, A.9.2.15.92, WP.

27. Modeling himself upon his uncle, Warren mentored younger men. When Hall J. Howe asked Warren to "cast a helpful eye" upon his son, who had taken to sail for his health, Warren took the boy under his wing. He took him to Canton, showing him China and providing him with new clothes when he outgrew his old during the course of the voyage. Reported Maria, "Warren seems to have been actuated by the purest principles of [Christianity] in the matter,—saying naively that it was just what he longed in vain to have done for him by some good Samaritan when he was a boy" (Maria Weston Chapman to Caroline Weston, n.p., [1842], A.9.2.4.23, WP).

28. Bates also established Maria's son, his grandnephew Henry Grafton Chapman Jr., in business in 1858, providing £10,000 ($48,600) with which to purchase a partnership in the New York City banking firm of Ward, Campbell, & Company. At the same time, Thomas Charles Baring also bought into the company. See Diary of Joshua Bates, 3 June 1838, 1 January 1854, 26 November 1858, Baring Brothers DEP 74, BA; and Anne Warren Weston to Debora Weston, Weymouth, 22 April 1842, A.9.2.17.58; Caroline Weston to Debora Weston, n.p., 3 May [1842], A.9.2.3.99; Caroline Weston to Debora Weston, Boston, 24 June 1842, A.9.2.17.75, WP. See also Hidy, "Organization and Functions." Barrett's *Old Merchants of New York City* shows the dissolution of the firm Goodhue & Co. in December 1861, with two of the partners, Richard Warren Weston and Horace Gray, forming a new partnership in the firm Weston and Gray on 1 January 1862.

29. Bates sent numerous commissions to Chapman and Company. See, for example, Henry G. Chapman to Joshua Bates, Boston, 21 November 1831, HC 5.1.17, BA. Here Chapman advised Bates of the death of Mr. Charles Twey, agent of Mr. Shears, copper factor. In high demand by the shipbuilding industry in New England, copper was then a primary consignment for Chapman and Company. Wrote Chapman: "It is very

desirable for Msrs Chapman & Co. to be their *sole agents* in this place. Would you be kind enough to use your influence with them in advising their future shipments to HC & Co. as the fewer competitors, and the larger our assortment the better command we have of the market." Baring Brothers ledgers show a Chapman and Company account beginning in 1831 with commissions and consignments worth a high of £11,000 in 1833 down to £86 by the time of Chapman's death in 1842. Barings also did business with Ezra Weston in the thousands of pounds. See Henry G. Chapman to Joshua Bates, Liverpool, 19 April 1831, 28 May 1831; Boston, 28 June 1831, 29 July 1831, 30 October 1831, 21 November 1831, HC 5.1.17, BA.

30. Lucretia Cowing to Debora Weston, Cherry Grove, Md., 28 September 1838, A.9.2.10.56, WP. Lucretia was the daughter of Cynthia Bates Cowing. At the time this letter was written, she worked as governess in the home of Maryland's governor, a position disapproved of by her abolitionist cousins for its indirect support of slaveholders.

31. Maria Weston Chapman to sisters, London, 22 October [between 1825 and 1828], A.9.2.5.63, WP.

32. The first Boston high school for girls was founded in 1825. There was sufficient opposition to the idea of educating girls that the concerted effort of "the most prominent and influential citizens" was required for the "experiment." Some 286 students applied for admission, but many were not sufficiently prepared to go beyond grammar school. Of those qualified, 135 students were accepted, as many as could be accommodated. The school continued until 1827, when the numbers of applicants, and the potential costs, so rose that Mayor Josiah Quincy recommended the school be discontinued. It was. One cause of the controversy was that a significant number of Irish girls not only attended but did well, a factor some commentators feared would make them unfit for domestic service. Girls had been admitted part time to the town grammar schools when founded in 1789. After the high school closed, girls were allowed to attend the grammar schools full time until sixteen years of age (boys left for high school at fourteen). Ebenezer Bailey was so disappointed at the closing of the public high school for girls that he opened a private school. It continued for some ten years. The city did not reintroduce a public high school for girls until 1852. See Winsor, *Memorial History of Boston*, 242–51, 343–45.

33. Weston careers in teaching covered the broad spectrum of possibilities in antebellum New England. These included teaching girls in schools run by a male teacher for male students; establishing their own schools, singly and together; and teaching in a setting established by a local committee of parents or town fathers. The largest expansion of such schools occurred in New England between 1830 and 1850. At midcentury, some 25,000 students attended 6,000 academies. See Solomon, *In the Company of Educated Women*, 15.

34. The *Catalogue* lists Maria as preceptress, Caroline as an assistant, and Caroline and Anne as students. See Henry G. Chapman to Joshua Bates, 29 July 1831, HC 5.1.17, BA.

35. Caroline Weston to Debora Weston, Boston, 14 January 1834, A.9.2.7.33, WP. Among those from whom she borrowed were William L. and Helen B. Garrison, who left many of their household effects (and pets) with the Westons when leaving Boston for Connecticut for a period of rest and recuperation. See also Anne Warren Weston to Debora Weston, Boston, 21 January 1834, A.9.2.7.34, in which she asks whether she is

needed yet in Boston, describes talking up the new school, and asks whether Caroline has settled the property issue yet and whether the school will commence.

36. Southwick, *Reminiscences*, 37.

37. Caroline Weston to Debora Weston, Boston, [1836], A.9.2.3.28, WP.

38. Debora Weston to Caroline Weston, New Bedford, 1836, A.9.2.8.1, WP.

39. Ebenezer Bailey (1795–1839) left Boston's high school for girls to found a boys' school in Roxbury in 1838. The following year, Caroline left Boston to take up a girls' school in Roxbury. By 1840 she had thirty-three students, including her younger sister Emma and her niece Lizzy (Elizabeth B. Chapman). Bailey's recommendation surely contributed to her success there. Another academician, George Wilder, offered the girls' department of his school in Dorchester to Anne after the sisters closed their Boston school.

40. Edmund Quincy, who moved from Boston to Dedham in 1840, encouraged Anne to establish a school there. Samuel J. May urged Caroline to take the Derby Academy in Hingham. See Edmund Quincy to Maria Weston Chapman, Dedham, 26 April 1840, A.9.2.13.57; and Anne Warren Weston to Mary Weston, Boston, 16 May 1839, A.9.2.11.106, WP.

41. A year younger than Lucia Weston, Sarah Southwick became fast friends with the younger Westons. "During our residence of nearly twenty years in Boston," she recalled, "I had no young friend for whom I had the affection that I had for Lucia Weston. She and her sisters were constantly at our house. Lucia Weston and I circulated petitions together for several successive years, going to every house, rich and poor; taking a different ward each year as our sphere of labor. We read together and slept together, sometimes on the attic floor, when crowded out of our own rooms by guests attending anti-slavery conventions" (*Reminiscences*, 34–35).

42. Ibid., 37–38. During this period, Caroline, Lucia, and possibly Anne also taught adult night school at the Belknap Street School in Boston, a segregated public primary school established for black students in 1831. The impact of their teaching and their political example may have added to Sarah Southwick's motivation for joining the faculty of the Belknap School. She assisted Ambrose Wellington in the 1840s during the abolitionist effort to desegregate Boston's public schools. When that failed, she became a teacher in Boston's Smith School for black children, sharing the position with Susan Paul, another member of the BFAS, a favorite of the Westons, and daughter of Rev. Thomas Paul, founder in 1805 of the First African Baptist Church in Boston. Sarah Southwick never married, and Susan Paul died in 1841 at the relatively young age of thirty-two. See Levesque, *Black Boston*, 169.

43. Anne Warren Weston to Debora Weston, 21 January 1834, A.9.2.7.34; Anne Warren Weston to Debora Weston, Boston, 18 April 1837, A.9.2.9.28, WP.

44. Debora Weston to Anne Warren Weston, New Bedford, 15 January 1836, A.9.2.8.6, WP. She figured she was making about a dollar a day. They had charged $10.00 a quarter or $2.50 a week to their boarding students in Boston. See Anne Warren Weston to Debora Weston, Boston, 18 April 1837, A.9.2.9.28, WP.

45. Printed Circular, Ms. 1290, Blagden Collection, HL. Debora continued to teach in New Bedford on and off until 1850, by which time her nursing skills were required by her brothers and the family could afford to support her in that private occupation.

46. Mary Kelley argues the reverse causation, that education provided the motivation and identity women enacted as reformers, bringing such skills as writing, lecturing, editing, and publishing to abolition. See *Learning to Stand and Speak*, 14. In the Weston case, political consciousness and socialization began at home. Reform and schooling (as one another's students and teachers) proved mutually reinforcing. Debra Gold Hansen argues that many self-supporting women of the BFAS utilized the social skills involved in reform work to create paid employment as moral reform agents, lecturers, editors, and social workers. See *Strained Sisterhood*, 80.

47. Lucia Weston to Debora Weston, Boston, 28 April 1839, A.9.2.11.91, WP.

48. Anne Warren Weston to Lucia Weston, Boston, 21 September 1840, A.9.2.14.23–24, WP.

49. Solomon (*In the Company of Educated Women*, 33) adds to this list recalcitrant students, indifferent school boards, inhospitable communities, and the isolation of teachers within those communities.

50. Preston, "Domestic Ideology," 536 n. 4; Vinovskis and Bernard, "Beyond Catharine Beecher," 868.

51. Preston, "Domestic Ideology," 536, 542; Melder, "Woman's High Calling," 22.

52. Quoted in Preston, "Domestic Ideology," 544.

53. Debora Weston to Maria W. Chapman, New Bedford, 13 April 1837, A.9.2.9.27, WP; Caroline Weston to Ann T. G. Phillips, New Bedford, March 9, 1844, 1483, Blagden Collection, HL; Debora Weston to Anne Warren Weston, New Bedford, 23 June 1839, A.9.2.11.122; Anne Warren Weston to Debora Weston, Groton, 17 March 1837, A.9.2.9.16; Anne Warren Weston to Debora Weston, [Dorchester], 11 July 1839, A.9.2.11.134; Anne Warren Weston to Debora Weston, n.p., 24 June 1839, A.9.2.11.118; Anne Warren Weston to Debora Weston, Weymouth, 29 July 1842, A.9.2.17.84, WP.

54. Anne Warren Weston to Debora Weston, Boston, 4 October 1836, A.9.2.8.56, WP. Farnsworth served as vice president of the MAS and provided financial support for the *National Anti-Slavery Standard*. His children were Amos Henry (1825–50), Mary Elizabeth (b. 1823), and George Bourne (1828–87). George served as a lieutenant in the Fifth Massachusetts African American regiment during the Civil War.

55. Nevertheless, teaching paid more than any female occupation other than factory work. See Wallace, "Feminization of Teaching"; Perlmann and Margo, *Women's Work?*, 7–8, 22; and Hansen, *Strained Sisterhood*, 51–52.

56. Caroline Weston to Debora Weston, Boston, n.p., n.d., A.9.2.11.7, WP.

57. Caroline Weston to Anne Warren Weston, n.p., 21 June 1836, A.9.2.8.33, WP.

58. Comments such as these illustrate the casual racism of many abolitionists, though it is difficult to tease out Caroline's full meaning and intent from such a short phrase.

59. By the following year the Westons had hired Mary Proctor, a far more efficient charwoman. See Caroline Weston diary, 8 October 1835, A.9.2.7.65–66; Anne Warren Weston to Mary Weston, 27 October 1835, A.9.2.7.71; Caroline Weston to Anne Warren Weston, 21 June 1836, A.9.2.8.33; Caroline Weston to Debora Weston, Boston, 12 October 1836, A.9.2.8.60; and Anne Warren Weston to Debora Weston, Boston, 18 April 1837, A.9.2.9.28, WP. See also Debora Weston to Caroline Weston, New Bedford, 19 January 1845, A.9.2.21.5, WP.

60. Caroline Weston to Anne Warren Weston, Boston, 13 August 1835, A.9.2.7.63, WP.

61. Debora Weston to Caroline Weston, New Bedford, 5 October 1836, A.9.2.8.58; Anne Warren Weston to Debora Weston, Boston, 19 October 1836, A.9.2.8.74; Anne Warren Weston to Debora Weston, Boston, 1 January 1837, A.9.2.9.2; Anne Warren Weston to Debora Weston, Boston, 29 April 1837, A.9.2.9.30; Debora Weston to Caroline Weston, New Bedford, 2 May 1837, A.9.2.9.32; John F. Emerson to Debora Weston, New Bedford, 24 May 1837, A.9.2.9.36, WP.

62. John F. Emerson to Debora Weston, New Bedford, 3 June 1837, A.9.2.9.38; J. K. Lord to Debora Weston, New Bedford, 27 July 1837, A.9.2.9.51; Anne Warren Weston to Debora Weston, n.p., 11 October 1837, A.9.2.5.80b; John F. Emerson to Debora Weston, New Bedford, 31 December 1838, A.9.2.10.90, WP.

63. Anne Warren Weston to Debora Weston, n.p., 23 and 25 February, 1839, A.9.2.11.45, WP.

64. Sophia [unknown] to Caroline Weston, St. Louis, 10 November 1836, A.9.2.8.70; Anne Warren Weston to Debora Weston, Boston, 19 November 1836, A.9.2.8.73; Lucia Weston to Debora Weston, Boston, December 1836, A.9.2.8.76; Debora Weston to Maria Weston Chapman, New Bedford, 13 April 1837, A.9.2.9.27, WP.

65. Caroline Weston to Debora Weston, [Roxbury], 23 and 24 February [n.y.], A.9.2.6.69, WP.

66. Emerson became principal with the school's founding in 1827. The public school was abolished in 1829, and he headed up a private high school for the next eight years. The public school was revived in 1837, and he again took the headship. Two years later, Emerson, a Whig, was elected to the Massachusetts House of Representatives.

67. Debora Weston to Anne Warren Weston, New Bedford, 22 January 1836, A.9.2.8.8, WP. Kathryn Grover has suggested that the Westons "seem to have been assigned to the city to whip up abolitionist fervor" of a "radical" kind and that Anne and Debora's presence there in August 1835 was to "size up the town" in preparation for an upcoming antislavery petitioning campaign across the North in which the BFAS assigned members to focus on particular counties. My reading of the Weston letters suggests at least a dual purpose for their presence in New Bedford: the sisters' economic need and professional opportunities. Three groups contributed to abolition in New Bedford: Quakers; a number of well-to-do merchants, manufacturers, and bankers; and African Americans. Grover found both social distance and a high level of cooperation between the first two and the third "in instances where immediate action was called for." Debora thought New Bedford's abolitionists insufficiently Garrisonian and socially uncongenial. "I have no pleasure in any of these brethren," she wrote, while identifying Emerson as "the stoutest of any of them. . . . I don't *fellowship* anything here. However what must be must be." This latter reflected the economic reality of her need to find paid work. See Grover, *Fugitive's Gibraltar*, 6, 129, 141.

68. Anne Warren Weston to Debora Weston, Groton, 8 September 1836, A.9.2.8.47; Anne Warren Weston to Debora Weston, Groton, 17 March 1837, A.9.2.9.16; Debora Weston to Maria Weston Chapman, New Bedford, 13 April 1837, A.9.2.9.27; Debora Weston to Mary Weston, New Bedford, 24 February 1839, A.9.2.11.47, WP.

69. Anne Warren Weston to Debora Weston, Weymouth, 5 October 1841, A.9.2.15.74, WP.

70. Caroline Weston to Debora Weston, Roxbury, 5 October 1841, A.9.2.15.75, WP.

71. Debora Weston to Lucia and Emma Weston, New Bedford, 21 October 1841, A.9.2.15.84; Debora Weston to Anne Warren Weston, New Bedford, 1 November 1841, A.9.2.15.88, WP.

72. Anne Warren Weston to Debora Weston, Weymouth, 27 October 1841, A.9.2.15.83, WP.

73. Caroline Weston to Debora Weston, Weymouth, 23 November 1841, A.9.2.3.37, WP.

74. Anne Warren Weston to Debora Weston, Weymouth, 28 November 1841, A.9.2.15.100, WP.

75. Caroline Weston to Ann and Wendell Phillips, New Bedford, 25 May 1843, 1290, Blagden Collection, HL.

76. Caroline Weston to Ann T. G. Phillips, New Bedford, 9 March 1844, 1483, Blagden Collection, HL.

77. Ibid. In the tale, Sambo rode an alligator by jabbing a thumb in its right eye to get it to turn left or the left eye to turn right, and when asked what should be done if the alligator swam downward replied, "Ah Massa, dat berry hard!" See Davis, "Negro Folk-lore in South Carolina," 244.

78. Caroline Weston to Debora Weston, Boston, [fall 1836], A.9.2.3.30; Debora Weston to Caroline Weston, n.p., [1837], A.9.2.3.115, WP. For an example of one detailed explanation of a mathematical problem, see Caroline Weston to Debora Weston, Boston, 3 March 1839, A.9.2.11.50, WP. This problem likely came from a mathematics textbook and was not constructed by Caroline; it seems unlikely that a temperance advocate would have used this calculation of quantities of rum to teach fractions involving pints and gallons. Her explanation more likely was directed more toward modeling how to teach a problem than toward showing Debora herself how to work it; no Westons demonstrated difficulty in calculating the costs of cambric, carpet, or wood for their own household.

79. Debora Weston to Caroline Weston, New Bedford, 5 October 1836, A.9.2.8.58; Debora Weston to Caroline Weston, New Bedford, September 1836, A.9.2.8.44, WP.

80. Caroline Weston to Anne Warren Weston, Boston, [1839], A.9.2.4.53-54, WP.

81. Debora Weston to Anne Warren Weston, New Bedford, 15 January 1836, A.9.2.8.6; Anne Warren Weston to Debora Weston, n.p., 9 January 1837, A.9.2.9.6, WP. Maria offered to support the lessons when they proved beneficial. See Debora Weston to Anne Warren Weston, New Bedford, 1 December 1839, A.9.2.12.101, WP.

82. Anne Warren Weston to Lucia Weston, Boston, 28 September 1840, A.9.2.14.32, WP.

83. Anne Warren Weston to Debora Weston, Weymouth, 7 June 1840, A.9.2.13.81; Anne Warren Weston to Debora Weston, Boston, 25 January 1842, A.9.2.17.27; Anne Warren Weston to Debora Weston, Boston, 11 April 1842, A.9.2.17.50, WP.

84. This was the land that J. John Eaton Jr. sold to Warren Weston and his mother in 1813.

85. Debora Weston to Caroline Weston, Weymouth, 21 October 1850, A.9.2.25.33, WP.

86. Anne Warren Weston to Wendell Phillips, n.p., n.d., 1289, folio 6, Blagden Collection, HL.

87. Debora Weston to Maria Weston Chapman, New Bedford, 1 August 1836, A.9.2.8.39; Maria Weston Chapman to Debora Weston, Boston, 6 December 1839, A.9.2.12.108, WP.

88. Anne Warren Weston to Wendell Phillips, Weymouth, 28 October [1852], Am 1953, 1289, folio 8, Blagden Collection, HL.

89. Debora Weston to Anne Warren Weston, New Bedford, 13 April 1839, A.9.2.11.80; Caroline Weston to Maria Weston Chapman and Henry Chapman, Roxbury, 15 January 1841, A.9.2.15.11–14, WP; Maria Weston Chapman to David L. Child, "Boston for the hour, Weymouth for the month," 24 August 1843, A.4.1.77, ASC.

90. Caroline Weston to Debora Weston, Roxbury, [December 1839], A.9.2.6.77, WP.

91. Debora Weston to Anne Warren Weston, New Bedford, 7 April 1842, A.9.2.17.49, WP. James S. Gibbons (1810–92) and Abigail Hopper Gibbons (1801–93) were married in 1833. Quaker abolitionists, they moved in 1835 from Philadelphia to New York City, where he conducted a dry goods business. When, in 1841 and 1842, the New York Monthly Meeting of Friends disowned Abigail's father, Isaac Hopper, and husband, James, for abolitionism, she resigned. She engaged in a wide variety of reform activism: antislavery, temperance, prison reform, and poor relief.

92. Anne Warren Weston to Debora Weston, Boston, 11 April 1842, A.9.2.17.50, WP.

93. Debora Weston to Anne Warren Weston, New Bedford, 14 April 1842, A.9.2.17.51, WP.

94. Ellis Gray Loring (1803–58) was a Boston lawyer. An early abolitionist, he supported the *Liberator* and helped found the NEAS. For his activism and that of his wife, Louisa Gilman Loring (1797–1868), a member of the BFAS, he was ostracized by much of Boston's elite.

95. David Lee Child (1794–1874) was a journalist, teacher, lawyer, and abolitionist. His wife, Lydia Maria Child (1802–80), was a prominent antislavery author, member of the BFAS, and friend of the Westons. Maria played a crucial role in acquiring the services of both at one time or another to edit the *Anti-Slavery Standard*.

96. Anne Warren Weston to Debora Weston, Weymouth, 22 April 1842, A.9.2.17.58; J. A. Collins to Caroline Weston, Boston, 28 April 1842, A.9.2.17.60; Caroline Weston to Debora Weston, n.p., 3 May 1842, A.9.2.3.99, WP.

97. Anne Warren Weston to Debora Weston, Weymouth, 10 March 1842, A.9.2.17.40, WP. For more on Chapman's illness and his nursing, see Chapter 3.

98. Debora Weston to Anne Warren Weston, New Bedford, 26 April 1842, A.9.2.17.59; Anne Warren Weston to Debora Weston, Weymouth, 22 April 1842, A.9.2.17.58, WP.

99. Anne Warren Weston to Debora Weston, Northampton, 4 May 1842, A.9.2.17.61, WP.

100. Anne Warren Weston to Debora Weston, Boston, 3 June 1842, A.9.2.17.66; Anne Warren Weston to Debora Weston, Weymouth, 19 June 1842, A.9.2.17.73, WP.

101. On sending such stores to Weymouth, see, for example, Henry G. Chapman to Debora Weston, Boston, 26 December 1840, A.9.2.14.84, WP.

102. Laugel also received an additional $19,000 from a trust established by her grandfather after her father's death in 1842. Of Elizabeth's two siblings, Ann Greene Chapman died in 1877 and Henry G. Chapman Jr. in 1883.

103. The record does not show who paid Lucia's living expenses in Europe. It may be that siblings Maria and Warren shared the cost, that Joshua Bates contributed, or that all three maintained her.

104. In contrast, for example, to the experience of Rebecca Dickinson (1787–1802), a single woman who lived her "part alone." Faced with the vagaries of income incumbent upon the seasonality of agricultural labor and sporadic demand for sewing, she bemoaned "how times vary with me." A contemporaneous fictional character questioned similarly, "What a present is mine, and what a prospect is my future. Labour and watching's in the busy season—hunger in the slack—and solitude in both." See Miller, "'My Part Alone.'"

CHAPTER 4

1. Anne Warren Weston to Mary A. Estlin, Weymouth, 25 February 1855, A.7.2.27, JBEP. She had written similarly five months earlier: "Lucia seems doing *pretty well*. I shall never be free from anxiety till I find she has safely weathered the winter. . . . It is now about 4 years since I have known an entire freedom from anxiety as to the health of somebody or other, & when I consider how large our family is & that we must all die some time, I don't suppose I ever am to be perfectly at ease again in this life" (Anne Warren Weston to Wendell Phillips, Weymouth, 30 September 1854, Am 1953, 1289, folio 5, Blagden Collection, HL).

2. Anne Warren Weston to Wendell and Ann Phillips, Weymouth, 25 July and 27 August 1852, Am 1953, folio 4, Blagden Collection, HL; Anne Warren Weston to Mary A. Estlin, Weymouth, 19 July 1852, A.7.2.18, JBEP.

3. Anne's growing anxiety may be followed in her letters: Anne Warren Weston to Mary A. Estlin, New York City, 25 March 1851, A.7.2.9; Anne Warren Weston to Mary A. Estlin, Weymouth, 30 September 1851, A.7.2.11; Weymouth, 4 April 1852, A.7.2.17; Weymouth, 19 July 1852, A.7.2.18; Weymouth, 26 October 1852, A.7.2.19, JBEP. See also Anne Warren Weston to Wendell Phillips, New York, 22 April 1851, 1289, folio 3, Blagden Collection, HL. Warren was invalided for about two years during which Anne and Debora took turns nursing him. His illness would continue to a lesser or greater degree for years.

4. Carter's study of single southern women during this period covers their obligations to family caretaking and the costs and benefits of family ties. See *Southern Single Blessedness*, 65–94.

5. Richard D. Webb to Anne Warren Weston, 26 September 1857, 8 February 1858, A.9.2.29.36, WP.

6. Debora Weston to Mary Weston, New Bedford, 6 November 1836, A.9.2.8.68; Anne Warren Weston to Debora Weston, n.p., n.d., A.9.2.3.51; Samuel J. May Jr. to Richard D. Webb, Leicester, 30 June 1857, A.9.2.3.29, WP.

7. Among wealthy families in the North, servants accomplished this labor as nannies, tutors, nurses, cooks, and housekeepers. In the South, slaves made it possible for

single women to engage in lives of benevolence. Although Carter does not explore the issue of how the labor of slaves sustained the moral and benevolent work among these women, the Drayton and Telfair sisters of Charleston offer a good example. See *Southern Single Blessedness*, 118–49.

8. Caroline Weston diary, 19 September 1835, A.9.2.7.65-66; Caroline Weston to Anne Warren Weston, [Boston], [1836], A.9.2.4.55; Anne Warren Weston to Mrs. Warren Weston, New Bedford, 30 May 1836, A.9.8.28; Debora Weston to Anne Warren Weston, Boston, 6 June 1836, A.9.2.8.4; Anne Warren Weston to Debora Weston, Boston, 1 January 1837, A.9.2.9.2; Anne Warren Weston to Debora Weston, Boston, 16 January 1837, A.9.2.9.7; Debora Weston to Caroline Weston, New Bedford, 5 April 1837, A.9.2.9.24; Anne Warren Weston to Debora Weston, Weymouth, 20 June 1838, A.9.2.10.30; Anne Warren Weston to Debora Weston, Weymouth, 26 July 1838, A.9.2.3.38; Anne Warren Weston to Debora Weston, Weymouth, 2 November 1838, A.9.2.10.65; Anne Warren Weston to Debora Weston, Weymouth, 18 April 1839, A.9.2.11.85; Anne Warren Weston to Debora Weston, Weymouth, 1 May 1839, A.9.2.11.93; Lucia Weston to Debora Weston, Boston, 3 August 1839, A.9.2.12.9; Caroline Weston to Debora Weston, n.p., 12 September 1839, A.9.2.12.32; Maria Weston Chapman to Debora Weston, Boston, 6 December 1839, A.9.2.12.108, WP. Lucia and Emma Weston, along with Lizzy Chapman, attended Caroline and Anne's Boylston Street school, Caroline's Roxbury school, and Debora's in New Bedford. See Debora Weston to Mrs. Warren Weston, n.p., spring [1836 or 1837], A.9.2.5.69; Debora Weston to Anne Warren Weston, n.p., [1838], A.9.2.6.34; Lucia Weston to Debora Weston, Boston, [24 June 1839], A.9.2.11.118; Caroline Weston to Maria Weston Chapman and Henry G. Chapman, Roxbury, 15 January 1841, A.9.2.15.11-14; Emma Weston to Debora Weston, n.p., 15 December 1836, A.9.2.8.87; and Emma Weston to Debora Weston, Weymouth, 18 April 1839, A.9.2.11.86, WP.

9. Lucia or Emma would come to Boston to help out with their new niece or nephew. See Anne Warren Weston to Debora Weston, Boston, 24 July [1837 or 1838], A.9.2.3.40; and Anne Warren Weston to Lucia Weston, 12 August 1837, A.9.2.9.61, WP. Hervey rarely contributed to the household domestic work; his schooling was deemed to take precedence over such female-gendered tasks.

10. Anne Warren Weston to Debora Weston, n.p., 23 February 1839, A.9.2.11.44; Anne Warren Weston to Debora Weston, Weymouth, 9 November 1841, A.9.2.15.90, WP. During Henry G. Chapman's long struggle with tuberculosis, when he and Maria traveled for his health, the children were cared for by their aunts and grandmother in Boston and Weymouth. See Anne Warren Weston to Maria Weston Chapman, Weymouth, 25 February 1841, A.9.2.15.27; Susan Taber to Debora Weston, New Bedford, 8 March 1841, A.9.2.15.30; Caroline Weston to Henry and Maria Weston Chapman, Boston, 5 April 1841, A.9.2.15.36; Anne Warren Weston to Debora Weston, Concord, 16 September 1841, A.9.2.15.67; Anne Warren Weston to Emma and Debora Weston, Weymouth, 5 October 1841, A.9.2.15.74; Lucia Weston to Debora Weston, Weymouth, January 1842, A.9.2.17.13; and Caroline Weston to Debora Weston, n.p., 3 May [1842], A.9.2.3.99, WP. The children of Richard Warren Weston were also cared for at Weymouth during his long illness in the early 1850s. See Anne Warren Weston to Mary A. Estlin, Weymouth, 30 September 1851, A.7.2.11, JBEP.

11. Anne Warren Weston to Debora Weston, Weymouth, 7 June 1840, A.9.2.13.81; Debora Weston to Mrs. Warren Weston, Boston, n.d., A.9.2.5.69; Caroline Weston to Debora Weston, Roxbury, [late November 1840], A.9.2.3.19; Anne Warren Weston to Debora Weston, Weymouth, 22 April 1842, A.9.2.17.58; Debora Weston to Anne Warren Weston, New Bedford, 26 April 1842, A.9.2.17.59, WP.

12. Lucia Weston to Debora Weston, Boston, [1840], A.9.2.5.74, WP.

13. Anne Warren Weston to Lucia Weston, New York, n.d., A.9.2.5.77; Debora Weston to Anne Warren Weston, New Bedford, 15 January 1836, A.9.2.8.6, WP.

14. Debora Weston to Mrs. Warren Weston, Boston, n.d., A.9.2.5.10; Debora Weston to Lucia Weston, n.p., n.d., A.9.2.3.112; Anne Warren Weston to Debora Weston, Groton, 13 July 1842, A.9.2.17.82, WP. See also Anne Warren Weston to Debora Weston, Weymouth, 20 June 1838, A.9.2.10.30, WP.

15. Anne Warren Weston to Debora Weston, [Weymouth], n.d., A.9.2.5.10, WP. See also Anne Warren Weston to Debora Weston, Weymouth, 5 October 1841, A.9.2.15.74, WP.

16. Anne Warren Weston to Debora Weston, Weymouth, 27 October 1841, A.9.2.15.90, 22 April 1842, A.9.2.17.58, 19 June 1842, A.9.2.17.73, WP.

17. Debora Weston to Mrs. Warren Weston, Boston, 8 May 1835, A.9.2.7.45; Anne Warren Weston to Debora Weston, Boston, [not before 1836], A.9.2.3.39, WP. The sisters hoped that if Lizzy were schooled with her younger aunts, Emma's style and decorum might rub off on Lizzy's "looks and actions" (Debora Weston to Anne Warren Weston, n.p., [1838], A.9.2.6.24, WP). See also Caroline Weston to Wendell and Ann Phillips, New Bedford, 30 June 1843, 1290, Blagden Collection, HL.

18. Mary G. Chapman to Debora Weston, [Boston], [1838], A.9.2.5.77; Debora Weston to Mrs. Warren Weston, Boston, n.d., A.9.2.5.69, WP.

19. Lucia Weston to Debora Weston, Weymouth, January 1842, A.9.2.17.13; Caroline Weston to Debora Weston, Roxbury, [late November 1840], A.9.2.3.19, WP.

20. Caroline Weston to Debora Weston, Roxbury, [June 1841], A.9.2.3.77, WP.

21. Henry G. Chapman to Debora Weston, Boston, 9 November 1841, A.9.2.15.87, WP.

22. Anne Warren Weston to Debora Weston, Boston, 15 December 1839, A.9.2.12.118, WP. This reference may signify that Henry had recently been breeched, moved from the genderless dress of childhood into pants as befitting a young man. He would have been about five years of age and doubtless exhilarated by his new status. Even if this was the case, the association of maleness with disorder was broadly applied in this family.

23. Anne Warren Weston to Debora Weston, n.p., [summer 1838], WP.

24. Anne Warren Weston to Debora Weston, Weymouth, 18 April 1839, A.9.2.11.85; Anne Warren Weston to Maria Weston Chapman, Weymouth, 25 February 1841, A.9.2.15.27, WP.

25. Maria Weston Chapman to Ann T. G. Phillips, Weymouth, [1860], Blagden Collection, HL.

26. Caroline Weston diary, 28 September 1835, A.9.2.7.65-66, WP.

27. The classic work on children of abolitionists is McPherson, *Abolitionist Legacy*. It focuses on those of the second and third generation who carried on the political activism of the first, not those who were traumatized by it. George Thompson's daughter

Amelia suffered nightmares after the family was forced to flee Salem in 1835. George Thompson Garrison was born in February 1836 after the riot in which his father was nearly lynched and his pregnant mother was warned that going to the jail to check on William's condition might hurt the baby. He proved as difficult and unruly as Elizabeth and Henry Chapman. Biographer Harriet Alonso, who also emphasizes the commitment to social justice learned by the Garrison children at their parents' knees, attributes George's misbehavior to his father's too-great affection. Garrison dedicated his son to abolition in a poem published in the *Liberator*: "For if, amid this conflict, fierce and wild, With stout foes of God and man, I fall, Then shalt thou early fill my vacant post." Despite Alonso's upbeat view of their childhood, all the Garrison children grew up trying to cope with their father's absence and their mother's anxiety. The Garrisons kept them in the house, ostensibly so they would not pick up the foul-mouthed speech of their urban neighborhood, although their safety was surely a concern. See George Thompson to Anne Thompson, 30 January 1836, Thompson Papers, John Rylands Library; Alonso, *Growing Up Abolitionist*, 50–53, 86–87; "Sonnets," *Liberator*, 20 February 1836; William L. Garrison to Helen Garrison, 23 July 1840, in Ruchames, *House Dividing*, 668; and William L. Garrison to Hannah Webb, 1 March 1843, in Merrill, *No Union with Slaveholders*, 131.

28. Anne Warren Weston to Mary Weston, n.p., 22 October 1835, A.9.2.4.26, WP.

29. Detailed discussions of their experience with mobs and feelings about these traumatic events can be found throughout the Weston sisters' correspondence. See, for example, the year 1836: Debora Weston to Caroline Weston, New Bedford, [1836], A.9.2.8.1; Lucia Weston to Debora Weston, Boston, 3 March 1836, A.9.2.8.15; Sophia Ammidon to Anne Warren Weston, St. Louis, 8 May 1836, A.9.2.8.27a; Debora Weston to Anne Warren Weston, Boston, 6 June, A.9.2.8.4, and 10 June 1836, A.9.2.8.31; Debora Weston to Caroline Weston, New Bedford, 5 October 1836, A.9.2.8.58; and Caroline Weston to Debora Weston, Boston, [fall 1836], A.9.2.3.30, and 12 October 1836, A.9.2.8.60, WP.

30. Debora Weston to Ann T. G. Phillips, Weymouth, 1 April 1856, 1484, folio 2, Blagden Collection, HL. The quotation came from Letitia Elizabeth Landon and was used as the preface to Felicia D. Hemans's poem "The Sicilian Captive." Maria placed the abolitionist in the position of the tormented slave. See Wolfson, *Felicia Hemans*, 407.

31. Caroline Weston to Anne Warren Weston, Boston, [1839], A.9.2.4.53-54, WP.

32. Caroline Weston to Henry G. Chapman and Maria Weston Chapman, Boston, 5 April 1841, A.9.2.15.36, WP.

33. Maria Weston Chapman to Elisabeth Pease, Boston, 15 January 1848, A.1.2.18.9, ASC.

34. Samuel J. May Jr. to John B. Estlin, Leicester, 16 July 1848, B.1.6.2.77, May Papers, BPL.

35. Anne Warren Weston to Caroline Weston, Boston, 22 May 1849, A.9.2.24.12; Anne Warren Weston to Maria Weston Chapman, Weymouth, 5 June 1849, A.9.2.24.77, WP. Maria's sister-in-law Mary G. Chapman accompanied them. Her relations with the Westons, however, were never as warm or as comfortable as those of her sister, Ann Gray Chapman, and Mary returned to Boston within the year. Emma followed in June 1849.

36. Caroline Weston to Rev. Samuel May, Paris, 2 December 1848, B.1.6.3.55, May Papers, BPL.

37. Maria Weston Chapman, n.p., [fall 1849], A.9.2.6.34, WP. Elizabeth was also linked to the Prince de Joinville, a son of Louis Philippe of France, then living in Tickenham near Joshua Bates. See Taylor, *Women of the Anti-Slavery Movement*, 77.

38. John B. Estlin to Anne Warren Weston, Bristol, 14 November 1850, A.9.2.1.12, WP.

39. Mary A. Estlin to Anne Warren Weston, Bristol, England, 15 November 1850, A.9.2.25.44, WP.

40. Caroline Weston to Wendell and Ann T. G. Phillips, Interlaken [Switzerland], 20 September [1851], 1290, folio 7, Blagden Collection, HL; Anne Warren Weston to John B. Estlin, Weymouth, 27 October 1850, A.7.2.5, JBEP.

41. Maria Weston Chapman to Mary A. Estlin, Paris, 24 January [1852], A.7.2.54, JBEP.

42. Maria Weston Chapman to Wendell and Ann Phillips, Paris, 28 September 1848, 394, folio 2, Blagden Collection, HL.

43. Caroline Weston to Samuel J. May Jr., Paris, 3 July 1850, B.1.6.4.5, May Papers, BPL; John B. Estlin to Anne Warren Weston, Bristol, 14 November 1850, WP.

44. There are hints not only that Maria disapproved of the young woman but also that her family found Henry unacceptable. In 1856 he traveled to London with his uncle Warren Weston and great-uncle Joshua Bates to begin his business education. Henry may not have returned to the United States again until 1858, when Bates helped him purchase a position with Ward Campbell and Co. of New York. Henry married Eleanor Jay, daughter of abolitionist John Jay, in June 1859 and settled permanently in New York. Joshua Bates eventually despaired of Henry, however, and disinherited him in his will (1864, no. 744, Somerset House, London).

45. Anne Warren Weston to Ann G. T. Phillips, Weymouth, 20 March 1855, 1482, folio 2, Blagden Collection, HL; Maria Weston Chapman to Lizzie Chapman Laugel, Boston, Christmas 1855, A.9.2.28.63, WP.

46. Anne Warren Weston to Debora Weston, Weymouth, 9 November 1841, A.9.2.15.90; Caroline Weston to Debora Weston, Weymouth, 23 November 1841, A.9.2.3.37, WP.

47. Debora remained in New Bedford over the Thanksgiving holiday. See Anne Warren Weston to Debora Weston, Weymouth, 28 November 1841, A.9.2.15.100, WP.

48. See, for example, Beecher, *Evils Suffered*, *Letters to the People*, and *Physiology and Calisthenics*.

49. Caroline Weston to Debora Weston, Boston, 20 July [1838], A.9.2.3.79, WP. Hannah Cranch Bond married Dr. Noah Fifield, a strong abolitionist and close friend of the Westons. Their son, William Cranch Bond Fifield (1828–96), went to Phillips Exeter Academy; studied medicine at Harvard Medical School, graduating in 1851; and practiced in Weymouth for sixty years. He attributed his role in gaining the admission of women to the Massachusetts Medical Society to the antislavery training of his youth. See *American Series of Popular Biographies*.

50. Anne noted their mother was "much calmer and firmer than ourselves in view of any impending calamity," asserting a fatalistic nature that looked on death not as

something with which to battle but rather as something to be accepted. See Anne Warren Weston to Friends [Wendell and Ann T. G. Phillips], Clifton, Staten Island, 9 July 1851, Am 1953, folio 3, Blagden Collection, HL.

51. Maria Weston Chapman to Mary A. Estlin, n.d., [late 1854 or early 1855], A.7.2.73, JBEP.

52. The Weston sisters also provided a supporting cast for their aunt Priscilla Weston's thirteen-year decline into paralysis and dementia and the brief but fatal illnesses of their grandmother Tirzah Bates Hunt and in-laws Ann, Sarah Greene, and Henry Chapman senior. Maria's "brain fever" is discussed in Chapter 6 because of the ways in which it was politicized by anti-Garrisonian abolitionists and those who generally opposed female political activism.

53. His sister Mary Chapman seems to have taken a lesser role in Henry's care. A nervous woman, she may have found nursing too anxiety producing, or perhaps the Westons found her more difficult than helpful and discouraged her involvement.

54. Anne had suggested the name: "I think Gertrude very good but if there be strong opposition in any quarter I would give it up. It might be named Caroline or Emma or even Maria. The name of Weston does not occur in any of the children's names. Caroline Weston Chapman would not be amiss or Harriet Martineau even" (Anne Warren Weston to Debora Weston, Duxbury, 22 June 1840, A.9.2.13.91, WP). The name was not universally popular. Wrote Emma, "You must kiss Gertrude for me, if she must be Gertrude, which I am very sorry for" (Emma Weston to Elizabeth Bates Chapman, Weymouth, n.d., A.9.2.3.91, WP). Quincy protested "against going to foreign parts after Gertrude . . . or any such heathenish appellations when so beautiful and well associated a name [as Maria Weston] is to be found at home" (Edmund Quincy to Maria Weston Chapman, Dedham, 8 July 1840, A.9.2.13.97-98, WP).

55. Edmund Quincy to Anne Warren Weston, Dedham, 21 May 1840, A.9.2.13.73, WP; Anne Warren Weston to Wendell and Ann T. G. Phillips, Boston, 15 October 1840, 1289, folio 1, Blagden Collection, HL. Debora returned to New Bedford for an all-expenses-paid visit in October.

56. Anne Warren Weston to Lucia Weston, Boston, [September 1840], A.9.2.14.31-32, September 1840, A.9.2.14.23-24, 28 September 1840, A.9.2.14.31-32, October 1840, A.9.2.6.33, WP.

57. S[usan] Tabor to Debora Weston, New Bedford, 8 March 1841, A.9.2.15.30; Caroline Weston to Maria Weston Chapman and Henry G. Chapman, Roxbury, 15 January 1841, A.9.2.15.11-14, WP.

58. Burgess, *Climate of Italy*, debunks what had become a common, and fashionable, assumption that consumption could be improved or cured by travel to warm climates such as Malta or Italy.

59. Maria Weston Chapman to Henry G. Chapman Jr., Bonaires, 14 March 1841, A.9.2.5.33; Caroline Weston to Maria Weston Chapman and Henry G. Chapman, Boston, 5 April 1841, A.9.2.15.36, WP.

60. Her sisters, believing such a retreat might become an annual necessity, tried to accept that "the entire sacrifice of two or three years would be cheaply made to secure subsequent health." By "sacrifice" they meant Maria's withdrawal from abolitionist activity into private nursing at a crucial moment in the conflict between the MAS and the

Massachusetts Emancipation Society. See Caroline Weston to Maria Weston Chapman and Henry G. Chapman, Boston, 5 April 1841, A.9.2.15.36, WP.

61. Anne Warren Weston to Debora Weston, Boston, 11 February 1842, A.9.2.17.33, WP.

62. Ibid., [21 January 1842]; Anne Warren Weston to Elizabeth Pease, Boston, 30 January 1842, A.1.2.12.2.19, ASC.

63. William L. Garrison to Richard D. Webb, Boston, 27 February 1842, A.1.2.3.24.53, ASC.

64. Debora Weston to Anne Warren Weston, New Bedford, 14 April 1842, A.9.2.17.50, WP.

65. Anne Warren Weston to Debora Weston, Weymouth, 22 April 1842, A.9.2.17.50, WP.

66. Maria Weston Chapman to Debora Weston, Boston, 22 April [1842], A.9.2.5.8; Caroline Weston to Debora Weston, n.p., 3 May [1842], A.9.2.3.99, WP. This last suggests that Henry's moody disposition was not merely the result of his illness but part of his personality or, as his political enemies put it, his character.

67. Anne Warren Weston to Debora Weston, Northampton, 4 May 1842, A.9.2.17.61, and New York, 11 May 1842, A.9.2.17.62, WP.

68. Caroline Weston to Debora Weston, Roxbury, [June 1842], A.9.2.3.77, WP.

69. Anne Warren Weston to Debora Weston, Boston, 3 June 1842, A.9.2.17.66; Caroline Weston to Debora Weston, Roxbury, 17 June 1842, A.9.2.17.71, and Boston, [24 June 1842], A.9.2.17.75, WP.

70. Anne Warren Weston to Debora Weston, Groton, 13 July 1842, A.9.2.17.82, WP.

71. Ware (1814–87) married Elizabeth Cabot Lee. He received his M.A. and Doctor of Medicine degrees from Harvard in 1837 and became a well-known physician in Boston.

72. Maria Weston Chapman to Debora Weston, Boston, 1 August 1842, A.9.2.17.85, WP.

73. Anne Warren Weston to Debora Weston, Boston, 23 March 1839, A.9.2.11.65-66, WP. See also Lucia Weston to Anne Weston, Boston, [1839], A.9.2.11.11; and Lucia Weston to Anne Warren Weston, Boston, [1839], A.9.2.11.10, WP. Taylor suggests that the drains there may have carried the disease. See Taylor, *Women of the Anti-Slavery Movement*, 5.

74. Evelina A. S. Smith to Caroline Weston, Dorchester, 8 December 1844, A.9.2.20.118, WP; Anne Warren Weston to Wendell Phillips, Weymouth, 5 April [n.y.], 1289, folio 7; Caroline Weston to Wendell Phillips and Ann T. G. Phillips, n.p., n.d., 1290, folio 5, Blagden Collection, HL.

75. Wendell Phillips to Elizabeth Pease, Nahant, October 1844, A.1.2.14.60, ASC; Samuel J. May Jr. to Anne Warren Weston, Boston, 2 February 1853, A.9.2.4.95; Anne Warren Weston to Debora Weston, Weymouth, 3 February 1853, A.9.2.27.9, WP.

76. Anne Warren Weston to Ann T. G. Phillips, Weymouth, 3 September 1853, Am 1953, 1289, folio 9; Anne Warren Weston to Wendell Phillips and Ann T. G. Phillips, Paris, 25 May 1856, Am 1953, 1289, folio 5, Blagden Collection, HL.

77. Sarah Southwick wrote that Lucia was buried in the European cemetery there.

78. Emma provided the most consistent company, although Caroline and Anne spent time with Lucia as well, and her brothers and Annie Chapman visited. See Edmund Quincy to Caroline Weston, Boston, 16 September 1844, A.9.2.20.61, WP; Wendell Phillips to Elizabeth Pease, Nahant, October 1844, A.1.2.14.60, ASC; Anne Warren Weston, journal, Weymouth, 8 January 1845, A.9.2.21.3, WP; Anne Warren Weston to Emma Weston, Boston, 2 January 1853, A.9.2.27.2; Anne Warren Weston to Debora Weston, Weymouth, 3 February 1853, A.9.2.27.9; and Samuel May Jr. to Anne Warren Weston, Leicester, 20 February 1853, A.9.2.27.10, WP.

79. Maria Weston Chapman to Mary A. Estlin, Paris, May 1854, A.7.2.10, JBEP. The term "selfishness" was gendered male in the Weston universe and was applied both to the men of the family Weston and to some of those in the antislavery family as well; see Chapter 8.

80. Such labor demanded considerable time and effort from antebellum women of all regions and in all but the wealthiest of households. For a description of nineteenth-century New England housework, see Boydston, *Home and Work*, and Susan Strasser, *Never Done*. There is a large literature on how capitalism changed both domestic manufacturing and women's work. Key works include Dublin, *Transforming Women's Work*; Jensen, "Cloth, Butter, and Boarders"; and Jensen, *Loosening the Bonds*.

81. Anne Warren Weston to Debora Weston, Weymouth, 27 October 1841, A.9.2.15.83, WP.

82. Anne Warren Weston to Ann T. G. Phillips, Weymouth, 20 March 1855, 1482, folio 2, Blagden Collection, HL.

83. See, for example, Hervey E. Weston to Debora Weston, n.p., 1 August 1834, A.9.2.7.36; Anne Warren Weston to Debora Weston, [Weymouth], [1837–38], A.9.2.3.50; Emma Weston to Lucia Weston, Weymouth, [1837–38], A.9.2.3.17; and Anne Warren Weston to Debora Weston, Weymouth, 9 November 1838, A.9.2.10.68, WP.

84. Anne Warren Weston to Debora Weston, [Weymouth], n.d., A.9.2.5.10; Anne Warren Weston to Lucia Weston, New York, n.d., A.9.2.5.77; Anne Warren Weston to Lucia Weston, Boston, 28 September 1840, A.9.2.14.31; Debora Weston to Caroline Weston, New Bedford, 19 January 1845, A.9.2.21.5; Debora Weston to Lucia and Emma Weston, n.p., n.d., A.9.2.5.68, WP.

85. Caroline Weston to Anne Warren Weston, n.p., 21 June 1836, A.9.2.8.33; Anne Warren Weston to Debora Weston, Weymouth, 18 April 1839, A.9.2.11.85; Anne Warren Weston to Mary Weston, Concord, 5 June 1846, A.9.2.22.59, WP. On occasion women were hired for specific tasks. When Maria and Henry gave up the West Street house, moved the children to the smaller Poplar Street house, and left for Haiti, a Mrs. Rowan came in to help the Westons clean the house and pack up their things. That Thanksgiving, they hoped to hire Mrs. White to help prepare the family dinner (to which not only the usual cohort of sisters and Hervey were coming but also Warren and his family, as well as Maria and hers) because Ma Weston was too ill "to do any thing." Aunt Mary pitched in and helped Caroline and Anne bake "mince pies and puddings," while Lucia roasted the beef. See Anne Warren Weston to Henry and Maria Weston Chapman, n.p., 15 January 1841, A.9.2.15.10; Caroline Weston to Maria Weston Chapman and Henry G. Chapman, n.p., 15 January 1841, A.9.2.15.11-14; Caroline Weston to

Debora Weston, Weymouth, 23 November 1841, A.9.2.3.37; and Anne Warren Weston to Debora Weston, Weymouth, 28 November 1841, A.9.2.15.100, WP.

86. Southwick, *Reminiscences*, 11.

87. Anne Warren Weston to Debora Weston, Weymouth, 23 November 1838, A.9.2.5.17, WP.

88. See Dudden, *Serving Women*; Palmer, *Domesticity and Dirt*; Lucy Salmon, *Domestic Service*; Sutherland, *Americans and Their Servants*; and Katzman, *Seven Days a Week*.

89. Anne Warren Weston to Debora Weston, Boston, [24 June 1839], A.9.2.11.118, WP.

90. Caroline Weston to Debora Weston, Roxbury, 17 June 1842, A.9.2.17.71, WP. Drunkenness was not taken lightly in this family.

91. Anne Warren Weston to Debora Weston, Weymouth, 20 June 1838, A.9.2.10.30, WP.

92. Anne Warren Weston to Emma Weston, Boston, 2 January 1853, A.9.2.27.2, WP.

93. The Weston correspondence speaks to sewing more than to other domestic labor, such as sweeping, cleaning fireplaces, laundry, or cooking. Sewing was often accomplished in groups as one sister sewed while others read aloud, and all discussed matters of political strategy or gossiped about events and individuals.

94. Some estimate a drop of 50–90 percent, with textile production leading the way. The evidence suggests a significant expansion of consumer goods after 1830, marketed by a growing number of retailers who displayed and sold these commodities. Elite women purchased custom-fit dresses, while working women bought ready-made. Secondhand clothing shops sprang up to fit a niche further down the socioeconomic ladder, particularly among the urban African American population. The change transformed the relationship among producers, consumers, and commodities, and revolutionized the lives of New England women as the processes of material production were gradually removed from the home. See Stansell, *City of Women*, and Lawes, *Women and Reform*, chap. 2. See also Stapp, *Afro-Americans in Antebellum Boston*, which suggests that dealing and trading in used clothing were among the most common and successful African American businesses in 1840s Boston.

95. Caroline Weston to Debora Weston, Roxbury, 17 June 1842, A.9.2.17.71, WP.

96. Anne Warren Weston to Debora Weston, Groton, 10 April 1838, A.9.2.10.22, WP.

97. Hervey E. Weston to Debora Weston, n.p., 1 August 1834, A.9.2.7.36, December 1834, A.9.2.7.39, WP.

98. For views of this task, see Kelly, *In the New England Fashion*, and Gamber, *Female Economy*.

99. Anne Warren Weston to Debora Weston, Weymouth, 15 November 1840, A.9.2.14.57; Anne Warren Weston to Debora Weston, n.p., [not before 1833], A.9.2.5.10; Anne Warren Weston to Debora Weston, Groton, 10 April 1838, A.9.2.10.22, WP.

100. Anne Warren Weston to Debora Weston, Boston, 15 January 1842, A.9.2.17.42; Caroline Weston to Maria and Henry Chapman, Roxbury, 20 January 1841, A.9.2.15.11-14; Emma Weston to Debora Weston, [Weymouth], 9 October 1836, A.9.2.8.59, WP.

101. Caroline Weston to Debora Weston, n.p., 12 September 1839, A.9.2.12.32, WP. See also Anne Warren Weston to Debora Weston, [written on the back of a printed BFAS circular dated 12 February 1838], A.9.2.10.7, WP, in which she reported, "As to my making Lizzy's chemises I don't know as I shall get time to. But if I don't I will bring them out."

102. Debora Weston to Caroline Weston, n.p., [1837], A.9.2.3.115, WP. The free labor philosophy rejected the purchase or consumption of produce or products of slave labor; see Faulkner, "Root of the Evil."

103. Debora Weston to Mary Weston, Boston, 15 June 1837, A.9.2.9.42; Caroline Weston to Debora Weston, Boston, 4 July 1843, A.9.2.18.69; Lucia Weston to Debora Weston, Boston, 24 June 1842, A.9.2.3.54; Emma Forbes Weston to Debora Weston, Boston, 9 July 1842, A.9.2.17.80, WP. See also Caroline Weston to Debora Weston, Boston, 12 October 1836, A.9.2.8.60, WP.

104. Anne Warren Weston to Debora Weston, Boston, 25 January 1842, A.9.2.17.27, WP.

105. Debora Weston to Mary Weston, Boston, 15 June 1837, A.9.2.9.42; Debora Weston to Mary Weston, New Bedford, 20 October 1836, A.9.2.8.62; Caroline Weston to Anne Warren Weston, Boston, [1839], A.9.2.4.53-54, WP. The strategy was commonplace among the middling orders; see Alcott, *Little Women*, chap. 3.

106. Caroline Weston to Debora Weston, Roxbury, 28 June 1842, A.9.2.3.55; Anne Warren Weston to Debora Weston, Boston, 25 January 1842, A.9.2.17.27, WP.

107. Anne Warren Weston to Debora Weston, New Bedford, 22 October 1842, A.9.2.17.99, WP. For a similar discussion of bonnet refurbishment, see Anne's communication: "Emma & I went & bought me an open work bonnet at Barnes's. I had it lined with pink [and] trimmed with pink & white & green flowers. For the bonnet I gave $3.50 & I think it pretty. Lucia has had her last summer straw trimmed with green & it looks sweetly. Emma has an open work lined & trimmed with blue in which she will make her transit. Debora a[n] open work lined with white trimmed with pink & with some of the beautiful flowers you sent in the box. So I have given you a list of our headgear. I should say too that Ma has modestly had a plain ribbon of brown put on a straw for herself" (Anne Warren Weston to Caroline Weston, Boston, 22 May 1849, A.9.2.24.122, WP).

108. Such household help were either relatives or others known to the household and were provided room and board in return for lessons in housewifery. See Ulrich, "Martha Ballard and Her Girls," 70–100.

109. Debora Weston to Lucia Weston, Boston, 8 January 1839, A.9.2.11.17, WP.

110. Problems with patterns haunted nineteenth-century dressmaking. A number of competing systems were invented to aid both the professional dress trade and the domestic seamstress. See Gamber, *Female Economy*.

111. Anne Warren Weston to Debora Weston, Boston, 3 June 1842, A.9.2.17.66; Anne Warren Weston to Debora Weston, Boston, 25 January 1842, A.9.2.17.27; Debora Weston to Anne Warren Weston, New Bedford, 1 December 1839, A.9.2.12.101, WP.

112. Anne Warren Weston to Debora Weston, Boston, 15 January 1842, A.9.2.17.24, WP.

113. Anne Warren Weston to Caroline Weston, Weymouth, 14 December 1846, A.9.2.22.137, WP. Debora also hired a mantua-maker. "My 'woodpecker' gown was cut and made, cape and all, for the woman brought a[n ap]prentice with her and I paid her the sum of 5 shillings and sixpence. I got her to cut and fit your cape too," she wrote to Anne in Weymouth, "and you shall have it very soon, looking very handsome; mine looks beautifully" (Debora Weston to Anne Warren Weston, New Bedford, 1 December 1839, WP). Coins from various countries widely circulated in the United States and were not demonetized until 1857. These were generally valued in British terms such that a shilling was worth twelve and a half cents.

114. Anne Warren Weston to Debora Weston, n.p., [July 1836], A.9.2.3.49; Emma Forbes Weston to Debora Weston, [Weymouth], 9 October 1836, A.9.2.8.59, WP.

115. Maria and Edmund Quincy were assigned the task by William Lloyd Garrison, who, suffering from a painful swelling of the side, had gone to the Northampton Water Cure to recuperate. Wrote Garrison to Chapman: "I see nothing, as yet, from your pen in the Liberator. I am sure that the omission has arisen from your other numerous engagements, for your good will is boundless, and your readiness to serve the cause almost beyond comparison or competition. There is scarcely one person in the wide world to whom I am so deeply indebted, in a variety of modes, as to yourself; and though I have given you in return few words expressive of my gratitude, be assured that my heart is none the less full of thankfulness" (William L. Garrison to Maria Weston Chapman, Northampton, 7 July 1843, A.1.2.41.32, ASC).

116. Eliza L. Follen to Maria Weston Chapman, West Roxbury, 13 August 1843, A.9.2.19.17, WP.

CHAPTER 5

1. Caroline Weston to Samuel J. May, Paris, 2 December 1848, B1.6.3.55, May Papers, BPL.

2. Ellen Hartigan-O'Connor makes this point with regard to commercial transactions among the Robinson sisters of Newport, Rhode Island. See "Abigail's Accounts," 42.

3. For references to weekly letters, see Lucia Weston to Debora Weston, Boston, 28 April 1839, A.9.2.11.91, WP; and John B. Estlin to Anne Warren Weston, Bristol, England, 14 November 1850, A.7.11.12, JBEP. A sample from April 1839 illustrates the pattern. This was an extraordinary time due to the battle within the BFAS between Garrisonians and anti-Garrisonians that would lead to the society's demise. Due to their political import and full of concern about board and society meetings called, denied, and held; petition campaigns; fund-raising; challenges to the usual allocation of funds from the BFAS treasury; and an effort to repeal the Massachusetts ban on interracial marriage, letters from this period were more likely to have been saved. And typical of Weston letters, interspersed with such weighty political matters were daily concerns about the health of family members, teaching school, paying bills, caring for and educating the Chapman children, and replacing lost books and recommending others. Anne in Boston or Weymouth wrote Debora in New Bedford on 8, 11, 23, 30 April and 1 May 1839; Debora wrote from New Bedford to Anne in Boston or Weymouth on 1,

13, 16, and 26 April 1839; Lucia in Boston wrote Anne in Weymouth in early April and Debora on 28 April 1839; Maria in Boston wrote to Debora in New Bedford on 4, 18, and 22 April 1839; Debora wrote to Maria on 18 and 28 April 1839; Emma in Weymouth wrote Debora in New Bedford on 18 April 1839. No (remaining) letters were sent to or from Caroline during this month. She was teaching in Roxbury but spent many weeknights and weekends with Anne and Maria in Boston, where she would have read any incoming letters. Two of her letters remain from March 1839 that were sent from Boston to Debora in New Bedford on 3 and 18 March. Debora sent one to Caroline, in Boston, dated 21 March.

4. Anne Warren Weston to John B. Estlin, Weymouth, 27 October 1850, A.7.2.5, JBEP.

5. Debora Weston to Lucia Weston, New Bedford, 25 April 1839, A.9.2.5.75; Lucia Weston to Debora Weston, Boston, 28 April 1839, A.9.2.11.91, WP.

6. Most Weston letters had multiple audiences, extending beyond the addressee. Usually the audience was the Weston circle, both those residing together in the same household and those siblings not at home but to whom missives were forwarded as a matter of course. However, the Westons also recognized, particularly as their reform work expanded, that letters with news of the cause might find an audience among other activists known to the family. For a discussion of letters as a genre and of the import of multiple audiences in stretching the boundaries of genre and its definition, see Gaul, *To Marry an Indian*, 23–45.

7. Note from Debora attached to letter from Anne Warren Weston, New York, 11 May 1842, A.9.2.17.62; Anne Warren Weston to Debora Weston, Boston, 3 June 1842, A.9.2.17.66, WP. Both Anne and Caroline had written Debora before leaving for New York, reporting on Henry's condition and the state of the household. See Caroline Weston to Debora Weston, n.p., 3 May [1842], A.9.2.3.99; and Anne Warren Weston to Debora Weston, Northampton, 4 May 1842, A.9.2.17.61, WP. Once she returned and checked on her school and on Henry, Caroline again wrote Debora with details. See Caroline Weston to Debora Weston, Roxbury, 17 June 1842, A.9.2.17.71, WP.

8. Note from Debora Weston attached to letter from Anne Warren Weston, New York, 11 May 1842, A.9.2.17.62; Anne Warren Weston to Debora Weston, New Bedford, 31 October 1842, A.9.2.177.103, WP.

9. Anne Warren Weston to Debora Weston, Weymouth, 3 February 1853, A.9.2.27.9, WP.

10. Debora Weston to Caroline Weston, Weymouth, 21 October 1850, A.9.2.25.33, WP.

11. Anne Warren Weston to Debora Weston, Groton, 10 April 1838, A.9.2.10.22, WP. Lucia used the closing "yours in bonds" in writing to Anne, [Weymouth], n.d., A.9.2.5.9, WP. See also Mary Weston to Debora Weston, Weymouth, 3 July 1836, A.9.2.3.89, WP. An interesting note from Anne to the abolitionist advocate and loyal Garrisonian Elizabeth Pease expressed the difference between sisters and friends: "When slave holders & their acknowledged abettors attack us & we receive assurance of the sympathy of distant friends, we are grateful in heart and strengthened in faith, but we have not the conviction that those distant friends are, as it were, *bound with us*" (Anne Warren Weston to Elisabeth Pease, Boston, 31 March 1841, A.1.2.1.134, ASC).

12. Debora Weston to Caroline Weston, "New Bedford no Boston," 1 June 1844, A.9.2.16.18, WP.

13. Debora Weston to Anne Warren Weston, New Bedford, 23 June 1839, A.9.2.11.122, WP.

14. Anne Warren Weston to Debora Weston, Groton, 10 April 1838, A.9.2.10.22, WP.

15. Debora's correspondence suggests that she ensured regular communication by scheduling it. "I was just thinking what a fool I had been not to make some arrangement as to when you should write, & when I should write to you," she explained to her aunt Mary Weston. "[Your letter] was just the thing I wanted, for if you do not write I shall not get much Weymouth news. I wish you would write pretty often, for it seems sometimes as if I should fly I want to hear so much, & you know I am troubled with a feeling that nothing can get on well without me" (Debora Weston to Mary Weston, New Bedford, 17 September 1836, A.9.2.8.50, WP). She proposed to Anne that she write every evening. See Debora Weston to Anne Warren Weston, New Bedford, 5 January 1840, A.9.2.13.5, WP.

16. Hansen, *Very Social Time*, 115.

17. Caroline Weston to Wendell and Ann T. G. Phillips, New Bedford, 30 June 1843, 1290, Blagden Collection, HL; Lucia Weston to Anne Warren Weston, Weymouth, 7 January 1842, A.9.2.17.18; Edmund Quincy to Anne Warren Weston, Dedham, 21 May 1840, A.9.2.13.73, WP.

18. Hansen, *Very Social Time*. 115.

19. Debora Weston to Anne Warren Weston, New Bedford, 17 March 1839, A.9.2.11.62, WP. Debora also urged her aunt to read and keep the enclosed letter from Anne as she would "want it when I come home." See also Debora Weston to Mary Weston, New Bedford, 2 September 1839, A.9.2.12.25, WP.

20. Anne Warren Weston to Debora Weston, New Bedford, 26 October 1842, A.9.2.17.100; Anne Warren Weston to Lucia Weston, New York, 11 May 1842, A.9.2.17.62; Mary G. Chapman to Debora Weston and Maria Weston Chapman, Boston, n.d., A.9.2.5.44, WP.

21. Anne Warren Weston to Debora Weston, New Bedford, 26 October 1842, A.9.2.17.100, WP.

22. Mary G. Chapman to Debora Weston and Maria Weston Chapman, [Boston], n.d., A.9.2.5.44, WP.

23. Anne Warren Weston to Mary Weston, Boston, 16 May 1839, A.9.2.11.106, WP. See also Anne Warren Weston to Debora Weston, Weymouth, 5 November 1838, A.9.2.10.66.

24. Caroline Weston to Debora Weston, Roxbury, 28 June 1842, A.9.2.3.55; Anne Warren Weston to Caroline Weston, Weymouth, 14 December 1846, A.9.2.22.137; Anne Warren Weston to Debora Weston, Boston, 25 January 1842, A.9.2.17.27; Edmund Quincy to Maria Weston Chapman, Dedham, 5 April 1844, A.9.2.20.24, WP.

25. Edmund Quincy to Maria Weston Chapman, 31 October 1846, Quincy, Wendell, Holmes, and Upham Family Papers, MHS. Similarly, he reported to Richard D. Webb that his letters had arrived from Dublin, had been read with much satisfaction, and had been sent the rounds of the "Boston clique," including the Westons. See Edmund

Quincy to Richard D. Webb, 26 March 1843, Quincy, Wendell, Holmes, and Upham Family Papers, MHS. See also Richard D. Webb to Maria Weston Chapman, Dublin, 17 October 1844, A.1.2.14.63, ASC.

26. Samuel May Jr. to Anne Warren Weston, Leicester, 20 February 1853, A.9.2.27.10, WP; Anne Warren Weston to Samuel May Jr., Weymouth, 19 June 1854, A.1.2.24.66, ASC.

27. Lucretia Mott to Richard D. Webb, 23 April 1843, ASC. Sarah Pugh (1800–1884) was a Philadelphia teacher and a Quaker active in the PFAS.

28. This practice was not uncommon elsewhere in America and Great Britain during the antebellum period. For a discussion, see Dublin, *From Farm to Factory*, introduction. Among abolitionists it contributed to the development of community and turned household living spaces into informal schools and clubs where antislavery doctrine and strategy were debated and clarified. This shared social activity made a somewhat diverse group of people (in class, religious background, race, and political orientation) more informed and committed antislavery actors.

29. Anne Warren Weston to Caroline Weston, n.p., [June 1840], A.9.2.6.42, WP. See also Caroline Weston to Anne Warren Weston, Boston, [1839], A.9.2.4.53-54, WP. The term "caroused" was used by the Westons and picked up by their closest friends and colleagues to indicate the oral performance and celebration of letters arriving from kin and fictive kin.

30. Anne Warren Weston to Debora Weston, New Bedford, 31 October 1842, A.9.2.177.103, WP. On reading aloud, see, for example, Anne Warren Weston to Mary A. Estlin, Weymouth, 21 January 1855, A.7.2.26; and Maria Weston Chapman to John Bishop Estlin, Boston, 7 October 1846, A.7.2.40, JBEP. The rules governing privacy were unclear (see the Appendix), and, to their great consternation, Weston letters that the writers deemed confidential not infrequently appeared in the British antislavery press. See, for example Anne Warren Weston to Wendell Phillips, Weymouth, 18 September [n.y.], Am 1953, 1289, folio 9, Blagden Collection, HL.

31. Anne Warren Weston to Caroline Weston, [June 1840], A.9.2.6.42, WP. Maria encouraged Mary Ann's correspondence in a message to her father, John Bishop Estlin, in which she reported, "I am sure she would be repaid for the kindness of writing it could she see the real joy it gave" (Maria Weston Chapman to John Bishop Estlin, Boston, 7 October 1846, A.7.2.40, WP).

32. Indeed, when Webb received letters from American abolitionists, he took "them to a little committee, where our very small 'faction' consisting of James Haughton, my two brothers, and sometimes Richard Allen, assemble every Wednesday morning to talk over Anti-Slavery, Teetotalism, Peace, etc.," and "read aloud such letters or portions of such letters as we have received during the past week, as bear upon the subject of our deliberations" (Richard D. Webb to Maria Weston Chapman, Dublin, 16 May 1846, A.9.2.22.51, WP).

33. For the limits that postage imposed on correspondence, see the Appendix.

34. Debora Weston to Anne Warren Weston, New Bedford, 17 March 1839, A.9.2.11.62; Wendell Phillips, Edmund Quincy, and Maria herself drew upon the journals for antislavery articles, speeches, and pamphlets. See Maria Weston Chapman to Wendell Phillips, n.p., n.d., 394, folio 6, Blagden Collection, HL; Maria Weston Chapman to William Lloyd Garrison, Cape Haitien, 19 January 1841, A.1.2.11.33, ASC; Edmund Quincy to Henry and Maria Weston Chapman, Dedham, 25 February 1841, A.9.2.13.26–28,

WP; Edmund Quincy to Caroline Weston, Dedham, 13 November 1844, Francis Jackson Papers, MHS; and Maria Weston Chapman, n.p., n.d. [probably August 1845], A.9.2.4.16, WP.

35. Caroline Weston to Maria Weston Chapman and Henry Chapman, Roxbury, 20 January 1841 [a lengthy letter she calls "Caroline Weston's–diary"], A.9.2.15.11-14, WP; Caroline Weston to Henry and Maria Weston Chapman, Roxbury, 21 January 1841, A.1.2.11.33, ASC.

36. Caroline Weston diary, 1835, A.9.2.7.65-66, WP.

37. Lucia Weston to Debora Weston, Boston, [November 1842], A.9.2.3.107, WP. These events followed directly upon the death of Henry G. Chapman, the nursing of whom provided the main reason for Lucia's stay in Boston.

38. Anne struggled with her belief in nonresistance even as she urged "breaking [into] the jail." Caroline accepted an invitation to attend the trial on the arm of Justice Story's nephew, E. Morfield. Maria, who was on the executive committee of the AAS at the time, took on editing the *Liberator* with Garrison out of town. See Anne Warren Weston to Debora Weston, 8 November 1842, A.9.2.17.106; Caroline Weston to Debora Weston, Boston, [late October 1842], A.9.2.17.111; and Samuel J. May Jr. to Maria Weston Chapman, 5 November [1842], A.9.2.20.90, WP.

39. Caroline Weston to Emma Weston and Maria Weston Chapman, [New Bedford], October 1845, A.9.2.21.64, WP. She notes that "Debora will send her journal up to Sat. noon."

40. Caroline Weston to Emma Weston and Maria Weston Chapman, October 1845, A.9.2.21.64; Anne Warren Weston to Lucia Weston, Boston, 28 September 1840, A.9.2.14.31, WP.

41. Debora Weston to Caroline Weston, New Bedford to Boston, 11 March 1839, A.9.2.11.56, WP.

42. Anne Warren Weston to Debora Weston, Weymouth, 8 June 1840, A.9.2.13.80, WP.

43. Caroline Weston to Debora Weston, Boston, [23 July 1842], A.9.2.3.88, WP.

44. Anne Warren Weston to Debora Weston, [Weymouth], [21 January 1842], A.9.2.3.3, WP. The small annuity she mentions came from funds provided each of the sisters by Henry Chapman Sr.

45. Anne Warren Weston to Debora Weston, Boston, 23 March 1838, A.9.2.10.15, WP.

46. Anne Warren Weston to Lucia Weston, Boston, 28 September 1840, A.9.2.14.31, WP.

47. Ibid. For custards from Weymouth, see Debora Weston to Anne Warren Weston, Boston, 6 June 1836, A.9.2.8.4, WP.

48. Caroline Weston to Debora Weston, [Roxbury], 12 September 1839, A.9.2.12.32, WP.

49. Debora Weston to Anne Warren Weston, New Bedford, 15 January 1836, A.9.2.8.6, WP. With Debora leading the charge, the issue was resolved so as to admit the women of color on equal terms with white members, in accordance with core Weston values of racial integration.

50. Anne Warren Weston to Emma Weston, Boston, 19 October 1841, A.9.2.15.81, WP.

51. Anne Warren Weston to Debora Weston, Weymouth, 5 November 1838, A.9.2.10.66, WP. Similarly, at Maria's request, Anne reviewed a letter Maria had written to Oliver Johnson; see Anne Warren Weston to Debora Weston, Weymouth, 9 November 1838, A.9.2.10.68, WP.

52. Debora Weston to Maria Weston Chapman, New Bedford, 4 March 1840, A.9.2.14.88, WP.

53. Anne Warren Weston to Debora Weston, Weymouth, 28 November 1841, A.9.2.15.100, WP. For Debora's concerns about undertaking a leadership role, see Debora Weston to Anne Warren Weston, New Bedford, 15 January 1836, A.9.2.8.6, WP.

54. Anne was among those who deprecated the tone of the *Liberator.* "All Yerrington's articles made me perfectly faint," she wrote. "If Garrison does not take the staff out of his hand I shall drop my Liberator for I am ashamed of it" (Anne Warren Weston to Caroline Weston and Debora Weston, Boston, 28 September 1843, A.9.2.19.40, WP). James Brown Yerrington (1800–1866) printed the *Liberator* from 1841 and assumed a variety of editorial responsibilities in Garrison's absence. See Merrill, *No Union with Slaveholders,* 158.

55. Maria Weston Chapman to Mary A. Estlin, Boston, 27 January 1846, A.7.2.32, JBEP. Maria envisioned a journal something like the sisters' *Liberty Bell.*

56. Anne Warren Weston to Debora Weston, Boston, 30 March 1839, A.9.2.11.71; Maria Weston Chapman to Debora Weston, Boston, 4 April 1839, A.9.2.11.75; Debora Weston to Maria Weston Chapman, New Bedford, 18 April 1839, A.9.2.11.83, WP. By "and mine" Maria meant her in-laws as well as her marital household.

57. Maria Weston Chapman to Debora Weston, Boston, 6 December 1839, A.9.2.12.108; Anne Warren Weston to Debora Weston, n.p., 25 February 1839, A.9.2.11.45, WP. Andrew Robeson [1787–1862] was a wealthy New Bedford whaling and textile merchant, a Quaker denied membership in the New Bedford Society of Friends, and an officer in both the Massachusetts and American Anti-Slavery Societies.

58. Debora Weston to Caroline Weston, New Bedford, 2 January 1840, A.9.2.13.3, WP.

59. Caroline Weston to Anne Warren Weston, Boston, c/o James Robbins, Esq., Brush Hill, 14 March 1840, A.9.2.13.39–40, WP.

60. Maria Weston Chapman to William L. Garrison, Cape Haitien, 19 January 1841, A.1.2.11.33, ASC.

61. Caroline Weston to Debora Weston, Boston, 3 March 1839, A.9.2.11.50, WP.

62. Maria Weston Chapman to Debora Weston, Boston, 14 March 1839, A.9.2.11.58, WP.

63. Caroline Weston to Emma Forbes Weston and Maria Weston Chapman, [New Bedford], October 1845, A.9.2.21.64, WP. Boot and shoe merchant Isaiah C. Ray [1804–82] of New Bedford and Nantucket embraced a number of antislavery controversies, including the 1845 battle of Nathanial Rogers and John Robert French with the New Hampshire Anti-Slavery Society over the *Herald of Freedom;* the custody battle between Elizabeth and William Wells Brown in 1847; and an 1851 challenge to the Fugitive Slave Act in which he asked "the colored people to send a fugitive to his house,

and he would protect him." See Sterling, *We Are Your Sisters*, 144–46; Guarneri, *Utopian Alternative*, 474, 507; Wesley and Uzelac, *William Cooper Nell*, 527; and Merrill, *No Union with Slaveholders*, 282.

64. The *National Anti-Slavery Standard* was the journal of the AAS.

65. Caroline Weston to Emma Forbes Weston and Maria Weston Chapman, [New Bedford], October 1845, A.9.2.21.63, WP. John F. Emerson was the New Bedford schoolmaster, abolitionist, and "dear friend" who brought the Westons to New Bedford. He was also treasurer of the New Bedford Anti-Slavery Society upon its founding in 1834.

66. Anne Warren Weston to Debora Weston, Boston, 18 April 1837, A.9.2.9.28; Anne Warren Weston to Debora Weston, Groton, 10 April 1838, A.9.2.10.22; Anne Warren Weston to Maria Weston Chapman, Weymouth, 5 November 1838, A.9.2.10.67; Anne Warren Weston to Debora Weston, Weymouth, 9 November 1838, A.9.2.10.68; Anne Warren Weston to Debora Weston, Weymouth, 16 November 1838, A.9.3.5.88; Debora Weston to Anne Warren Weston, Boston, 20 November 1838, A.9.2.10.73; Lucia Weston to Anne Warren Weston, Boston, [January 1839], A.9.2.11.10; Caroline Weston to Debora Weston, Boston, 3 March 1839, A.9.2.11.50; Anne Warren Weston to Debora Weston, Boston, 8 March 1839, A.9.2.11.53, WP.

67. Anne Warren Weston to Debora Weston, Boston [1836], A.9.2.3.49; Anne Warren Weston, n.p., 15 April 1836, A.9.2.8.19; Anne Warren Weston to Debora Weston, Boston, 4 September 1837, A.9.2.3.72; Caroline Weston to Anne Warren Weston, Boston, [1839], A.9.2.11.6; Anne Warren Weston to Debora Weston, Boston, [1840], A.9.2.3.21; Anne Warren Weston to Maria Weston Chapman, New York, 13 May 1840, A.9.2.13.74; Caroline Weston to Henry Chapman and Maria Weston Chapman, n.p., 15 January 1841, A.9.2.15.10; Anne Warren Weston to Debora Weston, Boston, 8 January 1842, A.9.2.17.67; Debora Weston to Emma Forbes Weston, Weymouth, 16 March 1842, A.9.2.17.43, WP.

68. Debora Weston to Caroline Weston, New Bedford, 2 January 1840, A.9.2.13.3, WP.

69. Anne Warren Weston to Debora Weston, New Bedford, 22 October 1842, A.9.2.17.99; Anne Warren Weston to Caroline Weston, Boston, 12 November 1848, A.9.2.24.43, WP.

70. Debora Weston to Anne Warren Weston, New Bedford, 1 January 1837, A.9.2.9.1; Anne Warren Weston to Debora Weston, n.p., 19 September 1837, A.9.2.9.71; Debora Weston to Anne Warren Weston, New Bedford, 25 November 1839, A.9.2.12.94; Debora Weston to Anne Warren Weston, New Bedford, 29 February 1840, A.9.2.13.31; Anne Warren Weston to Emma and Debora Weston, Weymouth, 4 October 1841, A.9.2.3.10; Anne Warren Weston to Ann T. G. Phillips, 3 August [1854], WP.

71. Anne Warren Weston to Debora Weston, Boston, 9 October 1837, A.9.2.9.78; Debora Weston to Emma Forbes Weston, Weymouth, 16 March 1842, A.9.2.17.43, WP. See also Anne Warren Weston to Caroline Weston, Boston, 12 November 1848, A.9.2.24.43, WP.

72. Anne Warren Weston to Debora Weston, New Bedford, 22 October 1842, A.9.2.17.99, WP.

73. Debora Weston to Caroline Weston, New Bedford, 11 March 1839, A.9.2.11.56, WP.

74. Caroline Weston to Debora Weston, Boston, 16 April 1842, A.9.2.17.54, WP.

75. Debora Weston to Anne Warren Weston, New Bedford, April 4, 1840, A.9.2.13.48; Anne Warren Weston to Debora Weston, Boston, 29 April 1837, A.9.2.9.30, WP. The fact that the sisters knew the contents of each other's wardrobes down to their underwear drawer suggests their ongoing struggle to retain middle-class status.

76. Anne Warren Weston to Debora Weston, Groton, 10 April 1838, A.9.2.10.22; Maria Weston Chapman to Debora Weston, Boston, Monday [January 1845], A.9.2.4.13, WP.

77. Debora Weston to Anne Warren Weston, New Bedford, 1 February 1837, A.9.2.9.12, WP.

78. Anne Warren Weston to Debora Weston, Boston, 6 December 1836, A.9.2.8.77, WP.

79. Emma Forbes Weston to Debora Weston, Boston, 6 December 1836, A.9.2.5.91, WP.

80. Anne Warren Weston to Debora Weston, Boston, 22 October 1836, A.9.2.8.63, WP.

81. Debora Weston to Anne Warren Weston, New Bedford, 22 January 1836, A.9.2.8.8, WP. Held by conservatives to be dangerous to young women, novel reading was believed to first stir and then indulge the emotions. The Westons were voracious readers of novels, as well as history, religious and reform tracts, autobiographies, biographies, and memoirs.

82. Anne Warren Weston to Debora Weston, Boston, 25 January 1842, A.9.2.17.27, WP.

83. Debora Weston to Anne Warren Weston, New Bedford, 19 November 1837, A.9.2.9.88; Caroline Weston to Debora Weston, Boston, [14 June] 1842, A.9.2.17.75; Lucia Weston to Debora Weston, Boston, 24 June 1842, A.9.2.3.54, WP.

84. Anne Warren Weston to Debora Weston, Groton, 17 March 1837, A.9.2.9.16, WP.

CHAPTER 6

1. Maria Weston Chapman to Debora Weston, Boston, [January 1845], A.9.2.4.13, WP. See also Maria Weston Chapman to Caroline Weston, n.p., [1846], A.9.2.6.35, WP.

2. Their stories are found in the gospels of Luke 10:38–42 and John 11:1–12:11.

3. The sisters spoke of the movement and the church as made up of "brothers and sisters in the same household," a common reference among abolitionists. See Anne Warren Weston to Wendell Phillips, Weymouth, 1 December 1850, 1289, folio 2, Blagden Collection, HL. See also Edmund Quincy to Caroline Weston, Dedham, 6 November 1843, A.9.2.19.73, WP.

4. Anne Warren Weston to Debora Weston, Groton, 10 April 1838, A.9.2.10.22, WP.

5. Maria Weston Chapman to Debora Weston, Boston, [January 1845], A.9.2.4.13; Maria Weston Chapman to Anne Warren Weston, Boston, 22 September 1839, A.9.2.6.30, WP. In writing the second annual history of the BFAS, Maria consciously utilized such language from the Sermon on the Mount. As Anne wrote, "In relating the Slave case (the runaways) Maria says 'They were sick & in prison—we visited them,

strangers & we took them in.' The Report is on the whole intended to be very cunning" (Anne Warren Weston to Debora Weston, 4 October 1836, A.9.2.8.56, Boston, WP).

6. Debora Weston to Maria Weston Chapman, New Bedford, 13 April 1837, A.9.2.9.27, WP.

7. Caroline Weston to Wendell and Ann T. G. Phillips, [New Bedford], n.d., 1290, folio 6, Blagden Collection, HL. A deeply religious man, George A. Avery was a successful Rochester, New York, wholesale grocer. He supported Lane Seminary until the trustees banned discussion of slavery. His brother Courtland Avery was one of the "Lane Rebels" who transferred to Oberlin College in protest. Avery participated in the Rochester and Monroe County Anti-Slavery Societies, serving variously as vice president and treasurer. See Czerkas, "Averys and the Stantons," 3114.

8. Lucia Weston to Anne Warren Weston, Boston, April 1839, A.9.2.11.72, WP.

9. As corresponding secretary of the BFAS, Maria exchanged letters with abolitionists in Great Britain and throughout the northern United States (Ohio, Rhode Island, Connecticut, New York, and Pennsylvania in particular). As her fame built, she also exchanged unofficial correspondence with a broad range of supporters and opponents of slavery. See, for example, Amelia A. T. Kirby to Maria Weston Chapman, Cincinnati, 2 July 1845, A.9.2.21.29; Mary G. Rice to Maria Weston Chapman, Northborough, 23 October 1839, A.9.2.12.57; William R. Chapman to Maria Weston Chapman, New Haven, 19 December 1839, A.9.2.12.123; and Anne Cropper, n.p., [December 1843], A.9.2.19.91, WP.

10. Caroline Weston to Debora Weston, Weymouth, 23 November 1841, A.9.2.3.37, WP. The emphasis on the word "cab" alluded to the Garrisonian quip that there were "not enough of us to fill a Cab." See Edmund Quincy to Richard D. Webb, Dedham, 23 May 1846, 14 July 1846, Quincy, Wendell, Holmes, and Upham Family Papers, MHS.

11. Maria Weston Chapman to Caroline Weston, Paris, 18 November 1852, WP. Boston merchant Charles F. Hovey (1807–59) was a financial supporter and active member of the governing boards of both the American and Massachusetts Anti-Slavery Societies. He willed a legacy to the cause for which Maria served as trustee.

12. Caroline Weston to Anne Warren Weston and Debora Weston, n.p., 11 September 1839, A.9.2.12.20, WP.

13. Debora Weston to Mary Weston, n.p., n.d., A.9.2.12.20, WP.

14. Maria Weston Chapman to Caroline Weston, [Boston], 1842, A.9.2.4.23, WP. Mary M. Brooks led the Concord Female Anti-Slavery Society and supported the Boston Female Anti-Slavery bazaar and Garrison. A Philadelphia Quaker, merchant, and Garrisonian, Edward Davis regularly corresponded with the Westons. Two years older than Lucia, Mary Fifield (1824–45) was a Weston neighbor and the daughter of Dr. Noah Fifield.

15. See Chapter 3.

16. Caroline Weston to Anne Warren Weston, Boston, 13 August 1835, A.9.2.7.63, WP.

17. Anne Warren Weston to Caroline Weston, Groton, 7 August 1837, A.9.2.9.59, WP.

18. Caroline Weston to Debora Weston, Boston, n.d. [back of 1841 call for antislavery fair], A.9.2.5.22, WP.

19. Caroline Weston to Emma Weston and Maria Weston Chapman, [New Bedford], October 1845, A.9.2.21.64, WP.

20. See Grover, *Fugitive's Gibraltar*, chap. 6, for discussion of this complex era in New Bedford's history and the role of the Weston sisters.

21. She complained, "I eat scarcely any thing but toasted bread, my free labour principles cutting me off from almost every thing good" (Debora Weston to Mary Weston, New Bedford, 6 November 1836, A.9.2.8.68, WP). See also Debora Weston to Anne Warren Weston, New Bedford, 19 November 1837, A.9.2.9.88, WP.

22. Caroline Weston to Wendell and Ann T. G. Phillips, New Bedford, 13 November 1843, Blagden Collection, HL.

23. The older sisters routinely attended meetings of the Weymouth Female Anti-Slavery Society when living at home and kept in frequent communication with their aunt Mary Weston on the society's doings while away. Maria and Anne came to help as called, but most of their time and effort went into the BFAS. Lucia and Emma contributed their share of labor to the Weymouth Female more regularly than their older sisters. See Anne Warren Weston to Debora Weston, Boston, 24 July [n.y.], A.9.2.3.40; Caroline Weston diary, 26 and 28 September 1835, A.9.2.7.65-66; Mary Weston to Anne Warren Weston, Weymouth, 3 July 1836, A.9.2.3.89; [Mary Weston] to Debora Weston, [Weymouth], 19 July 1836, A.9.2.4.94; Mary Weston to Debora Weston, Weymouth, 24 October 1836, A.9.2.8.65; Mary Weston to Debora Weston, Weymouth, 22 January [1837], A.9.2.5.82; Mary Weston to Bella [Debora Weston], Weymouth, 17 September 1837, A.9.2.3.71; Mary Weston to Debora Weston, Weymouth, 24 June [1838], A.9.2.5.51; Anne Warren Weston to Mary Weston, Boston, 9 January 1939, A.9.2.11.19; Anne Warren Weston to Debora Weston, Boston, 8 April 1839, A.9.2.11.77; Anne Warren Weston to Debora Weston, Weymouth, 18 April 1839, A.9.2.11.85; Emma Weston to Debora Weston, Weymouth, 18 April 1839, A.9.2.11.86; Mary Weston to Debora Weston, Weymouth, 18 April 1839, A.9.2.11.12; Anne Warren Weston to Debora Weston, Weymouth, 1 May 1839, A.9.2.11.93; Maria Weston Chapman to Mary Weston, Boston, 18 May 1839, A.9.2.11.103b; Emma Weston to Debora Weston, Weymouth, [1841], A.9.2.16.4; Anne Warren Weston to Maria Weston Chapman, Weymouth, 25 February 1841, A.9.2.15.27; Anne Warren Weston to Henry and Maria Weston Chapman, Weymouth, 18 May 1841, A.9.2.15.47; Anne Warren Weston to Debora Weston, Weymouth, 28 November 1841, A.9.2.15.100; Caroline Weston to Debora Weston, Weymouth, n.d., A.9.2.3.70; Lucia Weston to Debora Weston, Weymouth, January 1842, A.9.2.17.3; Anne Warren Weston to Debora Weston, Boston, 25 January 1842, A.9.2.17.27; Anne Warren Weston to Debora Weston, Weymouth, 29 July 1842, A.9.2.17.84; Debora Weston to Caroline Weston, Weymouth, 26 March 1843, A.9.2.18.24; [Debora Weston] to Caroline Weston, Weymouth, May 1846, A.9.22.41; Anne Warren Weston to Messrs. Bates, Hanson and White, Weymouth, February 1847, A.9.2.23.6; Samuel May Jr. to Anne Warren Weston, Boston, 28 September 1849, A.9.2.24.95, WP. Samuel May Jr. to Anne Warren Weston, n.p., 3 October 1848, A.4.6A.2.71; James Buffum to Anne Warren Weston, Lynn, 9 October 1848, A.4.6A.3.28, ASC. Anne Warren Weston to John B. Estlin, Weymouth, 27 October 1850, A.7.2.5; Anne Warren Weston to John B. Estlin, Weymouth, 11 November 1851, A.7.2.12, JBEP. Anne Warren Weston to Elizabeth Pease, Weymouth, 14 October 1845,

A.9.2.15.72; Maria Weston Chapman to Samuel May Jr., Weymouth, 22 September 1857, A.1.2.27.61, ASC. Anne Warren Weston to Wendell Phillips, Weymouth, 18 September [1854]; Anne Warren Weston to Ann T. G. Phillips, Weymouth, 26 July 1855, Blagden Collection, HL.

24. Anne Warren Weston to Debora Weston, Dorchester, 11 July 1839, A.9.2.11.134, WP.

25. Debora Weston to Anne Warren Weston, New Bedford, 23 June 1839, A.9.2.11.122, WP. Part of the difficulty for Debora had to do with Quaker dominance over abolition in New Bedford. As she told Caroline:

As for the soc[iety] here, the difficulty is just this. Quakerism unfits a man for action. *I* think just as transcendentalism does. Joseph Congdon by common consent is the factotum of the soc[iety], that is, is President & does all the writing, writes the resolutions &c—just at this crisis the thing that he is most afraid of, is that the holy calm of his mind should be disturbed & that the spirit of fight should get into the societies, that we should turn partisans, & such sort of trash. Sunday night I went up & gave him battle, gave him Maria's opinion as to what ought to be said in the resolutions (the regular meeting was to be held this week) & finally threatened to denounce him as a peeler, when he said that he would not go into the Bristol County meeting which is to be held here in April. The meeting has been held & the resolutions sent strait off to the Liberator, the Mass[achusetts] Ab[olitionist] & the Emancipator. I trust Wendell will come down here in April & do battle valiantly. All they want is a leader not but what Joseph [Richetson] is thorough enough. . . . the Lord deliver me from a *quaker.* I cant abide them. (Debora Weston to Caroline Weston, New Bedford, 21 March 1839, A.9.2.11.64, WP)

26. She told a marvelous story about a stage ride in which she sat on top and held the six horses every time the driver stopped and "never had such a good ride in my life" (Debora Weston to Anne Warren Weston, n.p., 12 March 1838, A.9.2.10.10, WP).

27. Mary Weston to Debora Weston, n.p., 22 January [1837], A.9.2.5.82; Anne Warren Weston to Mary Weston, New Bedford, 29 October 1842, A.9.2.17.102; Caroline Weston to Debora Weston, [Weymouth], [postmarked 19 July 1836], A.9.2.4.94, WP. The last is a fragment and anonymously authored; the Boston Public Library labels it as Caroline's but the handwriting is Mary Weston's.

28. Anne Warren Weston to Debora Weston, Weymouth, 10 March 1842, A.9.2.17.40; Anne Warren Weston to Debora Weston, Weymouth, 11 April 1842, A.9.2.17.46; Anne Warren Weston to Debora Weston, n.p., 19 June 1842, A.9.2.17.73; Debora Weston to Caroline Weston, Weymouth, May 1846, A.9.2.22.41, WP.

29. Caroline wished every member of every female association would give to the fair but acknowledged, "I think there will be but a few give a single thing" (Caroline Weston to Debora Weston, Weymouth, 26–29 July [n.y.], A.9.2.4.92, WP).

30. Maria Weston Chapman to Mary Weston, [Boston], [18 May 1839], A.9.2.11.103b, WP; Maria Weston Chapman to Samuel J. May Jr., Weymouth, 22 September 1857, A.1.2.27.61, ASC.

31. Anne Warren Weston to Debora Weston, Boston, 25 January 1842, A.9.2.17.27; Frederick Douglass to Anne Warren Weston, Holden, 1 July 1845, A.9.2.21.27, WP; Samuel J. May Jr. to Anne Warren Weston, 3 October 1848, A.4.6A.2.71, ASC; Anne Warren Weston to Messrs. Bates, Hanson and White, Weymouth, February 1847, A.9.2.23.6, WP; Anne Warren Weston to Mary A. Estlin, Weymouth, 2 November 1850, A.7.2.7, JBEP; Wendell Phillips to Debora Weston, Boston, [17 October n.y.], A.9.2.19.42; Debora Weston to Emma Forbes Weston, Weymouth, 16 March 1842, A.9.2.17.43, WP.

32. "Some Reminiscences of Mrs. Maria W. Chapman," Bigelow Collection, Essex Institute/Peabody Essex Museum.

33. Dickson, *Manual of Pathology*, 178–79; Mosely, *Eleven Chapters*, 123–40, quoted in Skultans, *Madness and Morals*, 41–50. Dr. Mosely believed that the suppression of bodily discharge caused by weaning an infant could excite intense emotions in the mother, increasing blood circulation to the brain and producing an attack of acute phrenitis.

34. Bartlett, *Physician's Pocket Synopsis*, 223–24. See also Dickson, *Manual of Pathology*, 180.

35. George Man Burrows, "Brain, Heart and Will," from his *Commentaries on Insanity* (London: Underwood, 1828), quoted in Skultans, *Madness and Morals*, 36.

36. William L. Garrison to George W. Benson, Boston, 25 May 1838, in Ruchames, *House Dividing*, 2:366. Both Garrison and George Thompson suffered various ailments that periodically required their withdrawal from the fray.

37. Caroline Weston to Mary G. Chapman, Stonington, Connecticut, [1838], A.9.2.3.32, WP.

38. See Lydia Maria Child to Caroline Weston, Northampton, 27 July 1838, A.5.1.35, Child Papers, ASC, in which Child wrote that she had had as yet no opportunity to counter such rumors and reassured Caroline that she would do so at every opportunity. "This world-babble is of little consequence," she wrote. "Can one be deep, or high, or even simply true, without misrepresentation?"

39. Caroline Weston to Lucia Weston, Stonington, Connecticut, [1838], A.9.2.3.66, WP.

40. Anne W. Weston to [Philadelphia gentleman], [1838], A.9.2.5.21, WP.

41. Caroline Weston to Lucia Weston, Stonington, Connecticut, [1838], A.9.2.3.32, WP.

42. "Some Reminiscences of Mrs. Maria W. Chapman," Bigelow Collection, Essex Institute/Peabody Essex Museum.

43. Lydia Maria Child to Caroline Weston, Northampton, 13 August 1838, A.5.1.39, Child Papers, ASC. The exact nature and cause of Maria's illness remained a subject of debate as late as 1885. Even admirers still thought of her illness as a bout of temporary madness brought on by her fanaticism and the excitement of the mob, although they were willing to ascribe something to the too sudden weaning of her daughter. One obituary writer stated: "I had long been on the most friendly terms, while rather lamenting her enthusiastic devotion to the cause of the slave as a piece of amiable fanaticism. She had left her young child to attend the meeting, at great risk of her health, and this, with the excitement of the preceding night, had nearly thrown her into a fever. She only just escaped with her life from this exposure, but she did more towards making one

convert to abolitionism than any other conjunction of circumstances could have done." See "Some Reminiscences of Mrs. Maria W. Chapman," Bigelow Collection, Essex Institute/Peabody Essex Museum. Clare Taylor (*Women of the Anti-Slavery Movement*, 102 n. 4, 138) has asserted postpartum depression; however, Maria's high fever and resulting delirium weigh against this interpretation.

44. [Emma Mitchell to Maria Weston Chapman], Bristol, 13 January 1852, A.7.3.40, JBEP.

45. Anne Warren Weston to Debora Weston, Boston, 21 December 1836, A.9.2.8.79–80, WP; Anne Warren Weston and Caroline Weston to Wendell and Ann Phillips, Boston, 25 January 1840, 1290, Blagden Collection, HL; Anne Warren Weston to Elizabeth Pease, Boston, 31 May 1841, A.1.2.12.1.36, ASC. The politics of abolition informed the political meanings ascribed to sickness. For example, in the face of criticism for the supposed toll her public activism took upon her family and household, Maria cast her husband's death as an authorizing narrative legitimating a widow's choice not to mourn in household seclusion but rather to honor her dead spouse by returning to the political work he valued. For a discussion of Henry Grafton Chapman's death and the abolitionist propaganda Maria made of her widowhood, see Chambers, "'Great Was the Benefit of His Death.'"

46. Anne Warren Weston to Debora Weston, Boston, 6 January 1837, A.9.2.9.7, WP. Such fears were common at the time among childbearing women and their female kin and friends. See Leavitt, "Under the Shadow of Maternity."

47. Maria Weston Chapman to William Lloyd Garrison, Cape Haitien, 19 January 1841, A.1.2.11.33, ASC; Maria Weston Chapman to Debora Weston, Boston, 19 April 1841, A.9.2.3.82, WP.

48. Mary Gray Chapman confirmed that Sarah Greene Chapman was ill with a "positive fever" in a letter she wrote to Debora Weston, [Boston], 16 April 1841, A.9.2.15.42, WP.

49. Anne Warren Weston to Maria Weston Chapman, Boston, 15 April 1841, A.9.2.15.42, WP.

50. *True History*, 40, 45. "The Martyr Age of the United States of America" was originally published in the *London and Westminster Review* in Britain in 1838 and republished in Boston by Weeks, Jordan & Co. in 1839.

51. Anne Warren Weston to Debora Weston, Weymouth, 3 February 1853, A.9.2.27.9, WP; Anne Warren Weston to Mary A. Estlin, Weymouth, 23 February [1853], A.7.2.22, JBEP. See also Anne Warren Weston to Debora Weston, n.p., 19 September 1837, A.9.2.9.71, WP.

52. Today the herb, a form of mint, is used in some teas.

53. Maria Weston Chapman to Caroline Weston, Boston, 7 December 1843, A.9.2.19.85, WP.

54. Anne Warren Weston to Samuel J. May Jr., Paris, 24 June 1856, A.1.2.26, ASC. Charles Sumner (1811–74) served as senator from Massachusetts from 1851 until his death. On 22 May 1856, Representative Preston S. Brooks of South Carolina attacked Sumner with a cane. The viciousness of the incident convinced many northerners that the South's aggressive defense of slavery had to be stopped, a determination that helped arm the Free State settlers in Kansas and increased support for John Charles

Frémont as a Republican presidential candidate opposing the extension of slavery into the West.

55. Debora Weston to "dear folks," Weymouth, 2 June 1854, A.9.2.28.14, WP. The case of the fugitive slave Anthony Burns roiled Boston in the summer of 1854. Benjamin Franklin Hallet (1797–1862) had been editor of the *Boston Daily Advocate* but retired from the newspaper business to practice law after the paper merged with the *Boston Post* in 1838. The Westons saw him as an opponent of both emancipation and racial equality.

56. Anne Warren Weston to Debora Weston, 15 May 1839, A.9.2.11.105, WP.

57. Maria Weston Chapman to Caroline Weston, Boston, 7 December 1843, A.9.2.19.85, WP.

58. Anne Warren Weston to Mary A. Estlin, Weymouth, 30 September 1851, A.7.2.11; Anne Warren Weston to John B. Estlin, Weymouth, 11 November 1851, A.7.2.12, JBEP.

59. Anne Warren Weston to Mary A. Estlin, Weymouth, 18 January 1852 [mislabeled 18 November 1852], A.7.2.13, JBEP.

60. Anne Warren Weston to Mary A. Estlin, Weymouth, 15 February 1852, A.7.2.14, JBEP.

61. Anne Warren Weston to Debora Weston, Boston, 3 September 1837, A.9.2.3.69, WP.

62. Debora Weston to Anne Warren Weston, New Bedford, 25 November 1839, A.9.2.12.94, WP. See also Anne Warren Weston to Debora Weston, Weymouth, 2 November 1838, A.9.2.10.65, WP: "I was anxious to get Lizzy off because though we can do very well with Henry alone; or Lizzy alone; or with both together can manage, if either of them be ill enough to be confined to their room, yet with both well enough to be together I need not tell you there was no rest or peace."

63. Anne Warren Weston to Debora Weston, Boston, [1840], A.9.2.3.21; Lucia Weston to Debora Weston, Boston, n.d., A.9.2.3.106, WP; Maria Weston Chapman to Mary A. Estlin, Weymouth, 4 July 1858, A.7.2.83, JBEP; Maria Weston Chapman to "friends," Weymouth, 27 August 1841, Blagden Collection, HL.

64. This 31 March 1841 convocation at the Chardon Street Chapel, Boston, followed a previous meeting held in November 1840 at which such topics were discussed among progressive thinkers and Garrisonian abolitionists. The issues divided the Weston women. As Mary Weston told her niece, "Your mother & Maria was [*sic*] here—Maria[,] Phebe & Priscilla had a hot dispute—she (Maria) ran full tilt against the sabbath & the clergy in *toto*. You might just as well have written when the confusion of tong[ue]s took place. Your mother & I took no part. Phebe & Maria became very personal used great plainness of speech—They left it an adjourned meeting—she professing her intention of renewing the discussion & trying to emancipate them from the thraldom of the clergy—they to convince her of the horrid impiety of desecrating the sabbath. I have heard enough & shall take myself off at the next meeting. In truth dear D I am sorry that this subject of the sabbath has got in among the abolitionists" (Mary Weston to Debora Weston, Weymouth, 11 September [n.y.], A.9.2.3.24, WP).

65. Susan Tabor to Debora Weston, New Bedford, 8 March 1841, A.9.2.15.30; Caroline Weston to Henry Grafton and Maria Weston Chapman, Boston, 5 April 1841, A.9.2.15.30, WP. Ann Bates Weston, coping with her mother's death three weeks

earlier, had less capacity than usual to cope with her rambunctious grandchildren, her husband's antics, and the housekeeping.

66. Catherine Sargent left Anne $100 in her will. See Anne Warren Weston to Wendell Phillips, Weymouth, [1852], 1289, folio 7, Blagden Collection, HL. The Weston correspondence reveals Anne frequently visiting the Sargents, staying often for some time. See Anne Warren Weston to Debora Weston, Boston, 22 October 1836, A.9.2.8.63, 18 April 1837, A.9.2.9.28, 24 July [1837], A.9.2.3.40, 15 January 1842, A.9.2.17.24, 16 January 1842, A.9.2.17.25, 21 January 1842, A.9.2.3.3, 3 June 1842, A.9.2.17.66; Anne Warren Weston to Caroline Weston, Boston, 30 May 1844, A.9.2.20.33; Samuel J. May Jr. to Anne Warren Weston, Boston, 16 February 1849, A.9.2.24.62, WP; and Anne Warren Weston to Samuel J. May Jr., 1 October 1852, B.1.6.4.52, May Papers, BPL.

67. Caroline Weston to Henry and Maria Weston Chapman, 5 April 1841, A.9.2.15.36, WP.

68. Anne Warren Weston to Debora Weston, [Boston], 12 February 1838, A.9.2.10.7, WP. See also Debora Weston to Anne Warren Weston, New Bedford, 7 April 1842, A.9.2.17.49; and Lucia Weston to Anne Warren Weston, Boston, [January 1839], A.9.2.11.10, WP.

69. Anne Warren Weston to Debora Weston, Boston, 26 July 1838, A.9.2.10.41, WP.

70. Anne Warren Weston to Mary Weston, Boston, 27 February 1839, A.9.2.11.48; Anne Warren Weston to Debora Weston, Boston, 8 March 1839, A.9.2.11.53; Debora Weston to Caroline Weston, New Bedford, 11 March 1839, A.9.2.11.56, WP.

71. Caroline Weston to Debora Weston, Boston, October 1842, A.9.2.17.101, WP. Francis Jackson (1789–1861) was a well-regarded adviser to Garrison and provided solid financial support for the *Liberator* from his own funds. He served as president of the MAS and several New England conventions, and vice president of the NEAS. When he died he left $10,000 for aid to newly freed slaves and $5,000 to the woman's rights movement. Henry B. Stanton (1805–87), was among the "Lane Rebels" from Lane Theological Seminary who joined the AAS. He organized the Rhode Island Anti-Slavery Society. In the late 1830s, he became a critic of Garrison and would, eventually, join the Liberty Party and then the Republican Party as an advocate of political means to end slavery. He practiced law in Boston before removing to upstate New York to make a successful run for the Senate. Joshua Leavitt (1794–1873) helped found the AAS. By the early 1840s, he also had joined the political abolitionists. He edited their newspaper, the *Emancipator*.

72. Lucia Weston to Debora Weston, Boston, [November 1842], A.9.2.3.107, WP.

73. The timing of this event also had to do with her changed financial situation. The death in 1847 of Sarah Greene Chapman, her mother-in-law, left her with a substantial inheritance (approximately $40,750 worth of stocks and bonds) plus the monthly rent on a Boston townhouse inhabited by her sister-in-law. Maria explained her departure to Boston abolitionists as related to her children's well-being. Sarah Southwick, a close friend of Lucia Weston, noted: "I think [Maria's] sacrifices of social position when she allied herself to the antislavery cause, were very great. She has told me how her fashionable neighbors ignored her acquaintance, refusing even to bow. . . . I don't think she regretted the loss of social position for herself, but she probably did for her children, and it was the feeling that they were shut out by their anti-slavery from the more cultivated

circles of Boston that partly induced her to take them to Europe for education" (South-wick, *Reminiscences*, 35).

74. Maria Weston Chapman to Mary A. Estlin, Weymouth, 8 March 1858, A.8.2.78, [also A.7.2.79], JBEP.

75. Maria Weston Chapman to William Lloyd Garrison, Weymouth, n.d., A.1.2.28.1, ASC. Internal data suggest that the date was between 25 November and 31 December 1855.

76. Anne W. Weston to John B. Estlin, Weymouth, 15 February 1852, A.7.2.14, JBEP. Both Maria and Caroline read and spoke French well enough to translate documents, from antislavery novels to technical manuals. Edmund Hunt gave a marvelous picture in his memoirs of Maria's fluency. Hunt wanted to manufacture fireworks, as he found store-keeping boring. In 1856, he ordered a book on the subject, *Feu d'Artifice*, by Chertier, a Frenchman advanced in the skills of the trade: "I could not then read French, and impatient to know its contents, I went to the Westons' [house] and met Mrs. Chapman, who, upon my telling her my troubles, read off several chapters. This gave me some knowledge of the value of the book; so having a French-English dictionary, I went to work and translated the whole book, gaining a knowledge of its contents" (Hunt, *Weymouth Ways*, 433). The sisters had avidly followed the political situation in France—not only the emancipation of slaves in its colonies but also the conflict between royalists and republicans that resulted in the uprising of 1848. They continued to do so while in Paris.

77. Maria Weston Chapman journal, 20 November 1855, A.9.2.6.29, WP. The term "butterfly life" was used by abolitionists Sarah Grimké and Juliana Tappan to describe a life largely concerned with society and fashion. In trying to educate the wealthy of Hudson Square in New York City, for example, Tappan wrote: "There is so much aristocracy here, so much walking in Broadway to exhibit the butterfly fashions, that we can seldom gain access to the consciences of women" (Juliana A. Tappan to Anne Warren Weston, New York, 21 July 1837, A.9.2.9.49, WP).

78. Emma Michell to Maria Weston Chapman, Bristol, 13 January 1852, A.7.3.40, JBEP. Michell was Estlin's aunt and, like her niece, a great admirer of the Westons.

79. See, for example, R. R. Madden to Maria Weston Chapman, London, 27 August 1842, A.9.2.17.93; and Mary Carpenter to Maria Weston Chapman, Bristol, 17 October 1846, A.9.2.22.100, WP.

80. Anne and Emma joined Maria and Caroline in London in May. While there they saw the Bateses, and the Estlins traveled to Portland Place to visit with them. See John B. Estlin and Mary A. Estlin to Miss Weston, Bristol, 16 May 1857, A.9.2.29.10, WP. In September, Caroline and Maria again went to London and also to Bristol, where they met with antislavery activists. See Mary A. Estlin to Anne Warren Weston, Bristol, 19 September 1851, A.9.2.25.124, WP.

81. Mary A. Estlin to Anne Warren Weston, Bristol, 3 October 1851, A.9.2.25.124; Mary A. Estlin to Anne Warren Weston, Bristol, 11 October 1851, A.9.2.23.126; Mary A. Estlin to Maria Weston Chapman, Bristol, 17 October 1851, A.9.2.29.13, WP.

82. Mary A. Estlin to Emma Weston, Dublin, 9 July 1852, A.8.3.52, JBEP. On Lucia's health, see Anne Warren Weston to Ann Phillips, Weymouth, 3 September 1853; and Anne Warren Weston to Wendell and Ann Phillips, Paris, 25 May 1856, Blagden Collection, HL.

83. George Thompson to Richard D. Webb, London, 22 December 1851, GB 133.4.3, Raymond English Anti-Slavery Collection, John Rylands Library; Caroline Weston to Samuel J. May, Paris, 3 July 1850, B.1.6.4.5; Anne W. Weston to Samuel J. May Jr., Weymouth, 5 September 1849, B.1.6.3.66, May Papers, BPL; Sarah Pugh to Maria Weston Chapman, Bristol, 2 April 1853, A.9.2.27.22, WP. See also Taylor, *Women of the Anti-Slavery Movement*, 61–85.

84. Chamerovzow made a semiofficial call in 1854, bringing a letter of introduction from the Estlins asking Maria to speak frankly to him. "He may not see so strongly as we do the importance of the aims & measures of the American A. S. Socy as *the moral movement* of the Cause in America," wrote Mary Estlin; "& he may not as yet be able to do all that *he* hopes, & that *we* hope, may in time be effected, towards directing the Anti-slavery energy of this country to the aid of the labors of the American Anti-slavery Socy" (Mary A. Estlin to Maria Weston Chapman, Clevedon, 6 August 1854, A.7.3.84, JBEP). For a report on the visit from the Westons' perspective, see Caroline Weston to Mary A. Estlin, Paris, 20 August 1854, A.1.2.25, ASC; and Maria Weston Chapman to Elizabeth Pease Nichol, Bristol, 6 May 1855, A.9.2.25.29, WP.

85. Maria Weston Chapman to Mary A. Estlin, n.p., 26 December 1853, A.7.2.67, JBEP.

86. Harriet Beecher Stowe wrote about her visit with the Westons in her work *Sunny Memories of Foreign Lands*. Among other visitors were Bostonians Eliza Follen and her sister Susan Cabot, Charles P. Hovey, and Mrs. Robert Lowell; Philadelphians Sarah Pugh, J. Miller McKim, and E. M. Davis; and the expatriate Caroline B. Hunt. See Anne W. Weston to John B. Estlin, Weymouth, 3 February 1850, A.7.2.2, JBEP; Elizabeth Neall Gay to Lucia Weston, Staten Island, 1 February 1852, Gay Papers, Rare Book and Manuscript Library; Sarah Pugh to "dear friends," Bristol, n.d., A.9.2.16.90, WP; Maria Weston Chapman to John B. Estlin and Mary A. Estlin, Paris, 4 July 1853, A.7.2.64, JBEP; and Maria Weston Chapman to John B. Estlin, Paris, 14 December 1853, A.7.2.66, WP.

87. Anne Warren Weston to John B. Estlin, Weymouth, 27 October 1850, A.7.2.5, JBEP. This was not an unusual feeling among abolitionists. Sarah Otis Ernst acknowledged to Anne Warren Weston that she too would have liked to take her children abroad, "out of this proslavery atmosphere. We must otherwise consent to almost total separation from such society as our intellectual tastes would choose—suffer, as it were, social Outlawry—for the sake of principle, for slavery binds all ranks in its embrace" (Sarah Otis Ernst to Anne Warren Weston, Spring Garden, Ohio, 13 January 1856, A.9.2.28.69, WP).

88. Edmund Quincy to Richard D. Webb, Dedham, 5 August 1854, Quincy, Wendell, Holmes, and Upham Family Papers, MHS. Quincy believed there to be "very good Society, as Society in Boston, taking in Cambridge and the come-at-able towns. It is a sort of cross between Edinburgh and Liverpool or Bristol, consisting of professors and literary men, a few men of independent fortunes, but chiefly of prosperous merchants and professional men" (ibid). Maria had experienced some of what passed for "society" in Boston as the daughter-in-law and niece of such wealthy men as Henry Chapman, Ezra Weston, and Joshua Bates. An author and intellectual in her own right, she was considered (and rejected), along with Lydia Maria Child, for membership in Ralph

Waldo Emerson's Town and Country Club. This men's club embraced as members a range of reformers, literary men, and transcendentalists, including Henry Wadsworth Longfellow, Robert Lowell, Bronson Alcott, William Lloyd Garrison, and Theodore Parker. Most of Boston's social and intellectual elite viewed Chapman as too passionate a political partisan for comfort. She, on the other hand, vociferously rejected the intellectual disengagement with slavery that she saw as characterizing the "Athens of America" and carried on a rather public disagreement about abolition with William Ellery Channing. She did the same in France. In his diary, Crabb Robinson described her as "an enthusiast; and there is this drawback in the society of all enthusiasts, that they are discontented if you do not go all lengths with them, and they will seldom allow themselves to talk on any other than their own special topic" (13 June 1850 entry, in Sadler, *Henry Crabb Robinson*, 365).

89. Edmund Quincy to Richard D. Webb, Dedham, 5 August 1854, Quincy, Wendell, Holmes, and Upham Family Papers, MHS.

90. George Thompson to Amelia Thompson, Paris, 14 November 1851, Raymond English Anti-Slavery Collection, 133, 2.2.29, John Rylands Library. See also O'Meara, *Madame Mohl*; Simpson, *Letters and Recollections*; and Lesser, *Clarkey*. See Stowe, *Sunny Memories*, 154–55, for a description of Chapman's salon.

91. Bates never felt comfortable among the aristocracy and was quick to take offense when he, or his wife, felt unappreciated or ill-used. The following diary entries are typical: "I am quite aware that too much falls on me. . . . I have all the disadvantage of not being supported by my partners no one lends a helping hand to render myself or my family more respectable, and they never take the least notice of my countrymen unless I request it" (Diary of Joshua Bates, 27 December 1835, Baring Brothers DEP 74, BA). Having been invited to dinner at Lord Ashburton's to meet a representative of the Bank of the United States, he wrote: "It is very mortifying to be invited in this style only when some American is invited, and then my wife is not included which is very mortifying to her" (ibid., 30 April 1836).

92. Anne Warren Weston to Ann Phillips, Weymouth, 26 July 1855, 1482, folio 2, Blagden Collection, HL.

93. Maria Weston Chapman to Elizabeth Pease, Paris, 25 December 1849, A.2.1.18.88, WP. Maria quotes the *Liberator* motto.

94. Ibid.

95. Maria Weston Chapman to Wendell and Ann Phillips, Paris, 28 September 1848, 394, folio 2, Blagden Collection, HL; Maria Weston Chapman to Elizabeth Pease, Paris, 29 November 1848, A.1.2.18.41, ASC. Chapman believed she could raise more money from Europe, particularly with select fair goods from Paris, than she could in Boston on the receiving end of others' choices.

96. Caroline Weston to Wendell and Ann T. G. Phillips, Interlaken [Switzerland], 20 September [1851], 1290, folio 7; Anne Warren Weston to Wendell and Ann T. G. Phillips, Vevey, 31 October 1856, 1289, folio 5, Blagden Collection, HL.

97. Maria Weston Chapman to John B. Estlin, Paris, 4 January 1850, A.7.2.48, JBEP.

98. These included Madame Bremer, wife of the former *minister des affairs étrangères*; Madame Vavin, wife of Louis Philippe's *directeur de la hôtel de ville*; Mademoiselle de Montjolssier, a friend of Madame Louise Swanton Belloc and daughter

of Seranant; Madame Louise Marie Swanton Belloc, wife of Hilaire Belloc, a Britisher who lived in France and translated *Uncle Tom's Cabin* into French; Louise Marie Swanton Belloc's daughters Madame Millet and Madame Redelsperger; the Baronesse de Channe; and Madame de Lamartine, the British-born artist (Marianne Elisa Brick) and wife of French poet and politician Alphonse de Lamartine.

99. Maria Weston Chapman to Elizabeth Pease, London, 24 May 1851, A.1.2.20.39, ASC. Toward the end of the Civil War, Mary Clarke Mohl wrote to Elizabeth Reid, the founder of Bedford College for Women in London, that "Mrs. Chapman one day declared if I were American I should work for the slaves. Now I hate slavery, but as to spending all my life about it, I could not," a not uncommon view from Paris during these years. See Lesser, *Clarkey*, 174.

100. Maria Weston Chapman to Mary A. Estlin, Boston, 20 January 1847, A.7.2.43, JBEP. The advertisement for the December 1846 fair emphasized that "a very great proportion of this unusually large collection of beautiful articles from all parts of the world, are such as cannot be elsewhere procured on this side of the Atlantic, and may properly be classed as works of genius and art." The items included drawings from Lady Byron and the Carpenter sisters, rare editions of Milton, silver jewel boxes, Scottish tartan shawls, Parisian writing materials, and De La Rue stationery, tapestries, bronzes, etc.

101. Sarah Houghton to Maria Weston Chapman, n.p., 30 March 1847, A.9.2.23.1, WP. For similar comments, see Jane Wigham to Maria Weston Chapman, Edinburgh, 4 January 1847, A.9.2.23.4; Lucy Browne to Maria Weston Chapman, Bridgewater, 14 April 1847, A.9.2.23.26; Mary Carpenter to Maria Weston Chapman, Bristol, 31 October 1847, A.9.2.23.58; Anna Carpenter to Maria Weston Chapman, Bristol, 2 November 1847, A.9.2.23.64; and Richard Allen to Maria Weston Chapman, Brooklawn, Ireland, 16 November 1847, A.9.2.23.75, WP. See also Jane Wigham to Maria Weston Chapman, Edinburgh, 16 November 1847, A.4.6A.3.1&2, ASC.

102. Mary A. Estlin to Maria Weston Chapman, Bristol, 18 October 1847, A.9.2.23.54, WP.

103. Maria Weston Chapman to Elizabeth Chapman Laugel, Boston, 1855, A.9.2.28.63, WP.

104. Maria Weston Chapman to Anne, Debora, Lucia, and Emma Weston, Paris, 14 November 1848, A.9.2.24.48, WP; Maria Weston Chapman to Elizabeth Pease, Paris, 25 December 1849, A.1.2.18.88, ASC. For calculation of contemporary equivalent purchasing power see, http://www.measuringworth.com/uscompare/relativevalue.php.

105. Maria Weston Chapman to Elizabeth Pease, Paris, 25 December 1849, A.1.2.18.88, ASC.

106. Such a computation of hands and bodies offered an easy rationale for coworkers to parcel their social and domestic time and labor as needed and to rely upon Weston numbers to do the necessary. Seeing their labor as a calling, the Westons demanded a great deal of themselves in terms of labor, competence, and execution, both as individuals and as a group. And they knew that numbers mattered in both the personal and political context. Thus Caroline couched her lamentation on Emma's absence from Paris in terms of her own guilt: "I think I hear you exclaim against the removal of any more abolitionists—I confess that it is very *hard*—I hope not very *wrong*, to subtract

even the smallest quantity from the value of American abolitionism" (Caroline Weston to Samuel J. May Jr, Paris, 2 December 1848, B.1.6.3.55, May Papers, BPL). May replied so as to increase expectations. He urged Anne not to "go over to the side of 'the foreign Westons'" and remain abroad. "It will be hard to break away from so many, that are all so near to your heart,—very hard to turn away and bid them goodbye. But whenever you do so, I am sure you will have the consolation and support of feeling how much there is for you to do in America, how much that nobody but you can do. We cannot willingly consent long to lose your immediate participation in the Anti-Slavery work" (Samuel J. May Jr. to Anne Warren Weston, Leicester, 2 November 1856, A.9.2.28.72, WP).

107. The latter information points to 1851 or 1853, when Debora left her New Bedford school and, with the additional help of Lucia and Anne, nursed Warren at his home in Staten Island. In 1851 Debora accompanied him to the Northampton Water Cure for eight months of treatments and nursing care. In 1853, Debora again went to New York in February to care for Warren and stayed for a couple of months. While Maria was living in France at the time, she returned to the United States several times for brief visits during these years.

108. Maria Weston Chapman to Mary A. Estlin, Paris, 12 December 1852, A.7.2.6, JBEP.

CHAPTER 7

1. Debora Weston to Caroline Weston, Weymouth, 21 October 1850, A.9.2.25.33, WP; Debora Weston to Maria Weston Chapman, n.p., [October 1850], A.9.2.6.47, WP. Debora wrote of the passage of the Fugitive Slave Bill and the pursuit of fugitive slaves that followed. The restive population of Boston witnessed significant conflict between slave hunters and abolitionists, erupting in civil unrest over the cases of Shadrack in February and Thomas Sims in April 1851, for example. The Boston Vigilance Committee opposed the work of slave hunters and the courts that supported these actions. Among those involved were Wendell Phillips and Hervey Weston.

2. Scholars of metaphor have suggested that individuals organize their social world into "domains of belonging" that are bridged by the use of metaphor. The mind furnishes one domain (that of politics, for example) with items, concerns, and tasks belonging to another (such as the household), enabling a play of mind between the two, each helping to make sense of the other. See Fernandez, *Persuasions and Performances*, ix, xii; and Lakoff and Johnson, *Metaphors We Live By*, 3.

3. Anne Warren Weston to Mary Weston, Concord, 5 June 1846, A.9.2.22.59, WP; Maria Weston Chapman to Mary A. Estlin, Paris, 11 November 1854, A.7.2.72, JBEP. See also Maria Weston Chapman to Wendell Phillips, Boston, 10 July 1846; Caroline Weston to Wendell and Ann Phillips, Interlaken [Switzerland], 2 September [1851], 1290, folio 7, Blagden Collection, HL; and Anne Warren Weston to Maria Weston Chapman, Weymouth, 25 February 1841, A.9.2.15.27, WP.

4. There has been considerable scholarly interest in mapping the geography of cities with a view to understanding how the emergence of public and semipublic spaces, such as the Chapman household, contributed to the growth of reform and supported the development of political subjectivity. See, for example, Debora Cherry's discussion

of the geographies of art and feminism in London's West End in the 1850s and 1860s in *Beyond the Frame*, 20–33, esp. Figure 1.2.

5. Anne Warren Weston, [Weymouth], 15 April 1836, A.9.2.8.19; Anne Warren Weston to Debora Weston, Boston, 8 April 1839, A.9.2.11.77; Anne Warren Weston to Henry G. Chapman and Maria Weston Chapman, Weymouth, 18 May 1841, A.9.2.15.47; Anne Warren Weston to Debora Weston, Weymouth, 1 April 1842, A.9.2.17.46; Emma Weston to Debora Weston, [Weymouth], n.d., A.9.2.16.4, WP; Anne Warren Weston to Elizabeth Pease, Weymouth, 14 October 1845, A.1.2.15.72, ASC; Anne Warren Weston to Ann T. G. Phillips, Weymouth, 26 July 1855, 1482, folio 2, Blagden Collection, HL.

6. It was not always possible to offer overnight accommodation. Anne had wanted to put up Sydney H. Gay during the MAS annual meeting but knew "we could not ask him to go to Weymouth as I rather thought I was going home to be sick as Lucia was in her chamber" (Anne Warren Weston to Debora Weston, Weymouth, 3 February 1953, A.9.2.27.9, WP).

7. Nevertheless they felt obliged to "stir" him up on those occasions when he manufactured an "obstacle" to the opening of their home to abolitionists. See Anne Warren Weston [to unknown recipient], n.p., 15 April 1836, A.9.2.8.19; and Anne Warren Weston to Debora Weston, Boston, 6 December 1836, A.9.2.8.65, WP.

8. Anne Warren Weston to Debora Weston, Weymouth, 1 April 1842, A.9.2.17.46; [Debora Weston] to Lucia Weston, Weymouth, 6 March 1851, A.9.2.25.69; Debora Weston to Anne Warren Weston, Weymouth, 15 April 1851, A.9.2.25.81, WP. Henry C. Wright (1797–1870) attended Andover Seminary from 1819 to 1823 and then married Elizabeth LeBreton Stickney, a well-to-do widow with four daughters, to whom Wright was quite attached. They lived in Newburyport, Massachusetts, where he wrote for the *Liberator*. He served as one of the original agents of the AAS but was fired in 1837 for his radical opinions. Among those were his ideas on family governance and nonresistance. Both would have confounded Warren Weston. Wright helped found the Non-Resistance Society in 1838, although in December 1859, he published the *Natick Resolutions*, which called upon abolitionists to arm slaves so as to aid them in resisting slavery. His critique of male power over the family and of married women's sexual rights in marriage earned him considerable public condemnation. His own affairs caused concern among such friends as the Weston sisters and the orthodox Quaker family of Elizabeth Pease, with whom he became quite close during an agency to Great Britain. See, for example, his journal entries of 25 May 1834, 29 November 1834, 12 August 1835, and 28 May 1847 in Henry Clarke Wright Papers, Am 514-15, HL. Warren Weston Sr. found neither his personality nor his manner congenial. While women enjoyed Wright, Capt. Weston would have found his manner more familiar and confiding than he was comfortable with among men.

9. Debora Weston to Lucia Weston, Weymouth, 6 March 1851, A.9.2.25.69, WP. Ann Bates Weston may have sympathized with abolition and with her daughters' political activism, although she was not herself an activist. Her name appeared on an early antislavery petition from "359 Ladies of Massachusetts." See Antislavery petitions, HR24A-H1.3, National Archives.

10. Anne Warren Weston to Debora Weston, Weymouth, 20 July 1838, 1 May 1839, A.9.2.11.93, WP.

11. Caroline Weston to Henry G. Chapman and Mary Weston Chapman, Roxbury, 29 January 1841, A.9.2.15.11–14, WP.

12. Francesco Foscari, elected doge in 1423, allied Venice with Florence and engaged in a series of ruinous wars against Milan and Bologna. He was brought down and his son Jacobo forced into exile by accusations of their involvement in the murder of the Venetian admiral Piero Loredan. Accused of treason and banished to Crete, Jacobo died before his father could clear his name. News of his son's death caused Francesco to withdraw from politics into a grief so debilitating that his peers pushed him into retirement in 1457. His death eight days later drew such a public outcry that city leaders were forced to give him a state funeral. The conjoined political fates, forced separation, and tragic deaths of father and son were celebrated in Byron's poem "The Two Foscari" (1821), Mary Russell Mitford's play *Foscari: A Tragedy* (1826), and Francesco Hayez's painting *The Parting of the Two Foscari* (1842).

13. Debora Weston to Anne Warren Weston, New Bedford, 1 February 1837, A.9.2.9.12, WP.

14. Edmund Quincy to Richard D. Webb, n.p., 3 October 1848, Quincy, Wendell, Holmes, and Upham Family Papers, MHS. See also ibid., Dedham, 1 February 1849. Lawrence Friedman notes the importance of the Chapman home to Garrisonian sociability in his discussion of the "Boston clique" as a pseudofamily with Garrison as its father. Friedman calls the Chapman home a place "warm and stimulating yet informal and unpretentious," where "Chapman and her sisters were usually at home to receive callers with a warm pot of tea." He acknowledges its role as an information center as well, where "one could always count on learning the latest news concerning Clique-sponsored antislavery ventures." Nevertheless, his view limits the household's function to the traditionally feminine roles of hospitality and conversation. See Friedman, *Gregarious Saints*, 55–57. Maria continued to rent in the city after Henry's death and that of his parents, who left the Chauncy Place house to Mary Chapman and Maria Weston Chapman in joint tenancy. Maria never lived there. When she returned from Paris in 1855, she went to Weymouth and lived with her mother, except for episodic visits to New York, where she rented domestic space to be near her son and grandchildren.

15. Petitioning was a household project. Antislavery women went door-to-door gathering signatures, a process that clustered signatures on the form according to household. Pressure among peers or family members, as well as shared values, encouraged all or many of those present to sign—or to resist signing.

16. It was not unusual for abolitionists to conduct business or hold meetings in private homes. Anne, for example, noted, "This morning, I called at Miss Parkers to call a [BFAS] Board meeting to see about giving Mr May his call to labour as our agent. We finally agreed to hold it tomorrow afternoon, after the Female prayer meeting at Miss Sullivans" (Anne Warren Weston to [Lucia Weston], n.p., 15 April 1836, A.9.2.8.19, WP). Other private homes also served such a role for groups and committees of BFAS women: those of Thankful Hussey Southwick, the Sargent sisters, and the Ball sisters, and the Parker sisters' boardinghouse at 5 Hayward Place. For references to such meetings, see, for example, Anne Warren Weston to Debora Weston, Boston, 19 October 1836, A.9.2.8.74, and 25 October 1837, A.9.2.9.83, WP; and Francis Jackson to the Westons, Boston, 6 January 1843, A.4.6A.1.72, ASC. In Weymouth, the household of the

Weston aunts functioned similarly to that of the Weston sisters. As Debora Bingham Van Broekhoven notes, antislavery women were more likely, certainly in the 1830s, to meet in their homes than in halls or churches. The imposition from 1834 of an informal ban on antislavery talk in the Quaker households of Providence, Rhode Island, by the Quaker Meeting therefore offered a barrier to the formation of female antislavery societies in the area. See Van Broekhoven, *Devotion of These Women*, 84.

17. [Debora Weston] to Caroline Weston, Weymouth, May 1846, A.9.2.22.41, WP.

18. Edmund Quincy to Maria Weston Chapman, Dedham, 16 December 1844, A.9.2.20.126, WP.

19. For example, Francis Jackson, as chairman of the *Liberator* Committee and seeking to expand the newspaper's circulation in the aftermath of the division among abolitionists, invited various Garrisonians to "a meeting to be held at my house No. 7 Hollis Street" (Francis Jackson to Maria Weston Chapman, Caroline Weston, Ann [*sic*] Weston, Deborah [*sic*] Weston, Boston, 6 January 1843, A.4.6A.1.72, ASC).

20. Anne Warren Weston to [Lucia or Emma Weston], n.p., 15 April 1836, A.9.2.8.19, WP. May's use of the term "ladies" was a reflexive courtesy. Born in 1797, May was a Unitarian clergyman and early supporter of Garrison and the abolitionist cause as a founding member of the NEAS in 1832 and the AAS in 1833. His family background commanded respect. The terms "ladies" and "women" were infused with political meaning in a context in which the public activism of women was widely condemned. This was a high-level gathering. Joseph Southwick, Samuel Sewall, Ellis Gray Loring, and Isaac Knapp were all founding members of the NEAS in 1832 or the AAS in 1833, members of the board of managers, and officers of one or another society for many years. Sewall, Loring, and Kimball were Boston Brahmins. Isaac Knapp and Drury Fairbanks, who had been with Garrison since the beginning, were businessmen—a printer and shoe seller. Follen was a Harvard professor. Lydia Maria Child was already well known in Boston for her antislavery writings. Louisa Loring and Eliza Follen would be active in the cause throughout their lives. Ange Ammidon married a Baptist minister, Rev. Joseph Parker, and broke from the Westons in 1839 because her husband and brother-in-law opposed women's public activism.

21. Anne Warren Weston to [Lucia or Emma Weston], n.p., 15 April 1836, A.9.2.8.19, WP.

22. Anne Warren Weston to Debora Weston, Boston, 8 March 1839, A.9.2.11.53, WP. They met at other houses as well, Thankful Southwick's, for example. See Anne Warren Weston to Lucia Weston, Boston, 21 September 1840, A.9.2.13.23–24, WP.

23. Anne Warren Weston to Lucia Weston, Boston, October 1840, A.9.2.6.33; Caroline Weston to Debora Weston, Roxbury, June 1841, A.9.2.3.77; Emma Forbes Weston to Debora Weston, [Weymouth], [1841], A.9.2.16.4; Lucia Weston to Debora Weston, Boston, 20 October 1839, A.9.2.11.9, WP.

24. Anne Warren Weston to Debora Weston, Boston, 15 September 1837, A.9.2.9.67, WP.

25. Theodore Weld (1803–95) left Lane Theological Seminary when the school forbade abolitionist debate and became an antislavery lecturer. He helped train the agents of the AAS and edited many of its publications and tracts. In 1838 he married Angelina Grimké, the first female agent of the AAS. William Goodell (1792–1878) began a general reform newspaper, the *Investigator and General Intelligencer*, in 1826. The journal

merged with Garrison's *National Philanthropist* and became the *Genius of Temperance* in 1830. Goodell helped found the AAS and its magazine, the *Emancipator*, in 1834. He left New York City for Utica in 1836 to edit the *Friend of Man*, an antislavery paper, until 1842. He left the AAS in 1840 to help found the Liberty Party and then, in 1847, the Liberty League.

26. Anne Warren Weston to Debora Weston, Boston, 15 September 1837, A.9.2.9.67, WP. The Reverend Charles Fitch became the first minister of the First Free Congregational Church, founded as an antislavery body when most churches in New England resisted what they saw as politicization of the slavery question. Fitch broke with Garrison in 1837 and condemned Henry and Maria Weston Chapman, the latter of whom took him to task for refusing to stand on the antislavery ground before a body of orthodox ministers whose approval was required to grant the institution membership in the Congregational denomination. While Fitch would later regret the violence of his condemnation of Garrison, he never apologized to Maria and continued to attack what he saw as the Chapmans' lack of courtesy.

27. Anne Warren Weston to Debora Weston, Boston, 23 March 1839; Anne Warren Weston to Debora Weston, Boston, 30 March 1839, A.9.2.11.71; Anne Warren Weston to Caroline and Debora Weston, [Boston], [April 1840], A.9.2.16.13, WP.

28. The Reverend James Boyle preached in Vermont. Although he became interested in the ideology of perfectionism advocated by John Humphrey Noyes, he did not follow him to Oneida, New York, or join Noyes's experiment in communal living and complex marriage. Boyle became the agent of the Ohio Anti-Slavery Society in 1839.

29. Maria Weston Chapman to Anne Warren Weston, n.p., [1843], A.9.2.4.14, WP. See also Anne Warren Weston, journal, Weymouth, 8 January 1845, A.9.3.21.3; and Anne Warren Weston to "misses Weston," Boston, 23 January 1845, A.9.2.121.7, WP.

30. Caroline Weston to Anne Warren Weston, Boston, [1839], A.9.2.4.53–54; Caroline Weston to Debora Weston, Boston, [1836], A.9.2.3.49, WP.

31. Lucia, for example, stopped in and saw Oliver Johnson and Edmund Quincy and asked if they had any news for her to dispense among family and friends. See Lucia Weston to Anne Warren Weston, Boston, [1839], A.9.2.11.11, WP.

32. Debora Weston to Anne Warren Weston, Boston, 10 June 1836, A.9.2.8.31; Caroline Weston to Anne Warren Weston, 21 June 1836, A.9.2.8.33, WP.

33. Anne Warren Weston to Debora Weston, Boston, 11 December 1839, A.9.2.12.114, WP. See also Anne Warren Weston to Mary Weston, Boston, 27 February 1839, A.9.2.11.48; Anne Warren Weston to Debora Weston, Boston, 1 January 1837, A.9.2.9.2; and Anne Warren Weston to Debora Weston, Boston, 22 October 1836, A.9.2.8.63, and 11 December 1839, A.9.2.12.114, WP. Stephen S. Foster (1809–81) graduated from Dartmouth College. A professional reformer, he committed his efforts to abolition and nonresistance. He married antislavery lecturer Abigail Kelley in 1845. Francis Jackson (1789–1861) was a wealthy Boston merchant who served for many years as president of the MAS and vice president of the AAS. His views supported female activism and woman's rights. His wife, Harriet, was a member of the BFAS. His daughter Eliza Jackson Merriam (1814–45) served as treasurer in 1841 after the "peeling" away of the proclerical members.

34. William Lloyd Garrison to Helen Benson Garrison, March 5, 1836, in Ruchames, *House Dividing*, 55; William L. Garrison to Helen Benson Garrison, April 18, 1836, in Garrison and Garrison, *William Lloyd Garrison*, 2:106; Caroline Weston to Anne Warren Weston, Boston, [1836], A.9.2.4.55; Caroline Weston to Debora Weston, Boston, [1836], A.9.2.3.49; Debora Weston to Anne Warren Weston, Boston, 10 June 1836, A.9.2.8.31; Lucia Weston to Debora Weston, Boston, 20 October 1839, A.9.2.11.9; Lucia Weston to Anne Warren Weston, Boston, [January 1839], A.9.2.11.10; Anne Warren Weston to Debora Weston, Boston, 30 March 1839, A.9.2.11.71; extract of letter from Anne Warren Weston to sisters, Weymouth, 4 December 1839, A.9.2.12.106, WP. Oliver Johnson (1809–89) printed the *Liberator*, was a founder of the NEAS in 1832, and served as an agent of the MAS in 1836. He worked for several newspapers including the *Ohio Anti-Slavery Bugle* and the *Pennsylvania Freeman*. In 1853 he became associate editor of the *National Anti-Slavery Standard*.

35. Edmund Quincy to Maria Weston Chapman, Dedham, 26 April 1840, A.9.2.13.57, WP.

36. Ibid.

37. Caroline Weston to Debora Weston, n.p., n.d., A.9.2.4.93, WP; Edmund Quincy journal, 26 September 1839, Quincy, Wendell, Holmes, and Upham Family Papers, MHS; Anne Warren Weston to Debora Weston, Boston, 1 January 1837, A.9.2.9.2; Lucia Weston to Debora Weston, Boston, 1834, A.9.2.3.18; Caroline Weston to Debora Weston, Boston, [1836], A.9.2.3.49; Caroline Weston diary, 19 and 20 September 1835, A.9.7.65–66, WP. They offered to have the invalid Ann T. G. Phillips stay with them in an effort to free Wendell for speaking on the road but were refused: "We are truly grateful for your mothers kind offer to receive Ann & our self-devoted offer of offering yourselves . . . 'as sacrifices' to aid my going to Philad[elphia]. But you have all the glory—just the same. It is impossible for me to go" (Wendell Phillips to Maria Weston Chapman, n.p., [1845], A.9.2.21.41, WP). See also Caroline Weston to Wendell and Ann Phillips, New Bedford, 1 March 1845, 1290, folio 3, Blagden Collection, HL.

38. Maria Weston Chapman to Henry G. Chapman, n.p., n.d., A.9.2.5.53, WP.

39. Edward M. Davis to Maria Weston Chapman, Philadelphia, 25 April 1845, A.9.2.21.21; Evelina A. S. Smith to Caroline Weston, Hingham, 3 July 1837, A.9.2.9.44, and 25 October 1840, A.9.2.14.44, WP.

40. Caroline Weston to Maria Weston Chapman, New Bedford, [December 1843], A.9.2.20.137, WP.

41. Caroline Weston to Lucia Weston, Boston, [December 1840], A.9.2.6.20, WP.

42. Evelina A. S. Smith to Caroline Weston, Hingham, 3 July 1837, Dorchester, 8 December 1844, A.9.2.9.44, WP.

43. *Liberator*, 11 June 1836. Among the better-known writers of the day were Lydia Maria Child, Elizabeth Cabot Follen, Harriet Martineau, Felicia Hemans, and A[nna] L[etitia] Barbauld.

44. Debora Weston to Anne Warren Weston, New Bedford, 23 June 1839, A.9.2.11.122, WP.

45. Debora Weston to Maria Weston Chapman, New Bedford, 28 April 1839, A.9.2.3.60, WP.

46. Thereafter, Anne constructed the magazine in Weymouth. See Lucia Weston to Debora Weston, Boston, 20 October 1839, A.9.2.11.9; and Maria Weston Chapman to Debora Weston, Boston, 6 December 1839, A.9.2.12.108, WP. Fifteen volumes were published beginning in 1839; only in 1850, 1855, and 1857 was Anne unable to complete the task. Although there is a seeming gap between 1839 and 1841, this is an accident of timing. The Westons called the first *Liberty Bell*, "the 'Bell' of 1839 & 40" because it commemorated the fair of 1839 but was actually published in the new year. Thereafter, they dated the *Bell* in the year of printing rather than the year of the associated fair; hence, the second *Bell* was 1841. See Caroline Weston to Samuel J. May, Weymouth, 24 October 1871, May Papers, BPL. For discussion of its production and place in antislavery literature, see Thompson, "*Liberty Bell.*"

47. See Frances Drake's report of the value placed on copies of the *Bell* and the competition for them that emerged: Frances H. Drake to Maria W. Chapman, Leominster, 18 January 1846, A.9.2.22.8, WP.

48. For discussion of the role of such albums among African American women, see Armstrong, "Mental and Moral Feast."

49. Maria Weston Chapman to Wendell and Anne T. G. Phillips, 21 April 1840, Blagden Collection, HL.

50. Anne's piece was sent as a letter to "the Female Anti-Slavery Societies," at the bidding of the BFAS managing board. She assured her readers that "though the love of some of those who have been hither to esteemed as the firm supporters of the A. S. cause, seems to be waning cold, & though some who have put their hands to the plough seem to be looking back, and though the hearts of many appear failing them for fear, yet it is not so with us." She insisted that "the inconsistency, the fear & the timidity of others only supplies to us a new & urgent motive for labouring with ten fold zeal & devotedness." See Anne Warren Weston to the Female Anti-Slavery Society, Boston, 21 August 1837, A.9.2.9.62; and Anne Warren Weston to Debora Weston, Boston, 3 September 1837, A.9.2.3.69, WP.

51. Anne Warren Weston to Debora Weston, Boston, 8 March 1839, A.9.2.11.53; Anne Warren Weston to Debora Weston, Boston, 18 April 1837, A.9.2.9.28, WP.

52. The scope of correspondents and their subjects is striking. See, for example, a letter from a Mary F. Manter, who wrote: "Will you please excuse me for writing so often, the short visit I spent at your house had endeared you and your family to me and will not soon be forgotten by me your unworthy friend, I often think of you and your sisters it seemed to me that peace and love pervaded in your dear family, I felt so sick I did not enjoy myself as I otherwise should, but yet it was so pleasant being at your house that I cannot forbear to express my feelings though very imperfectly, I am quite poor as to the things of this world and undeserving of your notice yet I beg to have the privilege of being one of your friends though the least and hearing from you some times" (Mary F. Manter to Maria Weston Chapman, Walpole, 20 September 1840, A.9.2.14.89, WP).

53. Some of the letters were passed along: "Shoals of letters awaited us from England, which I send you herewith, & they will by their voluminousness, take up your idle time" (Maria Weston Chapman to Debora Weston, Boston, 22 April [1839], A.9.2.5.8, WP).

54. Anne Warren Weston to Debora Weston, Boston, 8 March 1839, A.9.2.11.53, WP.

55. Caroline Weston to Debora Weston, Boston, [1836], A.9.2.3.28, WP. See also Anne Warren Weston to Debora Weston, Boston, 15 December 1839, A.9.2.12.118, WP.

56. Harriet Miller to Maria Weston Chapman, Milton, 21 September 1840, A.9.2.14.22; S. Lincoln Gardner to Maria Weston Chapman, n.p., 23 September 1840, A.9.2.14.26, WP. For similar responses, see Experience Billings to Maria Weston Chapman, Foxborough, 31 August 1840, A.9.2.14.12; Lucy Daniels to Maria Weston Chapman, Ipswich, 24 September 1840, A.9.2.14.28, WP; Sarah M. Rhoads to Maria Weston Chapman, North Attleboro, 11 October 1840, A.4.6A.1.58; Lucia A. Bradford to Maria Weston Chapman, Duxbury, 12 October 1840, A.4.6A.1.59, ASC; and Harriet Pierce to Maria Weston Chapman, Lexington, 27 October 1840, A.9.2.14.45; Jerusha L. Bird to Maria Weston Chapman, Taunton, 1 November 1840, A.9.2.14.51, WP.

57. Indeed one wonders whether the appointment of Henry G. Chapman as MAS treasurer had not something to do with the Weston sisters' role in organizing and developing the BFAS fair into the primary financial support for the organization and its agents. Some historians have identified the first Boston antislavery fair as occurring in the Chapman home in 1835; however, Maria deferred to Lydia Maria Child and Louisa Loring, who had held a small sale of useful items a year earlier. See Pease and Pease, *Bound with Them in Chains*, 44; and *Liberator*, 25 January 1856 and 22 November 1834. In writing the history of the fair, Maria claimed $300 as the proceeds of the Child fair and $600 for that held in her home the following year. Receipts grew over the years. By 1854 the fair was bringing in $5,011 gross, or roughly $141,000 in the equivalent of 2012 purchasing power. See http://www.measuringworth.com /uscompare/relativevalue.php.

58. Lucia Weston to Debora Weston, Boston, 18 December 1836, A.9.2.8.89; Debora Weston to Caroline Weston, Weymouth, May 1846, A.9.2.22.41, WP. This too was usual practice among female antislavery society members. For the practice in New Bedford, see Caroline Weston, who commented on attending two meetings of the local women's antislavery sewing circle a week at the home of one or another member: Caroline Weston to Wendell and Anne T. G. Phillips, New Bedford, 13 November 1843, Blagden Collection, HL. For discussion of such a Weymouth meeting at the home of Mrs. Hanson, see Anne Warren Weston to Debora Weston, Weymouth, 1 April 1842, A.9.2.17.46, WP.

59. Caroline Weston to Anne Warren Weston, [Boston], [1836], A.9.2.4.55; Lucia Weston to Debora Weston, Boston, 15 September 1839, A.9.2.12, WP. Emma would also be "made instrumental in working for the Mass[achusetts] Fair this summer at Roxbury," under Caroline's supervision. See Emma Weston to Debora Weston, Weymouth, 18 April 1839, A.9.2.11.86, WP. See also Sarah R. May to Debora Weston, Leicester, 10 October 1848, A.9.2.24.36, WP.

60. Anne Warren Weston to Mary A. Estlin, Weymouth, 23 February [1853], A.7.2.22, 14 January 1851, A.7.2.8, JBEP. In 1855, Anne stayed with Mrs. Charles Hovey in Boston during the fair, then with Eliza Follen during the MAS annual meeting that followed. She suggested that the fair be moved from Boston to Philadelphia for ease and consistency of administration, an idea that Maria vetoed because she believed Philadelphia could not sustain the income produced in Boston. See Anne Warren Weston to

Mary A. Estlin, Weymouth, 21 January 1855, A.7.2.26, JBEP. Maria gave up her town house in 1847 and many worried that that would mean the end of the fair "as there will be no place in the whole City to store the Foreign goods, or domestic either I suppose" (Evelina A. S. Smith to Caroline Weston, Dorchester, 26 September 1847, A.9.2.23.44, WP). They found a carriage house to serve.

61. Anne Warren Weston to Mary A. Estlin, Weymouth, 21 January 1855, A.7.2.26, JBEP.

62. Anne Warren Weston to Samuel J. May Jr., n.p., n.d., B.1.6.13.1, May Papers, BPL; Anne Warren Weston to Caroline Weston, Boston, 1 January 1849, A.9.2.24.57, WP; Anne Warren Weston to John B. Estlin, Weymouth, 27 October 1850, A.7.2.26, JBEP.

63. Debora Weston to Ann Phillips, Weymouth, 8 September 1856, 1484, folio 2, Blagden Collection, HL. The "ghouls" were characters of Muslim folklore. This reference to desert spirits who assumed the shape of animals and fed on corpses may have come from Weston reading of the travelogue written by J[ames] A[ugustus] St. John, *Egypt and Nubia* (London: Chapman and Hall, 1845).

64. *Liberator*, 20 January 1854. Among the noble sacrifices of which she spoke were the deaths of beloved coworkers during the previous year, including those of her aunt Priscilla Weston and her dear friend Catherine Sargent.

65. Abby Kelley Foster to Anne Warren Weston, New York, 15 June [1850], A.9.2.29.15; [Sarah Otis Ernst] to Anne Warren Weston, Spring Garden, Ohio, 28 July 1850, A.9.2.25.16, WP. A Garrisonian in Cincinnati, Ohio, where Garrison was viewed as "disreputable," Ernst objected to innovations that would make her project of expanding "true" abolition there more difficult. A Boston friend of Anne Warren Weston, she married Andrew H. Ernst, a widower with six children, and relocated with him to Ohio in 1841. She helped organize and lead the Cincinnati Anti-Slavery Sewing Circle, organized in 1846 to aid the fugitive slaves who passed through Ohio to Canada, a group that, in 1849, undertook production of an annual fair. The earnings from this fair were used to support an annual conference that Frederick Douglass called "the most influential Anti-Slavery conventions ever held in the United States." Ernst occupied a position on the business committee for the convention, unusual for a woman in an area with a Garrisonian minority. In discussing women's antislavery fairs in the Western Reserve, Stacey M. Robertson has written, "A minority in the Old Northwest, Garrisonian abolitionists used traditional avenues, including sewing societies and fairs, to push their radical agenda in a region otherwise dominated by political and church abolitionists" (Robertson, *Hearts Beating for Liberty*, 90). For a discussion of the relationships between these women and the Westons and their role in building community among abolitionists, see Robertson, *Hearts Beating for Liberty*, 91–126.

66. This can be seen in the fair correspondence, where advice was given as to what sold well and what should, therefore, be contributed the following year, and in the fair reports, where table-by-table descriptions of best sellers were sometimes provided. See, as examples, Anne W. Weston to Mary A. Estlin, Weymouth, 14 January 1851, A.7.2.8, JBEP; and the fair report published in the *Liberator* of 25 January 1850.

67. *Liberator*, 30 January 1857, 12 February 1858.

68. Maria Weston Chapman to Elizabeth Pease Nichol, Weymouth, 25 January 1860 [misdated 1858], A.1.2.30.5, ASC.

69. Carolyn J. Lawes, in her study of Worcester, Massachusetts, discusses the movement in the 1850s among local sewing circles such as the large Center Mission Sewing Circle toward sewing for the fugitive, an object that met general concerns about the wrong of slavery without involving women in too close an association with the MAS or the Boston fair, as did the small Worcester Anti-Slavery Sewing Circle. See Lawes, *Women and Reform*, 72–76.

70. *Liberator*, 30 January 1857.

71. *Liberator*, 26 January 1855.

72. Increasingly, the Rochester, New York, fair that sustained Frederick Douglass's newspaper the *North Star* competed for British donations. Maria blamed the influence of Englishwoman Julia Griffiths on Douglass: "I know how difficult it has been to [the European friends of the fair] for years, to keep up their contributions. I knew that in some places they had greatly assumed, owing to 'fowls' like Julia Griffiths coming where there was no depth of earth, and scratching and destroying where we had planted— (such never seek new grounds, but follow the same)" (Maria Weston Chapman to Elizabeth Pease Nichol, Weymouth, 20 September 1858, A.9.2.29.133, WP). "Fowls [fouls] like Julia Griffiths" was a play on words; the Westons, who had an affection for Ann Douglass, Frederick's wife, disapproved of Griffith's behavior with Douglass. For a discussion of Douglass's relationships with women other than his wife, see Diedrich, *Love Across Color Lines*.

73. "I knew that all our French contributions—i.e. all our protestant ones," she wrote, "would never again be sent and *they* were a quarter of the whole for with the last they complained of *Mrs Stowe* as a heretic and told me they were about to send a pastor to collect for their new church on the Boulevard Sebastopol." Given such a worthy local cause as a building fund, and given their theological quibbles with America's most famous abolitionist, she admitted, "I could not but know the consequences" (*Liberator*, 26 January 1855).

74. Maria Weston Chapman to Mary A. Estlin, Weymouth, January 1858, 24.12.23.131, Estlin Papers, Dr. Williams's Library; Maria Weston Chapman to Mary A. Estlin, Weymouth, 8 March 1858, A.7.2.78, JBEP.

75. Nor, it should be said, without the full complement of sisters. By 1855, Lucia and Emma lived in Europe. In addition, Caroline and Anne made periodic visits, some lasting several months, to join Lucia and Emma in Italy or visit their niece, Elizabeth Chapman Laugel, in Paris.

76. Debora Weston to Anne Warren Weston, New Bedford, 26 April 1839, A.9.2.89, WP.

77. Anne Warren Weston to Samuel May Jr., Rome, 29 April 1857, B.1.6.6.56, May Papers, BPL.

78. Debora Weston to Maria Weston Chapman, New Bedford, 13 April 1837, A.9.2.9.27; Debora Weston to Anne Warren Weston, New Bedford, 15 January 1836, A.9.2.8.6, WP.

79. Debora Weston to Mary Weston, New Bedford, 5 January 1840, A.9.2.13.5, WP. See also Debora Weston to Caroline Weston, New Bedford, 2 January 1840, A.9.2.13.3, WP.

CHAPTER 8

1. Bold indeed. Anne knew that "Judge Weston & his wife of Augusta, Maine, have been excommunicated from the church, for letting a sewing circle dance at their house. They behaved worthy the name, & the Judge talked to the church Weston fashion." The judge was no relation but, as Anne said, "The name is destined to ecclesiastical proscription" (Anne Warren Weston to Debora Weston, Boston, 29 March 1841, A.9.2.15.22, WP).

2. Anne Warren Weston to Wendell Phillips, Weymouth, 28 October [1852], Am 1953, 1289, folio 8, Blagden Collection, HL. The society actually made $180 at its fair, $5 more than the previous year and well above Anne's projection. See Anne Warren Weston to Wendell Phillips, Weymouth, 22 November 1852, 1289, folio 4, Blagden Collection, HL. For additional instances of the appellation "household of faith" as used by the Westons or applied to them, see Edmund Quincy to Caroline Weston, Dedham, 6 November 1843, A.9.2.19.73, WP; Anne Warren Weston to Wendell Phillips, Weymouth, 1 December 1850, 1289, folio 2, Blagden Collection, HL; and Maria Weston Chapman to "the saints that be in Paris first, & afterwards saints that be in Rome," Weymouth, 30 December 1855, A.9.2.6.80, WP.

3. All the sisters had an impish wit. Caroline told a story about two "elite" women who called at Maria's in Boston to get subscriptions for the Sailor's Boardinghouse. Lucia recognized one of them as having "almost turned her out of the house" while petitioning against slavery, so Caroline donned a sympathetic demeanor and "politely assured her of my extreme interest in the matter & commiserated their sufferings in the good work they had undertaken—congratulated them on the general interest felt—& told them that it had been my duty to present to the community claims of a more unpopular nature—& you can't conceive says I how that adds to the fatigue & embarrassment of duties like those you have undertaken—wasn't it good?" (Caroline Weston to Debora Weston, Boston, 3 March 1837, A.9.2.9.15, WP).

4. Garrison and Garrison, *William Lloyd Garrison*, 2:137–38.

5. Debora Weston to Anne Warren Weston, New Bedford, 15 January 1836, A.9.2.9.15, WP. For another of Anne's sallies against Perkins, see Anne Warren Weston to Ann Phillips, Weymouth, 26 July 1855, 1482, folio 2, Blagden Collection, HL.

6. Mary Weston to Debora Weston, Weymouth, 24 October 1836, A.9.2.8.65, WP.

7. For the sobriquet, see Maria Weston Chapman to Caroline Weston, Boston, [1839], A.9.2.5.11, WP. The context was Maria's refusal to allow Perkins to speak at her grandmother's funeral.

8. Reverend Perkins was born in Bridgewater in 1790, as was his wife Rhoda Keith Perkins; he died in East Braintree in 1874.

9. [Mary Weston] to Bella [Debora] Weston, Weymouth, 17 September 1837, A.9.2.3.71, WP.

10. Perkins continued to provoke the Westons and attack the Weymouth and Braintree Female Anti-Slavery Society in an effort to shape local discourse. For example, in 1842, Anne told Debora, "Sunday Weymouth was again convulsed by Mr Perkins' iniquity. Lunsford Lane was coming & Cyrus Burleigh with him & E. Richards went for Mr Perkins' meeting house. Mr P. declined—'Why' said Elias Mr P. disapproved of

Burleigh's sentiments—would not let him into his pulpit." A slave in Raleigh, North Carolina, Lunsford Lane (1803–63), arranged for his wife's owner, Benjamin B. Smith, to purchase his freedom with money he had earned selling tobacco. Lane left the state but returned to purchase his wife and child. They lived in Raleigh until 1840, when he was expelled for violating a law prohibiting free blacks from entering the state. Although a mob tarred and feathered him, he managed to escape north with his mother, wife, and child. He spoke to abolitionist groups as a means of raising funds. Perkins agreed to tell Lundsford's story to his congregation and accepted $23 in donations from his parishioners. When Lundsford and Burleigh held their evening meeting at the Universalist Church, most of Perkins's congregation was there: "The house was thronged to suffocation, benches in all the aisles." Anne hoped that Perkins, "whose great meeting house was standing so quietly unoccupied while the church & congregation were nearly smothered in the Universalist," would be ousted for his petty grandstanding and obstructionism. See Anne Warren Weston to Debora Weston, Boston, 25 January 1842, WP; and Alice R. Cotton, "Biography of Lunsford Lane," in Powell, *Dictionary of North Carolina Biography*, 14. Charles Calistus Burleigh (1810–78) studied law but did not practice. He worked as an antislavery agent, lecturer, writer, and editor for the *Genius of Temperance*, the *Union*, and the *Pennsylvania Freeman*.

11. Wales Lewis was born in Bristol, Maine, in 1798 and died at Pittston, Maine, in 1869. His first wife died in Weymouth in 1846 at the age of twenty-seven, and he married Lucy Pratt (1812–91) of Weymouth that December. He served Weymouth's Second Parish from 1838 to 1847.

12. Debora Weston to Mary Weston, n.p., 23 February 1835, A.9.2.7.58, WP.

13. Mary Weston to Debora Weston, Weymouth, 19 July 1836, A.9.2.4.94, WP.

14. Emma Forbes Weston to Caroline Weston, Boston, n.d., A.9.2.5.7, WP.

15. Such announcements routinely included lectures, sermons, concerts, and meetings of church committees and missionary or benevolent societies. See Altschuler and Saltzgaber, *Revivalism*, for the case of a woman excommunicated by the First Presbyterian Church of Seneca Falls in 1843 on charges of "unchristian and unladylike" behavior when she challenged the authority and integrity of a minister who refused to read an announcement of Abby Kelley's forthcoming antislavery lecture.

16. Caroline demonstrated the breadth of a Sunday's efforts to give notice: "[I] went in the morning to Mr Pierpont's . . . got Mr Jackson to carry a notice of the meeting of the Boston Female Anti-Slavery Society . . . in the afternoon went over to Bowdoin Street . . . our notice was not read—though there were many others—Henry Ware read it through—at Mr Gannetts—but neither messrs Adams or Riley—noticed it at all" (Caroline Weston diary, 11 October 1835, A.9.2.7.65–66, WP). The battle of the notices may be followed in Weston correspondence. See, for example, Debora Weston to Anne Warren Weston, n.p., 10 June 1836, A.9.2.8.31; Anne Warren Weston to Mary Weston, n.p., 27 October 1835, A.9.2.7.71; Debora Weston to Anne Warren Weston, Boston, 6 June 1836, A.9.2.8.4; Caroline Weston to Anne Warren Weston, n.p., 21 June 1836, A.9.2.8.33; and Anne Warren Weston to Debora Weston, Groton, 17 March 1837, A.9.2.9.16, WP.

17. Caroline Weston to Anne Warren Weston, Boston, [1839], A.9.2.4.53–54, WP.

18. Ibid. Samuel E. Sewall (1799–1888) was a Boston attorney and Garrisonian. He served a term in the Massachusetts Senate as a Free-Soiler and developed a reputation for defending fugitive slaves and woman's rights. He belonged to Channing's Federal Street church.

19. Caroline Weston to Anne Warren Weston, Boston, [1839], A.9.2.4.53–54; Caroline Weston to Anne Warren Weston, Boston, [1836], A.9.2.4.55; Debora Weston to Mrs. Warren Weston, Boston, 5 June 1836, A.9.2.8.30; Debora Weston to Anne Warren Weston, Boston, 6 June 1836, A.9.2.8.4, WP. Maria was not named by the newspaper; however, such reticence would decline over time and Maria's name would become a household word.

20. George Bradburn to Maria Weston Chapman, Green Plain, Ohio, 31 August 1843, A.9.2.19.25, WP.

21. See, for example, David L. Child to Maria Weston Chapman, Washington, D.C., 11 January 1843, A.5.1.32; New York, 4 September 1843, A.4.1.81; Washington, D.C., 18 April 1844, A.4.2.3–4; Maria Weston Chapman to David L. Child, Weymouth, 2 September 1843, A.4.1.79, ASC.

22. Frederick Douglass to Maria Weston Chapman, Kilmarnock, Scotland, 29 March 1846, A.9.2.22.35a, WP.

23. Edmund Quincy to Caroline Weston, Dedham, 16 February 1846, A.9.2.8.30, WP. Given the number of times the board charged their "sister" with disciplining an agent, one wonders less at her impertinence than at their cowardliness.

24. Calvin Allen to Maria Weston Chapman, Roxbury, 5 January 1840, A.9.2.13.6, WP. Maria termed it "abuse" in a notation on the back of the letter.

25. [Unknown] to Caroline Weston, New Bedford, 3 November 1835, A.9.2.7.75, WP.

26. *True History*, 41. Evidence of Maria's prominent public profile may be seen in the idiosyncratic work of Thomas V. L. Wilson, who crafted and published a list of the wealthiest men in Boston. He described Henry Chapman in terms of his relationship to his daughter-in-law and her well-known political views: "CHAPMAN, HENRY. A retired ship-chandler. Late Chapman and Wainwright. Chapman married a Green [*sic*], and is father-in-law of Maria Chapman, the abolitionist" (Wilson, *Aristocracy of Boston*, 11).

27. The issue arose frequently during Weston petitioning. Unwed women entering the homes of married women were attacked for using abolition to seek husbands. In Hayward Place, Boston, Anne acquired ten names but "was told by a Mrs. Bailey that she hoped that all the young Ladies who interested themselves in this matter would get what she supposed they were after namely nigger husbands" (Anne Warren Weston to Debora Weston, Boston, 19 November 1836, A.9.2.8.73, WP). To some Bostonians, the two deviancies of singlehood and abolition suggested a potential third—transgressing the color line (as no white man would marry an unruly abolitionist, the Westons had no option but to seek husbands outside their race).

28. See Shammas, *History of Household Government*, for a discussion of the legal challenges to men as heads of household. Daniel Scott Smith ("Meanings of Family and Household") concurs that heads of household had more responsibilities and obligations than rights in this transitional period. See also Grossberg, *Governing the Hearth*. Massachusetts gave married women the right to hold property in their own names in 1845

and in 1855 enacted a more substantial law providing for their sole ownership of both real and personal property.

29. For a recent discussion of how these issues influenced partisan politics and party platforms in the 1840s and 1850s, see Pierson, *Free Hearts*.

30. *Liberator*, 4 August 1837. Nancy Isenberg has written that men viewed abolitionist women as meeting the normative gendered expectations of bourgeois publicity because, as Rep. John Adams saw it, their petitioning required male mediation—"a male representative presented the petitions and interpreted their meaning." Thus the petitioning of abolitionist women for an end to slavery was a sympathetic act, not a political one. Women's influence was contained by social circles. "Rather than restrict women to the home or family, the democratic variation of the bourgeois public sphere rationalized gender inequality [in the civic and legislative arenas] by making sure women were seen first as social rather than political beings." Yet many stories of female petitioning suggest that male heads of household viewed it as a potential challenge to male governance in the household, and thus a step down a slippery slope toward female rule at home and in the civic arena. See Isenberg, *Sex and Citizenship*, 59–69; quotation on p. 66.

31. *Liberator*, 4 August 1837. For discussions of antislavery petitioning, see Zaeske, *Signatures of Citizenship*, and Portnoy, *Their Right to Speak*, 81–86.

32. Debora Weston to Anne Warren Weston, Boston, [1836], A.9.2.8.4, WP.

33. Feminist theorists remind us that patriarchy has two parts, that of the fathers over sons and that of men over women. While the American Revolution overturned the rule of the king (the symbolic father), it left in place that of men over women and brothers over sisters. Feminist theorists interpret republics as fundamentally misogynist; republicanism based public participation on gendered forms of independence and dependence, in which the supposed dependency of women in family and household defined their relationship to the state through the father, husband, brother, master, and head of household. See Pateman, *Sexual Contract, Disorder of Women*, and *Fraternal Social Contract*; MacCannell, *Regime of the Brother*; and Matthes, *Rape of Lucretia*. For historical studies, see McCurry, "Two Faces of Republicanism"; Bloch, "Gendered Meanings"; Gundersen, "Independence"; and Fliegelman, *Prodigals and Pilgrims*. New work on childbearing by Susan Klepp and schooling by Mary Kelley offers a more nuanced view of increased female volition under republican rule. Women also increasingly challenged legal dependency during the second quarter of the nineteenth century in terms of married women's property rights, their rights to their children and to divorce, and their desire for the suffrage. Among other recent works, see Isenberg, *Sex and Citizenship*; Anderson, *Joyous Greetings*; Ginzberg, *Untidy Origins*; Kelley, *Learning to Stand and Speak*; and Klepp, *Revolutionary Conceptions*.

34. A. Brooke to Maria Weston Chapman, Ohio, 5 October 1843, A.9.2.19.46; Debora Weston to Anne Warren Weston, n.p., 16 April [1839], A.9.2.3.59, WP. During the 1838 National Anti-Slavery Women's Convention in New York City, the *New York Commercial Advertiser* editorialized on the routing of the delegates: "We are glad that the meeting was prevented by peaceable means. The females who so far forget the province of their sex, as to perambulate the country, and assemble for such purposes, should be gently restrained from their convocations, and sent to the best insane hospitals to be

found. Meantime the husbands and parents of these modern Amazons, should be arrayed in caps and aprons, and installed in their respective kitchens" (*Liberator*, 25 May 1838). The executive committee of the Massachusetts Abolition Society confirmed this linkage of Chapman with Garrison, charging them with being the "two leading minds" of the conspiracy against the movement. See *True History*, 18.

35. Roper and Tosh (*Manful Assertions*, 8) have made the case "for seeing masculine and feminine identities not as distinct and separate constructs, but as parts of a political field whose relations are characterized by domination, subordination, collusion and resistance." So too women's historians have shown that women and men did not compete for or share power in American society or any of its institutions as equals but rather came together as "heirs of a system of dominance and subordination based upon gender," a system first taught in the family. See Boydston, Kelley, and Margolis, *Limits of Sisterhood*, 6.

36. See, for example, [Debora Weston] to Caroline Weston, Weymouth, May 1846, A.9.2.22.41, WP.

37. Journal of Anne Warren Weston, 9 January 1845, A.9.2.21.3, WP.

38. Lucia Weston to Debora Weston, Weymouth, January 1842, A.9.2.17.13; Lucia Weston to Anne Warren Weston, Weymouth, 7 January 1842, A.9.2.17.18; Anne Warren Weston to Caroline Weston and Debora Weston, Boston, 10 November 1843, A.9.2.10.68, WP.

39. Maria Weston Chapman to Joshua Bates, Boston, 29 March 1837, HC 5.1.17, BA.

40. Maria Weston Chapman to Caroline Weston, n.p., [summer 1845], A.9.2.6.31, WP; Maria Weston Chapman to Sidney Gay, November 1845, Gay Papers, Rare Book and Manuscript Library; Maria Weston Chapman to Debora Weston, Boston, n.d., A.9.2.16.60; Maria Weston Chapman to Debora Weston, Boston, 14 March 1839, A.9.2.11.58, WP.

41. Caroline Weston to Maria Weston Chapman and Henry Chapman, n.p., [1839], A.9.2.6.70; Caroline Weston to Anne Warren Weston, Boston, [1839], A.9.2.4.53–54, WP; Caroline Weston to Wendell and Ann Phillips, [New Bedford], n.d., Blagden Collection, HL.

42. Like her sisters Maria and Caroline, Anne also had a combative streak. See Anne Warren Weston to Caroline Weston and Debora Weston, n.p., [April 1840], A.9.2.16.13, WP; Anne Warren Weston to Elizabeth Pease, Weymouth, 25 August 1841, A.1.21.12.1.104, ASC; Anne Warren Weston to Wendell and Ann Phillips, Weymouth, 1 June 1851, 1289, folio 3, Blagden Collection, HL; Anne Warren Weston to Elizabeth Pease, Boston, 30 January 1845, A.1.15.11, ASC; and Anne Warren Weston to Debora Weston, n.p., 30 January 1837, A.9.2.9.9, WP.

43. Maria Weston Chapman to Elizabeth Pease Nichol, Weymouth, 20 September 1858, A.1.2.28.133, ASC. Mathews preached in black churches, for which he was mobbed and almost drowned in Kentucky in 1851. He served as secretary of the Christian Anti-Slavery Convention. Garrisonians did not support evangelical efforts in the South, believing them fruitless in changing white behavior and potentially damaging to slaves, who might find in religion an acceptance of bondage that would undermine their potential for resistance. See Harrold, *Abolitionists and the South*, 98–103. Rev. John Scoble (1810–68) was appointed secretary of the British and Foreign Anti-Slavery

Society in 1842 and edited the *Anti-Slavery Reporter*. He emigrated to Canada in 1852 to work for the British and American Institute of Science, before returning to England in 1867.

44. Maria's attacks on Douglass's character, for example, were vicious. See Chapter 6.

45. Maria in particular attacked the antislavery field for this. In speaking of Louis A. Chamerovzow, new leader of the British and Foreign Anti-Slavery Society, she wrote: "He sees & knows what is right & loves it too perhaps,—feebly; of course would be happy indeed to be on the right side if he could afford it" (Maria Weston Chapman to Mary A. Estlin, 26 December 1853, A.7.2.67, JBEP). See her similar expressions with regard to the Reverend Samuel Ringgold Ward: "That individual looks upon the cause just as Mr Hemming does—solely with regard to its capacity for paying salaries. It is just as difficult for a black man to be an abolitionist as for a white one" (Maria Weston Chapman to Mary A. Estlin, 28 December 1854, A.7.2.74, JBEP). Ward had served as an agent of the AAS in 1839 but upon the influence of Lewis Tappan transferred to the New York Anti-Slavery Society in 1840 and served as an agent there until 1851, when, after aiding a fugitive slave, he fled to Canada. In 1853 he traveled to England, where, in 1855, he published his *Autobiography of a Fugitive Negro*.

46. Richard D. Webb to Maria Weston Chapman, Brooklawn, 8 July 1849, A.9.2.24.82, WP.

47. Debora Weston to Maria Weston Chapman, New Bedford, 7 May 1839, A.9.2.11.99, WP.

48. Anne Warren Weston to Debora Weston, Boston, 27 July [1837], A.9.2.3.40, WP. See the short biography of Knapp in Ruchames, *House Dividing*, xxvi.

49. Maria Weston Chapman to David L. Child, n.p., [December 1843], A.4.1.111, ASC.

50. Many, both friends of the cause and opponents of abolition, critiqued Maria, as well as her sisters. Lydia Maria Child urged Caroline Weston to take care in the handling of "new organizationists": "I am convinced that every move Garrison can make against the *Abolitionist* reacts against the Liberator. Friends at a distance *will* not believe that such men as Stanton and Phelps are plotters against the cause and if you prove their narrow sectarianism, nothing is gained, at least for the present; for this seems a virtue in their eyes" (Lydia Maria Child to Caroline Weston, Northampton, 7 March 1839, A.5.1.46–47, Child Papers, ASC).

51. "Rhadamanthine," meaning vigorously strict, referred to the Greek judge of the underworld. See Anne Whitney to Maria Weston Chapman, October 1880, Whitney Collection, Wellesley College Library. For some of the many expressions of Chapman's autocratic side, see Maria's "I am driving business I assure you," in Maria Weston Chapman to Debora Weston, Boston, 18 April 1839, A.9.2.11.83, WP; and Maria Weston Chapman to Mary Anne Estlin, Boston, 4 February 1857, A.1.2.27.4, JBEP. For responses, see, for example, Eliza Wigham to Samuel May, Dublin, 16 May 1858, B.1.6.6.93; Samuel J. May Jr. to Richard Dana Webb, Leicester, 6 June 1858, B.1.6.7.1, May Papers, BPL; Lydia Maria Child to Maria Weston Chapman, New York, 11 May 1842, A.5.1.28; Lydia Maria Child to Maria Weston Chapman, n.d. [June 1842], A.5.1.33, Child Papers, BPL; and James S. Gibbons to Caroline Weston, New York,

21 May 1842, A.9.2.17.63; George Bradburn to Maria Weston Chapman, Green Plain, Ohio, 31 August 1843, A.9.2.19.25, WP. For witty responses to Chapman's dressings-down, see Edmund Quincy to Maria Weston Chapman, Dedham, 6 November 1843, A.9.2.19.73, WP; and David L. Child to Maria Weston Chapman, Washington, D.C., 18 April 1844, A.4.2.3–4, ASC. See also Amos Farnsworth to Anne Warren Weston, Groton, 20 July 1845, A.9.2.21.36, WP, for a similarly teasing and colorful response to her acerbity.

52. Anne Warren Weston to Debora Weston, Boston, 30 January 1837, A.9.2.9.9; Anne Warren Weston to Debora Weston, Boston, 23 March 1838, A.9.2.10.15; Caroline Weston to Anne Warren Weston, Boston, [1839], A.9.2.4.53–54; Debora Weston to Maria Weston Chapman, New Bedford, [March 1838], A.9.2.16.9; Caroline Weston to Debora Weston, Boston, [Fall 1836], A.9.2.3.30, WP. Caroline was speaking of the daughters of a southern slaveholder who, when confronted by abolitionists seeking to take their slaves from them as they lingered in Boston on a trip, resisted even as their father gave in to the committee's demand.

53. Anne Warren Weston to Wendell Phillips, New York, 30 April 1851, Am1953, Folder 3, Blagden Collection, HL; Debora Weston to Maria Weston Chapman, n.p., [1850–51], A.9.2.6.47, WP.

54. Anne Warren Weston to Wendell Phillips, Weymouth, 1 June 1851, 1289, folio 3; Anne Warren Weston to Wendell Phillips, Weymouth, n.d., Blagden Collection, HL; Caroline Weston to Emma Weston and Maria Weston Chapman, n.p., October 1845, A.9.2.21.64, WP.

55. Lucia Weston to Debora Weston, Boston, 22 January 1837, A.9.2.3.90, WP.

56. Maria's interest was sparked by Harriet Martineau. Her sisters, particularly Anne, drew upon the advocacy of Sydney Howard Gay. Gay left the *Anti-Slavery Standard* in 1858 to work for the *New York Tribune* and later the *Chicago Tribune*. Anne's interest may be followed in Weston correspondence with Gay and his wife, Elizabeth Neall Gay, who had been an active member of the PFAS. That correspondence is housed in the Rare Book and Manuscript Library at Columbia University.

57. For excerpt of the letter, see Chapman, "Memorials of Harriet Martineau," 541.

58. Ibid. For discussion of such laws in the United States, see Connelly, *Response to Prostitution*; Butler, *Daughters of Joy*; Hobson, *Uneasy Virtue*; and Gilfoyle, *City of Eros*.

59. See the correspondence among Philadelphia abolitionist Sarah Pugh; New Yorker Elizabeth Neall Gay; Mary A. Estlin of Bristol, England; Maria W. Chapman; and Anne Warren Weston, in the Rare Book and Manuscript Library, Columbia University, and Dr. Williams's Library, London. They discussed the "rumbling of the storm" against the C.D. Acts on both sides of the Atlantic and exchanged support and information about the campaigns. See, for example, Sarah Pugh to Mary A. Estlin, 27 February 1871, 21 January 1872, 16 August 1873, 6 April 1876, 19 June 1876, 22 January 1877, 24.121; Elizabeth Neall Gay to Mary A. Estlin, 29 January 1881; Maria Weston Chapman to Mary A. Estlin, n.d., n.p., 24.122, Dr. Williams's Library; and Sarah Pugh to Elizabeth Neall Gay, 6 December 1876, and Elizabeth Neall Gay to Sarah Pugh, 9 October 1870, Gay Papers, Rare Book and Manuscript Library.

60. Chapman, *Right and Wrong in Massachusetts*, 53.

61. Maria drafted these words as a statement to be sent to the AAS executive committee, who, she charged, "have been laboring to sow the idea that because the Mass Soc. has not denied that women are persons, it therefore introduces the 'woman question.'" By insisting that women "are persons," she also insisted that they have the same voting rights as men on all issues before the MAS. See Maria Weston Chapman, draft [on back of letter from Lucinda Wilmerth], 30 April 1839, A.4.6A.1.48, ASC.

62. Ibid.

63. Anne Warren Weston to Debora Weston, Dorchester, 11 July 1839, A.9.2.11.134; Paulina Gerry to Maria Weston Chapman, Stoneham, 6 July 1839, A.9.2.11.131, WP.

64. Elizabeth Reid (1789–1866) was a Unitarian relative of Mary Ann Estlin, an ardent Weston correspondent, and an active abolitionist; Anne Knight (1790–1862) was a Quaker and Weston correspondent; and Harriet Martineau (1802–76) was another Unitarian and close personal friend of Maria Weston Chapman. Martineau chose Chapman to edit her autobiography. The Westons corresponded with all these women and visited them in England during the years they lived abroad.

65. Caroline Weston to Anne Warren Weston, n.p., 13 June 1846, A.9.2.22.61; Sarah Otis Ernst to Anne Warren Weston, n.p., 13 January 1856, A.9.2.28.69, WP.

66. In her "Memorials of Harriet Martineau," Chapman included a discussion of her childhood in which she attributed "the powers of a human being" to "the obstacles to be overcome." Chapman blamed Martineau's birth order (sixth of eight children) for her mother's neglect and her own emotional frailty and lack of self-worth, citing an incident when her mother blamed Harriet's carelessness for damage done when a "fly got into her eye." "An accusation of carelessness was in this way converted into a sort of moral support," she wrote, as Martineau thereafter took comfort in criticism as a sort of positive recognition of her value. Chapman then, in an odd aside, associated such coldness and neglect with New England families. "New England . . . has been thought by strangers no less cold and dry of heart than Old England. The distinguished French statesman and author, Gustave de Beaumont [whose abolitionist tale she translated for the American market], observing upon the extreme rarity of any demonstrations of tenderness in American households, declares that the few families in which he noticed them were called in derision 'the kissing families'" (143).

67. Anticipating shared sibling enjoyment, she noted, "I write this for your mother's [Maria's] benefit" (Bella [Debora Weston] to Henry Chapman Jr., New Bedford, 11 March 1839, A.9.2.11.56, WP). An appreciation of female independence and competence might have resonated with regard to their mother's situation as well. In like vein, Debora told Anne about an afternoon spent sledding with Lizzy Chapman down a quarter-mile slope from the top of a hill: "The boys . . . would have liked to steer for me, but I preferred to command my own ship" (Debora Weston to Anne Warren Weston, 12 March 1838, Groton, A.9.2.10.10, WP). So too she described with pride and pleasure learning to drive a carriage and horses.

68. Maria Weston Chapman to David L. Child, Boston, [26 October 1843], A.4.1.63, ASC.

69. Anne Warren Weston to Samuel J. May, Weymouth, 2 March [1852], B.1.6.3.44, May Papers, BPL; Sarah Pugh to Mary A. Estlin, St. Ann's, 13 October 1853, 24.121.48,

Estlin Papers, Dr. Williams's Library; Anne Warren Weston to Ann Phillips, Weymouth, 15 August [1866], Blagden Collection, HL.

70. *Liberator*, 18 May 1848.

71. Ibid.

72. Jeanne Deroin (1805–94) was Maria's contemporary. Of working-class origins, she began her adult life as an embroiderer and, briefly, a teacher of working-class children. Her primary interest was in the unionization of working women. Although her candidacy for France's legislative assembly died in 1849 when she failed to acquire the support of the democratic socialists, her election to the central committee of the Association Fraternelle et Solidaire de Toutes les Associations provided her with a political platform. Arrested for political activity associated with the revolution of 1848, she was imprisoned from May 1850 to July 1851. She sent a letter to the Massachusetts Women's Rights Convention of 1851, opening communication with American feminists. Deroin had written for *La Politique des Femmes,* but after the revolutionary government ruled that women could no longer participate in politics, the journal was renamed *L'Opinion des Femmes.* See Anderson, *Joyous Greetings,* 7. Deroin fled to Great Britain after the coup of December 1851.

73. Deroin received fifteen votes. Caroline's snide characterization of Queen Victoria as lacking in ability had to do with her public emphasis on her domestic relations as wife and mother. She ruled for sixty-four years but rarely opened or attended Parliament in person. See Caroline Weston to Wendell Phillips, Paris, 25 April 1849, 1290, folio 4, Blagden Collection, HL.

74. *Liberator*, 18 May 1848.

75. Caroline Weston to Wendell Phillips, Paris, 25 April 1849, 1290, folio 4, Blagden Collection, HL.

76. Nancy Isenberg and Elizabeth R. Varon have noted that disunionism had various meanings for abolitionists. It could be used as an attack on abolitionists, particularly Garrisonians, and could mean either "a moral and philosophical strategy for recalling the state back to its original principles of freedom and liberty" or "a radical act of dissent" requiring the constitution of a new social compact. See Isenberg, *Sex and Citizenship,* 23, 217 n. 39. For discussions of the various meanings of disunion by Garrisonians and the political antislavery movement, see Varon, *Disunion!,* esp. 123–24, 144–45.

77. Emma Michell to Anne Warren Weston, Bristol, 20 November 1853, A.9.2.7.26, WP. Hemphill (*Siblings,* 131) suggests that the importance of sibling relations in the antebellum period may be seen in the widespread application of sibling metaphors to other relationships: religious fellowship, close friendships, or other relations of love and loyalty, as well as new forms of association.

78. The quoted phrase is from Bodle, "Littlest Commonwealth?," 25.

APPENDIX

1. Correspondence between the Westons and other activists is also found in the Quincy, Wendell, Holmes, and Upham Family Papers at the Massachusetts Historical Society, the Sydney Howard Gay Papers at Columbia University, the Abby Kelley Foster Papers at the American Antiquarian Society, and the John Bishop Estlin Papers at both

the Boston Public Library and Dr. Williams's Library, London. Examples of antislavery correspondence written by the Westons in their official capacity reside not only in the Anti-Slavery Collection at the Boston Public Library but also in the Letterbooks of the BFAS in the Massachusetts Historical Society and among the papers of such female antislavery societies as the Salem Female Anti-Slavery Society at the Essex Institute/ Peabody Essex Museum and the Concord Female Anti-Slavery Society at the Concord Historical Society.

2. For example, Sylvia Ammidon was a student of Maria's from her days as principal of Bailey's Boston High School and was briefly a member of the BFAS. She wrote Debora Weston to expect a letter from Maria addressed to their mother, Ann Bates Weston. Enclosed in that missive, she wrote, would be a second letter from Maria addressed to Sylvia. She asked Debora to forward her letter on to Hingham, Massachusetts, where she was staying. Neither Maria's letter to Ann Bates Weston nor her letter to Sylvia Ammidon remains, nor does Debora's reply. See Sylvia A. Ammidon to Debora Weston, Hingham, 12 October 1830, A.9.2.7.19, WP.

3. Randolph, "On the Biography of the Bakunin Family Archive," 211.

4. Ibid. See also Fritzsche, "The Archive and the Case of the German Nation." Fritzsche reminds us that "the history of the archive is embedded in the recognition of loss" (187).

5. No such copy in Lizzy's hand exists, nor do many of Maria's letters from Haiti. See Edmund Quincy to Caroline Weston, Dedham, 12 November 1844, Jackson Papers, MHS.

6. Caroline Weston to Wendell and Ann Phillips, Weymouth, 13 November [n.y.], 1290, folio 5, Blagden Collection, HL.

7. Caroline Weston to Wendell Phillips, Weymouth, 27 October [1870], Blagden Collection, HL.

8. Garrison and Garrison, *William Lloyd Garrison*.

9. References to such letters, however, suggest that both were literate.

10. A few letters to Joshua Bates, their mother's brother and financial supporter, exist in the collection, but Bates's business connections with Henry G. Chapman are gathered with his business correspondence in the Baring Brothers manuscript collection at the Baring Archive, London.

11. Little remains to document Hervey's role in the Weymouth Society of the 1830s, the MAS of the 1840s, or the Boston Vigilance Committee of the 1850s. This may be because he lived in the Weston home in Weymouth and communicated with them orally.

12. There is a small collection of her correspondence with Edmund Quincy in the Quincy, Wendell, Holmes, and Upham Family Papers at the Massachusetts Historical Society.

13. Wendell Phillips died in 1884; Ann Terry Greene Phillips died in 1886.

14. See, for example, Edmund Quincy to Friends [Henry Chapman and Maria Weston Chapman], Dedham, 18 May 1841, A.9.2.13.71–72, WP.

15. Abigail Kelley to Maria Weston Chapman, Harveysburg, Ohio, 8 November 1845, A.9.2.21.89, WP. See also the words "private cut out" written by Helen Weston on Richard D. Webb to Maria Weston Chapman, Dublin, 26 February 1846, A.9.2.22.26, WP.

16. There are numerous redacted letters that bear no signature as to the editor but are noted as "extracts." A letter from Anne Warren Weston to Caroline Weston in Helen Weston's hand is dated 12 November 1848, A.9.2.24.43, WP.

17. For additional acts of censorship, see the missing first page and cut-off portion of the second page of a letter from Maria Weston Chapman to Mary A. Estlin, Weymouth, 8 March 1858, A.9.2.78, JBEP; and the letter in which Harriet Martineau's description of Maria is cut off, Anne Warren Weston to Caroline Weston, Boston, 12 November 1848, A.9.2.24.43, WP. See also "Extracts from a letter of A. W. W.," Weymouth, 2 September 1843, A.9.2.19.28, WP.

18. Lydia Maria Child to Maria Weston Chapman, Wayland, 26 July 1856, A.5.1.31, Child Papers, ASC; Debora Weston to Caroline Weston, Weymouth, 6 June 1854, A.9.2.28.16, WP.

19. Clearly in this case Debora did not burn the letter. See Caroline Weston to Debora Weston, Roxbury, 17 June 1842, A.9.2.17.71, WP. There is no way to know whether she, or her sisters, purposefully destroyed others.

20. Anne Warren Weston to Debora Weston, Boston, 3 October 1840, A.9.2.14.35, WP.

21. Maria Weston Chapman to Mary A. Estlin, Weymouth, 8 March 1858, A.8.2.78, JBEP.

22. The pages of this letter were separated and the pieces filed in both Estlin and Weston collections, making it difficult to connect them.

23. Note dated 10 September 1899 and attached to a letter from Richard D. Webb to Maria Weston Chapman, Dublin, 26 February 1846, A.9.2.22.26, WP. Other examples of missing sheets or fragments include A.9.2.22.28 and A.9.2.22.16, WP.

24. The Westons despised Julia Griffith and thought she had a deleterious effect on Douglass and his family. See, for example, Anne Warren Weston to Mary A. Estlin, 4 April 1852, A.7.2.17, JBEP; Richard D. Webb to Maria Weston Chapman, Dublin, 22 January 1854, A.9.2.28.4, WP; Maria Weston Chapman to William Lloyd Garrison, Weymouth, n.d., A.1.2.28.39, Garrison Papers, BPL; and Maria Weston Chapman to Mary A. Estlin, Leeds, 15 October 1855, A.7.2.75; Boston, 4 February 1857, A.7.2.77; Weymouth, 8 March 1858, A.8.2.78, JBEP.

25. Caroline Weston to Debora Weston, Boston, 4 July 1843, A.9.2.18.69, WP. The diaries of Madame D'Arblay (Frances Burney) were published in America in the 1840s and read by the Westons. See Caroline Weston to Henry G. Chapman and Maria Weston Chapman, Boston, 5 April 1841, A.9.2.15.36, WP; Anne Warren Weston to Ann T. G. Phillips, Weymouth, 11 June 1866, Blagden Collection, HL; and Anne Warren Weston to Mary A. Estlin, Weymouth, 19 July 1852, A.7.2.18, JBEP.

26. Caroline Weston diary, 16, 18, 28, 29 September 1835, A.9.2.7.65–66, WP.

27. See Sophia [unknown] to Caroline Weston, St. Louis, 10 November 1836, A.9.2.8.70; Caroline Weston diary, 19 and 20 September 1835, A.9.2.7.65–66; and Anne Warren Weston to Debora Weston, Brush Hill, 11 June 1846, A.9.2.22.60, WP.

28. Archival letters have long served as the primary sources of historical investigation and writing and have attracted serious scholarly attention. Some of the questions under discussion include the textual dimensions of letter writing; the performative and fictive aspects of correspondence; the construction of narrative over time between

correspondents; the role of letter writing in the establishment of literary culture; the varying discursive practices of men and women, and diverse races and classes; the political value of the epistolary form in various time periods; the assertion of power through epistolary definitions of self, other, and context; reconciliation and contention in correspondence; the contradictions involved in the publication of private correspondence; the "fictionalization" of correspondence; and the "authority" and "inclusiveness" of "official" and unofficial archives. For discussions of some of these matters, see Barton and Hall, *Letter Writing*; Beebee, *Epistolary Fiction*; Bower, *Epistolary Responses*; Burton, *Archive Stories*; Cook, *Epistolary Bodies*; Decker, *Epistolary Practices*; Ditz, "Formative Ventures"; Favret, *Romantic Correspondence*; Gaul, *To Marry an Indian*; How, *Epistolary Spaces*; and Smith, *Poetics of Women's Autobiography*.

29. Anne wrote to Henry and Maria, "I believe Caroline wrote you the last day of the year; with my journal at my side I will begin the 1st of Jan. & select such items as may seem the most important" (Anne Warren Weston to Henry G. Chapman and Maria Weston Chapman, Boston, 15 January 1841, A.9.2.15.10, WP).

30. Anne Warren Weston to Maria Weston Chapman, Weymouth, 25 February 1841, A.9.2.15.27, WP. See also Anne Warren Weston to Mary A. Estlin, Weymouth, 19 July 1852, A.7.2.18, JBEP; and Debora Weston to Caroline Weston, Boston, [1 June 1844], A.9.2.16.18, WP. See Chapter 5 for additional discussion.

31. Indeed, the term "journal letter" often connoted detailed coverage of organizational gatherings in which the sisters shared an interest. Anne used the term, for example, in offering her report of a Non-Resistant Society meeting in Boston for her siblings. See Anne Warren Weston to "Misses Weston," Boston, 23 January 1845, A.9.2.21.7, WP.

32. Nathaniel Peabody Rogers (1794–1846) was a lawyer turned newspaper editor. In 1838 he established the *Herald of Freedom* in Concord, New Hampshire. The Westons supported the paper until a dispute over its ownership caused them to sever relations in 1845.

33. Anne Warren Weston, Weymouth, 8 January 1845, A.9.2.21.3, WP.

34. Anne Warren Weston to Wendell and Ann T. G. Phillips, New York City, 23 March 1851, Am 1953, Folder 3, Blagden Collection, HL; Anne Warren Weston to Debora Weston, Boston, [1836], A.9.2.3.39, WP.

35. Yet she was careless about forwarding her sisters' correspondence, or perhaps too busy to attend to it properly, thus forcing her sisters to compensate. Debora complained, "Maria never gives us [our] letters but when we come in town we search the house" (Anne Warren Weston to Debora Weston, Boston, 7 July 1839, A.9.2.11.133, WP).

36. Caroline Weston to Emma Weston and Maria Weston Chapman, n.p., October 1845, A.9.2.21.64, WP.

37. Anne Warren Weston to Maria Weston Chapman, Weymouth, 2 April 1849, A.9.2.24.70, WP.

38. Debora Weston to [Caroline Weston], n.p., 21 October 1850, A.9.2.25.33, WP.

39. Anne Warren Weston to Wendell and Ann Phillips, Vevey, 31 October 1856, 1289, folio 5, Blagden Collection, HL.

40. Anne Warren Weston to Caroline Weston and Debora Weston, Boston, 19 June 1843, A.9.2.19.75; Edmund Quincy to Maria Weston Chapman, Dedham, 5 April 1844,

A.9.2.20.24; Anne Warren Weston to Debora Weston and Caroline Weston, n.p., 9 September 1843, A.9.2.19.34, WP.

41. Lucia Weston to Debora Weston, Boston, 20 October 1839, A.9.2.11.9; Debora Weston to Maria Weston Chapman, New Bedford, 30 December 1839, A.9.2.12.131, WP. For other calls to burn their letters, see Anne Warren Weston to Wendell and Ann Phillips, Vevey, 31 October 1856, 1289, folio 5, Blagden Collection, HL; and Caroline Weston to Debora Weston, Roxbury, 17 June 1842, A.9.2.17.71, WP.

42. E. A. S. Smith to Caroline Weston, Dorchester, 8 December 1844, A.9.2.20.118, WP.

43. Mary A. Estlin to Caroline Weston, Bristol, 3 June 1851, A.7.3.19, JBEP.

44. Anne Warren Weston to Debora Weston, New Bedford, 31 October 1842, A.9.2.17.103, WP. Exactly what Anne meant by "their injury" is not clear. However, Anne knew well her audience and their social and familial context and may have thought the Beanes lacked the political sophistication to understand the original text.

45. Anne Warren Weston to Caroline Weston, Boston, 12 November 1848, A.9.2.24.43, WP.

46. Richard D. Webb to Maria Weston Chapman, Dublin, 18 November 1854, A.9.2.32.40, WP.

47. A similar purpose, but more precipitate, was the phrase "Private—that is *dont leave it about*," which Caroline put on one of her letters. See Caroline to Emma, A.9.2.21.64, and Maria Weston Chapman, October 1845, A.9.2.4.19, WP.

48. Mary A. Estlin to Anne Warren Weston, Bristol, 16 January 1854, JBEP.

49. Anne Warren Weston to Wendell Phillips, Weymouth, 5 April [n.y.], Blagden Collection, HL.

50. Maria Weston Chapman to James S. Gibbons, 25 May 1843, A.9.2.18.44, WP. Gibbons (1810–92) was a Quaker merchant and Garrisonian who moved from Philadelphia to New York City in 1835. See also Maria Weston Chapman to Mary A. Estlin, Paris, 24 March 1853, A.7.2.63, WP.

51. Mary A. Estlin to Anne Warren Weston, Bristol, 30 November 1854, A.9.2.28.33, WP. Anne had shared in some detail the contents of a letter Garrison had forwarded to her from a Mr. Paton of Edinburgh. She commented on the details and cautioned Mary only that "as Mr Paton's letter to Garrison was marked 'Private' of course you will govern yourselves accordingly." On another occasion she remarked to Estlin, "By a letter marked 'Private' which Mr. Gay shewed me, I see that Andrew Paton is dealing with Pennington of whose dishonesty I feel fully persuaded" (Anne Warren Weston to Mary A. and John B. Estlin, n.p., n.d., A.9.2.2.10, WP).

52. Mary A. Estlin to Anne Warren Weston, Bristol, 30 November 1854, A.9.2.28.33, WP. For more on this debate, see Anne Warren Weston to Mary A. Estlin, New York, 15 March 1851, A.7.2.9, JBEP; and Mary A. Estlin to Anne Warren Weston, Bristol, 3 August 1854, A.9.2.28.25, WP.

53. Maria Weston Chapman to Mary A. Estlin, Paris, 24 March 1853, A.9.2.2.63, WP.

54. Ibid.

55. See, for example, Maria Weston Chapman to Debora Weston, 14 March 1839, A.9.2.11.58, WP. Her items regarded a possible agenda for the New Bedford Female Anti-Slavery Society meeting Debora was to lead.

56. Anne Warren Weston to Caroline Weston, [Boston], 12 November 1848, A.9.2.24.43, WP.

57. Debora Weston to Anne Warren Weston, New Bedford, 15 January 1836, A.9.2.8.6; Maria Weston Chapman to Anne Warren Weston, Paris, 10 January 1849, A.9.2.24.59, WP.

58. Anne Warren Weston to Caroline Weston, Boston, 30 May 1844, A.9.2.20.33, WP.

59. Harris, *American Women Writers*, 3–30.

60. Maria Weston Chapman to Mary A. Estlin, Paris, 24 March 1853, A.7.2.63, JBEP.

61. Debora Weston to Caroline Weston, New Bedford, 11 March 1839, A.9.2.11.55, WP.

62. Caroline Weston to Debora Weston, Boston, 14 January 1834, A.9.2.7.33, WP.

63. Caroline Weston to Ann and Wendell Phillips, [New Bedford], n.d., 1290, folio 6, Blagden Collection, HL.

64. Maria Weston Chapman to Mary A. Estlin, Paris, 24 March 1853, A.7.2.63, ASC.

65. Anne Warren Weston to Caroline Weston, Weymouth, 14 December 1846, A.9.2.22.137, WP.

66. Debora Weston to Anne Warren Weston, Boston, 6 June 1836, A.9.2.8.4; Anne Warren Weston to Debora Weston, Boston, 15 December 1836, A.9.2.8.87, WP.

67. Caroline Weston to Debora Weston, Boston, n.d. [postmarked 21 September 1838], A.9.2.3.25, WP.

68. As paper was made of rag through the middle of the nineteenth century, it was more expensive than in the early twentieth century. The first groundwood pulp mill in the United States was built in Massachusetts in 1867.

69. Lucia Weston to Debora Weston, Boston, n.d., A.9.2.4.86; Lucia Weston to Debora Weston, Boston, 20 October 1839, A.9.2.11.9, WP.

70. Anne Warren Weston to Debora Weston, Weymouth, 27 June [n.y.], A.9.32.3.74; Anne Warren Weston to Mary Weston, n.p., 9 January 1839, A.9.2.11.19; Anne Warren Weston to Debora Weston, n.p., n.d., A.9.2.5.18; Maria Weston Chapman to Nancy [Ann Bates] Weston, New York, 24 October [1857], A.9.2.5.91; Anne Warren Weston to Debora Weston, Dorchester, 11 July 1839, A.9.2.11.134, WP.

71. Nineteenth-century novels referred to this common practice as "crossing."

72. For an example of a letter written at ninety degrees, see a letter begun to Maria, dated 16 August 1836, in ASC, which was finished crosswise with a list of women who might be willing to pass petitions in Franklin County, Massachusetts.

73. Fuller, *American Mail*, 43.

74. Anne Warren Weston to Mary A. Estlin, Weymouth, 5 February 1853, A.7.2.21; Anne Warren Weston to Mary A. Estlin, Weymouth, 15 February 1852, A.7.2.14, JBEP.

75. Debora Weston to Anne Warren Weston, New Bedford, 1 April 1839, A.9.2.11.74, WP.

76. Debora Weston to Anne Warren Weston, New Bedford, 1 March 1840, A.9.2.13.33, WP. See also Anne Warren Weston to Debora Weston, Boston, 7 July 1839, A.9.2.11.133; Debora Weston to Anne Warren Weston, New Bedford, 15 January 1836, A.9.2.8.6, 1 January 1837, A.9.2.9.1, WP. In addition to forwarding, correspondence might also be kept for sharing later.

77. Anne Warren Weston to Debora Weston, New Bedford, 31 October 1842, A.9.2.17.103, WP.

78. The title to the appendix, "To Be Left at Capt Weston's Near Wales' Tavern," comes from an inscription on the exterior of a letter from Maria Weston Chapman to Caroline Weston, n.p., 6 August 1842, WP. Wales' tavern abutted Warren Weston's Weymouth Landing farm.

79. Betsy Newton to Mrs. Chapman, Worcester, 28 July 1837, A.9.2.9.52, WP.

80. See, for example, T. Packard Jr. to Caroline Weston, n.p., n.d., ASC. The letter provided a list of female contacts from every town in Franklin County, Massachusetts. These were individuals who would take responsibility for passing petitions seeking an end to slavery in the District of Columbia.

81. In 1847, the U.S. Post Office issued its first stamps for purchase by the sender: a five-cent stamp bearing the image of Benjamin Franklin and a ten-cent stamp with George Washington's visage.

82. Earle, *Epistolary Selves*, 8.

83. Anne Weston to Debora Weston, Groton, 17 September 1836, A.9.2.8.52, WP. See also Maria Weston Chapman to Mary A. Estlin, Paris, 2 March 1854, A.7.2.68, JBEP.

Bibliography

MANUSCRIPT SOURCES

The Baring Archive, London
    Diary of Joshua Bates, Baring Brothers DEP 74
    HC 5.1.5
    HC 5.1.17
Boston Public Library, Boston, Mass.
    Anti-Slavery Collection
        Lydia Maria Child Papers
    John Bishop Estlin Papers
    William Lloyd Garrison Papers
    Francis Jackson Papers
    Samuel J. May Papers
    Weston Papers
Dr. Williams's Library, London
    The Estlin Papers
Essex Institute/Peabody Essex Museum, Salem, Mass.
    Bigelow Collection
Historical Society of Pennsylvania, Philadelphia
    Philadelphia Female Anti-Slavery Society Papers
Houghton Library, Harvard University, Cambridge, Mass.
    Blagden Collection
    Journals of Henry C. Wright
John Rylands Library, University of Manchester, UK
    Raymond English Anti-Slavery Collection
Library of Congress, Washington, D.C.
Massachusetts Archives, Boston, Mass.
    Office of the Secretary of State, Vital Records
    Supreme Judicial Court, Archives and Records Preservation
Massachusetts Historical Society, Boston, Mass.
    Boston Female Anti-Slavery Society Letterbooks
    Henry Ingersall Bowditch Papers
    Francis Elizabeth Gray Papers
    Francis Jackson Papers
    Elizabeth Ann Oliver Papers
    Quincy, Wendell, Holmes, and Upham Family Papers
    Robie-Sewall Family Papers
    Wigglesworth Family Papers
National Archives, Washington, D.C.

Antislavery Petitions, HR24A-H1.3

Rare Book and Manuscript Library, Columbia University, New York
   Sydney Howard Gay Papers
Schlesinger Library, Harvard University, Cambridge, Mass.
Smith College Library, Northampton, Mass.
   Sophia Smith Collection
Somerset House, London, UK
   Principal Registry of the Family Division
Tufts Public Library, Weymouth, Mass.
   Concord Book Transcription, Weymouth Anti-Slavery Society
Wellesley College Library, Wellesley, Mass.
   Anne Whitney Collection

PRINTED PRIMARY SOURCES

An Account of the Interviews which Took Place on the Fourth and Eighth of March Between a Committee of the Massachusetts Anti-Slavery Society, and the Committee of the Legislature. Boston, 1836.

Alcott, Louisa May. *Little Women.* New York: Viking Penguin, 1989.

Altschuler, Glenn C., and Jan M. Saltzgaber. *Revivalism, Social Conscience, and Community in the Burned-Over District: The Trial of Rhoda Bement.* Ithaca: Cornell University Press, 1983.

American Series of Popular Biographies. Massachusetts Edition. Boston: Graves & Steinbarger, 1891.

Barber, John Warner. *Historical Collections, Being a General Collection of Interesting Facts, Traditions, Biographical Sketches, Anecdotes, etc., Relating to the History and Antiquities of Every Town in Massachusetts.* Worcester: Dorr, Howland, 1839.

Barnes, Gilbert H., and Dwight L. Dumond, eds., *Letters of Theodore Dwight Weld, Angelina Grimké Weld and Sarah Grimké, 1822–1844.* New York: D. Appleton-Century, 1934.

Barrett, Walter. *The Old Merchants of New York City.* Second Series. New York: Carleton, 1863.

Bartlett, J. S., M.D. *The Physician's Pocket Synopsis: Affording a Concise View of the Symptoms and Treatment of the Medical and Surgical Diseases Incident to the Human Frame. Compiled from the Best Authorities, with References to the Most Approved Modern Authors. Together with the Properties and Doses of the Simples and Compounds of the National Pharmacopoeia of the United States. Alphabetically Arranged.* Boston: Munroe and Francis, 1822.

Beecher, Catharine E. *The Evils Suffered by American Women and American Children: The Causes and the Remedies. Presented in an Address by Miss C. E. Beecher, to Meetings of Ladies in New York, and Other Cities.* New York: Harper, 1846.

———. *Letters to the People on Health and Happiness.* New York: Harper, 1855.

———. *Physiology and Calisthenics. For Schools and Families.* New York: Harper & Brothers, 1856.

Birney, Catherine H. *The Grimké Sisters: Sarah and Angelina Grimké: The First American Women Advocates of Abolition and Women's Rights.* Philadelphia: Lee and Shepard, 1885.

Burgess, T. H., M.D., *Climate of Italy in Relation to Pulmonary Consumption: With Remarks on the Influence of Foreign Climates upon Invalids.* London: Longman, Brown, Green, & Longmans, 1852.

Case of the Slave-Child, MED. Report of the Arguments of Counsel, and of the Opinion of the Court, in the Case of Commonwealth vs. Aves: Tried and Determined in the Supreme Judicial Court of Massachusetts. Thomas Aves. Boston: I. Knapp, 1836. Cornell University Library Digital Collections.

Chamberlain, George W. *Genealogies of the Early Families of Weymouth, Massachusetts.* Baltimore: Genealogical Publishing Co., 1984.

Chapman, Maria Weston. "Memorials of Harriet Martineau." In *Harriet Martineau's Autobiography.* Vol. 2, edited by Maria Weston Chapman. Boston: James R. Osgood, 1877.

———. *Pinda: A True Tale.* New York: American Anti-Slavery Society, 1840.

———. *Right and Wrong in Boston, in 1836. Annual Report of the Boston Female Anti-Slavery Society, Being a Concise History of the Cases of the Slave child, Med, and of the Women Demanded as Slaves of the Supreme Judicial Court of Mass.* Boston: Isaac Knapp, 1836.

———. *Right and Wrong in Boston. Annual Report of the Boston Female Anti-Slavery Society, with a Sketch of the Obstacles Thrown in the Way of Emancipation by Certain Clerical Abolitionists and Advocates for the Subjection of Woman, in 1837.* Boston: Isaac Knapp, 1837.

———. *Right and Wrong in Massachusetts.* 1839. New York: Negro Universities Press, 1969.

———. *Right and Wrong in the Anti-Slavery Societies. Seventh Annual Report of the Boston Female Anti-Slavery Society.* Boston: W. H. Dorr, 1840.

Clarke, James Freeman. *Anti-Slavery Days.* New York: J. W. Lovell, 1883.

Dickson, S. Henry, M.D. *Manual of Pathology and Practice, Being the Outline of the Course of Lectures Delivered.* Charleston: Published by the Author, 1842.

Eliot, Samuel A. *Theodore Lyman.* Republished from Barnard's American Journal of Education, March 1861.

Forbes, A[bner] and J. W. Greene. *The Rich Men of Massachusetts, Containing a Statement of the Reputed Wealth of about Fifteen Hundred Persons, with Brief Sketches of More than One Thousand Characters.* Boston: W. V. Spencer, 1851.

Formation of the Massachusetts Abolition Society. Boston, 1839.

Garrison, Wendell Phillips, and Francis Jackson Garrison. *William Lloyd Garrison, 1805–1879. The Story of His Life Told by His Children.* 4 vols. New York: Century, 1885–89.

Higginson, Thomas Wentworth. *John Greenleaf Whittier.* New York: Macmillan Co., 1902.

Howe, M. A. Dewolfe. *John Jay Chapman and His Letters.* Boston: Houghton Mifflin, 1937.

Humphrey, Heman, D.D. *Parallel Between Intemperance and the Slave Trade: An Address Delivered at Amherst College, July 4, 1828*. Amherst, Mass.: J. S. and C. Adams, Printers, 1828.

Hunt, Edmund Soper. *Weymouth Ways and Weymouth People. Reminiscences*. Boston: Privately Printed, 1907.

Lesser, Margaret. *Clarkey: A Portrait in Letters of Mary Clarke Mohl*. New York: Oxford University Press, 1984.

Lyman, Theodore, Jr. *Memoir of Theodore Lyman, Jr., Prepared at the Request of the New England Historic Genealogical Society, and Privately Reprinted from Their Volume of Memoirs*. Cambridge: John Wilson and Son, 1881.

——. *Papers Relating to the Garrison Mob*. 3d ed. Cambridge: Welch, Bigelow, 1879.

Martineau, Harriet. *The Martyr Age of the United States*. Boston: Weeks, Jordan, 1839.

Meltzer, Milton, and Patricia G. Holland, eds. *Lydia Maria Child, Selected Letters, 1817–1880*. Amherst: University of Massachusetts Press, 1982.

Merrill, Walter, ed. *I Will Be Heard!* Volume 1 of *The Letters of William Lloyd Garrison, 1822–1835*. Cambridge: Belknap Press of Harvard University Press, 1971.

——. *No Union with Slaveholders*. Volume 4 of *The Letters of William Lloyd Garrison, 1841–1849*. Cambridge: Belknap Press of Harvard University Press, 1971.

Merrill, Walter, and Louis Ruchames, eds. *Let the Oppressed Go Free, 1861–1867*. Cambridge: Belknap Press of Harvard University Press, 1979.

——. *To Rouse the Slumbering Land, 1868–1879*. Cambridge: Belknap Press of Harvard University Press, 1981.

Mosely, William Willis. *Eleven Chapters on Nervous and Mental Complaints*. London: Simpkin, Marshall, 1838.

O'Meara, Kathleen. *Madame Mohl: Her Salon and Her Friends*. Boston, 1886.

Other Merchants and Sea Captains of Old Boston. Boston: State Street Trust, 1919.

Prince, Nancy. "Narrative of the Life and Travels of Mrs. Nancy Prince." In *Collected Black Women's Narratives*, edited by Henry Louis Gates Jr. New York: Oxford University Press, 1988.

A Quarter-Century Record of the Class of 1839. New Haven: Yale College, 1865.

Report of the Boston Female Anti-Slavery Society; with a Concise Statement of Events, Previous and Subsequent to the Annual Meeting of 1835. Boston: Published by the society, 1836.

Ruchames, Louis, ed. *From Disunionism to the Brink of War*. Volume 5 of *The Letters of William Lloyd Garrison, 1850–1860*. Cambridge: Belknap Press of Harvard University Press, 1975.

——. *A House Dividing against Itself*. Volume 2 of *The Letters of William Lloyd Garrison, 1836–1840*. Cambridge: Belknap Press of Harvard University Press, 1971.

Sadler, Thomas, ed. *Henry Crabb Robinson, Diary, Reminiscences, and Correspondence*. Vol. 3. Boston: Fields, Osgood, 1869.

Salmon, Lucy. *Domestic Service*. 1897. New York: Arno Press, 1972.

Scudder, Horace E. *Justin Winsor: A Memoir*. Cambridge: University Press, 1899.

Shattuck, Lemuel. *Report to the Committee of the City Council Appointed to Obtain the Census of Boston for the Year 1845*. Boston: John H. Eastburn, 1846.

Simpson, M[ary] C[harlotte] M[air]. *Letters and Recollections of Julius and Mary Mohl*. London: Kegan Paul, Trench, 1887.

Sixth Annual Report of the Boston Female Anti-Slavery Society. Boston: Dow & Jackson, 1839.

Skultans, Vieda. *Madness and Morals: Ideas on Insanity in the Nineteenth Century*. Boston: Routledge & Kegan Paul, 1975.

Smith, Adam. *The Theory of Moral Sentiments*. Edited by D. D. Raphael and A. L. Macfie. 1759. Oxford: Clarenden Press, 1976.

Southwick, Sarah H. *Reminiscences of Early Anti-Slavery Days*. Cambridge: Riverside Press, 1893.

Stimpson's Boston Directory; Containing the Names of the Inhabitants, Their Occupations, Places of Business, and Dwelling Houses, and the City Register, with Lists of the Streets, Lanes and Wharves, the City Officers, Public Offices and Banks, and Other Useful Information. Boston: Stimpson and Clapp. 1832.

Stoddart, Anna M. *Elizabeth Pease Nichol*. London: J. M. Dent, 1899.

Stowe, Harriet Beecher. *Sunny Memories of Foreign Lands*. Boston: Phillips, Sampson, 1854.

Thompson, Ralph. "*The Liberty Bell* and Other Anti-Slavery Gift-Books." *New England Quarterly* 7 (March 1934): 154–68.

The True History of the Late Division in the Anti-Slavery Societies, Being Part of the Second Annual Report of the Executive Committee of the Massachusetts Abolition Society. Boston: David H. Ela, 1841.

Weston, Edmund Brownell. *In Memoriam: My Father and Mother, Hon. Gershom Bradford Weston and Deborah Brownell Weston of Duxbury, Massachusetts. Memoirs of Capt. Ezra Weston (I), Ezra Weston (II), Gershom Bradford Weston, Alden Bradford Weston, Ezra Weston (IV), and Deborah Brownell Weston*. Providence, R.I.: Privately Printed, 1916.

Weston, Ezra, III. "Weston Family of Duxbury, Mass." New England Historic and Genealogical Society.

Weston, Thomas, Jr. *The Descendants of Edmund Weston of Duxbury*. Boston: George E. Littlefield, 1887.

Wilson, Thomas V. L. *Aristocracy of Boston; Who They Are, and What They Were. Being a History of the Business and Business Men of Boston For the Last Forty Years. By One Who Knows Them*. Boston: Published by the Author, 1848.

Winsor, Justin, ed. *The Memorial History of Boston, Including Suffolk County, Massachusetts, 1630-1880*. Vol. 4. Boston: Ticknor, 1886.

Woodwell, Roland H. *John Greenleaf Whittier: A Biography*. Haverhill: Trustees of the John Greenleaf Whittier Homestead, 1985.

SECONDARY SOURCES

Alexander, Adele. *Ambiguous Lives: Free Women of Color in Rural Georgia, 1789–1829*. Fayetteville: University of Arkansas Press, 1991.

Allgor, Catherine. "'A Lady Will Have More Influence': Women and Patronage in Early Washington City." In *Women and the Unstable State in Nineteenth-Century America*, edited by Alison M. Parker and Stephanie Cole, 37–60. College Station: Texas A & M University Press, 2000.

———. *Parlor Politics: In Which the Ladies of Washington Help Build a City and a Government*. Charlottesville: University Press of Virginia, 2000.

Alonso, Harriet Hyman. *Growing Up Abolitionist. The Story of the Garrison Children*. Amherst: University of Massachusetts Press, 2002.

Anderson, Bonnie S. *Joyous Greetings: The First International Women's Movement, 1830–1860*. Oxford: Oxford University Press, 2000.

Anderson, Godfrey T. "The Captain Lays Down the Law." *New England Quarterly* 44 (June 1971): 305–9.

Anderson, Michael. *Family Structure in Nineteenth Century Lancashire*. Cambridge: Cambridge University Press, 1971.

Appleby, Joyce. *Inheriting the Revolution: The First Generation of Americans*. Cambridge: Belknap Press, 2000.

———. "The Personal Roots of the First American Temperance Movement." *Proceedings of the American Philosophical Society* 141 (June 1997): 141–59.

Armstrong, Erica R. "A Mental and Moral Feast: Reading, Writing, and Sentimentality in Black Philadelphia." *Journal of Women's History* 16 (Spring 2004): 78–102.

Atkins, Annette. *We Grew Up Together: Brothers and Sisters in Nineteenth-Century America*. Urbana: University of Illinois Press, 2001.

August, Thomas. *The Clerk's Tale: Young Men and Moral Life in Nineteenth-Century America*. Chicago: University of Chicago Press, 2003.

Balleisen, Edward J. *Navigating Failure: Bankruptcy and Commercial Society in Antebellum America*. Chapel Hill: University of North Carolina Press, 2001.

Balsam, Rosemary H., M.D. "Sisters and Their Disappointing Brothers." In *Brothers and Sister: Developmental, Dynamic, and Technical Aspects of the Sibling Relationship*, edited by Salman Akhtar and Selma Kramer, 71–100. Northvale, N.J.: Jason Aronson, 1999.

Baptist, Edward E. "The Migration of Planters to Antebellum Florida: Kinship and Power." *Journal of Southern History* 62 (August 1996): 527–54.

Bardaglio, Peter. *Reconstructing the Household: Families, Sex, and the Law in the Nineteenth Century South*. Chapel Hill: University of North Carolina Press, 1995.

Barnes, Gilbert Hobbs. *The Antislavery Impulse, 1830–1844*. New York: D. Appleton-Century, 1933.

Barton, David, and Nigel Hall, eds. *Letter Writing as a Social Practice*. Philadelphia: John Benjamins, 2000.

Beattie, Betsy. *Obligation and Opportunity: Single Maritime Women in Boston, 1870–1930*. Montreal: McGill-Queen's University Press, 2000.

Beattie, Cordelia. *Medieval Single Women: The Politics of Social Classification in Late Medieval England*. Oxford: Oxford University Press, 2007.

Beebee, Thomas O. *Epistolary Fiction in Europe, 1500–1850*. Cambridge: Cambridge University Press, 1999.

Bell, Rudolph M., and Virginia Yans-McLaughlin, eds. *Women on Their Own: Interdisciplinary Approaches.* New Brunswick, N.J.: Rutgers University Press, 2008.

Bennett, Judith M., and Amy M. Froide. *Singlewomen in the European Past, 1250-1800.* Philadelphia: University of Pennsylvania Press, 1998.

Bent, Mary Woodburn. *"Miss Lizzie": A Portrait of A New England Teacher.* Boston: Chapman & Grimes, 1937.

Berend, Zsuzsa. "'The Best or None!' Spinsterhood in Nineteenth-Century New England." *Journal of Social History* 33 (2000): 935–57.

Billingsley, Carolyn Earle. *Communities of Kinship: Antebellum Families and the Settlement of the Cotton Frontier.* Athens: University of Georgia Press, 2004.

Bloch, Ruth. "The Gendered Meanings of Virtue in Revolutionary America." *Signs: A Journal of Women in Culture and Society* 13 (Fall 1987): 37–58.

Bodle, Wayne. "The Littlest Commonwealth? The Neglected Importance of Sibling Relations in American Family History." *Reviews in American History* 30 (2002): 22–30.

Bower, Anne. *Epistolary Responses: The Letter in 20th Century American Fiction and Criticism.* Tuscaloosa: University of Alabama Press, 1997.

Boydston, Jeanne. *Home and Work: Housework, Wages, and the Ideology of Labor in the Early Republic.* New York: Oxford University Press, 1990.

Boydston, Jeanne, Mary Kelley, and Anne Margolis. *The Limits of Sisterhood: The Beecher Sisters on Women's Rights and Woman's Sphere.* Chapel Hill: University of North Carolina Press, 1988.

Boylan, Anne M. *The Origins of Women's Activism: New York and Boston, 1797-1840.* Chapel Hill: University of North Carolina Press, 2002.

——. "Timid Girls, Venerable Widows, and Dignified Matrons: Life Cycle Patterns among Organized Women in New York and Boston, 1797–1840." *American Quarterly* 38 (Winter 1986): 779–97.

——. "Women in Groups: An Analysis of Women's Benevolent Organizations in New York and Boston, 1797–1840." *Journal of American History* 71 (December 1984): 497–523.

Browne, Patrick T. J. *King Caesar of Duxbury: Exploring the World of Era Weston, Shipbuilder and Merchant.* Duxbury: Duxbury Rural & Historical Society, 2006.

Bullette, Margaret M. "The Puzzling Case of the Deceased Wife's Sister: Nineteenth Century England Deals with a Second-Chance Plot." *Representations* 31 (Summer 1990): 49.

Burton, Antoinette. *Archive Stories: Facts, Fictions, and the Writing of History.* Durham: Duke University Press, 2005.

Butler, Anne M. *Daughters of Joy, Sisters of Misery: Prostitutes in the American West, 1865-1890.* Urbana: University of Illinois Press, 1985.

Carr, Jacqueline Barbara. *After the Siege: A Social History of Boston, 1775-1800.* Boston: Northeastern University Press, 2005.

——. "A Change 'as Remarkable as the Revolution Itself': Boston's Demographics, 1780-1800." *New England Quarterly* 73 (2000): 583–602.

Carter, Christine Jacobson. *Southern Single Blessedness: Unmarried Women in the Urban South, 1800-1865.* Urbana: University of Illinois Press, 2006.

Cashin, Joan E. "'Decidedly Opposed to *the Union*': Women's Culture, Marriage, and Politics in Antebellum South Carolina." *Georgia Historical Quarterly* 78 (Winter 1994): 735–59.

———. *A Family Venture: Men and Women on the Southern Frontier*. New York: Oxford University Press, 1991.

———. "The Structure of Antebellum Planter Families: 'The Ties that Bound Us Was Strong.'" *Journal of Southern History* 56 (February 1990): 55–70.

Ceplair, Larry, ed. *The Public Years of Sarah and Angelina Grimké: Selected Writings 1835–1839*. New York: Columbia University Press, 1989.

Chadwick, John White. *A Life for Liberty: Anti-Slavery and Other Letters of Sallie Holley*. New York: G. P. Putnam's Sons, 1899.

Chamberlain, George Walter. *Genealogies of the Early Families of Weymouth, Massachusetts*. Baltimore: Genealogical Publishing Co., 1984.

———. *History of Weymouth*. Boston: Weymouth Historical Society, 1923.

Chambers, Lee V. "'Great Was the Benefit of His Death': The Political Uses of Maria Weston Chapman's Widowhood." In *Women on Their Own: Interdisciplinary Approaches*, edited by Rudolph M. Bell and Virginia Yans-McLaughlin, 157–79. New Brunswick, N.J.: Rutgers University Press, 2008.

Chambers-Schiller, Lee V. "The Cab, A Trans-Atlantic Community: Aspects of Nineteenth-Century Reform." Ph.D. diss., University of Michigan, 1976.

———. "'A Good Work among the People': The Political Culture of the Boston Antislavery Fair." In *The Abolitionist Sisterhood: Women's Political Culture in Antebellum America*, edited by Jean Fagan Yellin and John C. Van Horne, 249–74. Ithaca: Cornell University Press, 1994.

———. *Liberty, a Better Husband: Single Women in America: The Generations of 1780–1840*. New Haven: Yale University Press, 1984.

———. "Married to Each Other; Married to the Cause: Singlehood and Sibship in Antebellum Massachusetts." *Women's History Review* 17 (July 2008): 341–57.

Cherry, Deborah. *Beyond the Frame: Feminism and Visual Culture, Britain 1850–1900*. London: Routledge, 2000.

Clawson, Mary Ann. *Constructing Brotherhood: Class, Gender, and Fraternalism*. Princeton: Princeton University Press, 1989.

Clinton, Catherine. "Maria Weston Chapman (1806–1885)." In *Portraits of American Women From Settlement to the Civil War*, edited by G. J. Barker-Benfield and Catherine Clinton, 147–67. New York: St. Martin's Press, 1991.

———. *The Plantation Mistress: Woman's World in the Old South*. New York: Pantheon Books, 1982.

Cohen, Michael. *Sisters: Relation and Rescue in Nineteenth-Century British Novels and Paintings*. London: Associated University Presses, 1995.

Collison, Gary. "The Boston Vigilance Committee: A Reconsideration." *Historical Journal of Massachusetts* 12 (1984): 104–16.

———. *Shadrach Minkins: From Fugitive Slave to Citizen*. Cambridge: Harvard University Press, 1997.

Connelly, Mark Thomas. *The Response to Prostitution in the Progressive Era*. Chapel Hill: University of North Carolina Press, 1980.

Connolly, Brian J. "Domestic Intercourse: Incest, Family, and Sexuality in the United States, 1780–1871." Ph.D. diss., Rutgers University, 2007.

Cook, Elizabeth Heckendorn. *Epistolary Bodies: Gender and Genre in the Eighteenth-Century Republic of Letters.* Stanford: Stanford University Press, 1996.

Coser, Rose L., ed. *The Family: Its Structures and Functions.* New York: St. Martin's Press, 1974.

Cott, Nancy F. *The Bonds of Womanhood: "Women's Sphere" in New England, 1780–1835.* New Haven: Yale University Press, 1977.

———. "Giving Character to Our Whole Civil Polity: Marriage and the Public Order in the Late Nineteenth Century." In *U.S. History as Women's History: New Feminist Essays,* edited by Linda K. Kerber, Alice Kessler-Harris, and Kathryn Kish Sklar, 107–21. Chapel Hill: University of North Carolina Press, 1995.

———. "Marriage and Women's Citizenship in the United States, 1830–1934." *American Historical Review* 103 (December 1998): 1440–74.

———. *Public Vows: A History of Marriage and the Nation.* Cambridge: Harvard University Press, 2000.

Cover, Robert M. *Justice Accused: Antislavery and the Judicial Process.* New Haven: Yale University Press, 1975.

Crocker, Matthew H. *The Magic of the Many: Josiah Quincy and the Rise of Mass Politics in Boston, 1800–1830.* Amherst: University of Massachusetts Press, 1999.

Curry, Leonard P. *The Free Black in Urban America, 1800–1850: The Shadow of the Dream.* Chicago: University of Chicago Press, 1981.

Curry, Richard. O. *The American Abolitionists: Reformers or Fanatics?* New York: Holt, Rinehart and Winston, 1965.

Curry, Richard. O., and Lawrence Goodheart. "The Complexities of Factionalism: The Letters of Elizur Wright, Jr., on the Abolitionist Schism, 1837–1840." *Civil War History* 29 (September 1983): 243–59.

Czerkas, Jean. "The Averys and the Stantons, Family Ties That Bind." *Epitaph* 22 (Spring 2002).

Dalzell, Robert F., Jr. *Enterprising Elite: The Boston Associates and the World They Made.* Cambridge: Harvard University Press, 1987.

Davidoff, Leonore. "Kinship as a Categorical Concept: A Case Study of Nineteenth Century English Siblings." *Journal of Social History* 39 (2005): 411–28.

———. *Thicker than Water: Siblings and Their Relations, 1780–1920.* Oxford: Oxford University Press, 2012.

———. "Where the Stranger Begins: The Question of Siblings in Historical Analysis." Chapter 7 of *Worlds Between: Historical Perspectives on Gender and Class.* New York: Routledge, 1995.

Davidoff, Leonore, and Catherine Hall. *Family Fortunes: Men and Women of the English Middle-Class, 1780–1850.* London: Routledge, 2003.

Davidoff, Leonore, Meagan Dolittle, Janet Fink, and Katherine Holden. *The Family Story: Blood, Contract, and Intimacy, 1830–1960.* New York: Longman, 1991.

Davis, Asa J. "Two Autobiographical Fragments of George W. Latimer (1820–1896): A Preliminary Assessment." *Journal of the Afro-American Historical and Genealogical Society* 1 (Summer 1980): 3–18.

Davis, Henry C. "Negro Folk-lore in South Carolina." *Journal of American Folklore* 25 (July–September 1914): 241–54.

Dawley, Alan. *Class and Community: The Industrial Revolution in Lynn*. Cambridge: Harvard University Press, 1976.

Decker, William Merrill. *Epistolary Practices: Letter Writing in America before Telecommunications*. Chapel Hill: University of North Carolina Press, 1998.

DeLamotte, Eugenia C. *Perils of the Night: A Feminist Study of Nineteenth-Century Gothic*. New York: Oxford University Press, 1990.

Diedrich, Maria. *Love Across Color Lines: Ottilie Assing and Frederick Douglass*. New York: Hill and Wang, 1999.

Dillon, Lisa. "Women and the Dynamics of Marriage, Household Status, and Aging in Victorian Canada and the United States." *History of the Family* 4 (2000): 447–83.

Ditz, Toby L. "Formative Ventures: Eighteenth-Century Commercial Letters and the Articulation of Experience." In *Epistolary Selves: Letters and Letter-writers, 1600–1945*, edited by Rebecca Earle, 59–78. Brookfield, Vt.: Ashgate, 1999.

———. "Shipwrecked; or, Masculinity Imperiled: Mercantile Representations of Failure and the Gendered Self in Eighteenth-Century Philadelphia." *Journal of American History* 81 (June 1994): 51–80.

Dixon, Chris. *Perfecting the Family: Antislavery Marriages in Nineteenth-Century America*. Amherst: University of Massachusetts Press, 1997.

Dorsey, Bruce. *Reforming Men and Women: Gender in the Antebellum City*. Baltimore: Johns Hopkins University Press, 2002.

Duberman, Martin B., ed. *The Antislavery Vanguard: New Essays on the Abolitionists*. Princeton, N.J.: Princeton University Press, 1965.

———. "Behind the Scenes as the Massachusetts 'Coalition' of 1851 Divides the Spoils." *Essex Institute Historical Collections* 99 (April 1963): 152–60.

Dublin, Thomas. *Farm to Factory: Women's Letters, 1830–1860*. New York: Columbia University Press, 1993.

———. *Transforming Women's Work: New England Lives in the Industrial Revolution*. Ithaca: Cornell University Press, 1994.

DuBois, Ellen. *Feminism and Suffrage: The Emergence of an Independent Women's Movement in America, 1848–1869*. Ithaca: Cornell University Press, 1978.

Dudden, Faye E. *Serving Women: Household Service in Nineteenth-Century America*. Middletown: Wesleyan University Press, 1983.

Dumond, Dwight L. *Antislavery: The Crusade for Freedom in America*. Ann Arbor: University of Michigan Press, 1961.

Earle, Jonathan H. *Jacksonian Antislavery and the Politics of Free Soil, 1824–1854*. Chapel Hill: University of North Carolina Press, 2004.

———. "Marcus Morton and the Dilemma of Antislavery in Jacksonian Massachusetts, 1817–1849." *Massachusetts Historical Review* 2 (2002): 61–88.

Earle, Rebecca, ed. *Epistolary Selves: Letters and Letter-writers, 1600–1945*. Brookfield, Vt.: Ashgate, 1999.

Farber, Bernard. *Guardians of Virtue: Salem Families in 1800*. New York: Basic Books, 1972.

Farrell, Betty G. *Elite Families: Class and Power in Nineteenth-Century Boston.* Albany: State University of New York Press, 1993.

Faulkner, Carol. "The Root of the Evil: Free Produce and Radical Antislavery, 1820–1860." *Journal of the Early Republic* 27 (Fall 2007): 377–405.

Favret, Mary A. *Romantic Correspondence: Women, Politics, and the Fiction of Letters.* Cambridge: Cambridge University Press, 1993.

Feree, Myra Marx. "Beyond Separate Spheres." *Journal of Marriage and Family* 52 (1990): 866–84.

Fernandez, James W. *Persuasions and Performances: The Play of Tropes in Culture.* Bloomington: Indiana University Press, 1986.

Fliegelman, Jay. *Prodigals and Pilgrims: The American Revolution against Patriarchy.* Cambridge: Harvard University Press, 1985.

Foner, Eric. *Free Soil, Free Labor, Free Men: The Ideology of the Republican Party before the Civil War.* New York: Oxford University Press, 1970.

———. *Politics and Ideology in the Age of the Civil War.* New York: Oxford University Press, 1980.

Foner, Philip S. *History of Black Americans: From the Emergence of the Cotton Kingdom to the Eve of the Compromise of 1850.* Westport, Conn.: Greenwood Press, 1993.

Formisano, Ronald P. *The Transformation of Political Culture: Massachusetts Parties, 1790s–1840s.* New York: Oxford University Press, 1983.

Foucault, Michel. "The Eye of Power." In *Power and Knowledge: Selected Interviews and Other Writings*, edited by Colin Gordon. New York: Pantheon Books, 1980.

Frank, Stephen M. *Life with Father: Parenthood and Masculinity in the Nineteenth-Century American North.* Baltimore: Johns Hopkins University Press, 1998.

Fraser, Nancy. *Unruly Practices.* Minneapolis: University of Minnesota Press, 1989.

Frawley, Maria H. *Invalidism and Identity in Nineteenth-Century Britain.* Chicago: University of Chicago Press, 2004.

Freehling, William W. *The Road to Disunion: Secessionists at Bay, 1776–1854.* New York: Oxford University Press, 1990.

Friedman, Lawrence J. *Gregarious Saints: Self and Community in American Abolitionism, 1830–1870.* Cambridge: Cambridge University Press, 1982.

Fritzsche, Peter. "The Archive and the Case of the German Nation." In *Archive Stories: Facts, Fictions, and the Writing of History*, edited by Antoinette Burton, 182–209. Durham: Duke University Press, 2005.

Froide, Amy M. *Never Married: Singlewomen in Early Modern England.* New York: Oxford University Press, 2007.

Fuller, Wayne E. *The American Mail: Enlarger of Common Life.* Chicago: University of Chicago Press, 1972.

Gamber, Wendy. *The Female Economy: The Millinery and Dressmaking Trades, 1860–1930.* Urbana: University of Illinois Press, 1997.

Gaul, Theresa Strouth, ed. *To Marry an Indian: The Marriage of Harriett Gold and Elias Boudinot in Letters, 1823–1839.* Chapel Hill: University of North Carolina Press, 2005.

Gerteis, Louis S. *Morality and Utility in American Antislavery Reform.* Chapel Hill: University of North Carolina Press, 1987.

Gilfoyle, Timothy. *City of Eros: New York City, Prostitution, and the Commercialization of Sex, 1790–1920*. New York: W. W. Norton, 1992.

Gilje, Paul A. *Liberty on the Waterfront: American Maritime Culture in the Age of Revolution*. Philadelphia: University of Pennsylvania Press, 2003.

Ginzberg, Lori D. "Pernicious Heresies: Female Citizenship and Sexual Respectability in the Nineteenth Century." In *Women and the Unstable State in Nineteenth-Century America*, edited by Alison M. Parker and Stephanie Cole, 139–61. College Station: Texas A & M University Press, 2000.

———. *Untidy Origins: A Story of Woman's Rights in Antebellum New York*. Chapel Hill: University of North Carolina Press, 2005.

———. *Women and the Work of Benevolence: Morality, Politics, and Class in the Nineteenth-Century United States*. New Haven: Yale University Press, 1990.

Gittins, Diana. "Marital Status, Work and Kinship: 1850–1930." In *Labour and Love: Women's Experience of Home and Family, 1850–1940*, edited by Jane Lewis, 249–65. Oxford: Blackwell, 1996.

Glenn, Myra C. "Troubled Manhood in the Early Republic: The Life and Autobiography of Sailor Horace Lane." *Journal of the Early Republic* 26 (Spring 2006): 59–93.

Glick, Wendell P. "Thoreau and the 'Herald of Freedom.'" *New England Quarterly* 22 (June 1949): 193–204.

Glickstein, Jonathan A. *Concepts of Free Labor in Antebellum America*. New Haven: Yale University Press, 1991.

Glover, Kathryn. *The Fugitive's Gibraltar: Escaping Slaves and Abolitionism in New Bedford*. Amherst: University of Massachusetts Press, 2001.

Glover, Lorri. *All Our Relations: Blood Ties and Emotional Bonds among the Early South Carolina Gentry*. Baltimore: Johns Hopkins University Press 2000.

Goodheart, Lawrence B. *Abolitionist, Actuary, Atheist: Elizur Wright and the Reform Impulse*. Kent, Ohio: Kent State University Press, 1990.

Goodman, Paul. *Of One Blood: Abolitionism and the Origins of Racial Equality*. Berkeley: University of California Press, 1998.

Gordon, Eleanor, and Gwyneth Nair. "Middle Class Family Structure in Nineteenth-Century Glasgow." *Journal of Family History* 24 (October 1999): 468–77.

———. "The Myth of the Victorian Patriarchal Family." *History of the Family* 7 (2002): 125–38.

———. *Public Lives: Women, Family, and Society in Victorian Britain*. New Haven: Yale University Press, 2003.

Gough, Robert. "Close-Kin Marriage and Upper-Class Formation in Late Eighteenth-Century Philadelphia." *Journal of Family History* 14 (1989): 119–36.

Grimsted, David. *American Mobbing, 1828–1861: Toward Civil War*. New York: Oxford University Press, 1998.

Grossberg, Michael. *Governing the Hearth: Law and the Family in Nineteenth-Century America*. Chapel Hill: University of North Carolina Press, 1985.

Grover, Kathryn. *The Fugitive's Gibraltar: Escaping Slaves and Abolitionism in New Bedford, Massachusetts*. Amherst: University of Massachusetts Press, 2001.

Guarneri, Carl J. *The Utopian Alternative: Fourierism in Nineteenth-Century America*. Ithaca: Cornell University Press, 2002.

Gundersen, Joan. "Independence, Citizenship, and the American Revolution." *Signs: A Journal of Women in Culture and Society* 13 (Fall 1987): 59–77.

Hall, Nigel. "The Materiality of Letter Writing: A Nineteenth Century Perspective." In *Letter Writing as a Social Practice*, edited by David Barton and Nigel Hall, 83–108. Philadelphia: John Benjamins, 2000.

Hall, Peter D. "Family Structure and Economic Organization: Massachusetts Merchants, 1700–1850." In *Family and Kin in Urban Communities 1700–1930*, edited by Tamara K. Hareven, 38–61. New York: New Viewpoints, 1977.

———. "Marital Selection and Business in Massachusetts Merchant Families, 1700–1900." In *The Family: Its Structures and Functions*, edited by Rose L. Coser, 226–40. New York: St. Martin's Press, 1974.

Hamand, Wendy F. "The Woman's National Loyal League: Feminist Abolitionists and the Civil War." *Civil War History* 35 (1989): 39–58.

Hampel, Robert L. *Temperance and Prohibition in Massachusetts, 1813–1852*. Ann Arbor: UMI Research Press, 1982.

Hansen, Debra Gold. "The Boston Female Anti-Slavery Society and the Limits of Gender Politics." In *The Abolitionist Sisterhood: Women's Political Culture in Antebellum America*, edited by Jean Fagan Yellin and Van Horne, 45–65. Ithaca: Cornell University Press, 1994.

———. *Strained Sisterhood: Gender and Class in the Boston Female Anti-Slavery Society*. Amherst: University of Massachusetts Press, 1993.

Hansen, Karen V. *A Very Social Time: Crafting Community in Antebellum New England*. Berkeley: University of California Press, 1994.

Hareven, Tamara K., ed. *Family and Kin in Urban Communities, 1700–1930*. New York: New Viewpoints, 1977.

Harlow, Ralph V. *Gerrit Smith, Philanthropist and Reformer*. New York: Holt, 1939.

Harris, Sharon M. *American Women Writers to 1800*. New York: Oxford University Press, 1996.

Harrold, Stanley. *The Abolitionists and the South, 1831–1861*. Lexington: University of Kentucky Press, 1995.

Hartford, William F. *Money, Morals, and Politics: Massachusetts in the Age of the Boston Associates*. Boston: Northeastern University Press, 2001.

Hartigan-O'Connor, Ellen. "Abigail's Accounts: Economy and Affection in the Early Republic." *Journal of Women's History* 17 (2005): 35–58.

Hartog, Hendrik. *Man and Wife in America: A History*. Cambridge: Harvard University Press, 2000.

Heffernan, Nancy Coffey, and Ann Page Stecker. *Sisters of Fortune. Being the True story of How Three Motherless Sisters Saved Their Home in New England and Raised Their Younger Brother While Their Father Went Fortune Hunting in the California Gold Rush*. Hanover, N.H.: University Press of New England, 1993.

Hemphill, C. Dallett. "Fun with Ben and Jane: Brothers, Sisters, and Kin Work in Colonial America." Paper given at the Berkshire Conference of Women's Historians, 13 June 2008, Minneapolis, Minnesota.

———. *Siblings: Brothers and Sisters in American History*. New York: Oxford University Press, 2011.

Hersh, Blanche Glassman. *"The Slavery of Sex": Feminist-Abolitionists in America*. Urbana: University of Illinois Press, 1978.

Hewitt, Nancy. *Women's Activism and Social Change: Rochester, New York, 1822–1872*. Ithaca: Cornell University Press, 1984.

Hidy, Ralph W. *The House of Baring in American Trade and Finance*. Cambridge: Harvard University Press, 1949.

———. "The Organization and Functions of Anglo-American Merchant Bankers, 1815–1860." *Journal of Economic History* 1 (1941): 53–66.

Hill, Bridget. *Women Alone: Spinsters in Britain, 1660–1850*. New Haven: Yale University Press, 2001.

Hobson, Barbara. *Uneasy Virtue: The Politics of Prostitution and the American Reform Tradition*. New York: Basic Books, 1987.

Hoffert, Sylvia D. *When Hens Crow: The Woman's Rights Movement in Antebellum America*. Bloomington: Indiana University Press, 1995.

Hoganson, Kristin. "Garrisonian Abolitionists and the Rhetoric of Gender, 1850–1860." *American Quarterly* 45 (December 1993): 558–95.

Holden, Katherine. *The Shadow of Marriage: Singleness in England, 1914–1960*. Manchester: Manchester University Press, 2008.

Holt, Michael F. *The Political Crisis of the 1850s*. New York: Wiley, 1978.

———. *The Rise and Fall of the American Whig Party: Jacksonian Politics and the Onset of the Civil War*. New York: Oxford University Press, 1999.

Horton, James Oliver, and Lois E. Horton. *Black Bostonians: Family Life and Community Struggle in the Antebellum North*. New York: Holmes and Meier, 1979.

———. *In Hope of Liberty: Culture, Community, and Protest among Northern Free Blacks*. New York: Oxford University Press, 1997.

How, James. *Epistolary Spaces: English Letter Writing from the Foundation of the Post Office to Richardson's Clarissa*. Burlington, Vt.: Ashgate, 2003.

Howe, Anthony. *The Cotton Masters, 1830–1860*. Oxford: Oxford University Press, 1984.

Howe, Daniel Walker. *The Political Culture of the American Whigs*. Chicago: University of Chicago Press, 1979.

Isenberg, Nancy. *Sex and Citizenship in Antebellum America*. Chapel Hill: University of North Carolina Press, 1998.

Jabour, Anya. "'It Will Never Do for Me to Be Married': The Life of Laura Wirt Randall, 1803–1833." *Journal of the Early Republic* 17 (Summer 1997): 193–236.

Jeffrey, Julie Roy. *Abolitionists Remember: Antislavery Autobiographies and the Unfinished Work of Emancipation*. Chapel Hill: University of North Carolina Press, 2008.

———. *The Great Silent Army of Abolitionism: Ordinary Women in the Antislavery Movement*. Chapel Hill: University of North Carolina Press, 1998.

———. "The Liberty Women of Boston: Evangelicalism and Antislavery Politics." *New England Quarterly* 85 (March 2012): 38–77.

――. "Permeable Boundaries: Abolitionist Women and Separate Spheres." *Journal of the Early Republic* 21 (Spring 2001): 79–93.

Jensen, Joan M. "Cloth, Butter, and Boarders: Women's Household Production for the Market." *Review of Radical Political Economics* 12 (Summer 1980): 14–24.

――. *Loosening the Bonds: Mid-Atlantic Farm Women, 1750-1850.* New Haven: Yale University Press, 1980.

Johansen, Shawn. *Family Men: Middle-Class Fatherhood in Early Industrializing America.* New York: Routledge, 2001.

Johnson, Allan G. *Privilege, Power, and Difference.* New York: McGraw Hill, 2006.

Johnson, Joan Marie. "'How Would I Live Without Loulie?' Mary and Louisa Poppenheim, Activist Sisters in Turn-of-the-Century South Carolina." *Journal of Family History* 28 (October 2003): 561–77.

Kaster, Gregory L. "Labor's True Men: Organized Workingmen and the Language of Manliness in the USA, 1827-1877." *Gender and History* 12 (April 2001): 24–64.

Katzman, David. *Seven Days a Week: Women and Domestic Service in Industrializing America.* New York: Oxford University Press, 1978.

Kelley, Mary. "Catharine Maria Sedgwick." *New England Quarterly* 66 (1993): 366–98.

――. *Learning to Stand and Speak: Women, Education, and Public Life in America's Republic.* Chapel Hill: University of North Carolina Press, 2006.

――. "Negotiating a Self: The Autobiography and Journals of Catharine Maria Sedgwick." *New England Quarterly* 66 (September 1993): 366–98.

Kelly, Catherine E. *In the New England Fashion: Reshaping Women's Lives in the Nineteenth Century.* Ithaca: Cornell University Press, 1999.

Kevitt, Chester B. *Weymouth, Massachusetts: A New England Town.* Weymouth, Mass., 1981.

Kierner, Cynthia A. *Beyond the Household: Women's Place in the Early South, 1700-1835.* Ithaca: Cornell University Press, 1998.

――. "Hospitality, Sociability, and Gender in the Southern Colonies." *Journal of Southern History* 62 (August 1996): 449–80.

Klepp, Susan E. *Revolutionary Conceptions: Women, Fertility, and Family Limitation in America, 1760-1820.* Chapel Hill: University of North Carolina Press, 2009.

Kraditor, Aileen S. *Means and Ends in American Abolition: Garrison and His Critics on Strategy and Tactics, 1834-1850.* New York: Vintage Books, 1967.

Kurtz, Donn M., II. *Kinship and Politics: The Justices of the United States and Louisiana Supreme Courts.* Baton Rouge: Louisiana State University Press, 1997.

Lakoff, George, and Mark Johnson. *Metaphors We Live By.* Chicago: University of Chicago Press, 1980.

Laslett, Peter, Karla Oosterveen, and Richard M. Smith. *Bastardy and Its Comparative History: Studies in the History of Illegitimacy and Marital Nonconformism.* Cambridge: Harvard University Press, 1980.

Lasser, Carole. "'Let Us Be Sisters Forever': The Sororal Model of Nineteenth-Century Female Friendships." *Signs: A Journal of Women in Culture and Society* 14 (Autumn 1988): 158–81.

Laurie, Bruce. *Beyond Garrison: Antislavery and Social Reform*. New York: Cambridge University Press, 2005.

Lawes, Carolyn J. *Women and Reform in a New England Community, 1815–1860*. Lexington: University Press of Kentucky, 2000.

Leavitt, Judith Walzer. "Under the Shadow of Maternity: American Women's Responses to Death and Debility Fears in Nineteenth-Century Childbirth." *Feminist Studies* 12 (Spring 1986): 129–54.

Lerner, Gerda. *The Feminist Thought of Sarah Grimké*. New York: Oxford University Press, 1998.

——. *The Grimké Sisters from South Carolina: Rebels against Slavery*. Boston: Houghton Mifflin, 1967.

——. *The Grimké Sisters of North Carolina: Pioneers for Women's Rights and Abolitionism*. New York: Oxford University Press, 1967.

——. *The Majority Finds Its Past: Placing Women in History*. New York: Oxford University Press, 1979.

Levesque, George A. *Black Boston: African American Life and Culture in Urban America, 1750–1860*. New York: Garland Publishing, 1994.

Levy, Leonard W. "The 'Abolition Riot': Boston's First Slave Rescue." *New England Quarterly* 25 (March 1952): 85–92.

Lockley, Timothy James. *Welfare and Charity in the Antebellum South*. Gainesville: University Press of Florida, 2007.

Lumpkin, Katherine DuPre. *The Emancipation of Angelina Grimké*. Chapel Hill: University of North Carolina Press, 1974.

Lutz, Alma. *Crusade for Freedom: Women of the Antislavery Movement*. Boston: Beacon Press, 1968.

MacCannell, Juliet F. *The Regime of the Brother: After the Patriarchy*. London: Routledge, 1991.

Magdol, Edward. *The Antislavery Rank and File: A Social Profile of the Abolitionists' Constituency*. Westport, Conn.: Greenwood Press, 1986.

Main, Gloria. "Rocking the Cradle: Downsizing the New England Family." *Journal of Interdisciplinary History* 37 (2006–7): 35–58.

Marilley, Suzanne M. *Woman Suffrage and the Origins of Liberal Feminism in the United States, 1820–1930*. Cambridge: Harvard University Press, 1996.

Marshall, Megan. *The Peabody Sisters: Three Women Who Ignited American Romanticism*. Boston: Houghton Mifflin, 2005.

Matthes, Melissa. *The Rape of Lucretia and the Founding of Republics*. University Park: Pennsylvania State University Press, 2000.

May, Leila Silvana. *Disorderly Sisters: Sibling Relations and Sororal Resistance in Nineteenth-Century British Literature*. Lewisburg, Pa.: Bucknell University Press, 2001.

Mayer, Henry. *All On Fire: William Lloyd Garrison and the Abolition of Slavery*. New York: St. Martin's Press, 1998.

McCurry, Stephanie. "Two Faces of Republicanism: Gender and Proslavery Politics in Antebellum South Carolina." *Journal of American History* 78 (March 1992): 1245–64.

McDaniel, W. Caleb. *The Problem of Democracy in the Age of Slavery: Garrisonian Abolitionists & Transatlantic Reform*. Baton Rouge: Louisiana State University Press, 2013.

McPherson, James M. *The Abolitionist Legacy from Reconstruction to the NAACP*. Princeton, N.J.: Princeton University Press, 1975.

McWilliams, Wilson Carey. *The Idea of Fraternity in America*. Los Angeles: University of California Press, 1973.

Melder, Keith F. *The Beginnings of Sisterhood: The American Women's Rights Movement, 1800–1850*. New York: Schocken Books, 1977.

——. "Woman's High Calling: The Teaching Profession in America, 1830–60." *American Studies* 13 (1972): 19–32.

Melish, Joanne Pope. *Disowning Slavery: Gradual Emancipation and "Race" in New England, 1780–1860*. Ithaca: Cornell University Press, 1998.

Miller, Marla R. "'My Part Alone': The World of Rebecca Dickinson, 1787–1802." *New England Quarterly* 71 (September 1998): 341–77.

Morris, Thomas D. *Free Men All: The Personal Liberty Laws of the North, 1780–1861*. Baltimore: Johns Hopkins University Press, 1974.

Motz, Marilyn Ferris. *True Sisterhood: Michigan Women and Their Kin, 1820–1920*. Albany: State University of New York Press, 1983.

Mulkern, John R. *The Know-Nothing Party in Massachusetts: The Rise and Fall of a People's Movement*. Boston: Northeastern University Press, 1990.

Murphy, Teresa Anne. *Ten Hours' Labor: Religion, Reform, and Gender in Early New England*. Ithaca: Cornell University Press, 1992.

Muzzey, Artemus B. *The Young Maiden*. Boston, 1840.

Newman, Richard S. *The Transformation of American Abolitionism: Fighting Slavery in the Early Republic*. Chapel Hill: University of North Carolina Press, 2002.

Newmyer, R. Kent. *Supreme Court Justice Joseph Story: Statesman of the Old Republic*. Chapel Hill: University of North Carolina Press, 1986.

O'Brien, Michael. *An Evening When Alone: Four Journals of Single Women in the South, 1827–1867*. Richmond: University of Virginia Press, 1993.

O'Connor, Thomas H. *The Athens of America: Boston, 1825–1845*. Amherst: University of Massachusetts Press, 2006.

O'Day, Rosemarie. *The Family and Family Relationships, 1500–1900: England, France, and the United States of America*. New York: St. Martin's Press, 1994.

Osterud, Nancy, and John Fulton. "Family Limitation and Age at Marriage: Fertility Decline in Sturbridge, Massachusetts, 1730–1850." *Population Studies* 30 (November 1976): 481–94.

Palmer, Phyllis. *Domesticity and Dirt: Housewives and Domestic Servants in the United States, 1920–1945*. Philadelphia: Temple University Press, 1989.

Parsons, Elaine Frantz. *Manhood Lost: Fallen Drunkards and Redeeming Women in the Nineteenth-Century United States*. Baltimore: Johns Hopkins University Press, 2003.

Pateman, Carole. *The Disorder of Women*. Stanford: Stanford University Press, 1989.

——. *Fraternal Social Contract*. Malden, Mass.: Blackwell Publishing, 2006.

——. *The Sexual Contract*. Stanford.: Stanford University Press, 1988.

Pease, Jane H., and William H. Pease. *Bound with Them in Chains: A Biographical History of the Antislavery Movement.* Westport, Conn.: Greenwood Press, 1972.

——. *A Family of Women: The Carolina Petigrus in Peace and War.* Chapel Hill: University of North Carolina Press, 1999.

——. *The Fugitive Slave Law and Anthony Burns: A Problem in Law Enforcement.* Philadelphia: Lippincott, 1975.

——. *Ladies, Women, and Wenches: Choice and Constraint in Antebellum Charleston and Boston.* Chapel Hill: University of North Carolina Press, 1990.

Perlmann, Joel, and Robert A. Margo. *Women's Work? American Schoolteachers, 1650–1920.* Chicago: University of Chicago Press, 2001.

Perlmann, Joel, Silvana R. Siddali, and Keith Whitescarver. "Literacy, Schooling, and Teaching among New England Women, 1730–1820." *History of Education Quarterly* 37 (Summer 1997): 118–39.

Perry, Lewis. *Radical Abolitionism: Anarchy and the Government of God in Antislavery Thought.* Ithaca: Cornell University Press, 1973.

Perry, Mark. *Lift Up Thy Voice: The Grimké Family's Journey from Slaveholders to Civil Rights Leaders.* New York: Viking, 2001.

Petrulionis, Sandra Harbert. *To Set This World Right: The Antislavery Movement in Thoreau's Concord.* Ithaca: Cornell University Press, 2006.

Pierson, Michael D. *Free Hearts and Free Homes: Gender and American Antislavery Politics.* Chapel Hill: University of North Carolina Press, 2003.

Porter, Susan Lynn. "Victorian Values in the Marketplace: Single Women and Work in Boston, 1800–1850." In *Women of the Commonwealth: Work, Family, and Social Change in Nineteenth-Century Massachusetts,* edited by Susan L. Porter, 17–41. Amherst: University of Massachusetts Press, 1996.

Portnoy, Alisse. *Their Right to Speak: Women's Activism in the Indian and Slave Debates.* Cambridge: Harvard University Press, 2005.

Powell, William S., ed. *Dictionary of North Carolina Biography.* Vol. 4. Chapel Hill: University of North Carolina Press, 1991.

Preston, Jo Anne. "Domestic Ideology, School Reformers, and Female Teachers: Schoolteaching Becomes Women's Work in Nineteenth-Century New England." *New England Quarterly* 66 (December 1993): 531–51.

Quarles, Benjamin. *Black Abolitionists.* New York: Oxford University Press, 1969.

Rael, Patrick. *Black Identity and Black Protest in the Antebellum North.* Chapel Hill: University of North Carolina Press, 2002.

Randolph, John. "On the Biography of the Bakunin Family Archive." In *Archive Stories: Facts, Fictions, and the Writing of History,* edited by Antoinette Burton, 209–31. Durham: Duke University Press, 2005.

Richards, Leonard L. *"Gentlemen of Property and Standing": Anti-Abolitionist Mobs in Jacksonian America.* New York: Oxford University Press, 1970.

Robertson, Stacey M. *Hearts Beating for Liberty: Women Abolitionists in the Old Northwest.* Chapel Hill: University of North Carolina Press, 2010.

Roper, Michael, and John Tosh, eds. *Manful Assertions: Masculinities in Britain Since 1800.* New York: Routledge, 1991.

Rorabaugh, Walter J. *The Alcoholic Republic: An American Tradition.* New York: Oxford University Press, 1981.

Rothman, Sheila M. *Living in the Shadow of Death: Tuberculosis and the Social Experience of Illness in American History.* New York: Basic Books, 1994.

Rotundo, E. Anthony. *American Manhood: Transformations in Masculinity from the Revolution to the Modern Era.* New York: Basic Books, 1993.

Ruchames, Louis. "Race, Marriage and Abolition in Massachusetts." *Journal of Negro History* 40 (1955): 250–73.

Ruggles, Steven. *Prolonged Connections: The Rise of the Extended Family in Nineteenth-Century England and America.* Madison: University of Wisconsin Press, 1987.

———. "The Transformation of the American Family Structure." *American Historical Review* 99 (February 1994): 103–28.

Ryan, Mary P. *Cradle of the Middle Class: The Family in Oneida County, New York, 1790–1865.* New York: Cambridge University Press, 1981.

———. "The Power of Women's Networks: A Case Study of Female Moral Reform Societies in Antebellum America." *Feminist Studies* 5 (Spring 1979): 66–86.

———. "A Woman's Awakening: Evangelical Religion and the Families of Utica, New York, 1800–1840." *American Quarterly* 30 (Winter 1978): 602–23.

———. *Women in Public between Banners and Ballots, 1825–1880.* Baltimore: Johns Hopkins University Press, 1990.

Salerno, Beth A. *Sister Societies: Women's Antislavery Organizations in Antebellum America.* DeKalb: Northern Illinois University Press, 2005.

Sanchez-Eppler, Karen. "Bodily Bonds: The Intersecting Rhetorics of Feminism and Abolition." *Representations* (Fall 1988): 28–59.

Sandage, Scott A. *Born Losers: A History of Failure in America.* Cambridge: Harvard University Press, 2005.

Sanders, Valerie. *The Brother-Sister Culture in Nineteenth-Century Literature.* New York: Palgrave, 2002.

Scott, Anne Firor. *Natural Allies: Women's Associations in American History.* Urbana: University of Illinois Press, 1993.

Sewell, Richard H. *Ballots for Freedom: Antislavery Politics in the United States, 1837–1860.* New York: Oxford University Press, 1976.

Shammas, Carole. *A History of Household Government in America.* Charlottesville: University of Virginia Press, 2002.

Shields, David S. *Civil Tongues and Polite Letters in British America.* Chapel Hill: University of North Carolina Press, 1997.

Sklar, Kathryn Kish. *Women's Rights Emerges within the Antislavery Movement, 1830–1870.* Boston: Bedford/St. Martin's, 2000.

Smith, Daniel Scott. "'All in Some Degree Related to Each Other': A Demographic and Comparative Resolution of the Anomaly of New England Kinship." *American Historical Review* 94 (February 1989): 44–79.

———. "American Illegitimacy and Prenuptial Pregnancy." In *Bastardy and Its Comparative History*, edited by Peter Laslett, Karla Oosterveen, and Richard M. Smith. Cambridge: Harvard University Press, 1980.

———. "Family Limitation, Sexual Control, and Domestic Feminism in Victorian America." *Feminist Studies* 1 (1973): 40–57.

———. "Female Householding in Late Eighteenth-Century America and the Problem of Poverty." *Journal of Social History* (1994): 83–107.

———. "The Meanings of Family and Household: Change and Continuity in the Mirror of the American Census." *Population and Development Review* 18 (September 1992): 421–56.

Smith, Daniel Scott, and Michael S. Hindus. "Premarital Pregnancy in America, 1640–1971: An Overview and Interpretation." *Journal of Interdisciplinary History* 5 (Winter 1975): 537–70.

Smith, Judith. *Family Connections: A History of Italian and Jewish Immigrant Lives in Providence, Rhode Island, 1900–1940*. Albany: State University of New York Press, 1985.

Smith, Sidonie. *A Poetics of Women's Autobiography: Marginality and the Fictions of Self-Representation*. Bloomington: Indiana University Press, 1987.

Solomon, Barbara Miller. *In the Company of Educated Women*. New Haven: Yale University Press, 1985.

Stack, Carol B. *All Our Kin: Strategies for Survival in a Black Community*. New York: Harper & Row, 1974.

Stange, Douglas C. *Patterns of Antislavery among American Unitarians, 1831–1860*. Rutherford, N.J.: Fairleigh Dickinson University Press, 1977.

Stansell, Christine. *City of Women: Sex and Class in New York, 1789–1860*. Champaign-Urbana: University of Illinois Press, 1987.

Stapp, Carol Buchalter. *Afro-Americans in Antebellum Boston: An Analysis of Probate Records*. New York: Garland Publishing, 1993.

Stauffer, John. *Black Hearts of Men: Radical Abolitionists and the Transformation of Race*. Cambridge: Harvard University Press, 2002.

Sterling, Dorothy. *Ahead of Her Time: Abby Kelley and the Politics of Antislavery*. New York: W. W. Norton, 1991.

———. *We Are Your Sisters: Black Women in the Nineteenth Century*. New York: W. W. Norton, 1997.

Stewart, James Brewer. *Holy Warriors: The Abolitionists and American Slavery*. New York: Hill and Wang, 1976.

———. *William Lloyd Garrison and the Challenge of Emancipation*. Arlington Heights, Ill.: H. Davidson, 1992.

Still, William. *The Underground Railroad*. New York: Arno Press, 1968.

Strasser, Susan. *Never Done: A History of American Housework*. New York: Pantheon Books, 1982.

Sutherland, Daniel E. *Americans and Their Servants: Domestic Service in the United States from 1800 to 1920*. Baton Rouge: Louisiana State University Press, 1981.

Tadmor, Naomi. *Family and Friends in Eighteenth-Century England: Household, Kinship, and Patronage*. Cambridge: Cambridge University Press, 2001.

Tager, Jack. *Boston Riots: Three Centuries of Social Violence*. Boston: Northeastern University Press, 2001.

Tate, Gayle T. "Political Consciousness and Resistance among Black Antebellum Women." *Women and Politics* 13 (1993): 67–89.

Taylor, Alice. "From Petitions to Partyism: Antislavery and the Domestication of Maine Politics in the 1840s and 1850s." *New England Quarterly* 77 (March 2004): 70–88.

——. "Selling Abolitionism: The Commercial, Material, and Social World of the Boston Antislavery Fair, 1834–58." Ph.D. diss., Western Ontario University, 2007.

Taylor, Clare. *Women of the Anti-Slavery Movement: The Weston Sisters.* New York: St. Martin's Press, 1995.

Thomas, John L. *The Liberator: William Lloyd Garrison.* Boston: Little, Brown, 1963.

Tilly, Charles. *Social Movements, 1768-2004.* Boulder: Paradigm, 2004.

Trinterud, Leonard J. *The Forming of an American Tradition.* Philadelphia: Westminster Press, 1949.

Tyrrell, Ian R. *Sobering Up: From Temperance to Prohibition in Antebellum America, 1800-1860.* Westport, Conn.: Greenwood Press, 1979.

Uhlenberg, Peter. "A Study of Cohort Life Cycles: Cohorts of Native Born Massachusetts Women, 1830–1920." *Population Studies* 23 (1969): 420.

Ulrich, Laurel. "Martha Ballard and Her Girls: Women's Work in Eighteenth Century Maine." In *Work and Labor in Early America*, edited by Stephen Innes, 70–105. Chapel Hill: University of North Carolina Press, 1988.

Van Broekhoven, Deborah Bingham. "'Better than a Clay Club': The Organization of Anti-Slavery Fairs, 1835-60." *Slavery and Abolition* 19 (April 1998): 24–45.

——. *The Devotion of These Women: Rhode Island in the Antislavery Movement.* Amherst: University of Massachusetts Press, 2002.

——. "'Let Your Names Be Enrolled'": Method and Ideology in Women's Antislavery Petitioning." In *The Abolitionist Sisterhood: Women's Political Culture in Antebellum America*, edited by Jean Fagan Yellin and John C. Van Horne, 179–99. Ithaca: Cornell University Press, 1994.

Varon, Elizabeth R. *Disunion! The Coming of the American Civil War, 1789-1859.* Chapel Hill: University of North Carolina Press, 2008.

——. "Tippecanoe and the Ladies, Too: White Women and Party Politics in Antebellum Virginia." *Journal of American History* 82 (September 1995): 494–521.

——. *We Mean to Be Counted: White Women and Politics in Antebellum Virginia.* Chapel Hill: University of North Carolina Press, 1998.

Vicinus, Martha. *Independent Women: Work and Community for Single Women, 1850-1920.* London: Virago, 1985.

Vickers, Daniel. *Farmers and Fishermen: Two Centuries of Work in Essex County, Massachusetts, 1630-1850.* Chapel Hill: University of North Carolina Press, 1994.

Vickers, Daniel, and Vince Walsh. *Young Men and the Sea: Yankee Seafarers in the Age of Sail.* New Haven: Yale University Press, 2005.

Vinovskis, Maris A., and Richard M. Bernard. "Beyond Catherine Beecher: Female Education in the Antebellum Period." *Signs: A Journal of Women in Culture and Society* 3 (1978): 856–69.

———. "Trends in Massachusetts Education, 1826–1860." *History of Education Quarterly* 12 (Winter 1972): 501–29.

Von Frank, Albert. *The Trials of Anthony Burns: Freedom and Slavery in Emerson's Boston.* Cambridge: Harvard University Press, 1998.

Voss-Hubbard, Mark. "Slavery, Capitalism, and the Middling Sorts: The Rank and File of Political Abolitionism." *American Nineteenth Century History* 4 (Summer 2003): 53–76.

Wallace, Anthony E. C. *Rockdale: The Growth of an American Village in the Early Industrial Revolution.* New York: Alfred A. Knopf, 1978.

Wallace, James M. "The Feminization of Teaching in Massachusetts: A Reconsideration." In *Women of the Commonwealth: Work, Family, and Social Change in Nineteenth-Century Massachusetts,* edited by Susan L. Porter, 43–61. Amherst: University of Massachusetts Press, 1996.

Walters, Ronald. *The Antislavery Appeal: American Abolitionism after 1830.* Baltimore: Johns Hopkins University Press, 1976.

Webb, Robert K. *Harriet Martineau: A Radical Victorian.* New York: Columbia University Press, 1960.

Weeks, Jeffrey. "Pretended Family Relationships." In *Marriage, Domestic Life, and Social Change: Writings for Jacqueline Burgoyne (1944–1988),* edited by David Clark, 187–230. New York: Routledge, 1991.

Wellman, Judith. *The Road to Seneca Falls: Elizabeth Cady Stanton and the First Women's Rights Convention.* Urbana: University of Illinois Press, 2004.

———. "Women and Radical Reform in Antebellum Upstate New York: A Profile of Grassroots Female Abolitionists." In *Clio Was a Woman: Studies in the History of American Women,* edited by Mabel E. Deutrich and Virginia C. Purdy, 112–27. Washington, D.C.: Howard University Press, 1980.

Wells, Robert V. "Illegitimacy and Bridal Pregnancy in Colonial America." In *Bastardy and Its Comparative History: Studies in the History of Illegitimacy and Marital Nonconformism,* edited by Peter Laslett, Karla Oosterveen, and Richard M. Smith, 349–61. Cambridge: Harvard University Press, 1980.

Wesley, Dorothy Porter, and Constance Porter Uzelac, eds. *William Cooper Nell: Nineteenth Century African-American Abolitionist, Historian, Integrationist; Selected Writings, 1832–1874.* Baltimore: Black Classic Press, 2002.

Wiecek, William M. "Latimer: Lawyers, Abolitionists, and the Problem of Unjust Laws." In *Antislavery Reconsidered: New Perspectives on the Abolitionists,* edited by Lewis Perry and Michael Fellman, 219–35. Baton Rouge: Louisiana State University Press, 1979.

Wilentz, Sean. *Chants Democratic: New York City and the Rise of the American Working Class, 1788–1850.* New York: Oxford University Press, 1984.

Winter, Kari J. *Subjects of Slavery, Agents of Change: Women and Power in Gothic Novels and Slave Narratives, 1790–1865.* Athens: University of Georgia Press, 1992.

Withey, L. E. "Household Structure in Urban and Rural Areas: The Case of Rhode Island, 1774–1800." *Journal of Family History* 3 (1978): 37–50.

Wolfson, Susan J. *Felicia Hemans: Selected Poems, Letters, Reception Materials.* Princeton, N.J.: Princeton University Press, 2000.

Wulf, Karin. *Not All Wives: Women of Colonial Pennsylvania*. Ithaca: Cornell University Press, 2000.

Wyatt-Brown, Bertram. *Lewis Tappan and the Evangelical War against Slavery*. Baton Rouge: Louisiana State University Press, 1997.

Yasuba, Yasukchi. "Birth Rates of the White Population in the United States, 1800–1860." *Johns Hopkins University Studies in Historical and Political Science* 79 (1961): 109.

Yee, Shirley J. *Black Women Abolitionists: A Study in Activism, 1828-1860*. Knoxville: University of Tennessee Press, 1992.

Yellin, Jean Fagan. *Women and Sisters: The Antislavery Feminists in American Culture*. New Haven: Yale University Press, 1989.

Zaeske, Susan. *Signatures of Citizenship: Petitioning, Antislavery, and Women's Political Identity*. Chapel Hill: University of North Carolina Press, 2003.

——. "'The South Arose as One Man': Gender and Sectionalism in Anti-Slavery Petition Debates, 1835-1845." *Rhetoric & Public Affairs* 12 (Fall 2009): 341-68.

Zboray, Ronald J., and Mary Saracino Zboray. "Books, Reading, and the World of Goods in Antebellum New England." *American Quarterly* 48 (December 1996): 587-622.

——. "Political News and Female Readership in Antebellum Boston and Its Region." *Journalism History* 22 (Spring 1996): 2-14.

——. "Whig Women, Politics, and Culture in the Campaign of 1840: Three Perspectives from Massachusetts." *Journal of the Early Republic* 17 (1997): 277-315.

Index

Barring Brothers: temperance ship, 236 (n. 22)

Bates, Col. Joshua, 47, 48; identified, 223 (n. 12)

Bates, Joshua, 4, 44, 162, 225 (n. 26), 234 (n. 7); economic assistance to Westons, 49, 64, 65, 67, 80, 225 (n. 25), 235 (n. 16), 235 (n. 17); on social position, 54, 135, 271 (n. 91); occupation, 65; economic assistance to Tirzah Bates Pratt Hunt, Cynthia Bates Cowing, and Henry Cowing, 65, 235 (n. 10), 235 (n. 14), 236 (n. 21); and temperance, 66, 210 (n. 16), 236 (nn. 22–23); economic assistance to Chapmans, 227 (n. 52), 237 (nn. 28–29), 248 (n. 44); economic assistance to Elizabeth [Betsy] Sturgis, Harriet Sturgis, and John Sturgis, 234 (n. 10)

Bates, Lucretia Sturgis, 54, 67, 235 (n. 10), 236 (n. 21)

Bates, Tirzah Pratt, 47, 224 (n. 20), 235 (n. 10), 235 (n. 14)

Beaumont, Gustave de, 136, 290 (n. 66)

Belknap Street School, 239 (n. 42)

Benson, Anna Elizabeth: as antislavery sibling, 9

Benson, Frances: as antislavery sibling, 9

Benson, George W., 55, 218 (n. 87)

Benson, Mary: as antislavery sibling, 9

Benson, Sarah Thurber: as antislavery sibling, 9

Birney, James G., 35, 37, 38; identified, 196 (n. 3), 217 (n. 84)

Blagden, George W., 30, 217 (n. 86)

"Boston clique," 59, 143, 145, 231 (n. 85), 256 (n. 25), 275 (n. 14)

Boston Female Anti-Slavery Society (BFAS), 19, 38, 122, 142, 218 (n. 89), 284 (n. 16); membership, 1, 195 (n. 1), 210 (n. 19); division of, 4, 36, 195 (n. 1), 196 (n. 3); fairs, 9, 42, 43, 211 (nn. 24–25); male participation in, 213 (n. 47). *See also* Fair, Boston Female Anti-Slavery Society

Boston High School for Girls, 238 (n. 32)

Boston literary and social elite, 270–71 (n. 88)

Boston Vigilance Committee, 6, 199 (n. 30), 273 (n. 1), 292 (n. 11); and Hervey Weston, 273 (n. 1)

Bowditch, Henry I., 39, 40, 163

Boylan, Anne M., 14, 15; on single female abolitionists, 206 (n. 81), 207 (n. 84)

Boyle, Laura, 144

Boyle, James, 144; identified, 277 (n. 28)

Bradburn, George, 41, 140; on Chapman's "insolence," 158

British & Foreign Anti-Slavery Society, 37, 42, 134, 164, 178, 287 (n. 43), 288 (n. 45)

Brooks, John, 57

Brooks, Lucy, 57

Brooks, Mary Merrick, 53, 120, 227 (n. 56); identified, 262 (n. 14)

Brooks, Nathan, 53, 227 (n. 56); and Weston beau ideal, 53–54

Brown, William W., 123, 259 (n. 63)

Browning, Elizabeth Barrett, 135, 232 (n. 91)

Browning, Robert, 135

Buffum, Lucy, 115

Burleigh, Charles C., 37; identified, 284 (n. 10)

Burns, Anthony, 128, 177, 200 (n. 31), 217 (n. 82), 267 (n. 55)

Butler, Fanny Kemble, 147

Cabot, Frederick S., 39

Cabot, Susan, 86, 105, 195 (n. 1); as antislavery sibling, 9, 15

Carter, Christine Jacobson, 244 (n. 4)

Chace, Eliza J., 55, 229 (n. 68)

Chace, William M., 55–56, 229 (nn. 67–70)

Chamerovzow, Louis Alexis, 134, 270 (n. 84), 288 (n. 45)

Channing, William Ellery, 24–25, 32, 56, 212 (n. 34), 271 (n. 88)

Channing, William F., 39–40

Chapman, Ann Greene, 22, 25, 142, 146, 147, 210 (n. 18); as antislavery sibling, 9

Chapman, Ann Greene (Dicey), 5, 44, 83, 85–86, 124, 135, 228 (n. 57); fears of anti-abolitionist behavior, 85

Chapman, Elizabeth Bates, 5, 70, 82, 176; courtship and marriage, 43, 61, 86, 87, 248 (n. 37); behavioral problems of, 82–86; anti-abolitionist roots of rebelliousness, 84–85; inheritance, 244 (n. 102). *See also* Laugel, Auguste

Chapman, Gertrude, 40, 82, 90, 107, 125–26, 130

Chapman, Henry, 41, 64, 76, 79, 92, 186, 223 (n. 16), 249 (n. 52), 285 (n. 26)

Chapman, Henry Grafton, 6, 24, 39, 79, 84, 159, 177, 202 (n. 48), 225 (n. 23); identified, 226 (n. 52); as founder of "Free Church," 26; as treasurer of MAS, 31, 38, 90; illness of, 41, 78, 89–92, 249–50 (n. 60); as husband, 53, 54; recuperation in Haiti, 90–91, 126; household governance of, 159–60; harassment of, 212 (n. 32); temperament and character of, 226 (n. 43), 250 (n. 66); occupation of, 226–27 (n. 52), 237–38 (n. 29)

Chapman, Henry Grafton, Jr., 44, 82, 86, 135, 227 (n. 53), 246 (n. 22), 244 (n. 102), 245 (n. 10); behavioral problems of, 82–86, 118, 206 (n. 78); schooling of, 84, 86; and courtship, 87–88, 248 (n. 44); occupation, 88; identified, 226–27 (n. 52)

Chapman, Maria Weston: attributes and reputation, 2, 8, 42, 126–27, 158, 165, 197 (n. 13), 254 (n. 115), 271 (n. 88); reaction to "Pastoral Letter," 29; move to Paris, 43, 86; female friendships, 43, 86, 132, 197 (n. 12); as teacher, 63, 67, 68; education of, 67, 68; harassment of, 212 (n. 32); on Sabbath reform, 267 (n. 64). *See also* Chapman town house

—antislavery: leadership role in, 1, 2, 4, 5, 6, 11, 19, 27, 28, 31, 33, 37, 40, 41, 43, 44, 161; as antislavery author, 1, 5, 28, 32, 38, 44, 106, 147, 244 (n. 102); early activism, 22, 23, 24; and petitioning, 25; and slave rescue, 26; and division among abolitionists, 30, 42, 110, 231 (n. 85); and Elizur Wright, 31; nonresistance of, 33; as editor, 40, 41, 219 (n. 110); and Frederick Douglass, 41; and George Bradburn, 42; and Haitian journals, 106; and European antislavery activism, 134, 135–37

—courtship and marriage, 6, 53, 159, 202 (n. 48); financial circumstances following, 41, 79–80, 86; effect of antislavery mobs on children, 85; and politics of pregnancy and childbearing, 124–26; spousal governance, 159; widowhood, 138, 275 (n. 14); childbearing, 225 (n. 23)

—feminism, 1, 290 (n. 61); on woman's rights, 167–68, 170; on Jeanne Deroin, 170–71

—France: children's education in, 86; travel companions in, 86; role of inheritance in move to, 86, 268 (n. 73); on social freedom of Europe, 87; on butterfly life, 132; impact of move to on sibling antislavery labor, 132; purpose and timing of Europe, 132, 134, 135, 268 (n. 73); and Parisian abolitionists, 271–72 (n. 98)

—fund-raising, 22, 24, 38, 42, 110; and aid to individuals and societies, 22, 208 (n. 4), 213 (n. 43), 220 (n. 109); and antislavery fairs, 122, 150, 151, 280 (n. 57)

—illness, 123–25, 127, 265–66 (n. 43); and rumors of insanity and rumor management, 124–25, 265 (n. 38), 265–66 (n. 43), 266 (n. 45); used to attack character, 126–27; doctored by Hervey, 127; attributed to antislavery work, 265–66 (n. 43)

Chapman, Mary Gray, 88, 104, 124, 130, 142, 144, 249 (n. 53); as antislavery sibling, 9; and antislavery fairs, 22, 149; courtship, 55–57, 229 (n. 67); inheritance, 79, 229–30 (n. 72); social relations with Westons, 230 (n. 72), 247 (n. 35)

Chapman, Sarah Greene, 107; and abolition, 24, 26, 149, 211 (n. 23); and Gertrude Chapman, 126, 130, 266 (n. 48)

Chapman town house, 39, 43; and mob violence, 84; as antislavery workplace, 142–43, 144, 145–47, 149, 262 (n. 9); impact of loss of, 149–50; Lawrence Friedman on, 275 (n. 14)

Chase, Aaroline, 111

Chase, Matilda: as antislavery sibling, 9

Chase, Lucy: as antislavery sibling, 9

Child, David Lee, 40, 78, 163; rejects Chapman's political discipline, 158–59; identified, 196 (n. 10), 243 (n. 95); Chapman's dissatisfaction with, 220 (n. 110)

Child, Lydia Maria, 2, 22, 27, 38, 40, 124, 142, 145, 158, 211 (n. 25), 219 (n. 38), 270 (n. 88), 276 (n. 20), 278 (n. 43); on "new organizationists," 36, 288 (n. 50); on AAS executive committee, 37; identified, 196 (n. 10), 243 (n. 95); response to Chapman's criticism, 196–97 (n. 10); conflict over *National Antislavery Standard*, 219 (n. 107); Anne Warren Weston on, 219–20 (n. 107)

Children of abolition, 246 (n. 27)

Choate, Rufus: identified, 213, (n. 42)

Church, Ministry and Sabbath Convention, 130

Clark, Mary, 27

Clerical abolitionists, 34. *See also* "Appeal of Clerical Abolitionists on Anti-slavery Measures"

Cohen, Michael, 201 (n. 45)

Collins, John A., 8, 41–42, 58, 78, 140, 144; and Weston hospitality, 140; identified, 231 (n. 81)

Combe, George, 147

Commissions, Weston, 107–14; in constructing Weymouth sisterhood, 107; on expenditures, 108; in manufacturing and sustaining affection, 108; as domestic assistance, 108–9; political, 109–13; overlapping domestic and political, 113

Congdon, Susan, 107

Congdon, Mary, 110, 111

Contagious Diseases Acts, 166–67, 289 (n. 56), 289 (n. 58)

Conventions, antislavery: American Women, 18, 29, 214 (n. 48)

Cooke, Parsons, 29

Correspondence, antislavery, 104, 115

Correspondence, Weston:

—censorship, 176–79, 229 (n. 70); on propriety and reputation 177; on privacy, 177, 178–79, 295 (n. 47, 51); on destruction of letters, 178, 181, 293 (n. 19), 295 (n. 41); of private diaries, 178–79; self-censorship, 181; on redacted material, 292 (n. 15), 293 (nn. 16–17)

—constructing a collection, 176; and concerns about revisionist history, 176; priorities in selection, 176; reliance upon Weston retention, 176; on representativeness, 176; safekeeping, 176; brothers' letters, 199 (n. 27); and preservation, 293 (n. 22), 294 (n. 35)

—epistolary practice: structure of, 102; expectations as to frequency, 102, 179–83; in shaping interpretation, 179–80; on privacy, 180–81, 182; on distribution of letters, 182; selectiveness and transformation of meaning, 182; and conditions for writing, 183; on use of journals, 294 (n. 29), 294 (n. 31)

—materiality, 183–86; graphic strategies, 183; signs of interruption,

Liberty Bell, 20, 42, 76, 77, 110, 113, 129, 136, 147, 150, 176, 279 (n. 47); contributors, 208 (n. 3); publication history, 279 (n. 46)

Liberty Party, 38, 42, 156, 158, 196 (n. 3), 215 (n. 68), 217 (n. 84), 268 (n. 71), 276–77 (n. 25)

Little, Caroline: as antislavery sibling, 9

Little, Susan: as antislavery sibling, 9

Loring, Ellis Gray, 78, 142, 219 (n. 107), 276 (n. 20); and rescue of Med Sommersett, 26; and reprimand of Douglass, Remond, and Collins, 42; Weston view of, 163; identified, 213 (n. 41), 243 (n. 94)

Loring, Louisa Gilman, 142, 150, 179, 195 (n. 1), 211 (n. 25), 276 (n. 20), 280 (n. 57); identified, 243 (n. 94)

Loud, Eliza S., 156, 157

Louge, Janette: as antislavery sibling, 9

Louge, Rebecca: as antislavery sibling, 9

Lovejoy, Elijah, 32

Lyman, Theodore: and Boston mob, 1835, 23–24, 211–12 (n. 30); son's defense of, 176

Lynn Female Anti-Slavery Society, 28, 111–12, 216 (n. 79)

Marriage: "to the cause," 16, 227 (n. 55); sibling exchange marriages, 13, 204 (n. 65), 205 (n. 74), 232 (n. 89); to a dead wife's sister, 13, 205 (n. 74); cousin marriage, 13, 205–6 (n. 74); average age in Massachusetts, 46; as category of analysis, 208 (n. 88); rate in Massachusetts, 222 (n. 3); fertility, 224–25 (n. 23)

Martineau, Harriet, 4, 147, 166–67, 168, 249 (n. 54), 278 (n. 43); Chapman opinion of, 2, 127, 147; identified, 197 (n. 11), 290 (n. 64), 290 (n. 66); on Contagious Diseases Acts, 289 (n. 56)

Massachusetts Abolition Society, 1, 218 (n. 87), 287 (n. 34); alliance with Massachusetts Female Emancipation Society, 1; as "new organization," 35, 196 (n. 3), 217 (n. 86)

Massachusetts Abolitionist, 32, 35, 213 (n. 45)

Massachusetts Anti-Slavery Society (MAS), 1, 26–27, 31, 34, 35, 112; division, 35, 36, 38, 41, 131, 143, 231 (n. 81)

Massachusetts Anti-Slavery Society Fair, 42, 44, 221 (n. 118)

Massachusetts Female Emancipation Society (MFES), 1, 35, 36; alliance with Massachusetts Abolition Society, 196 (n. 3)

Mathews, Edward, 164, 287 (n. 43)

May, Samuel J., 19, 29, 54, 142, 150; and Chapman hospitality, 142, 145; on abolitionist women, 166; identified, 198 (n. 16)

May, Samuel J., Jr., 3, 105, 140, 163

McKim, J. Miller, 145, 270

Meigs, Rosamond Weston, 176

Merriam, Eliza Jackson: as antislavery sibling, 202 (n. 51); BFAS treasurer, 277 (n. 33)

Michell, Emma, 105, 125, 166, 172; on Chapman, 197 (n. 12)

Mobs, anti-abolitionist, 19, 22–24, 33, 121, 151, 179, 287 (n. 43); Weston experience of, 4–5, 84–85, 123, 160, 166, 247 (n. 29), 265 (n. 43); impact on children, 84–85, 206 (n. 78); in Boston, 176, 211 (n. 29)

Mohl, Mary Clarke, 134–35, 136, 137, 272 (n. 99)

Mott, Lucretia, 27, 33, 105, 145, 218 (n. 92); on AAS executive committee, 37

Nash, Hannah, 98

National Anti-Slavery Standard, 20, 40, 41, 112, 159

National Bazaar of the American Anti-Slavery Society Fair, 42

New Bedford: abolitionism, 109, 112, 264 (n. 25); fair, 110–11; Lyceum, 112, 121

New England Anti-Slavery Society
(NEAS), 2, 8, 22, 33, 84, 131, 202
(n. 52), 210 (n. 18), 211 (n. 24)
New England Freedom Association, 199
(n. 30)
New Hampshire Anti-Slavery Society, 41
"New organization,"196 (n. 3); Child on
Weston critique of, 288 (n. 50)
Newport Female Anti-Slavery Society, 36
Nichol, Elizabeth Pease, 34, 43, 104, 135,
166, 274 (n. 8)
Non-Resistance Society: meetings in
Chapman home, 33, 143; founding,
33, 274 (n. 8)
Non-Resistant, 20, 199 (n. 31)
North Star, 42, 282 (n. 72)

Parker, Abigail: and division in BFAS, 1;
as antislavery sibling, 9; vote to end
BFAS, 35; political role household,
275 (n. 16)
Parker, Anna Sargent, 14, 57, 105; identified, 230 (n. 74)
Parker, Eliza: and division in BFAS, 1;
as antislavery sibling, 9; vote to end
BFAS, 35; political role of household
of, 275 (n. 16)
Parker, Lucy: and division in BFAS, 1;
as antislavery sibling, 9; vote to end
BFAS, 35; political role of household
of, 275 (n. 16)
Parker, Lydia Cabot, 150
Parker, Mary S., 1, 24, 27, 30, 127, 143,
195 (n. 1), 214 (n. 49); and division
in BFAS, 1; as antislavery sibling, 9;
on leadership, 15; vote to end BFAS,
35; on Chapman, 127; political role of
household of, 275 (n. 16)
Parker, Theodore, 40, 130, 132, 200
(n. 31), 271 (n. 88)
"Pastoral Letter" (General Association
of Congregational Ministers), 28–29,
30, 143, 148, 195 (n. 1)
Patriarchy, 18, 286 (n. 33)
Peck, Harriett: as antislavery sibling, 9

Peck, Joanna: as antislavery sibling, 9
Peck, Mary Ann: as antislavery sibling, 9
Perkins, Jonas, 13, 154–56, 162, 217
(n. 86), 283–84 (n. 5, 7, 10); as signa-
tory to "Appeal of Clerical Abolitionists on Anti-slavery Measures,"
30–32, 214 (n. 64); identified, 155,
283 (n. 8)
Perkins, Rhoda Keith (Mrs. Jonas), 32,
155, 156
Petitions, antislavery, 15, 25, 32, 111,
160–61, 186, 216 (n. 76–77), 275
(n. 15), 286 (n. 30), 297 (n. 80); and
Weston brothers, 5, 6, 199 (n. 33); by
Weston sisters, 13–14, 20, 40, 239
(n. 41), 241 (n. 67), 274 (n. 9); by
Latimer Committee, 39
Phelps, Amos, 30, 31, 34, 36, 37, 147, 155,
156, 217 (n. 86);on "Pastoral Letter,"
30; Westons on, 165
Philadelphia Female Anti-Slavery Society, 9, 27, 38
Phillips, Ann Terry Greene, 104, 105, 210
(n. 17); identified, 22, 292 (n. 13); invalidism of, 198 (n. 18), 278 (n. 37)
Phillips, Wendell, 32, 41, 140, 147, 154,
200 (n. 31), 218 (n. 87), 220 (n. 109),
257 (n. 34), 273 (n. 1), 292 (n. 13);
as Chapman lawyer, 79; and circulation of antislavery correspondence,
104, 105; feminism, 168; and "Lyman
Mob," 176; marriage, 177, 215 (n. 73),
278 (n. 37)
Pillsbury, Parker, 134
Pratt, Ann: as antislavery sibling, 202
(n. 52)
Pratt, Sarah: as antislavery sibling, 202
(n. 52)
Pregnancy, premarital: rates of, 48; of
Ann Bates, 47; of Tirzah Pratt, 48; of
Cynthia Bates Cowing, 48; definition
of full term, 224 (n. 18); and social
disapprobation, 224 (n. 22)
Prigg v. Pennsylvania, 39, 218 (n. 99)
Prince, Nancy Gardner, 208 (n. 4)

Pugh, Sarah, 3, 27, 105, 214 (n. 49), 270 (n. 86), 289 (n. 59); identified, 257 (n. 27)

Quincy, Edmond, 2, 3, 7, 36, 37, 39, 40, 41, 56, 134, 140, 144, 165; on Westons, 8; on Chapman salon, 16–17, 141, 145; and *Non-Resistant*, 34; on siblings, 45, 61; on Weston marriage-ability, 54; on gossip, 103, 145; and Weston correspondence, 104, 176, 177, 181; and *Liberty Bell*, 150; on Chapman as MAS disciplinarian, 159; and antislavery division, 218 (n. 87); on *Latimer Journal*, 219 (n. 105); on kinship ties, 222 (n. 1)

Ray, Isaiah C., 112–14; identified, 259 (n. 63)
Reid, Elizabeth, 166, 168; identified, 290 (n. 64)
Remond, Caroline, 44; as antislavery sibling, 9
Remond, Charles L., 41–42; identified, 218 (n. 92)
Remond, Nancy, 9
Remond, Sarah: as antislavery sibling, 9
Remond, Susan: as antislavery sibling, 9
Right and Wrong in Boston (1836), 19, 146
Right and Wrong in Massachusetts (1839), 19, 38, 167
Robeson, Andrew, 110, 113; identified, 259 (n. 57)
Rogers, Nathanial, 41, 162, 209 (n. 10), 259 (n. 63); Weymouth hospitality, 140; Anne Warren Weston on, 163, 180; identified, 294 (n. 32)
"Rule of the brother," 16, 161, 169
"Rule of the sister," 12, 205 (n. 71)
Ruggles, Steven, 223–24 (n. 17)
Ryan, Mary, 13, 206 (n. 75)

Samaritan Asylum, 208–9 (n. 4)
Sargent, Catherine, 14, 57, 78, 105, 115, 130, 170, 195 (n. 1), 268 (n. 66), 281

(n. 64); as antislavery sibling, 9; identified, 230 (n. 74); political role of household of, 275 (n. 16)
Sargent, Henrietta, 14, 57, 78, 90, 97, 105, 109, 115, 130, 170, 195 (n. 1), 218 (n. 89), 220; as antislavery sibling, 9; identified, 230 (n. 74); and sibling exchange marriage, 232 (n. 89); po-litical role of household of, 275 (n. 16)
Sargent, John T. and Mary, 44
Scoble, John, 133, 287–88 (n. 43)
Sewall, Samuel E., 26, 39, 142, 157, 205 (n. 74), 210 (n. 18), 276 (n. 20); iden-tified, 285 (n. 18)
Shaw, Lemuel, 26, 39
Siblicity: model for social relations, 10, 203 (n. 55), 261 (n. 3); "elective sisters," 10; sisters as friends, 10, 61; as political entity, 11; and politi-cal consciousness, 11; as economic corporation, 11; as domestic concern, 11; cohabitation and affection, 11; and "rule of the brother," 12, 18; and female equality, 172, 205 (n. 72); an-tislavery recruitment and retention, 14; in service of political innovation and female independence, 18; and emotional primacy, 61, 114; costs and benefits, 81; mobility, 116; nomencla-ture, 204 (n. 64), alternate view, 205 (n. 72)
Siblings, antislavery, 9, 202 (n. 51)
Singlehood, 222–23 (nn. 3–4), 232 (n. 94), 233 (n. 97); and sororal prac-tice of abolitionism, 8, 15, 208 (n. 92); historiography of, 15–16; and sibship, 16, 233 (n. 95); in Massachusetts demographics, 45, 222 (n. 3); and factors contributing to Weston, 46; "single blessedness," 52–53; role in female reform and benevolence, 206 (n. 81), 207 (n. 84), 244–45 (n. 7)
Sibling exchange marriage, 13, 204 (n. 65), 205 (n. 74), 232 (n. 89)
Sisson, Anna: as antislavery sibling, 9

Sisson, Hannah: as antislavery sibling, 9

Sisson, Lydia: as antislavery sibling, 9

Sisson, Sarah: as antislavery sibling, 9

Sisson, Susan: as antislavery sibling, 9

Sisterhood: gender consciousness and, 200 (n. 39); sisters and friends, 255 (n. 11). *See also* Weymouth sisterhood

Smith, Daniel Scott, 10, 11, 18, 203 (n. 59), 285 (n. 28)

Solomon, Barbara, 240 (n. 49)

Sommersett, Med, 26

Sororal model of social activism, 8; examples of, 9–10, 201–2 (n. 47), 202 (n. 51)

Spear, Catherine: as antislavery sibling, 9, 202 (n. 52)

South Weymouth Female Anti-Slavery Society, 23, 155, 156

Southwick, Abby, 27; as antislavery sibling, 9

Southwick, Anna: as antislavery sibling, 9

Southwick, Elizabeth: as antislavery sibling, 9

Southwick, Joseph, 24, 130, 142, 276 (n. 20); identified, 202 (n. 50), 211 (n. 22), 212 (n. 33)

Southwick, Sarah, 2, 34, 38, 69, 130; on Westons, 3, 239 (n. 41); as antislavery sibling, 9; identified, 196 (n. 8); and teaching 239 (n. 42)

Southwick, Thankful Hussey, 24, 130, 276 (n. 20): identified, 202 (n. 50), 212 (n. 33), 215 (n. 72), 218 (n. 89); political role of household of, 275 (n. 16), 276 (n. 22)

Spacial geography of abolition, 16–17; and Chapman townhouse, 17

Spear, Catharine: as antislavery sibling, 202 (n. 51)

Stanton, Henry B., 34, 36, 37, 132; dismissed as Weston suitor, 59; Weston view of, 162; identified, 268 (n. 71)

Stewart, Maria Miller, 20

Story, Joseph, 39, 40, 205 (n. 74)

Sturgis, Elizabeth [Betsy], 234 (n. 10)

Sturgis, Harriet, 234 (n. 10)

Sturgis, John, 234 (n. 10)

Sturgis, William, 235 (n. 10)

Sumner, Charles, 266 (n. 54)

Taber, Susan, 110, 130

Tappan, Arthur, 35, 37; identified, 217 (n. 84)

Tappan, Eliza Aspinwall: as antislavery sibling, 9; and Chapman hospitality, 145

Tappan, Ellen: as antislavery sibling, 9; and Chapman hospitality, 145

Tappan, Georgiana: as antislavery sibling, 9; and Chapman hospitality, 145

Tappan, Juliana: as antislavery sibling, 9; response to "Pastoral Letter," 29; and Chapman hospitality, 145

Tappan, Lewis, 35, 36, 37, 220 (n. 10), 288 (n. 45); identified, 217 (n. 84)

Taylor, Clare, 173, 198 (n. 18), 266 (n. 43)

Taylor, Jeremy: on friendship, 10, 18

Teaching profession: in Massachusetts, 70; pay, 240 (n. 55); of Westons, 68–75; Weston's Boston boarding school, 68; governesses as teachers, 70–71; and John F. Emerson, 72–89 passim; impact of antislavery politics on, 120–21, 214 (n. 59); Weston range of experience in, 238 (n. 33), 239 (n. 39); economics of, 239 (n. 44); Weston sharing of lesson plans, 242 (n. 78)

Temperance: reform, 21, 110; Massachusetts Society for the Suppression of Intemperance, 209 (n. 6); Weymouth meeting, 209 (n. 10); and Martha Washington Relief Society of Duxbury, 209 (n. 11); Heman Humphrey on, 210 (n. 15); and William Lloyd and James Holly Garrison, 210 (n. 15); and economic success, 210 (n. 16); of Ezra Weston, Gershom B. Weston, Joshua Bates, 234 (n. 6); and temperance ships, 236 (n. 22), 236 (n. 23)

Thompson, George, 23, 26, 43, 102, 134, 135, 136, 142, 145, 163, 165, 265 (n. 36); death threats against, 22, 24; and American antislavery societies, 23; and Anne W. Weston, 58–59, 179; and trauma of Amelia Thompson, 85, 246–47 (n. 27)

Thoreau, Cynthia Dunbar, 9

Thoreau, Helen: as antislavery sibling, 9

Thoreau, Susan: as antislavery sibling, 9

Thurber, Abby: as antislavery sibling, 9, 202 (n. 52)

Thurber, Rachel: as antislavery sibling, 9, 202 (n. 52)

Tocqueville, Alexis de, 134, 137

Union Religious Society of Weymouth, 31, 162

Varon, Elizabeth R., 38–39; on disunion, 291 (n. 76)

War of 1812, 47, 63

Ward, Samuel Ringgold, 288 (n. 45)

Ware, Charles Eliot, 92; identified, 250 (n. 71)

Washington Total Abstinence Society of Weymouth and Braintree, 21

Webster, Daniel, 236 (n. 20)

Weeks, Jeffrey, 203 (n. 55)

Webb, Richard Dana, 34, 43, 105

Weld, Angelina Grimké. *See* Grimké, Angelina

Weld, Theodore, 33, 143; identified, 276 (n. 25)

Weston and Gray, 237 (n. 28)

Weston, Ann (Nancy) Bates, 46, 53, 143, 223 (n. 12); and abolitionism, 5, 199 (n. 25), 274 (n. 9); on premarital pregnancy, 47; spacing of children, 48, 224 (n. 23); Chapman child care, 50; and annuities from brother, 64; illnesses of, 88, 89; fatalism of, 89, 248–49

(n. 50), 267–68 (n. 65); and domestic servants, 94–95; will, 230 (n. 78)

Weston, Anne Warren: attributes of, 3, 81, 154; leadership role in abolitionism, 5, 6, 41; political philosophy of, 8; and antislavery fairs, 8, 43, 154, 149–53; and antislavery petitioning, 25; and Anti-Slavery Convention of American Women, 27; and nonresistance, 33, 34, 39, 200 (n. 31), 258 (n. 38), 219 (n. 101); and *Latimer Journal*, 39–41; illness and nursing duties, 40, 49, 127–28, 244 (n. 1), 244 (n. 3); and George Thompson, 58–59; on courtship and marriage, 60, 61; on teaching, 63, 68, 69; inheritance, 80; on correspondence, 101; on antislavery correspondence, 115; and "Pastoral Letter," 143, 148, 279 (n. 50); and *Songs of the Free*, 146; lack of propriety of, 154; on feminists and woman's rights, 168, 169; on political rights and moral imperatives, 169–70; on relationships with men, 231 (n. 83); and Sargent sisters, 268 (n. 66)

Weston, Caroline, 1, 4, 23, 31, 54, 81, 83, 142, 176, 195 (n. 1), 211 (n. 29); attributes of, 2–3, 8; antislavery leadership, 5, 6, 37, 41; antislavery labors, 25, 118, 121, 148–49; and Peace Congress, 34; suitors, 58; financial concerns, 63; teaching, 63, 68, 69, 70, 118; inheritance, 80; caretaking and child-rearing duties, 81–84, 118; apprehensions of mob, 85; illness, 88; nursing, 89; to Europe, 43, 132; and *Songs of the Free*, 146; on Jeanne Deroin, 170–71; on female enfranchisement, 171–72; and Belknap Street School, 239 (n. 42); fluency in French, 269 (n. 76); on Queen Victoria, 291 (n. 73)

Weston correspondence: frequency of, 100–101, 254 (n. 3), 256 (n. 15);

exchange among sisters, 101, 103–4; as sibling responsibility, 102; multiple audiences of, 103, 104, 255 (n. 6), 256 (n. 19); importance of preservation of, 105, 106, 176; practice of reading aloud, 105, 257 (n. 28–29), 257 (n. 32); and uses for political speaking and writing, 106, 176, 211 (n. 29), 257–58 (n. 34); and "journal letters," 179–80; and privacy considerations, 257 (n. 30)

Weston, Debora, 2, 31, 142; attributes of, 3–4, 127, 290 (n. 67); antislavery fundraising of, 4, 5, 111, 114, 121; refuses leadership role in abolition, 109; antislavery petitioning, 25, 121; teaching, 43, 118, 132; and marital eligibility, 54, 55; as educated in sisters' boarding school, 69; caretaking and child-rearing duties, 81–82; on correspondence, 101, 102, 106; nursing duties, 118; and "free" produce movement, 121

Weston, Deborah Nash, 47, 64; identified, 223 (n. 10); will, 223 (n. 16), 230 (n. 77)

Weston, Eliphaz, 46; military and political service, 64; identified, 223 (n. 9), 233 (n. 3)

Weston, Emma Forbes, 2, 52, 81, 83, 130; attributes of, 4–5; advice on marriage, 54; coming out in European society, 54–55; Italian romance, 55; enrolled in sisters' schools, 69, 70; inheritance, 80; reared with nieces and nephews, 82, 199 (n. 23); and nursing, 88, 132; and fair work, 149, 280 (n. 59)

Weston, Ezra, 47; as shipbuilder, 64; on temperance and success, 234 (n. 6)

Weston, Ezra, II: cousin to Warren Weston, 64; as shipbuilder, 64; potential cost of success, 234 (n. 4)

Weston, Gershom Bradford: as Boston Brahmin, 64; identified, 64, 234 (n. 5); on temperance and success, 234 (n. 6)

Weston, Helen, 176

Weston, Hervey Eliphas: role in abolitionism, 5–6, 31, 36–37; schooling, 50; health, 50–51; medical training and practice, 50–51; and Lucia's illness, 51; and authority of the brother, 162; study of numismatics, 226 (n. 42); on Vigilance Committee, 273. *See also* Boston Vigilance Committee

Weston homestead(s): capital construction and improvements in town, 78; in Weymouth Landing, 225 (n. 25); in Weymouth town, 225 (n. 25)

Weston household, 48; as political, 105; governance, 162

Weston, Lucia, 2, 5, 81; attributes of, 4; president of MAS, 6; and tuberculosis, 41, 51, 92–93, 128, 198 (n. 18), 198 (n. 19), 225 (n. 24), 251 (n. 78); and schooling, 69; reared with nieces and nephews, 82, 199 (n. 23); on correspondence, 101; journalizing, 106; as sounding board, 118; nursing Priscilla, 129; and fair work, 149; on friendship Sarah Southwick, 239 (n. 41); and Belknap Street School, 239 (n. 42)

Weston, Mary, 10, 46, 52, 74, 155, 157; leadership of Weymouth and Braintree Female Emancipation Society, 23, 32, 122, 211 (n. 27); and antislavery petitions, 25, 199 (n. 25); singlehood, 57, 230 (n. 76); and will, 57, 230 (n. 77); on fair work, 149; identified, 223 (n. 10); and Henry Chapman legacy, 223 (n. 16)

Weston, Phebe, 10, 46; and 1836 antislavery petition, 199 (n. 25); identified, 223 (n. 10); and Henry Chapman legacy, 223 (n. 16); and will, 230 (n. 77); singlehood, 230 (n. 76); and Sabbath reform, 267 (n. 64)

Weston, Priscilla, 10, 46, 74, 128–29; and 1836 antislavery petition, 199 (n. 25); identified, 223 (n. 10); and

Henry Chapman legacy, 223 (n. 16); singlehood, 230 (n. 76); as intestate, 230 (n. 77); and Sabbath reform, 267 (n. 64)

Weston, Richard Warren, 162, 225 (n. 24); and abolition, 6; marriage and children, 49; employment, 49, 50; intemperance, 49, 50, 66; health, 49, 81, 92; mentored by Joshua Bates, 66, 225 (n. 26); fraternal authority, 67, 162; as president of New York Stock Exchange, 225, (n. 27); and temperance ships, 236–37 (n. 24), 237 (n. 25); as mentor, 237 (n. 27)

Weston sisters, 3, 8, 27; assumptions of interchangeability of, 7, 8, 109, 201 (n. 45); and politics and health, 127–28; significance of number of, 137, 272–73 (n. 106); and value of Boston base of operations, 139, 141; and temperance, 162; as readers, 261 (n. 81)

—antislavery labor: organization of female antislavery societies, 1, 9, 19; fund-raising, 5, 19, 22, 44, 76–77, 98, 109–10, 114, 119, 121, 122, 128, 129, 130, 132, 136–37, 147–53, 264 (n. 29), 271 (n. 95), 272 n. 100), 280 (n. 57), 280 (nn. 60–61), 281 (n. 65), 281 (n. 66), 282 (n. 69); as antislavery society officers, 6, 20, 113; and fugitive slaves, 6, 34, 73, 121, 140–41, 172, 217 (n. 82); educating black children, 20, 21, 239 (n. 42); early interest in abolition, 20–21; writing, 19–20, 147, 259 (n. 51); negotiating public engagements, 77–78; importance of appearance to, 113–14; antislavery activities in Europe, 136–37, 269 (n. 80); and racial integration of female societies, 258 (n. 49)

—domestic labor, 251 (n. 80), 251 (n. 85), 252 (n. 93), 252 (n. 94), 253 (n. 101), 253 (n. 105), 253 (nn. 107–8), 254 (n. 113); fraternal

care, 50; nursing, 88–93; housework, 93–94, 97, 95–98; juggling with political work, 127, 128, 129–30; domestic manufacturing, 204 (n. 60); and clothing exchange, 261 (n. 75)

—and patriarchal authority, 13, 285 (n. 27); and "impudence," 18, 157–59; and temperance, 21, 22, 162; and opposition to personal liberty law, 40; on character of antislavery brethren, 41–42, 162–66; and relationship with parents, 132; and harassment, 157, 159, 164; and Contagious Diseases Acts, 166–67; and feminism, 168–69; and enfranchisement, 171–72; sibship and rejection of, 172

—sibling relations: role of correspondence and journalizing in, 100–107; and visitation, 105–6; and siblicity, 114, 115; negotiation of duties and responsibilities, 131–32; and isolation, 152–53; and religious disagreement, 201 (n. 46)

—significance of shared household, 43, 162, 167, 168; on habitual sympathy, 62; on shared labor and productivity, 152

—singlehood, 45, 57, 61, 62; factors contributing to, 46, 51; on suitors and beau ideal, 53, 60; and activism and marital eligibility, 54; and courtship, 58–60; impact of, on activism, 61, 285 (n. 27)

—as teachers, 62, 63, 71; and family economy, 63, 64, 76–77, 78–79; on correlation between reform and teaching, 240 (n. 46); and finances, 258 (n. 44). *See also* Teaching profession

Weston, Warren, 89; alcoholism of, 1, 48, 52, 63, 130, 162, 223 (n. 15); and abolition, 5, 147; and family governance, 46; occupation, 47; and household authority, 51–52, 159, 162; impact of War 1812 on, 63; and male abolitionists, 140; and antislavery hospitality, 140, 274 (n. 7); and dry rages, 209–10 (n. 14); and economic standing, 233 (n. 2); and male selfishness, 251 (n. 79)

Weston, Warren (shipwright of Duxbury), 233 (n. 3)

Weymouth, 47; temperance movement in, 21, 162; shipbuilding in, 47; Union Religious Society, 162; population, 200 (n. 33); shoemaking in, 235 (n. 14)

Weymouth and Braintree Female Emancipation Society, 9, 23, 32, 122, 155; sewing circle, 211 (n. 27), 215 (n. 71), 280 (n. 58)

Weymouth sisterhood: as appellation, 7; as family culture, 7–8; as labor exchange, 11; as political practice, 14, 16; maintenance through correspondence, 11, 100–102; through

visitation, 105–6; by journalizing, 106–7; by fulfilling commissions, 107–13; and integration of political relations and kinship ties, 114, 117–18

Whitney, Anne, 165, 197 (n. 13)

Whittier, John Greenleaf, 163; dismissed as Weston suitor, 59; and gossip with Westons, 145

Wigham, Jane and Eliza, 166

Wilentz, Sean, 237 (n. 25)

Williams, Charles D., wife of, 199 (n. 30)

Wollstonecraft, Mary, 168

Woman's rights: NEAS Convention (1838), 33; in antislavery societies, 34, 35, 290 (n. 61)

Wright, Elizur, Jr., 13, 27, 31, 34, 35, 143, 231 (n. 85); identified, 213 (n. 45)

Wright, Henry C.: and Weymouth hospitality, 140; identified, 274 (n. 8)

Yerrington, James Brown: identified, 259 (n. 54)